WORLD WAR II

WORLD WAR II

A 50th Anniversary History

by the writers and photographers of
THE ASSOCIATED PRESS

Foreword by
Harrison Salisbury

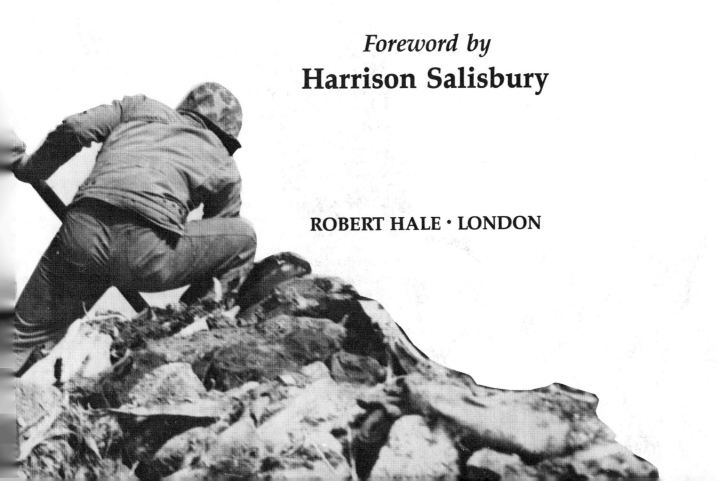

ROBERT HALE · LONDON

DEDICATION

Fifty years later, as we recall the worst war the world has endured, we remember, too, those who armed themselves with pen, typewriter and camera to record the events and report the truth as they saw it, despite the dangers.

Nearly 200 Associated Press men and women covered the war. They earned six Pulitzer Prizes—in the front lines and the foxholes, at sea and in the air, from the North Atlantic to the South Pacific. Five were killed, many more injured. Some 600 others from The AP served in the armed forces.

This book is dedicated to all those, who, by their talent, dedication, and sacrifice, thus enhanced the profession of journalism.

Louis D. Boccardi
President and General Manager
The Associated Press

PROJECT DIRECTOR: Dan Perkes
EDITOR: Nate Polowetzky
ASSOCIATE EDITOR: Norm Goldstein
WRITERS: John Barbour, Rick Hampson, Charles J. Hanley, Sid Moody
PHOTO EDITOR: Sandy Colton
PHOTO RESEARCHER: Elma Masut
Unless otherwise credited, all photos are Associated Press photos. Some credited to other sources are from the Wartime Pool, of which AP was a member.

Designed by Combined Books Inc.
26 Summit Grove Avenue, Suite 207
Bryn Mawr, Pennsylvania 19010

Produced by Wieser & Wieser, Inc.
118 East 25th Street
New York, New York 10010

Copyright © 1989 by The Associated Press, Inc.
First published in Great Britain 1990

Robert Hale Limited
Clerkenwell House
Clerkenwell Green
London ECIR OHT

ISBN 0-7090-3991-3

Printed in the United States of America

1 ROAD TO WAR

The world was out of work, out of hope. Three million were unemployed in Britain. In Germany they carted nearly worthless Deutsche marks to market in wheelbarrows. In wealthy America, a third of the work force, was out of work. There were some 400,000 jobless nomads riding the rails. Everywhere, the homeless and the hungry. In America a glut of apples were sold to the unemployed on credit, and shivering men and women were on street corners, hawking apples for a nickel. In New York City with a million jobless and eighty-two breadlines, some 7,000 men and boys were on the streets shining shoes for pennies.

It could only lead to disaster. In Washington, D.C., cavalry led by Major George S. Patton, under the overall command of the nation's only active four-star general, Douglas MacArthur, routed a ragtag "army" of veterans, their wives and children, there to beseech Congress for promised bonuses.

In 1932, it was a desperate world in search of saviors. To this stage came a patrician American crippled by polio and a failed German artist who had lived much of his youth in Viennese flophouses and had survived on charity soup.

On March 4, 1933, Franklin Delano Roosevelt was inaugurated as president of the United States. A day later, Adolf Hitler's National Socialist (Nazi) Party won enough of an edge in the last free elections of Germany's enfeebled democracy to allow him to power his way through to Chancellor.

Roosevelt and Hitler, along with Winston Churchill, would symbolize the conflict between democracy and dictatorship, between freedom and subservience; an unyielding, unfriendly polarity born in desperate days to bring to the world the greatest cataclysm it had ever known. Before it was over, some 70 million men and women would answer the call to arms, and 17 million of them would die; two-thirds of the homes and factories of the Axis nations would go up in smoke and dust. The Soviet Union alone would lose 20 million people and something called the atomic bomb would be born.

Worldwide, some 50 million human beings would vanish from the face of the earth, and two of them, Hitler and Roosevelt, would die within eighteen days of each other in April of 1945. One would be self-shot in the head next to his poisoned

In the Depression, Americans sold apples. Out of economic chaos in Germany, Adolf Hitler sold something else.

mistress-bride in an embattled bunker within hearing of Soviet artillery, and the other dead of a massive stroke while sitting for his portrait and looking forward to an international conference that would charter the United Nations.

On that blustery March 4, 1933, in the alabaster capital of the United States, leaning on the arm of his eldest son, his painful legs in braces, the man they called FDR, who grew up behind pruned shrubs and went to exclusive schools, stood before the nation. His hand on the old Dutch family Bible in which were recorded the births and deaths of 263 years of his kin, he took an oath as president:

"I, Franklin Delano Roosevelt, do solemnly swear that I will faithfully execute the office of President of the United States, and will, to the best of my ability, preserve, protect and defend the Constitution of the United States, so help me God."

No sooner had the cheering quieted, than Roosevelt got down to the dark facts of his Depression-stifled nation with first things first. He told his countrymen, "Let me assert my firm belief that the only thing we have to fear is fear itself, nameless, unreasoning, unjustified terror which paralyzes needed efforts to convert retreat into advance. . . ."

He promptly outlined his program to put the country to work. He said he expected the full cooperation of Congress, and if that were not forthcoming, "I shall not evade the clear course of duty that will then confront me. I shall ask Congress for the one remaining instrument to meet the

"I solemnly swear..." Roosevelt takes presidential oath in 1933.

crisis, broad executive power to wage a war against the emergency as great as the power that would be given me if we were in fact invaded by a foreign foe."

It was met by cheers and applause. With the power of an overwhelming mandate and a pliant Congress, Roosevelt, as some feared he might, could have taken a road to authoritarianism. Instead, he chose Americanism.

In fact, the world was filling up with dictators. In the Soviet Union, the son of a cobbler, Josef Stalin was knee-deep in a five-year purge in which tens of thousands were killed, tens of thousands more exiled, the army decimated and humbled, the officer corps purged. It would leave Stalin alone the cold-blooded master of the Soviet Union.

U.S. cavalry breaks up Bonus Army. Army head: MacArthur. Staff aide: Eisenhower.

As the world polarized, where stood Russia's enigmatic Josef Stalin?

And in Italy, a vain and pompous Benito Mussolini coveted the Mediterranean and dreamed of a new Roman Empire.

The day after Roosevelt's inauguration, the people of a splintered, impoverished Germany voted for their last chance to rehabilitate their Democratic Republic. Even by intrigue, propaganda, strongarm tactics by his brown-shirted storm troopers, the full power of the state and the unlimited funds provided by German industrialists, Adolf Hitler's Nazi party could not win a majority. But its 44 percent was enough.

By subterfuge, by burning the Reichstag, the German parliament, and blaming it on the communists, Hitler would forge a dictatorship as absolute as Stalin's.

Roosevelt's first hundred days attacked the Depression head on. His first bill, run through Congress, created the Civilian Conservation Corps (CCC). Shortly thereafter came the Public Works Administration, each intended in one way or another to put America back to work.

No one knew exactly how to make the CCC work. It was only a vague idea in Roosevelt's head: Take the unemployed and set them to doing something for the republic, thereby getting them off of state relief rolls, giving the young and uneducated a new start in life, but just as important, giving a sign of motion.

It was Frances Perkins, the Secretary of Labor, who suggested the Army as the government arm with the means to handle the thousands of volun-

Out of the ashes of the Reichstag fire, Hitler consolidated power.

teers. The Army had the field kitchens, the tents, the structure; it also had an abundance of out-of-work reserve officers who could supervise the operation.

There it was, a pseudo-military operation, paying young men a dollar a day, feeding them, housing them, educating them and putting them to work. The CCC bought up more land for the national forests and by summer nearly a quarter of a million of them were planting millions of trees, fighting forest fires (in which a few perished), building lookout towers, trails, ranger stations in national parks, installing telephone lines and learning how to do a job; most had never worked before.

Before the CCC was terminated in 1942, the Army had organized 2.5 million men, many of who would be the citizen-soldiers in a new, expanded Army. George C. Marshall, who would lead that Army in war, built and organized almost a score of CCC camps in the Southeast. He called it "the most instructive service I ever had, and the most interesting . . . the best antidote for mental stagnation that an Army officer in my position can have."

The Public Works Administration also served a military purpose, at a time when Congress, pacifists, isolationists and the general public opposed military spending. Roosevelt saw to it that PWA funds built a pair of aircraft carriers for the Navy, the *Yorktown* and the *Enterprise.* The Army was not as enterprising, Marshall was to note when he became deputy chief of staff.

While America found and applied its leaders to its war against poverty and economic stagnation, Hitler, taking a different road, was feverishly rebuilding the German Reich. If Hitler's Nazis were

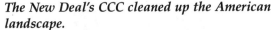

The New Deal's CCC cleaned up the American landscape.

The powers behind the swastika: (l. to r.) *Goebbels, Hitler, Hess, Goering.*

short on rational ideology, they were long on power and hatred. They had already singled out their enemies, primarily the Jews.

National Socialism was neither national nor socialist. Even Mussolini's state-only fascists looked on the German version as perversion.

In a series of laws and actions in 1933, the new German chancellor did what no previous German ruler or government had dared. He dissolved the powers of the self-governing German states and made them subservient to central authority. By 1934 he had effectively eliminated all the political parties, except his own. It was legitimatized by law.

His coterie would become the ruling ranks of both party and state: Hermann Goering, Joseph Goebbels, and Dr. Robert Ley among them.

Then, in June of 1934, Hitler flew to Venice to meet Mussolini for the first time. Not much came of it. Mussolini took one look at the mustachioed man in homburg and brown mackintosh jacket and said to an aide, "I don't like the look of him."

But the two later were to link arms against the world.

Hitler's Nazis and Mussolini's fascists forged an unholy alliance, the Axis.

Sowing the Dragon's Teeth

Albert Einstein was one of many Jewish scientists who fled Europe for America.

Before Roosevelt's first hundred days were done, Hitler had made himself master of Germany. His private army of 2 million storm troopers dwarfed the 100,000-man Wehrmacht (armed forces) and his storm troopers ruled the streets. Death was their easy answer whenever intimidation (Hitler called it education) failed.

The labor unions were effectively dissolved, just months after they were reassured they would be safe. The state would handle labor business.

The industrialists were appeased by reassurances that they were again the masters of their houses, and that Hitler had great plans for them. But Hitler needed not only the industrialists, but the financiers and the army.

In Germany, in the rumbling of random violence in the streets and sweeping political surprises, no one felt safe.

Least of all, the Jews. From his early twenties, Hitler had vented his hatred for the Jews in everything from beer hall speeches to *Mein Kampf*. This was no secret loathing, and it played to an easily aroused anti-Semitism in the German people. Over and again, Hitler listed his three main enemies, democracy, Marxists and Jews. The Jews, he said, were not Germans, but an inferior race destined for exile from Germany. He said they had too long preyed on the German people, had betrayed Germany in the war against the allies in 1918. On April 1, 1933, he ordered a national boycott of all Jewish shops, while his Brown Shirts beat, robbed and murdered Jews in the streets. That was only a beginning.

Roosevelt noted the atrocities with rue, but told his ambassador that the United States could protect only American Jews. So far as the general persecution went, all he could do was try to moderate it by persuasion.

Meanwhile, Jewish professors were being dismissed without pensions, and Jews were beaten when they failed to salute the Brown Shirts. There was already a concentration camp at Dachau, and incredibly the Nazis announced in the November 1933 elections that almost all the 2,242 inmates had voted for the government that had imprisoned them.

Hitler did not have eyes to see the long term effects of anti-Semitism on Germany, nor could Mussolini guess the incredible loss to Italy.

The University of Gottingen was the world center for theoretical physics. Its beacon was Professor Max Born. Albert Einstein, born of Jewish parents, studied at Gottingen before winning the 1921 Nobel Prize for his theories, opening the mind of the world to the relationship of matter and energy. He was on a lecture tour in California, when Hitler made his January 1933 move to power. Einstein never returned to Germany, taking a position with the Institute for Advanced Study in Princeton, New Jersey.

Born himself fled to Great Britain in 1933 and became a British citizen, teaching at Cambridge. A student of his, an Italian named Enrico Fermi, won the 1938 Nobel Prize for his work on the creation of radioactive isotopes by neutron bombardment.

To Hitler, Germany's Jews were a "problem." His solution: "The Jews will be hanged one after another, and they will stay hanging until they stink."

When he took his Jewish wife with him to Stockholm to receive the prize, out of concern for her safety under Mussolini's anti-Semitic laws on the German model, they continued on to the United States where he was offered a professorship at Columbia University. The next year he began working on nuclear fission.

Indeed the Thirties were a watershed for the Western democracies which received the benefit of incredible scientific and academic talent, Jews and others who fled in fright the upraised arms of Hitler and Mussolini.

In a major 1933 speech, Roosevelt outlined America's hopes for disarmament, and called for an abolition of all offensive arms. On the very next day, Hitler stood before the Reichstag and offered the American president his "warmest thanks" for "this ray of comfort for all who wish to cooperate in the maintenance of peace." One could almost hear Europe heave a sigh of relief. Germany, Hitler said, would be ready to disband the small force left to her, if her neighbors would do the same. All Germany wanted was security, and had no wish to "Germanize" other peoples. But he carefully outlined the conditions: Germany wanted equal treatment with other nations, and that included armaments. If this could not be, it would withdraw from the disarmament conference and the League of Nations.

Five months later, almost to the day, he did just that. Then he prepared to rearm, the Treaty of Versailles be damned. He reckoned, rightly, that the divided Allies would do nothing.

The decision made to rearm, his private army became a problem. It had acquired a life of its own, and its leaders, although old comrades of the fuehrer, considered themselves the guardians of

Hitler, the former corporal, was elected chancellor of Germany in 1933 over his former commander, Field Marshal Paul von Hindenberg.

Ernst Roehm, head of Hitler's Brown Shirts, was part of the fuehrer's 1934 purge of party leaders.

the National Socialist revolution, with or without Hitler.

By summer, the SA, as the Brown Shirts were called, had 2.5 million men in uniform. Within the SA was an elite corps called the Black Shirts, or the SS, under a former chicken farmer named Heinrich Himmler. It served as a bodyguard to Hitler and was confirmed in its loyalty. Hitler would have preferred to build up the army and keep the Brown Shirts as well, but it would be a luxury that neither he nor the Army could afford.

On June 30, 1934, in what became known as "The Night of the Long Knives," Hitler, with Goering's aid, personally led an attack on the SA leaders, executing most on the spot. From Berlin to Munich the firing squad volleys rang out through the night. Hitler said that sixty-one persons were shot. But postwar testimony put the figure between 1,000 and 7,000. Hitler was secure again, and the army, which had pressed him to rein in the Brown Shirts, was safely and gratefully in his grasp until the fall of his Third Reich.

In the month that followed, Hitler coerced the cabinet to cede to him the powers of president, with old Field Marshal Paul von Hindenburg ailing. The old man died on August 2. Seventeen days later, 95 percent of the registered voters went to the polls and 90 percent, more than 38 million, approved Hitler's seizure of power. Only some four million voted against him.

For the armed forces, there was a new, required oath that left no room for ambiguity: "I swear by God this sacred oath, that I will render unconditional obedience to Adolf Hitler, the Fuehrer of the German Reich and people, Supreme Commander of the Armed Forces, and will be ready as a brave soldier to risk my life at any time for this oath."

Hitler's plans for rearmament had been kept a not-so-careful secret in 1934. He promised the army conscription by April 1935. Publicly there was no general staff; the rosters of officers were no

American hero Charles Lindbergh was much impressed with Hitler's growing air force, the Luftwaffe.

longer published, while their numbers increased. Quietly the army tripled to 300,000 men.

Admiral Erich Raeder was warned by Hitler himself not to mention the two 26,000-ton battle cruisers, *Scharnhorst* and *Gneisenau,* under construction, each more than twice the size permitted by Versailles. And no submarines. But some U-boats had been secretly built and Raeder had stored the parts for a dozen of them at Kiel.

The boldest activity was Goering's. He was training military pilots under the aegis of the League for Air Sports. As head of civil aviation, he had German manufacturers designing a new generation of warplanes, while their pilots trained in small craft and gliders.

The major German armorers were also at work. Krupp, although forbidden to build guns, had already designed them, as well as the major components of a new generation of German tanks. I.G. Farben, the chemical giant, had devised ways to make synthetic gasoline and rubber from coal, to make the Reich independent of outside supplies, self-sufficient should war come.

If there was confusion elsewhere, there was none in Winston Churchill, still a non-government legislator because of his outspoken position against giving into the demands of Mohandas Gandhi for Indian independence. Arguing for more funds for the Royal Air Force in early 1934, he said:

"Germany is arming fast and no one is going to stop her. That seems quite clear. No one proposes a preventive war to stop Germany breaking the Treaty of Versailles. She is going to arm; she is doing it; she has been doing it. I have no knowledge of the details, but it is well known that those very gifted people, with their science and with their factories—with what they call their 'Air Sport'— are capable of developing with great rapidity the most powerful Air Force for all purposes, offensive and defensive, within a very short period of time.

"I dread the day when the means of threatening the heart of the British Empire should pass into the hands of the present rulers of Germany . . ."

One of the most outspoken opponents of appeasement of Nazi Germany from the back benches of Parliament was the political maverick Winston Churchill.

In January 1935, the coal-rich Saar, under League of Nations administration, voted to rejoin the Reich, and Hitler said Germany would make no more territorial claims. Hitler made his usual reassurances.

Finally, on March 16, 1935, Hitler went public with his military build-up. He established universal military service to create an army of thirty-six divisions, half a million men. Allied protests went unheeded. And Hitler kept promising peace.

Meanwhile, Mussolini's troops teased the borders of Ethiopia and Hitler's Nazi supporters organized in Austria, despite his assurance that Germany had no interest in its ancestral neighbor.

Guarded by its oceans and its uncontested borders, the United States had relied on relatively small armed forces in peacetime, considering its size and its underlying economic strength.

Until World War I, the United States had had few foreign obligations which would require a large army. And a sizable portion of the population,

whether pacifist or isolationist, wanted to keep it that way.

The armed forces were on the fringes of Roosevelt's thoughts, but he tended to take American strength for granted. When a congressional committee criticized the Post Office's air mail contracts with commercial lines, Roosevelt summarily cancelled those contracts and ordered the Army flying service to carry the mail. Of two hundred eighty-one pilots available, only thirty-one had more than fifty hours of night flying. The planes were ill-equipped and few of the pilots instrument trained. After losing twelve fliers in two months of crashes, and incurring the criticism of a national idol, Charles Lindbergh, who had flown the mail before flying the Atlantic, an angry Roosevelt returned the contracts to private hands.

Out of his Navy Department background, Roosevelt was a sea power partisan. He once told an audience that no airplane, nor fleet of them, could successfully battle warships.

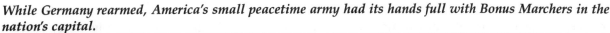

While Germany rearmed, America's small peacetime army had its hands full with Bonus Marchers in the nation's capital.

America's 1930s Army: helmets and rifles from World War I, cannons from trees.

Roosevelt aimed to keep military spending down. Chief of Staff Douglas MacArthur and Secretary of War George Dern tried to get Roosevelt to reconsider in the light of Germany's rearming and Japan's heightened activities on mainland Asia. A frustrated MacArthur finally said something about when the United States lost the next war and an American boy was lying in the mud with a bayonet through his belly and an enemy boot on his dying throat, uttering his last curse, he would rather the name on the boy's lips be Roosevelt and not MacArthur. Roosevelt was enraged and shouted, "You must not talk that way to the president!" But that was all that came of it. When next he dealt with MacArthur, it was to send him to the Philippines to establish a defense force there. No one believed the Philippines could be defended if the Japanese attacked, no one except MacArthur. But he would be thwarted by Congress.

It was no time for Roosevelt to broaden military spending or extend his horizons beyond the Atlantic shore. In the beginning, he even found something to like in what the fascist Mussolini was doing for the Italian economy, and he once said that what Hitler was doing was much the same as what his New Deal was doing. "But we are doing them in an orderly way."

Rehearsals

From Ethiopia to the Rhineland, from Spain to Nanking, the world was rehearsing for war.

Japan, despite its natural and verdant beauty, was not richly endowed with iron, oil and food, the essentials of industrial society. In the 1920s, certain elements eyed Manchuria in China as breadbasket, market, factory and homeland for a swelling 70 million population.

In 1931, the Japanese army, already stationed in Manchuria to protect the nation's interest, killed the ruling Chinese warlord. Soon, the Japanese occupied the whole territory, one the size of the U.S. West Coast. Japanese naval forces also seized Shanghai.

The League of Nations tut-tutted. The Japanese walked out and explained to the United States that they were sorry, but that Manchuria, renamed Manchukuo by them, had been "an incident," not a war.

In Japan, democracy was a home-grown hybrid. There were elders in Tokyo who disapproved of this aggression. Rivalries among young officers in the military, some contented with Manchukuo, others who felt Japan would never be "secure" until China was taken, set off waves of political assassinations. Above it all stood the emperor, standing just where ancient tradition required him to stand: above it all. He reigned. He did not rule. Hirohito had been raised from childhood to believe his role was as father to his people. They in turn idealized him as the embodiment of the national spirit. He was not even to be gazed upon by commoners.

Actually, Hirohito was an unprepossessing man happiest on Mondays and Saturdays when he could retire to his laboratory and study marine biology. Born in 1901, he had become emperor in 1926 after a European tour from which he returned with an admiration for Britain's constitutional monarchy. He and Empress Nagako had four daughters in a row, then two sons.

This mild man in baggy pants was the grandson of Emperor Meiji who had swept away the feudal framework of ancient Japan, one result of which left Hirohito as commander in chief of Japan's military.

Thus, he was technically in charge of a stubborn, aggressive, relentless overachiever named Hideki Tojo, a hard five-foot-two man who had risen by virtue of drive to become head of secret police in the Kwangtung army. He hated the United States dating to 1905 when Theodore Roosevelt's peace efforts in the Russian war denied many of the fruits 1f victory to Japan. Tojo's animus was rekindled by the "insult" of the 1924 immigration act.

To Tojo, Japanese expansion should be to the north against her obvious enemy, Russia. The Imperial navy, on the other hand, favored maximizing its fleet by moving the other way to the rice bowls and oil fields of Southeast Asia.

The army argued, with commendable foresight,

that the "southward movement" would inevitably bring the United States and the European colonial powers into a war. The fleet would have to take the Philippines to guard its flanks. Conversely, no one could object outside of Moscow to a war against communism. As the military exercised increasing control of the Cabinet, this decision would ultimately be made, in the summer of 1941.

But in July 1937, Japanese and Chinese troops had begun firing at each other near the Marco Polo bridge outside Peking. Japan sent in reinforcements, and war with China began in earnest.

In December, the Japanese, who already had shown themselves brutal conquerors, marched into Nanking. In an orgy surpassing that of Mongol hordes of the past, they raped and murdered, leaving perhaps 300,000 civilians dead.

Upriver from Nanking, on Sunday, December 12, 1937, Lieutenant Commander James Joseph Hughes was idling his 450-ton U.S. gunboat *Panay* in the Yangtze River, escorting three tankers and giving refuge to Western nationals. His gunboat was plainly marked with an American flag at its masthead and two more clearly painted on deck awnings. A demanding Japanese officer boarded, uninvited. Hughes outlined what the *Panay* was doing and then told the Japanese: "And now would you kindly leave my deck."

Then, shortly after lunch, two flights of Mitsubishi bombers, six planes in all, emblazoned with the Rising Sun, attacked the American vessels. They bombed and strafed until all four sank.

Then, as lifeboats carried survivors to shore, the planes machine-gunned them. Three sailors and a civilian were killed, eleven more crew members wounded.

A U.S. court of inquiry established that it had been a willful attack. Roosevelt rightly assessed it as a test of American determination in that part of the world. Ambassador Grew had expected the United States to attack in retaliation of the *Panay* assault. But instead America turned the other cheek.

Quietly, the Japanese awarded the commander of the *Panay* attack a medal. And in Tokyo, a seat was readied in the Cabinet for a new war minister, Hideki Tojo.

Europe was weaving a fabric of paper alliances as the Treaty of Versailles unravelled. But there was little or no will to confront Germany, and one year after he ordered national rearmament, one year punctuated with promises of peace, Hitler decided to test the will of the West.

On March 7, 1936, German troops, only three battalions, crossed the bridges over the Rhine into the demilitarized Rhineland. It was an act of perfidy and derring-do. The French could have, and

were entitled to have, blown the Germans away. Britain was obligated to back up the French. They did not. The Rhineland safely in his grasp, suddenly a hero at home, Hitler could design the future to suit himself. The chance the West had to stop him had passed.

Before January 1937 was out, Hitler withdrew Germany's signature to the Treaty of Versailles, a gesture more than anything else. It was the last vestige of the World War of 1914, the one they called "the war to end all wars." They also called it a war to make the world safe for democracy.

Hitler's brash move into the Rhineland showed that the armistice of 1918 had silenced only the guns.

The justness of the Treaty of Versailles was being tested by history. France wanted reparations and security against the Germans who had advanced on Paris five times in little more than a century. Great Britain looked for colonial spoils and coveted the German High Seas Fleet, the latter to no avail. The German ships were scuttled by their crews.

The United States asked for nothing in terms of territory or reparations, and in fact would loan Germany funds for recovery. It did insist, however, that its war loans be repaid with interest, thereby imposing a huge economic burden on its former allies, which the victors quickly passed on to the vanquished. All the more ironic, because President Woodrow Wilson had called for "peace without victors or vanquished." With the guns quiet he pressed with fierce idealism for the League of Nations. Ironically his own Congress would block entry into that essay at world government, dooming it eventually.

Versailles left the Teutonic ego bereft and bitter. Even old Marshal Foch, who had led the victory on the Western front, said, "This is not peace. It is an armistice for twenty years."

In 1936, Winston Churchill and his wife were taking a deliberate holiday from British politics, torn as the British government was between action and inaction. His friends told him he could not at that point change the course, so he bided their advice, took his paints to Spain. He later wrote:

"Our comfortable Barcelona hotel was the rendezvous of the Spanish Left. In the excellent restaurant where we lunched and dined were always several groups of eager-faced, black-coated young men purring together with glistening eyes about Spanish politics, in which quite soon a million Spaniards were to die."

Two months after Hitler's Rhineland coup, Italian troops, which had invaded Ethiopia eight months earlier, marched into the Ethiopian capital, Addis Ababa.

Two weeks after the fall of Ethiopia, Generalissimo Francisco Franco rebelled against the weak Spanish Republican government, ostensibly to save Spain from communism. In the ensuing civil war the Italians and the Germans had a new arena to test their military muscle.

Franco had the support of the army and most of the Catholic Church. He needed more and he turned to his fellow fascists in Europe to ask for it.

Mussolini sent up to 70,000 troops, and vast numbers of planes and other armaments. Germany spent half a billion marks, providing planes, tanks, technical help and the Condor Legion, whose major contribution was the aerial destruction of the town of Guernica, spiritual center of Spain's Basques, and most of its people.

It was an election year for Franklin Delano Roosevelt in a nation so anti-war and isolationist that even Ernest Hemingway warned against becoming involved in Spain. The bells had not tolled for him yet either.

FDR's "I hate war" speech was a reassurance to the isolationists, and yet he had some delicate manuevering. Theoretically, since the 1935 Neutrality Act did not apply to civil war, he could have allowed Franco to buy U.S. arms, which would probably have pleased pro-Franco Catholic voters. On the other hand it would have the look of American involvement and irritate the liberals. In the absence of Congress, he applied a moral embargo on all shipments to Spain, which Congress later confirmed by extending the Neutrality Act.

It was, however, an emotional time for many Americans. Some went to fight with the leftist Loyalists as volunteers. Some were moved by stories of Loyalist atrocities against Catholics. The

Brown Shirts marched in Germany for Nazism while the Bonus Army in the U.S. paraded for money.

U.S. State Department was staunchly anti-communist and at one point Secretary of State Cordell Hull would not even sign passports for an American volunteer ambulance unit planning to support the Loyalists.

The fear of communism led to a controversial decision by FDR that would affect Americans for years to come, including some academics, like a liberal young physicist named J. Robert Oppenheimer who would one day be faced with his idealist past. Roosevelt told FBI chief J. Edgar Hoover to extend his surveillance of communist groups beyond discerned threats against the president. He wanted to know more broadly what they were up to. In the years ahead the FBI would compile files on all sorts of Americans. The one on Oppenheimer would eventually reach the height of four-and-a-half feet.

Healing at Home, Heeling Abroad

As the Thirties edged on, there were signs of healing in America.

The Okies, dispossessed Oklahomans and others fleeing their dusty farms with their mattresses tied to the tops of their cars, managed to find a new life in California despite the hardships, their struggle later vividly captured in John Steinbeck's *The Grapes of Wrath*. Passengers on transcontinental trains had to wade through a foot of dust between cars on their way to the dining car. Even the sky over Chicago darkened with the windblown topsoil.

The two-engine DC-3 was becoming an alternative to cross-country travel. But it required several stops and overnight lodging.

American movies seemed obsessed with crime and Humphrey Bogart and James Cagney. They had begun the decade with anti-war and pacifist films like *All Quiet on the Western Front*, which starred Lew Ayres as a disillusioned young German soldier who survived the horrors of trench warfare, only to die in the final frames, reaching out to touch a butterfly. Ayres would become most liked as the affable, idealistic young Dr. Kildare. His popularity would haunt him when his nation went to war. A pacifist, he registered as a conscientious objector, volunteered for the ambulance service and nevertheless distinguished himself under fire.

Americans got used to night baseball and beer in cans, Gallup polls and Shirley Temple, movie house bank nights and bingo, bubble gum and Tootsie Rolls, sweater girl Lana Turner and sweet Ginger Rogers, ventriloquist Edgar Bergen and a wise-cracking not-so-dumb dummy Charlie McCarthy, sit-down strikes and miner-chief John L. Lewis, heavyweight Joe Louis and slinky Mary Martin, and dance halls and pop music by Benny Goodman, Tommy Dorsey, Glenn Miller, Artie Shaw, Guy Lombardo, Kay Kyser and Spike Jones. A dangerous music, a psychologist said, because the tempo is faster than the human pulse.

The first Alfred Hitchcock thrillers hit the silver screen and there was a radio in 27.5 million of America's 32 million family living rooms. Americans listened avidly to the shifting fortunes of the Barbours on "One Man's Family," and "The Shadow," a radio drama of a detective who could become invisible to those around him. The role of Lamont Cranston was played at one point by a twenty-year-old actor named Orson Welles.

There was an appeal to Americans in the omniscient crimefighter who knew what evil lurked in the hearts of men and that the seed of crime bears bitter fruit.

Radio also provided serious drama and commentary. Archibald MacLeish wrote "The Fall of the City," a story of a mythical metropolis, conquered by its own fear. A symbol of what seemed to be happening to the world.

But the radio was destined for far more than entertainment. It would open American minds to the rumblings of Europe, just as newsreels would open their eyes to the unbelievable image of a ranting, fiery Adolf Hitler who had half the world frightened near to death

The *Panay* incident did serve some purpose. It enabled Roosevelt to get a congressional OK for a billion-dollar two-ocean Navy. And, despite his earlier predilection for warships, he heeded the warnings of Air Force General Henry (Hap) Arnold that Germany's air fleet of 8,000 planes was a real threat. Arnold told him that the U.S. Army Air Corps with obsolete aircraft and something over 1,600 pilots was woefully inadequate. Roosevelt was becoming increasingly certain that war would eventually draw in America and that air power was a key to defense. He said in 1938 that the United States would need 8,000 warplanes. And the United States ordered its first thirteen B17s.

Repeatedly, Hitler reassured Europe that he had no plans to annex more territory. The German foreign minister Freiherr von Neurath told the American ambassador in London, William C. Bullitt, that Germany would do nothing else in Europe until it had finished its consolidation in the Rhineland.

Within months of promising Austria he would not interfere in its affairs, Hitler ordered his general staff to draw up contingency plans for the occupation of his neighbor.

By 1938, the Siegfried Line facing France was bristling with armaments and Hitler felt snug behind it. It would cost France or Britain dearly to cross that path. In a purge of his top generals (one because he had married a prostitute and another on trumped-up charges of homosexual activities), Hitler took over direct command of the army. In addition he got rid of Neurath, replacing him with a more obedient Joachim von Ribbentrop. The day after this spurt of activity, the official Nazi newspaper headlined, "Strongest Concentration of All Powers in the Fuehrer's Hands!" It was the beginning of what the Austrian chancellor, Dr. Kurt von Schuschnigg, remembered as "The Four Weeks Agony."

On February 12, 1938, Hitler met the Austrian chancellor at the border and took him to his mountain retreat at Berchtesgaden, alone to the second floor study where a huge picture window looked out on the Alps and Austria. Hitler's apparent good humor melted and he tore into the genteel Austrian, accusing him of obstructionism, accusing Austria of treason, lecturing him on Austrian and German history. The chancellor remembered the rhetoric like a combination of Julius Caesar and Jesus Christ. "I have a historic mission, and this mission I will fulfill because Providence has destined me to do so. . . . I have made the greatest achievement in the history of Germany, greater than any other German. And not by force, mind you. I am carried along by the love of my people. . . ."

He accused Schuschnigg of fortifying the border against Germany, which Schuschnigg denied.

Schuschnigg was given an ultimatum, demanding that his ban on the Austrian Nazi party be lifted, that amnesty be given all Nazis in jail, that pro-Nazis be named ministers of Interior, War and Finance. Steps would be taken to ensure close relations between the two armies and to assimilate the Austrian economy into the German. If he did as asked, there would be no further trouble from Hitler. When Schuschnigg told Hitler that only the Austrian president could sign such a document, Hitler blew up, and calling his generals, stalked out of the room. It was all bluff. The generals found Hitler chuckling over the plight of the lone Austrian grasping his hands.

The Austrians, including President Wilhelm Miklas, gave in to the German demands, and the pro-Nazis, released from prison, immediately began to take over the provinces. Hitler told the Reichstag that he would pledge the liberation of the ten million Germans who live in Austria and Czechoslovakia.

The Austrians tried to settle the question by plebiscite.

It caught Hitler and his generals by surprise and the fuehrer raged. He would not permit it. He ordered his army to move into Austria in three days: "The whole operation will be directed by myself."

He was not only dashing to the rescue; he was creating the damsel in distress. An unaware Schuschnigg was wakened by his bedside telephone to be told that the Germans had sealed the border, stopped all rail traffic and were concentrating their forces. Hitler wanted Schuschnigg to resign and he wanted a telegram inviting the Germans in. The Austrians balked at the telegram, but eventually the Nazi puppet installed as chancellor Arthur Seyss-Inquart, who exceeded his authority and delivered the invitation to invade by phone. German troops crossed the border and the fuehrer returned to his homeland as a hero returns, on the wings of adulation. The anschluss, the political reunification of Germany, was complete. Austria was incorporated into the Third Reich.

The rest of the world did nothing, treaties to the contrary. Hitler had established a practice of winning by bluff. He said, "When I crossed the frontier there met me such a stream of love as I have never experienced. Not as tyrants have we come, but as liberators."

For the American public, the anschluss took on a certain immediacy as the radio brought the news home as it happened. Edward R. Murrow reported from Vienna:

"It was called a bloodless conquest and in some ways it was—But I'd like to be able to forget the haunted look on the faces of those long lines of people outside the banks and the travel offices. People trying to get away. I'd like to forget the tired, futile look of the Austrian army officers, and the thud of hobnail boots and the crash of light tanks in the early hours of the morning in the Ringstrasse. . . . I'd like to forget the sound of the smashing glass as the Jewish shop streets were raided; the hoots and jeers at those forced to scrub the sidewalk. . . ."

Churchill asked the House of Commons: "How many friends will be alienated, how many potential allies shall we see go one by one down the grisly gulf? How many times will bluff succeed until behind bluff ever gathering forces have accumulated reality?"

Everyone knew Czechoslovakia had to be next. It was the last, best example of a small democracy in Europe. It was a nation of minorities. Besides the 3 million Germans, there were a million Hungarians and 500,000 Ruthenians of Russian descent. And there were Poles as well. The Czechs and Slovaks

In 1933 Nazis were only burning "un-German" books. Germany's ovens came later.

made up most of the 10 million population, and although closely related, even they had different cultures and history. For all that, the Czechoslovak minorities all voted, shared full civil rights, and some even had their own schools to help preserve their cultural differences.

Still there was plenty of potential enmity for Hitler to work on. He set to the task at once, and ordered the military to dust off plans for the invasion. His foreign office secretly subsidized the Sudeten German Party, which represented the Germans in Czechoslovakia.

He would use propaganda and saber-rattling to intimidate the Czechs. If he had to use military force, he wanted the vaunted Czech industrial plant intact. He encouraged the Poles and Hungarians to cooperate militarily. They would get a share of the pie.

In May, the Czechs ordered a partial mobilization, and Britain and France warned that a move against Czechoslovakia meant war. Hitler was furious, his bluff called. So he delayed his plans.

But secretly Hitler had already set October 1, 1938, for his attack.

"UNRELIABLES"

In the wake of Hitler's triumphal entry into Austria, Heinrich Himmler's SS forces arrested some 79,000 "unreliables" in the streets of Vienna in the first few weeks of the anschluss. Half of the city's 180,000 Jews were able to "buy" the right to emigrate by surrendering their possessions to the new government, run from Berlin.

The agency that handled these "problems" was the Office for Jewish Emigration, run by an Austrian Nazi by the name of Karl Adolf Eichmann, who would ultimately terminate the lives of some 4 million people, mostly Jews. Himmler and Reinhard Heydrich of the SS decided it was too expensive to ship Austrian prisoners back to concentration camps in Germany. So part of the benefit of the anschluss was that Austria got a concentration camp of its own at Mauthausen, where 35,318 people were executed in the six-and-a-half years it operated.

Less formally, the Nazi street mobs used the Danube as a burial ground.

The Road to Munich

Roosevelt's friends noticed changes in his behavior. His Secretary of the Interior Harold Ickes, a blunt, faithful aide-de-camp, said the president seemed a beaten man, somehow adrift. His own vice president, John Nance Garner, who had eyes on the presidency himself, called FDR "scared and tired" to his face. Ickes, who was present, was astonished.

Midway in his first term, having survived another recession and constant obstructionism by conservatives and big business, the random railings of extremists, Roosevelt told Secretary of Treasury Henry Morgenthau, Jr., at lunch, "The next two years really don't count. They are over the dam."

But the transient paranoia and the lassitude were passing things, the product of being tied to that chair constantly, he once said, not being able to get up and walk around the room. A sitting duck.

When it came to foreign affairs, he was guarded at best. He did not want another war, least of all one that involved America. He adopted a wait-and-see attitude on the appeasement policies. As he told one of his envoys, "if the Chief of Police makes a deal with the leading gangsters and there are no more hold-ups, that Chief of Police will be called a great man—but if the gangsters do not live up to their word the Chief of Police will go to jail."

The State Department was of little help. It considered communists the real enemies, Nazis acceptable alternatives. Roosevelt kept asking them why they didn't use what powers they had to curb the Japanese, or at least give them pause.

He distrusted, even disliked, some of his appointees, for instance, Joe Kennedy, his wealthy ambassador to London. And British Prime Minister Neville Chamberlain. Everyone, it seemed, was telling Roosevelt that Hitler was merely readjusting the evil wrought by Versailles, and the United States should stay out of it. So far as Hitler's anti-Semitism went, there were a lot of anti-Semites in the American diplomatic corps.

At one point, he balked at the thought of a huge influx of Jewish refugees. He thought of them as a domestic political problem, and considered somewhere else for them, Mexico maybe, or Venezuela or West Africa. Then he changed his mind and found a way to expedite their entry into the United States.

With resolution failing, the French asked British Prime Minister Chamberlain to make the best bargain possible with Hitler. Chamberlain wired the fuehrer that he wanted to talk peace face to face. They agreed to meet at Berchtesgaden on September 15.

Goering said of Czech crisis talks in 1938 with Chamberlain: "We got everything we wanted, just like that."

Chamberlain landed at Munich in the afternoon. He had been traveling since dawn by plane and train, arriving at Hitler's retreat in time for tea, after which he was led up to the second floor study where the Austrian chancellor had been pilloried a few months before. Through that great picture window, dark rain clouds gathered over the mountains.

Hitler began by lecturing Chamberlain on his record. On his agenda, there was only one problem left. The return of the Sudetenland to the Reich. Chamberlain agreed personally to let the Sudeten Germans decide for themselves by plebiscite whether to cede themselves to Germany.

Now the powers proceeded to mull the fate of the Czechoslovakians who were somehow not invited to the party. The British and French, dealing with the impatient and unpredictable fuehrer, were in a hurry. So they told the Czechs that if they did not agree to the return of the Sudetenland, they could expect no further help. The Czechs finally were forced to acquiesce with the bitter words, "We have been basely betrayed."

Chamberlain thus went to meet Hitler again in the little town of Godesberg on the Rhine, now ready to present the German with everything he had asked for. He had been stung by criticism at home and approached the meeting as a man with a mission; save the world from war at all costs.

He offered all Hitler wanted and more, ceding the Sudetenland now without plebiscite in return for an international guarantee against any unprovoked attack on the remainder of Czechoslovakia. Chamberlain's self-satisfied smile faded quickly.

The fuehrer said it would not be enough.

Chamberlain retreated in dismay to consult with his allies. The Czechs were told their erstwhile allies could no longer ask that they not mobilize.

Now Hitler demanded German occupation of the entire Sudetenland immediately, not later and not step by step as Chamberlain had proposed. While he and Chamberlain were meeting the next day, Hitler got the news that the Czechs had mobilized.

"Now, of course the whole affair is settled," Hitler said. "The Czechs will not dream of ceding any territory to Germany."

Finally Hitler, as if he were doing Chamberlain a favor, said he would wait until October 1 for the Czechs to abandon the Sudetenland, no later. He promised it would be his last territorial demand in Europe.

But the Czechs balked, the French ordered a partial mobilization and the British tried to get Hitler back to the table, to no avail. It looked again as if this were the end. Britain and France would have to honor their commitments.

On September 27, Hitler secretly ordered seven divisions to the Czech frontier, and mobilized five new divisions to face France.

Roosevelt, the king of Sweden, even Mussolini made appeals to Hitler. Combined, the Czechs and French outnumbered the Germans two-to-one. The British declared a state of emergency. Air raid ditches were dug in London parks and school children were evacuated.

Then Hitler stopped at the brink again. He telegraphed Chamberlain, denying he was threatening Czechoslovakia's existence, saying he was ready to negotiate a formal guarantee, and hoping Chamberlain could bring Prague "to reason at the very last hour."

The letter had its intended effect. Chamberlain messaged back that he thought Hitler could get what he wanted without war. He was ready to meet with Hitler, the Czechs, the French and the Italians, if Hitler desired. "I feel convinced we can reach agreement in a week. I cannot believe that you will take responsibility of starting a world war which may end civilization for the sake of a few days delay. . . ."

All the parties, save the Czechs and Russians, would meet in Munich with Mussolini's good offices. In London, when Jan Masaryk, the son of the Czech founder and now its ambassador to Britain, was told the Czechs were not invited to what looked like their own funeral, he said: "If you have sacrificed my nation to preserve the peace of the world, I will be the first to applaud you. But if not, gentlemen, God help your souls."

Mussolini thought it odd that Hitler had no wife, not even a mistress, but hailed Berlin-Rome Axis as marriage of "the greatest and most genuine democracies."

Chamberlain returns from Munich bearing—he believed—"peace in our time."

The conference ended at 2 a.m., September 30. Munich gave Hitler the Sudetenland. As they adjourned, Chamberlain asked Hitler if they might meet briefly in private. He presented him with a draft of what he hoped Hitler would make a joint declaration. It said in part:

"We regard the agreement signed last night, and the Anglo-German Naval Agreement, as symbolic of the desire of our two peoples never to go to war with one another again.

"We are resolved that the method of consultation shall be the method adopted to deal with any other questions that may concern our two countries, and we are determined to continue our efforts to remove possible sources of difference, and thus to contribute to assure the peace of Europe."

Hitler signed it quickly. It was only paper.

But that little piece of paper, which Chamberlain would wave to the crowds outside 10 Downing Street, gave rise to his pitiable summation, "This is the second time in our history that there has come back from Germany to Downing Street peace with honour. I believe it is peace in our time."

The Czechs were told, agree or deal with the Germans alone. When the final terms were delivered, Dr. Kamil Krofta, the foreign minister, said in anger and sadness, ". . . now everything is at an end; today it is our turn, tomorrow it will be the turn of others."

THE FEAST

In the wake of Munich, the feast began.

Poland got 650 square miles of Czechoslovakia and a population of 228,000, more than half of whom were Czechs. Hungary took 7,500 square miles in which lived 500,000 Hungarian Magyars and 272,000 Slovaks. Germany got 11,000 square miles with 2,800,000 Sudeten Germans and 800,000 Czechs, and a pro-German government in Prague.

The bluff won Hitler Germany 66 percent of Czechoslovakia's coal, 80 percent of its lignite and cement and textiles, 86 percent of its chemicals, 70 percent of its iron, steel and electrical power and 40 percent of its timber.

Kristallnacht

America heard it all on radio, live from Prague, London, Paris, Munich. And they read it in the big, black headlines. The events in Europe were becoming a clear and present danger.

Once more the instrument that brought Americans "Jack Armstrong," "The Green Hornet," "The Lone Ranger," and "Kay Kyser's Kollege of Musical Knowledge," now set the adrenalin racing with the threat of war.

After Munich, a poll showed that three-quarters of Americans thought their country would be drawn into a war in Europe, three times as many as a poll taken a year-and-a-half earlier. And only one in ten Americans thought good things could come of the pact at Munich.

They heard Winston Churchill say of his own country, "Britain and France had to choose between war and dishonor. They chose dishonor. They will have war."

Even President Roosevelt remarked, "The dictator threat from Europe is a good deal closer to the United States."

In fact the nation was so jittery that when dial-spinners tuned into CBS one night after 8:30 and heard that the nation had been invaded by Martians, otherwise rational folk panicked. Hundreds of thousands took to the streets, only to learn later that it was a dramatization of H.G. Wells' *War of the Worlds*.

Hitler's gold star. After war began, all Jews had to wear Star of David.

German street sign in 1935: "Jews not wanted in this place!"

The American mind was changing, however, and what came next would shock them further. Roosevelt would tell his 500th press conference, "I myself could scarcely believe that such things could occur in a 20th-century civilization."

And the worried German ambassador would report home that "the respectable patriotic circles, which are thoroughly anti-communist and, for the greater part, anti-Semitic in their outlook, also begin to turn away from us. . . . That men like Dewey, Hoover, Hearst, and many others who have hitherto maintained a cooperative reserve and have even, to some extent, expressed sympathy toward Germany, are now publicly adopting so violent and bitter an attitude against her is a serious matter."

What was the furor about?

It began in Paris. A seventeen-year-old Jewish refugee, seeking revenge for his father who was among 10 thousand Jews deported to Poland by boxcar, shot and mortally wounded the third secretary of the German embassy, Ernst Vom Rath. The young refugee, Herschel Grynszpan, had intended to kill the ambassador, but fired at the first embassy official he saw.

Thereby began a reign of cataclysm and terror that the Nazis would call "The Week of Broken Glass," beginning with what the Jews still remember as "Kristallnacht"—Crystal Night, for the shattered glass store windows.

Handwriting on the wall: 1935 sign says "Germans Don't Buy in Jewish Shops."

With Hitler's approval, the top Nazis gathered at the end of the annual celebration of the Munich Beer Hall Putsch, Hitler's abortive 1924 power grab, and set about planning the revenge for Vom Rath's murder. On the night of November 9, Goebbels called for the destruction of Jewish businesses and private apartments and synagogues wherever fire or other damage would not threaten German

November 10, 1938, was a national "Day of Vengeance" in Germany. Broken glass of Jewish shops gave it the name Kristallnacht.

life or property. Demonstrations would not be hindered by police, and "as many Jews, especially rich ones, are to be arrested as can be accommodated in the existing prisons. . . . Upon their arrest the appropriate concentration camps should be contacted immediately, in order to confine them in these camps as soon as possible." There was one caveat: no looting; that would come later by more legal means.

In a first report by the SS, at least 815 shops, 117 houses, 195 synagogues had been destroyed or set afire. Twenty thousand were imprisoned and at least thirty-six killed. The murders were considerably higher, and a day later the number of Jewish shops looted was put at 7,500.

The next step was to banish the Jews from the German economy, confiscate their businesses and property, including jewelry and works of art (Goering was angry when he had heard so many valuables had been destroyed). They left until later the decision of how to ban the Jews from every public facility from schools to forests, and how to expel them or confine them in ghettos or impress them as forced labor.

POEMS

After the close of World War I, William Butler Yeats wrote a haunting and prophetic, although short, poem, "The Second Coming." Reading it in the context of its time, one might wonder if he meant resurrection or war. It said in part:
> Things fell apart; the center cannot hold,
> Mere anarchy is loosed upon the world,
> The blood-dimmed tide is loosed, and everywhere
> The ceremony of innocence is drowned,
> The best lack all conviction, while the worst
> Are full of passionate intensity.

In the tide of poems that captured the horrors of World War I was one that in 1939 would seem so ironic. By John McRae, it evoked voices from the graves of that first cataclysm:
> To you from failing hands we throw
> The torch; be yours to hold it high.
> If ye break faith with us who die
> We shall not sleep, though poppies grow
> In Flanders Fields.

2 INVASION: 1939

On the last day in January 1939 at the White House, President Roosevelt called in the Senate Military Affairs Committee to confide his fearful appraisal of the world. He told the senators:

"About three years ago we got the pretty definite information that there was in the making a policy of world domination between Germany, Italy and Japan. . . . There are two ways of looking at it. The first . . . is the hope that somebody will assassinate Hitler or that Germany will blow up from within; that somebody will kill Mussolini or he will get a bad cold in the morning and die. . . . The other attitude is that we must try to prevent the domination of the world."

He offered a geography lesson. America's first line of defense, he said, is a thin line of islands in the Pacific from which, somehow, the Navy, Army and their planes can stop the Japanese. The first line of defense in the east is a very large group of nations in Europe and the Mediterranean.

He said Hitler was a "wild man" who thinks he is "a reincarnation of Julius Caesar and Jesus Christ." "A nut."

"Now if he insists on going to the westward . . . and the French and British . . . decide to fight, then you come to the question of arms. . . . It is a fifty-fifty bet that they would be put out of business and that Hitler and Mussolini would win. . . . Then the next step, which Brother Hitler suggested in the speech yesterday, would be Central and South America. . . . Do not say it is just a pipedream. Would any of you have said six years ago . . . that Germany would dominate Europe?"

He had drawn the line. Hitler was the enemy,

whether the nation knew it or not. Peace was slipping through the trembling fingers of Europe.

In America, two weeks after Munich, George C.

A STORYBOOK PHANTOM

On the eve of the Polish invasion, a Swedish envoy, a last minute friend-of-the-peace, described a futile midnight meeting with the fuehrer who had been roused from bed by Goering. It is more interesting as an insight into Hitler's madness than it was for any chance of success. He said the German leader walked up and down excitedly almost talking to himself, then:

"Suddenly he stopped in the middle of the room and stood there staring. His voice was blurred, and his behavior that of a completely abnormal person. He spoke in staccato phrases: 'If there should be war then I shall build U-boats, U-boats, U-boats, U-boats.' His voice became more indistinct and finally one could not follow him at all. Then he pulled himself together, raised his voice as though addressing a large audience and shrieked: 'I shall build airplanes, airplanes, airplanes, and I shall annihilate my enemies.' He seemed more like a phantom from a storybook than a real person."

Then Hitler confronted his visitor and asked why he couldn't make an agreement with the British. The Swede suggested they might lack confidence in him. Hitler struck his breast with his left hand and said, "Idiots! Have I ever told a lie in my life?"

The fuehrer gets a model of the new "people's car," a Volkswagen, on his 49th birthday in 1938.

Marshall, under whom had trained most of the prime members of the U.S. officer corps, was appointed Deputy Chief of Staff. At an early White House meeting, he had the audacity to tell his frustrated president he didn't think much of his plan to build 10,000 planes a year to catch up with Hitler and the rest of the world.

Some old hands wondered if Marshall hadn't doomed his career, but five months later Roosevelt would bypass thirty-four more senior officers and name him Chief of Staff. It was the beginning of a relationship that would cost Marshall his dream of leading combat troops, but would keep him nearby in Washington, a loyal and steady hand that Roosevelt could depend on.

The year 1939 was full of anomalies.

Adolf Hitler, between conquests, posed with a model of the Volkswagen, "The People's Car," that he was said to have helped design. He promised one for every German worker, another promise unkept. He also showed his gratitude for Chamberlain's role at averting war by criticizing the British for interference in Germany's affairs. "We cannot tolerate any longer the tutelage of governesses," he said. Meanwhile, he turned the huge Skoda works

in what had been Czechoslovakia to producing arms for his burgeoning armed forces, the Wehrmacht. And in January he ordered his generals to make plans for Poland by September.

General Hap Arnold, who had been taught to fly by the Wright brothers, inherited an Army Air Corps that had 20,000 men and a few hundred planes inferior to any combat aircraft in the modern world.

Congress, unwilling to risk offending the Japanese, would not vote the funds to fortify the U.S. base at Guam in the Marianas, and MacArthur's plans for the defense of the Philippines was scaled down to a defense of Manila harbor and the fortress island of Corregidor.

While Hitler was cowing Europe and manipulating the Western powers at Munich, the Japanese landed in South China forcing Chiang Kai-shek to retreat inland and establish a new capital at Chungking. A sharp-minded Colonel Joseph Stilwell, an old China hand, was U.S. military attache and had watched and reported Chiang's ineptness against the Japanese for years. When he and his family returned home in 1939, the ship's radio brought the news that Marshall had promoted him to brigadier general.

From his seat in Commons, Winston Churchill continued to press his government to beef up British arms, and deplored what he later called "a line of milestones to disaster . . . a catalogue of surrenders." "By this time next year we shall know whether the policy of appeasement has appeased, or whether it has only stimulated a more ferocious appetite."

He was not entirely unsuccessful. Britain began replacing its old biplane fighters with more modern Hurricanes and ultimately Spitfires. With 1939 half over, Britain could count twenty-six squadrons of eight-gun fighters, not equal to the 1,100 fighters and 1,500 bombers of the Luftwaffe, but closing the gap. America's most modern fighters, the early model P-40s, still mounted two machine guns firing through the propeller as old World War I fighters did, not wing-mounted as were the British, German and Japanese planes.

Chamberlain visited Mussolini to buttress the "peace." He showed the text he would deliver to Parliament, which led Mussolini, Il Duce, to wonder privately, "I believe this is the first time that the head of the British government has submitted to a foreign government the outlines of one of his speeches. It's a bad sign for them."

Japanese soldiers in China fly the Rising Sun battle flag near Hankow in 1938.

Winston Churchill was a lonely voice of protest against Hitler in 1938.

A grim Dr. Emil Hacha, president of Czechoslovakia, accepts the inevitable as Hitler occupies the nation in March 1939 for its own "protection."

Meanwhile, the weakened Czechs searched for one iota of good will in Hitler's heart, willing to give almost anything away for some semblance of national existence.

The Czechs tried their own brand of appeasement. They dissolved the Communist Party, yanked all Jewish teachers from German schools.

Nevertheless their days were numbered. On March 15, 1939, Hitler would have his day of pride.

How he got there is as cynical a story as he could write. First German propaganda and agents provocateurs whipped up disturbances in the remnants of Czech territory. Accusations of brutality against Germans, down to the smallest detail: a pregnant German woman struck down in the streets by "Czech beasts." Charges of murder of defenseless Germans.

Such was the backdrop for the visit by the Czech president, Emil Hacha, on March 14. Unable to fly because of a heart condition, Hacha and his party arrived in Berlin by train late that evening.

The Germans laid out the red carpet, a military honor guard, flowers and chocolates for Hacha's daughter and the swankest suite at the posh Adlon Hotel. It belied what was to follow.

Hacha was summoned to the fuehrer's presence at 1:15 in the morning. He had heard before he left Prague that German troops lined the border of his little state, and had occupied an industrial town. He was reduced to begging for some semblance of a "national life" for his tiny emasculated country.

Hitler was not buying. He had already given his troops orders to march at 6 a.m., so time was precious. Coexistence had been impossible. Czech territory would become part of the Third Reich. In fact, initial resistance at a military barracks "had been ruthlessly broken."

Fight and we will destroy you, Hitler said. Stand back and let us enter peacefully and perhaps you

will have some degree of autonomy. This was "the last good turn" he could do for the Czech people.

He would leave Hacha and his foreign minister to think about it. But Hacha said immediately in desperation, "The position is quite clear. Resistance would be folly."

Nevertheless, how could he notify all the Czech people in just four hours? Hitler said that was up to him, and left the Czechs to the tender ministrations of Goering and Foreign Minister Joachim von Ribbentrop. Hitler also thoughtfully provided his personal physician Theodor Morrell who was good at giving shots. It was now 2:15 in the morning. One report describes the heartless humiliation:

"The German ministers were pitiless. They literally hunted (them) around the table on which the (surrender) documents were lying, thrusting them continually before them, pushing pens into their hands, repeating that if they continued in their

Too late...British Prime Minister Neville Chamberlain makes anti-Nazi speech after disastrous Munich pact in 1938.

refusal, half of Prague would lie in ruins from bombing within two hours, and that would only be the beginning. Hundreds of bombers were waiting the order to take off, and they would receive that order at 6 in the morning if the signatures were not forthcoming."

Suddenly the ailing president fainted, and Goering and Von Ribbentrop, alarmed at what the world might say about murder in the German Chancellery, paused long enough to allow Morrell to give Hacha an injection. It brought him to long enough to talk to his Cabinet in Prague over a special line, advising surrender. A second injection sustained him long enough to walk him into another room where he signed the surrender papers in Adolf Hitler's presence.

Once out of sight of the weary Czechs, Hitler was delighted. He hugged his secretaries and shouted, "Children! This is the greatest day in my life. I shall go down in history as the greatest German." That evening the fuehrer made his triumphal entry into the Czech capital.

Hitler outlines his demands for Czechoslovakia to the Reichstag prior to the Munich negotiations. Goering presides behind him.

They Would Get War

If governments were slow to react, public outrage was not. So strong was the outcry from public and press that Chamberlain's hold on the British government was in danger. He now threw out a prepared speech and admonished Hitler for breaching the Munich agreement.

"I am convinced," he said on the eve of his seventieth birthday, "that after Munich the great majority of the British people shared my honest desire that that policy should be carried further, but today I share their disappointment, their indignation, that those hopes have been so wantonly shattered.

Almost two weeks later he informed Parliament that Britain and its Commonwealth and France would be "bound at once to lend the Polish government all support in their power," should Poland resist attack.

In March, Hitler personally liberated the former German port of Memel, it and its German population wrested from little Lithuania by threat. In April, an inspired Mussolini swept through little Albania.

Roosevelt's frustration at all this would not keep. Still hamstrung by his Neutrality Act which he rued ever signing, he sent a note to Hitler and Mussolini in mid-April. It said:

"Are you willing to give assurance that your armed forces will not attack or invade territory of the following independent nations?"

The list of thirty-one countries included all of Europe, the Baltic States, Soviet Union and, of course, Poland. "You have repeatedly asserted that you and the German people have no desire for war. If this is true there need be no war."

Hitler responded in a speech to the Reichstag thirteen days later, a speech replete with sarcasm and hypocrisy. It went on for more than two hours and was broadcast worldwide, including in the United States. In short, it made fun at Roosevelt's efforts to maintain the peace.

And in passing he mentioned that Poland's mobilization had negated the German-Polish non-aggression pact.

Roosevelt was incensed, but kept publicly quiet.

Meanwhile there were strange doings that would have further reinforced the American isolationist notion that Europe was a snake's nest of perfidy. They would make Germany and Italy forget that they were allied against Russia and communism. They would show the West that it wasn't wise to snub Josef Stalin as Britain had done at least twice through the Austrian and Czechoslovak crises. It made Stalin wonder if the West wasn't trying to provoke an angry confrontation between the Soviets and the Germans.

The first clue would have been the sudden resignation of Foreign Minister Maxim Litvinov, a Jew, who had been a devotee of the containment of Germany by treaty with the West. He was replaced by Vyacheslav Molotov, a close associate of Stalin. Some noted a bow to German anti-Semitism.

Before mid-May the French government was aware of rumors in Berlin of an impending agreement between the Germans and the Soviets to split Poland between the two of them. It was overshadowed by the signing in late May of "the Pact of Steel," tying Italian fortunes to Hitler's.

Hitler reminded his generals and admirals that "further successes can no longer be attained without the shedding of blood. . . . It is a question of expanding our living space in the East, of securing food supplies and also of solving the problem of the Baltic States. . . . If fate forces us into a showdown with the West it is invaluable to possess a large area in the East. In wartime we shall be even less able to rely on record harvests than in peacetime."

That meant Poland, and not just for food, but as a source of labor. Hitler's deadline for Poland was September 1. Meanwhile the allies dilly-dallied over a possible treaty with Stalin who was being secretly wooed by, of all people, Hitler.

Then the unthinkable came to pass.

On August 20 Hitler telegrammed his acceptance of a Soviet-drafted non-aggression pact. The two countries would divide Poland between them and the Russians were to have a free hand in the eastern Baltic.

Hitler then put Case White, the Polish operation, on automatic. If the West went to war, Italy promised it would make noises in the south to occupy some French troops without actually joining the battle.

Suddenly on August 31, the Polish ambassador's phone lines to Warsaw were cut. That night Hitler broadcast to his people peace proposals to Poland which he had never given to the Poles, his usual ploy to prepare the German mind for war.

Finally he launched Operation Canned Goods, planned months before. SS troops in Polish uniforms staged a mock attack on a German radio station at Gleiwitz on the Polish border, leaving a drugged concentration camp inmate, smeared with blood, as a German casualty of the attack. There were other such "provocations" along the border. Berlin was calmly asleep, but all communications to the outside world were cut. It would awaken to a war that would eventually destroy it and much of Europe as well.

War: "God Help Us All"

It was 5:20 a.m., September 1, 1939, smack on Hitler's timetable. A German warplane attacked the Polish fishing village of Puck and an adjacent air base on the Gulf of Danzig. Twenty-five minutes later a naval shell from the *Schleswig-Holstein* made a direct hit on a Polish amunition dump at Westerplatte. It was dawn as the Wehrmacht began a motorized march toward Warsaw, and a new word, blitzkrieg, lightning war, became part of the

Dashing but futile, Polish lancers would soon be pitting their horses against the steel of Hitler's tanks.

military lexicon.

At 2:30 a.m., Washington time, four hours after the attack began, the phone at President Roosevelt's bedside rang. It was his ambassador in Paris, Bill Bullitt.

"Tony Biddle has just got through from Warsaw, Mr. President. Several German divisions are deep in Polish territory, and fighting is heavy. Tony said there were reports of bombers over the city. Then he was cut off. . . ."

"Well, Bill, it's come at last. God help us all."

In London, mobilization was ordered and Winston Churchill was called to 10 Downing Street where Chamberlain asked him to join a small War Cabinet of ministers. But that was all he heard from Chamberlain until September 3, when the prime minister in a broadcast informed the nation that Britain was at war.

In a reshuffle of his government, Chamberlain not only gave Churchill a seat on an expanded War Cabinet, but also the Admiralty, which he had once served as First Lord, and at which he arrived at 6 p.m. to take charge. The signal had already gone out to the fleet: "Winston is back."

That same day in Berlin, Hitler received the news of Britain's declaration with an immobile stare. The bluffs had run out. Goering, when he heard, said, "If we lose this war, then God have mercy on us!"

Hitler donned a military uniform and pledged to his people he would not return to civilian clothes until victory was won, a promise he would keep to his death.

The French played for time, adding a few insignificant hours to its mobilization before declaring war. A last minute peace appeal by Germany's ally to the south failed.

There were those in the West who thought the Poles could hold out for a couple of months. Even the Germans were thinking in terms of weeks. But German power and speed had not been measured. It became a war of horse-drawn artillery against motorized guns that rolled down bad roads at forty miles an hour, a war of lances against tanks. The Polish air force was destroyed in forty-eight hours by German bombers. Stukas punctuated the sky, dive bombing Polish troops who quickly learned to lie low until the planes came out of their dives and machine gun them as they struggled for altitude again. Cracow, Poland's second city, fell on September 6. That same night the Polish government fled the capital. Within one week Poland's thirty-five divisions had been either surrounded or defeated by fast moving German panzers. It was all over in seventeen days.

The Germans kept trying to hurry up the Russians into the fray to move to the prearranged borders as their part of the spoils, and to take some of the international blame. Stalin had other ideas. He wanted the approval of the Germans to a statement that the Soviets had moved into Poland to save the White Russians and others from Nazi rule. The flabbergasted Germans would not agree. So Stalin redrew the occupation zones, giving Hitler a small slice of his Poland in return for suzerainty over the Baltic countries of Latvia, Estonia and Lithuania. After publicly and jointly pledging to re-establish law and order to permit the people to enjoy their pursuit of a normal life according to their own cultural heritage, both German and Soviet agreed on a reign of terror to suppress any semblance of freedom or national life.

Stalin got more than the Germans wanted to give him, Ukrainian wheat and Romanian oil, and a buffer of countries against likely German perfidy. Hitler had no choice. He could not afford immediately an aggressor at his rear, and he had to turn quickly to face Britain and France in the west. Just as the Rhineland was the beginning of the beginning, one could say that Poland was the beginning of the end, although it was not immediately evident.

The expected clash of the giants in the west didn't happen. The French army, brought to the front by a divided government, sat behind the Maginot Line, the fortifications on the eastern frontier, unwilling to force the issue. Poland had been a demonstration of incredible military force. It had an effect. Everyone was afraid to commit. The first British troops could not be expected in France until October. Even Hitler, grateful for the time, used restraint. Any incursion, including any air raid on Britain, would require his personal approval. The navy, however, was given carte blanche against the British.

With the war with Britain only ten hours old, the British liner *Athenia* with 1,400 passengers aboard was torpedoed without warning and sunk some 200 miles west of Scotland's Hebrides Islands. Of the 112 lost, twenty-eight were Americans.

The Germans denied that any submarine had fired (but it had, as was later proved) and accused Churchill of putting a time bomb aboard the ship to blame the Germans. In the first week of the war, the Germans sent eleven British ships to the bottom, and for all of September claimed twenty-nine ships sunk, twenty-six by U-boat and three by mines.

The land war that the German populace dreaded would be called, with some relief, a Sitzkrieg, a "sitting" war. But it gave Roosevelt the edge he had been looking for. He had sat politically silent when Hitler rubbed his nose in his last peace note, angry but silent. And he worked quietly behind the scenes to get the Neutrality Act lifted.

Publicly, in a radio fireside chat after the British declaration of war, he said, "This nation will remain a neutral nation, but I cannot ask that every American remain neutral in thought as well. Even a neutral has the right to take account of the facts. Even a neutral cannot be asked to close his mind or his conscience."

Privately he told House and Senate leaders of both parties that the German press was making hay

World-famed flier Charles A. Lindbergh, after Nazi invasion of Poland, urges America to keep out of the fighting.

with America's isolationist sentiments, citing every stay-at-home statement as pro-German. He called a special session of Congress on September 21 to join the battle.

Less than a week before, pursuing his heartfelt cause, Charles Lindbergh, the Lone Eagle, had emerged as a champion of isolationism. He described the European war as "a quarrel arising from the errors of the last war," although "quarrel" was trivializing it a bit. "This is not a question of banding together to defend the white race against foreign invasion."

There were many different voices, some patriotic, some not, defending the Neutrality Act. But there were also the shrill echoes of Father Charles Coughlin, the radio priest, and the march of home-bred Nazis of the German-American Bund, and the hidden fact that the campaign to retain neutrality was supported in part by German funds.

It became a month-long fight, Roosevelt's strategists insisting that the only issue before the Congress was the Neutrality Act. If there were other emergency issues, they would just have to wait. FDR called in senators one by one for presidential jawboning. He also asked the governor general of Canada to delay a planned visit: "I am almost literally walking on eggs. . . . I am at the moment saying nothing, seeing nothing, hearing nothing."

Finally on October 27 by a 63-30 vote the Senate repealed the Neutrality Act with the House following. Arms were now for sale, cash and carry, and the first British freighters began loading a week later.

While all this was going on, a curious, but terribly important, letter came across FDR's desk.

It was written in August by Leo Szilard, one of a now sizable contingent of displaced European scientists working in America. It was also to be signed by Albert Einstein. It recounted the rapidly growing science of atomic fission, and its potential as an explosive device of incredible power.

Its bearer, New Deal economist Alexander Sachs, told him that Napoleon had turned down Fulton's steamboat, not farsighted enough to see that it could carry his soldiers to England. The president got the point.

Slouching Toward War

It is 1940, a presidential election year. No American president has ever run for a consecutive third term, and two-term FDR lets anyone who will listen know that he is tired, wants out. It sets the political scene abuzz. Democrats like Postmaster General James Farley and Vice President John Nance Garner covet the presidency, and FDR does not like the prospect. A former Democrat and Roosevelt supporter named Wendell Willkie gets the Republican nomination. A former Republican, Henry Wallace, becomes Roosevelt's running mate.

America's isolationists see their cause fading. Newspaper ads for this cause or that blossom across the land. Roosevelt says he doesn't want war but he also does not want Europe under the sway of Hitler and Stalin. At the same time nobody, except West Coasters, notices that Japan continues to gnaw away at China.

Dictatorships are tidy, democracy is not. For FDR, compromise is necessary, allowing the rhetoric space. Yet the task of a statesman is to redefine the issues to form a consensus. And that, eventually, is what he and time did.

In January he confided to his Secretary of the Treasury over lunch: "I do not want to run unless between now and the convention things get very, very much worse in Europe."

The same month he sent Assistant Secretary of State Sumner Welles to all the old places for one last try at better answers. Would Chamberlain negotiate if Hitler pulled out of Poland and Czechoslovakia? Of course not, Chamberlain says, Hitler lies. Welles liked Hitler, even understood his German. Mussolini was even better. The French were dismayed that this was an envoy of FDR. The only one that Welles disapproved of was Winston Churchill who Welles said was smoking a two-foot cigar when they met and drinking a whiskey and soda with evidence that he had had a good many more.

Sumner Welles (by clock), Roosevelt's personal envoy to Europe, meets with Prime Minister Chamberlain of Britain and U.S. Ambassador Joseph P. Kennedy (r.).

A synonym for betrayal: Vidkun Quisling was named to head puppet government after Germany invaded Norway in April 1940.

Roosevelt and Churchill had helped run their nation's navies. Perhaps because of this, Roosevelt invited Churchill into a secret correspondence, epistles to be delivered by either's couriers. It was a correspondence that would weave a mutual fabric for action. Churchill would sign his communiques "Naval Person," until he became prime minister when he signed them "Former Naval Person."

Random events punctuate the Sitzkrieg.

—A trumped-up assassination attempt on Hitler, designed to rile up the German people against Britain.

—The British trap the pocket battleship *Graf Spee*, which has sunk nine British cargo ships in the South Atlantic. The German commander scuttles it in the harbor of Montevideo, Uruguay, after a running fight with outgunned British cruisers. The German press translates it into a heroic act.

—A German plane with a military courier aboard gets lost in bad weather, makes an emergency landing in Belgium. Although the courier torches his papers, enough are salvaged to disclose the entire German plan for the western invasion through the Lowlands.

—The western front remains quiet.

But the Germans cast covetous eyes at the coast and harbors of neutral Norway. They would give Germany another outlet to the sea and a haven for its northern fleet. They would also protect access to Swedish iron ore, and block the Allies from coming to the aid of the Finns who had been invaded by the Soviet Union.

The Germans had begun talks with a Norwegian-bred Nazi named Vidkun Quisling (the name now synonymous with traitor) to work out a bloodless takeover of Norway. And if Norway, why not Denmark, also neutral?

On April 9, 1940, before dawn, German ultimatums were handed to the respective foreign ministers in Oslo and Copenhagen. Denmark seemingly had no choice. It was indefensible, open to panzer attack by land and by bombardment from the sea. Indeed, two of the German commanders who would lead the operation had visited Copenhagen two days before the operation in civilian clothes to scout out the area. Denmark capitulated and in days the token resistance was run down.

Norway was a different matter. The British, hearing of the possible German action, were mounting a small landing force of their own, belatedly. The Norwegians would not lie down and play dead for the Germans. The king and the government fled to northern mountains to mount a resistance. Then, the German ships, prepared to fly the Union Jack as part of their subterfuge, came out of the night. Ten German destroyers with two battalions of soldiers beat the British to the port of Narvik where an ally of Quisling surrendered the garrison. Brave but hopelessly outgunned naval forces were quickly silenced with the loss of 300 Norwegian sailors. Trondheim fell easily. Bergen put up fire and damaged the cruiser *Koenigsberg* and another ship before the city fell. The British stood

Belgian Foreign Minister Paul Henri Spaak tells party officials of his message to Hitler that his nation "can not be vanquished." The date was May 10, 1940, that the world learned a new word: blitzkrieg.

Germany overwhelmed Norway in 1940 after a brief struggle.

offshore with a fleet that could have overcome the Germans, and in fact British dive bombers did sink the *Koenigsberg.* But Churchill called off the attack rather than risk his ships to German airpower, an action he later regretted.

By noon the Germans were in control of most of coastal Norway and the next day its paratroopers captured Oslo.

Two British attacks, including one by a destroyer task force, led by the aging battleship *Warspite,* all but eradicated the German cargo ships and destroyers at Narvik. The British landed, and with a force of 25,000, including a brigade of Poles, two battalions of French Foreign Legionnaires and two brigades of Norwegians, occupied Narvik. But time was against them. On the continent, there were developments that required all available men. Narvik was abandoned. The Norway adventure cost each side about 5,000 men, and German ship losses were high, and Norway would be worrisome to the German occupation force.

Another portentous day, May 10, 1940.

A three-day political crisis in Britain crested. Chamberlain stepped down as prime minister and Churchill took his place. Partly because of this, Britain and France were taken by surprise by the next German move.

That same day, the Germans notified Belgium and The Netherlands—both neutral nations—that in order to protect them they were marching in. But German troops preceded the words. Belgium Foreign Minister Paul Henri Spaak said the invasion was more odious than the attack in 1914. "No ultimatum, no note, no protest of any kind has ever been placed before the Belgian government. . . . Belgium is resolved to defend herself."

And she did. But there was no stopping the German might that returned to Flanders' fields.

More than walls crumbled as German panzers stormed through France in June 1940.

In six short weeks the German panzers, Stukas, Messerschmitts, parachute and glider troops and infantry hordes defeated four armies and took Paris. They had started almost numerically even, 135 divisions each. But the Allies with their split commands and no agenda were no match for the Germans with a unified command and a definite agenda.

The fall of Holland in five days was the first blow. The Germans, while negotiating for the surrender of Rotterdam, bombed the city off the map.

The main German units with massed tanks—three columns of them 100 miles long—forced the middle of the Allied line. The British and French, expecting the main drive to come from the north, had moved up to reinforce the Belgians. Thus most of the Allied armor and much of its strength were trapped when the Germans reached the English Channel.

There was still a chance to break through to the sixty-five divisions in the south, but France decided to change generals in midstream, and the three-day hiatus gave the Germans time to flesh out their gains. From then on German armor drove north to squash the trapped French, British and Belgians.

On May 15, five days after the invasion began, Churchill was wakened by a phone call from the French premier who shouted, "We have been defeated! We are beaten!"

Not quite, but very nearly so. King Leopold of Belgium surrendered his troops on May 28, to the great embarrassment of the French and British troops still fighting for survival. It left a twenty-mile gap in their lines. The Belgians had fought bravely against the new kind of warfare and it could be said that there was still fight left in them. But now German armor was twenty miles from Dunkirk, where Allied forces were trapped against the English Channel.

Churchill had taken the first steps toward evacuation, but just as the German advance had exceeded German expectations, now the evacuation would exceed British hopes, with a little help from the unpredictable Hitler. Inexplicably, the German

British evacuated 338,000 from the beaches of Dunkirk in May 1940.

armor stopped its advance. In ten days and nights by every marine conveyance possible, dories, pleasure craft, lighters, destroyers and larger, over 338,000 British and French troops were ferried to England safely and to fight again.

The reasons for the "grace" period were learned later. First Hitler didn't want to risk his armor; second, Goering said the Luftwaffe could wipe out the remaining troops from the air; third, Hitler did not want the decisive battle in Belgium because too many German-descended Flemish would die in the process, and he had plans for them in the peace to come.

Hitler staged armistice in rail car used in 1918.

What happened after Dunkirk is all denouement. The 143 available German divisions turned their attention to the sixty-five demoralized French divisions remaining. Smelling blood, Il Duce joined in from the south, but in a week of fighting from the Alps to the Riviera his thirty-five divisions could not budge six French.

On June 14, the undefended city of Paris fell to German armor and a swastika flew over the Eiffel Tower.

Hitler had been planning his final revenge for weeks, if not for months. On the warm afternoon of June 21 on the edge of the forest at Compiegne where the Germans submitted almost twenty-two years before, Hitler brought to the French a bitter defeat. He staged it. He walked to the small monument and read the inscription which said in French: "Here on the eleventh of November 1918 suc-

Hitler gleefully celebrates French surrender.

Hitler's legions paraded through the Arc de Triomphe in June of 1940.

cumbed the criminal pride of the German Empire—vanquished by the free peoples it had tried to enslave." With hate streaming from his eyes, he stepped down, and as historian William Shirer describes it, "snaps his hands on his hips, arches his shoulders, plants his feet wide apart. It is a magnificent gesture of defiance, of burning contempt."

War Clouds

When the last of the British and French were plucked from the waters of Dunkirk, Churchill, little more than a month prime minister, said:

"Even though large tracts of Europe and many old and famous states have fallen or may fall into the grip of the Gestapo and all the odious apparatus of Nazi rule, we shall not flag or fail. We shall go on to the end, we shall fight in France, we shall fight in the seas and oceans, we shall fight with growing confidence and growing strength in the air, we shall defend our island, no matter what the cost may be, we shall fight on the beaches, we shall fight on the landing grounds, we shall fight in the fields and in the streets, we shall fight in the hills; we shall never surrender, and even if, which I do not for a moment believe, this island or a large part of it were subjugated and starving, then our Empire beyond the seas, armed and guarded by the British fleet, would carry on the struggle, until, in God's good time, the New World, with all its power and might, steps forth to the rescue and the liberation of the old."

The Battle of Britain

Above: *Ed Murrow's measured voice brought the agony of the London blitz home to American listeners.* **At right:** *British Spitfires and Hurricane fighters filmed dogfights with German Heinkel and Dornier bombers during Battle of Britain.* **Below:** *German photo captures Messerschmitt 109 on tail of Spitfire during sky war.*

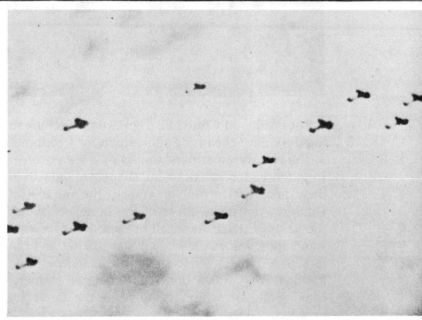

At left: *Londoners went underground while their city burned.* **Opposite top left:** *Luftwaffe was on verge of winning with attacks on RAF bases, then unwisely switched to bombing London.* **Opposite top right:** *Improved models of the Spitfire, to which so much was owed for winning the Battle of Britain.*

Willkie campaigns in St. Louis.

Knox draws number to begin national draft.

Roosevelt and Churchill. They would become in the dark days ahead the spokesmen for freedom.

The two were partners, united by a secret correspondence, dependent on but shapers of the will of their people. The fall of France, the miracle at Dunkirk, the doggedness of the besieged island, the valor of its air force, all of these molded what was happening in the United States. That and the fact that Hitler's conception of America, "The Melting Pot," was a bunch of "mongrel" Americans, many of whom came from the lands he invaded.

Even before France fell, Churchill pleaded with Roosevelt "to help us with everything short of actually engaging armed forces." He suggested the loan of forty or fifty old destroyers, a stopgap until British construction could catch up with needs. But Roosevelt would not try to push his balky Congress too fast, especially with the nominating conventions coming up in July.

As it was he had to buck the isolationists in Congress to pass the peacetime draft in an election year. He did it largely by making it a patriotic appeal in the interest of self-defense. The first draftee number, 158, was picked on October 30, 1940, on the eve of the election.

Naturally the most sensitive to the draft were those of conscription age. At Princeton University students formed a Veterans of Future Wars and asked the president to appoint an Unknown Sol-

dier "so we can know who he is before he gets killed." And at Vassar there was an association of Future Gold Star Mothers which said they would go to Europe to pick out appropriate grave sites for their future sons.

In August 1940, Roosevelt had come up with a political ploy to make the destroyer deal work. He would trade them for eight British bases in the Caribbean and Canada. The American people might buy that in the interest of national security. Besides, Roosevelt pointed out, the bases cost Britain some $25 million a year to maintain, and "they are nothing but a headache."

The deal went through, circumventing Congress. The destroyers were so old they were almost a liability to His Majesty's Navy, but it was a symbol that Britain was no longer alone.

Roosevelt faced a last ditch conservative stand in his own party, a bloc called "The Haters Club." Diverse as they were, hate of Roosevelt bound them together. He would not give them ammunition by breaking yet another tradition and running for a third term. He sent a message by way of his alter ego, Harry Hopkins, telling delegates he has no inclination to remain in any public office. Without their mutual hate object to run against, the various candidates were rudderless. Harry Hopkins maintained three hotel suites that summer in Chicago to receive various Democratic leaders while Roosevelt said he was "trusting in God." When Roosevelt's "no run" message was announced publicly, the convention erupted in a wild hour-long, not altogether spontaneous demonstration with cries of "We want Roosevelt." The next day's ballot gave Roosevelt 946 votes to 147 for the other four candidates.

It was not an easy campaign. Radical labor leader John L. Lewis, who devised the sit-down strike and organized the miners and the steel and auto workers, came out against Roosevelt, for Willkie. Doggedly, Willkie covered thirty states in fifty-one days, making 500 speeches. Roosevelt visited military bases as part of his job as president, and turned those visits into political messages.

Two phrases captured the nugget of the campaign:

"A vote for Willkie is a vote for Hitler."

"A vote for Roosevelt is a vote for war."

In a record turnout, 27.2 million out of 49 million voters went for Roosevelt, giving him a 449-82 electoral advantage, every large city except Cincinnati, the labor and the black vote.

Said New York City's politically-wise Mayor Fiorello La Guardia, "I would rather have FDR with his known faults than Willkie with his unknown qualities." He reflected the feeling of most Americans.

FDR'S FOES

Roosevelt's opposition was considerable and noisy. From a suburb of Detroit, Father Charles E. Coughlin, the Roman Catholic priest at Royal Oak's Shrine of the Little Flower and an early supporter of Roosevelt ("Roosevelt or ruin," he had shouted), turned against him.

When the Ku Klux Klan burned down his church in 1926, Father Coughlin took to the local CBS radio station to plea for rebuilding funds. His booming voice, his earnestness, his simple solutions, his mellifluous phrase-making not only rebuilt his church but made him a national celebrity, and, it later turned out, one of the leading silver price manipulators in the country.

When CBS dropped him because of his controversial views, he started his own sixty-station hookup with the money his followers sent in. He called Roosevelt an "anti-God" and the New Deal "the Jew Deal." He even went so far as to suggest in a speech that FDR be murdered. Under his banner he started the National Union for Social Justice. He was for Adolf Hitler, against freedom of speech, for anything "Christian," against anything Jewish, for isolation, against liberals, for Huey Long of Louisiana, against communism. He used the radio almost as well as the president did.

Huey Pierce Long, Jr., whom Roosevelt compared with Douglas MacArthur, matched Coughlin's demagoguery from his bastion in Louisiana and then on the floor of the U.S. Senate.

Unlike Coughlin, Long did something more than rant and rave. He revitalized his backward state, building thousands of miles of roads, a dozen bridges, establishing night schools for the illiterate, white and black alike, hospital care for the poor, free textbooks, free school buses. He abolished the poll tax, declared a debt moratorium, raised new business taxes, exempted the poor from the general property tax.

He was even-handed with blacks. When the Klan threatened to unseat him for this heresy, he said, "Quote me as saying that the Imperial Bastard will never set foot in Louisiana, and that when I call him a son of a bitch I am not using profanity, but am referring to the circumstances of his birth."

In the Senate he was instrumental in stopping some of the New Deal programs and reining in FDR. He helped pass the Neutrality Act of 1935 which required the president to embargo arms to any nation at war and forbid Americans to travel on ships belonging to any belligerent, except at their own hazard.

Father Charles E. Coughlin exploited radio in the 1930s to harangue a mass audience with attacks on Roosevelt, war and the Jews.

John L. Lewis, flamboyant head of the United Mine Workers and inventor of the sit-down strike, opposed Roosevelt's 1940 campaign for a third term.

Long rallied the conservatives in the Senate and Coughlin railed at his 45 million listeners to stop the United States participation in the World Court.

Huey Long was making himself important on the American political scene. People talked about him more and more. He was also brilliant. He finished Tulane's three-year law course in eight months, graduated at age twenty-one, and not much later argued constitutional law before the U.S. Supreme Court. He was an enigma, resorting to low comedy and pranks, called himself "Kingfish" after a radio character on "Amos 'n' Andy." Political cartoonists had a field day with his escapades.

But he sensed his exposed position, surrounded himself with bodyguards armed with revolvers and submachine guns, his own Secret Service.

He was clearly aiming for the presidency and may have made it. He sponsored a Share the Wealth program that would put a lid on fortunes at $5 million, set up old age pensions, free education through college, veterans' bonuses, cheap surplus food and no income less than $2,000. Every family would get a radio, a car and a washing machine, and $6,000 toward a home.

But he had premonitions and voiced them, talked of plots of assassination. And in fact on September 8, 1935, Carl Weiss, a young, idealistic doctor smoldering over a family grudge, stepped from behind a statehouse pillar and with one shot fatally wounded the "Kingfish." The assassin died with sixty-one bodyguard bullets in his body.

Roosevelt chats with reporters from his automobile in Warm Springs, Georgia.

The tone of the inaugural in January 1941 was military, a taste of "the Arsenal of Democracy," an overflight of 300 planes. That same month Roosevelt brought out the Lend Lease bill, taking isolationism head on.

The isolationist movement had at its heart the America First Committee, financed at the beginning by Robert E. Wood, chairman of Sears, Roebuck. It grew to 500 chapters and 800,000 members, punctuated by such names as Henry Ford, Teddy Roosevelt's daughter Alice Roosevelt Longworth, the author Kathleen Norris, the actress Lilian Gish and Kingman Brewster, Jr., who would become president of Yale. And Charles A. Lindbergh. Try as he might, Roosevelt could not lower the status of this American hero. Turns out, he had only to wait for Lindbergh to damage himself, which he did in a speech in Des Moines when he attacked the Jews as principal war agitators.

"Their greatest danger to this country lies in their large ownership and influence in our motion pictures, our press, our radio and our government." He said, although he admired both, "I am saying that the leaders of both the British and Jewish races, for reasons which are as understandable from their viewpoint as they are inadvisable from ours, for reasons which are not American, wish to involve us in the war."

With that he seemingly allied himself with Hitler and every white supremacist, pro-German group in America, from the German-American Bund to the Ku Klux Klan. It very nearly destroyed the isolationist movement.

Roosevelt's eyes were still on Europe and Hitler. He did everything possible to shore up Britain. He urged American boys to volunteer for the Royal Air Force. He turned over more ships to the British, sent them new P-40 fighter planes, met with

Churchill at Placentia Bay, Newfoundland, arranged for American military planners to meet secretly with their British counterparts to make contingency plans for a war in Europe, extended U.S. naval patrols halfway across the Atlantic, offered U.S. destroyers for convoy duty to ships of any nation threatened by Germany or Italy, froze Italian assets, unfroze Soviet assets, tried repeatedly to sell the public on the threat of a German invasion via South America.

Across the Pacific, Japanese intentions remained obscure despite U.S. code-breakers' eavesdropping on Tokyo's messages. Grew relayed a rumor that the Japanese planned a raid on Pearl Harbor. That was still only a concept in a few minds and even Tojo, then prime minister, was not to know of the attack until days before it happened. An embargo of Japan's oil was considered a consequence of Japanese belligerance, though Roosevelt was aware such an act almost inevitably meant war.

When the British ambassador, Lord Lothian, called the American hand on that continuing commerce with Japan, Treasury Secretary Henry Morgenthau, Jr., said, "Nobody has asked me or even suggested to me that we stop shipping aviation gasoline."

Lord Lothian's question brought Morgenthau up short. The British ambassador added that if the United States stopped shipping aviation gasoline to Japan, Britain would blow up the oil wells in the Dutch East Indies, and that would stymie the Japanese.

Roosevelt was persuaded by the State Department to limit an embargo against Japan to high octane gas and scrap steel, which he did in July 1940.

The State Department, sure the Japanese would attack the Soviet Union, continued to disregard the distant early warning signs posted regularly by its ambassador in Tokyo. Grew would say later that it was a lot like throwing pebbles into a lake at night, not being able to see the ripples.

In Japan the war faction led by General Tojo (front, third from left) won the upper hand in October 1941 when he became prime minister.

Famous photograph was taken in 1937.

Hirohito reigned but did not rule.

A CHINESE BABY

One picture focused American attention on China, and the ruthless march of the Japanese into her coastal cities.

Late in the afternoon of August 28, 1937, three Japanese bombers without contest circled the already stricken city of Shanghai and struck the South Railway Station, killing all but 300 of 1,800 mostly women and children awaiting evacuation.

The Japanese said their pilots thought it was a troop movement. Cameraman H.S. Wong captured the sight of a hurt and crying Chinese baby sitting in the tracks near its dead mother. The image touched American hearts, and they responded with charity to buy food and medicines for China's war victims.

But the Chinese baby lingered only briefly on the American consciousness. The United States continued to provide half of Japan's scrap steel requirements and oil, leading one critic to call it the filling station for fascism.

Japan's ambitions, fed by a burgeoning population and a paucity of natural resources, were clothed by the powers that ran the country in ancient tradition, and the symbol of that tradition was Emperor Hirohito.

A slight five-foot-three whose civilian clothes hung loosely on him, Hirohito was less than imposing in stature or demeanor. His name was derived from a Confucian saying: ''Make yourself broad-minded, and let people live in comfort.''

As emperor, he was said to be descended from the imperial line sprung from the Sun Goddess in the Shinto pantheon of gods. He did cut the imperial figure when he reviewed the troops on his white horse, Shiroyuki, or White Snow. That was the image on American newsreels.

The Japanese people would refer to him as ''Celestial Emperor Whom One Regards from Below the Staircase.'' Historically, however, the emperor's role was not always so exalted. His grandfather did much to re-establish imperial authority by putting down the military dictators, the shoguns, and opening up Japan to the 20th century and the Western world. But militarism is not so easily dismissed, in Japan or anywhere else.

Indeed, his grandfather had established Japanese power in Korea, Taiwan and Manchuria, with impressive victories over the Chinese and the Russians.

Hirohito pursued the study of marine biology as a young man, but his youthful pursuits were soon ended. He was barely twenty when he became Prince Regent, taking over for his ill father who died in 1926 at which time Hirohito was coronated.

It seems now, from the diaries of his Lord Keeper of the Privy Seal, that the young emperor was uneasy with military matters, and had in fact asked for a prime minister in 1932 who was moderate in thought and not militaristic. Nor was he pleased when Japan withdrew from the League of Nations. Although some historians disagree, Hirohito seemed to be less a man of war than a retiring and gentle monarch who was no match for the industrial-martial powers that would drive Japan through Asia in search of self-sufficiency and empire.

The actual plans for conquest had been laid down in the 1920s and Hirohito had little to say about them.

In 1936, Japan joined the Axis in an anti-Comintern pact. Hirohito was not happy with the treaty, worried that Japan might be drawn into a future war with the United States. Not so, however. Japan marched to its own tune, and its emperor did not hold the baton.

Captain D.D. Eisenhower (hat), West Point '15, took apart a tank with colleague George S. Patton and rebuilt it.

Race car driver and builder J. Walter Christie designed a tank that could travel 60 mph. The government bought only seven.

Army Chief of Staff MacArthur takes a coffee break after his soldiers dispersed the Bonus Marchers in Washington in 1932.

MEN OF WAR

When General Douglas MacArthur was Chief of Staff and routed the Bonus Army in 1932, his aide was then a young forward-thinking major named Dwight David Eisenhower.

Eisenhower had commanded a stateside tank battalion during the war, and the idea of an armored vehicle supporting infantry so fascinated him that in 1919 at Camp Meade, Maryland, he and George S. Patton, an avid horseman, took a tank completely apart and put it together again in working order. The two were to form a closeness which would lead Patton to write later on in another war, ''You are about my oldest friend.''

They supported as early as 1920 a tank designed by a race car driver and builder named J. Walter Christie. Christie's tank could do sixty miles an hour, leap a seven-foot trench and climb a two-and-a-half-foot wall. But the Army, despite endorsements from Patton and Eisenhower, bought only seven tanks and the idea languished, partly the victim of other American priorities. The Soviet Union, however, bought two Christie tanks and they became the prototype for thousands of Soviet manufacture.

Roosevelt once called General Douglas MacArthur one of the two most dangerous men in America (the other being Huey Long).

MacArthur, born on an Army post, the son of a Congressional Medal of Honor winner, had risen from colonel to brigadier general with the 42nd (Rainbow) Division in World War I, where he was awarded the second of what would become seven Silver Stars.

But he tended to run the Army as if he owned it. In Washington, he became identified politically with the far right at a time when the nation had sunk into poverty and the military was not high on the nation's list of priorities.

Perhaps the most ignominious mark in his long military record was the 1932 attack on the Bonus Expeditionary Force. President Hoover detailed him to maintain order in the capital, and the so-called Bonus Army was clearly a breach of order. The veterans, their wives and children, set up a tent city near the Anacostia River to persuade Congress to vote them a promised bonus. Taking a relatively minor communist-inspired scuffle with police as provocation, MacArthur led his several hundred infantry and cavalry into the encampment and sent the protesters packing. There were a number of injuries from bayonets, sabers, bricks and clubs, and an eleven-week-old baby died after exposure to tear gas. It was a far stronger reaction than President Hoover had authorized, but MacArthur said he hadn't heard the president's call for restraint.

In the mid-1930s, MacArthur, well-traveled and an expert in the Far East, served as military adviser to the Philippines, partly as a warning to the Japanese to stay away with the young republic only a decade from its independence, but defenseless against a modern military power.

If in the ranks of the Army there was a more clear contrast in personality and demeanor, it was between MacArthur and George Catlett Marshall. MacArthur admired pomp. Marshall was a devotee of simplicity. Indeed, MacArthur, as Army Chief of Staff, even blocked Marshall's promotion from colonel to general, in spite of fervent backing by General John J. Pershing.

The complexity of Army red tape, even down to battle orders, riled Marshall. He knew that, with the aversion of his nation to spend money on an up-to-date armed force, the Army would be only a cadre to be filled out by citizen soldiers in time of emergency. If such troops were called up,

Lieutenant Colonel George Marshall (center, front row) *rewrote the infantry manual at Fort Benning. Behind him is aide Omar Bradley.*

Major Eisenhower served under MacArthur when the latter led the Philippine army in the 1930s, respected him, but confided to his diary his boss could be a "big baby" and liked "boot lickers." (Credit: March of Time)

they would have trouble enough mastering their weapons and their commands without filling out forms in triplicate. He had landed in France with troops who were 85 percent recruits and who had only been handed their rifles on the troop train. They went into the line without proper uniforms and field kitchens.

Yet by his organizational flair and his pragmatism, he was able to accomplish incredible feats, such as moving 600,000 men and 2,700 field pieces sixty miles over three roads in two weeks to mount a final offensive. As assistant commandant at Fort Benning's infantry school, he revolutionized the training, cut the logistics and supply instruction manual from 120 pages to twelve.

Urging simplicity of command and operations that could be readily absorbed by citizen-soldiers thrown into the breach, his message was:

"Study the first six months of the next war. . . . I insist we must . . . expunge the bunk, complications and ponderosities; we must concentrate on registering in men's minds certain vital considerations . . . a technique and methods so simple that the citizen officers of good common sense can readily grasp the idea."

The Dutch were convinced Japanese ambitions were headed their way. The Japanese were buying record amounts of oil and rubber, tin and aluminum ore from the East Indies and demanding concessions and privileges in return. The Dutch also recognized that some Japanese engineers were military in disguise.

Oil was the driving force for the Japanese economy and expansion. So its logical path would be toward oil, which meant the shipping lanes to it, which meant the Philippines, which meant the United States, which meant war on a broad scale. The Japanese, however loose an alliance the Axis was with Germany and Italy, were clearly inspired by Hitler's successes in Europe. The die would be cast, without mutual consultation of any degree, when the Germans invaded Russia in June of 1941. Lend Lease was broadened to include the Soviet Union, and Roosevelt diverted fighter planes bound for Britain to the Russians who lost 2,000 aircraft on the ground on the first day. Thereupon, the Germans drove 500 miles into their heartland.

American cryptanalysts broke the Japanese diplomatic code, and delivered to the State Department almost the same day it was received a communication to Japanese embassies of strategy conferences in Tokyo. The decoders, using a system called Magic, clearly established that the Japanese would not attack the Soviet Union as Hitler would have wished, but would strike south toward the resources it needed, even though this would mean an inevitable clash with Britain and the United States.

In October 1941, Japan's so-called peace party that had proposed a summit meeting with Roosevelt fell. War Minister General Hideki Tojo took power. That same month at a formal meeting with his military leaders, Emperor Hirohito listened to their war plans and then solemnly brought out a slip of paper and read a stanza of a poem written by his grandfather, the Emperor Meiji:

> The seas surround all quarters of the globe and
>   my heart cries out to the nations of the world
> Why then do the winds and waves of strife
>   disrupt the peace between us?

It may have touched the hearts of those in full military dress assembled, but their minds were made up.

When Roosevelt finally turned his attention to Japan, he took steps that were quick and decisive. Japan's soldiers occupied Indochina, and Roosevelt, joined by the British and the Dutch colonial government in Jakarta, froze Japanese assets, which meant no more oil. Secretary of State Cordell Hull, whose actions and advice toward Europe were cautious, delivered an ultimatum to

THE SOVIET REVERSAL

Why did the Soviets quickly change course and join their enemy Hitler in his fateful Polish adventure?

Stalin told Churchill in Moscow later. He said the Soviets had become convinced that Britain and France would not go to war if Poland were attacked and that the proposed Triple Alliance would not deter Hitler. And there was the cost. France might field a hundred divisions, Britain two initially and two later. And how many divisions would the Soviet Union have to field? "More than three hundred."

And in fact the eventual battleline between the Soviet Union and Germany would be the longest in the history of the world, about 2,000 miles.

the Japanese that could not be misinterpreted:

Get out of China and Indochina, renounce the alliance with Germany and Italy and sign a non-aggression pact with your neighbors. There was no way the Japanese would agree. Their now dwindling oil supplies put a time limit for action. The Imperial navy's dive bombers at Kagoshima Bay in southern Kyushu began practicing skimming the mountains, and torpedo planes practiced with shallow water torpedos suitable for a harbor.

In November a slight, mustachioed Japanese envoy, Saburo Kurusu, arrived in the United States to join six-foot ambassador Kichisaburo Nomura who had already asked his government that he be relieved. "I do not want to continue this hypocritical existence, deceiving myself and other people." His request was denied. The two Japanese continued the charade.

At home, the Japanese reinforced armies in China, then set attack plans for Malaya, Java, Borneo, New Guinea, the Bismarck Archipelago, the Philippines.

On November 25, Cordell Hull rejected Japanese demands to rescind the American embargo and insisted on a pullout in China. On the same day, a large Japanese fleet put out under radio silence from an assembly point in the Kuriles Islands, heading southeast.

On Saturday, December 6, President Roosevelt was handed another intercept from Tokyo. His eyes darkened: "This means war." He sent one last appeal to Hirohito. The next afternoon (morning Hawaii time) Cordell Hull would be handed the same message by the Japanese envoys. Increasing their speed to twenty-four knots after a final refueling by tankers, the Japanese carrier task force in two parallel columns had already turned eastward toward Hawaii and Pearl Harbor.

3 PEARL HARBOR

The Sunday morning papers were full of news. Doris Duke, "the blue-eyed blonde American princess," laughed off reports she was getting a divorce. The Texas Longhorns walloped Oregon, 71-7, on the gridiron. And Little Orphan Annie was hurt in a car accident. (But she was going to be all right.)

For those Americans worried about the state of the world, especially the showdown with the Japanese, the papers that December 7, 1941, had a reassuring word from Navy Secretary Frank Knox.

"I am proud to report that the American people may feel fully confident in the Navy," the front pages quoted Knox as saying in his annual State-of-the-Navy message.

But out in the mid-Pacific, in the dark waters of the tropical night, the Navy was suddenly growing unsure of itself.

Just before 4 in the morning, Hawaii time, William W. Outerbridge, a Navy lieutenant on his first patrol as commander of the USS *Ward*, sounded general quarters on the old destroyer as it pounded through the waves off Pearl Harbor. A submarine conning tower had been spotted.

In the murky pre-dawn, the *Ward* crisscrossed the 800-foot-deep approaches to the harbor. Finally, at 6:45 a.m., it caught up with the intruder.

The destroyer's gunners swung their barrels to and put a four-inch shell through the conning tower. A depth charge followed, sending the mysterious sub to the bottom.

The young lieutenant flashed word back to Pearl Harbor: "Depth-bombed sub operating in defensive sea area."

The news slowly filtered up through channels. At 7:30 a.m., Admiral Husband E. Kimmel, commander in chief of the Pacific Fleet, was telephoned at his home on Makalapa Heights, overlooking Pearl Harbor, and told of the contact. The ramrod-correct Kimmel, a naval officer for thirty-seven years, questioned the submarine report, demanded confirmation, and waited. He had twenty-five minutes peace.

Five thousand miles to the east, in Washington, other Navy brass were on their own uneasy alert.

Coded messages from Tokyo to Japan's diplomats in Washington, deciphered by U.S. military cryptanalysts on Saturday and early Sunday, pointed to war, apparently within hours.

The cables, a formal reply to the latest demands the U.S. government had made on Japan, declared the long and frustrating negotiations a failure. A final message intercepted and decoded by 9 a.m. Eastern Standard Time instructed Ambassador Kichisaburo Nomura and special envoy Saburo Kurusu to deliver their climactic rejection to Secretary of State Cordell Hull at 1 p.m.

The precision of this timing alarmed military analysts. It could only mean Japan would open hostilities against the United States and Britain at about that time, probably in British Malaya or elsewhere in the western Pacific.

Rear Admiral Theodore Wilkinson, the Navy's intelligence chief, was one of those who sensed war was at hand. He pressed his boss for action.

"Why don't you pick up the phone and call Admiral Kimmel?" he asked Admiral Harold R. Stark, the Navy's top officer.

Tora, Tora, Tora! (Tiger, Tiger, Tiger!) was the pre-arranged code signal from Pearl Harbor planes meaning: We have succeeded in surprise attack.

But Stark chose not to put his Pacific commander on immediate alert. Instead, he phoned the White House. The president's line was busy.

It was shortly before 11 a.m. in Washington. Lieutenant Outerbridge was still hunting down his submarine.

Across the Potomac River, at Fort Myer, Virginia, the Army Chief of Staff, General George C. Marshall, was out on his Sunday morning horseback ride. An Army intelligence officer, convinced war would break out at 1 p.m., had been desperately trying to reach Marshall. Only the chief could put the Army on alert.

By 11:30, Marshall was in his office. Apprised of the Japanese messages, he wrote out a dispatch to his Hawaii and Philippines commanders, Lieutenant General Walter C. Short and General Douglas MacArthur. Admiral Kimmel was copied in.

The significance of the 1 p.m. deadline was unclear, Marshall told them, but, "Be on the alert accordingly."

The warning, classified as secret, was filed with the Army message center in Washington at noon. It would not be delivered in Hawaii for six-and-one-half hours.

While Marshall jotted down his final peacetime order, a soft pastel dawn was breaking over Pearl Harbor and the rest of Oahu.

At the island's rugged northern tip, two Army privates, Joe Lockard and George Elliott, manned a mobile radar station, part of a primitive network set up just four months earlier. At 7:02 a.m., as the more experienced Lockard instructed Elliott in reading the new device, a large blip of light appeared on its screen, a swarm of aircraft 130 miles out at sea, bearing down on Oahu.

Excited, they called the air-warning center at Fort Shafter, near Honolulu. But the lieutenant on duty, a trainee, told the radarmen not to worry: the planes must be either U.S. carrier aircraft or a flight of B-17 bomber reinforcements expected from the States.

The two privates could only watch the blip grow nearer. It finally disappeared, as the planes crossed a ridgeline on Oahu's northern shore.

At 7:45 a.m., from two miles up, high above the

jagged green of Oahu's Waianae Mountains and the brick-red earth of pineapple plantations, Commander Mitsuo Fuchida gazed down upon Pearl Harbor.

"Below me," he wrote later, "lay the whole U.S. Pacific Fleet in a formation I would not have dared to dream of in my most optimistic dreams."

Lined up in a neat file, some side by side like fat ducks in a small pond, seven of the fleet's battleships sat moored in calm sapphire waters beside Ford Island. Eighty-nine other cruisers, destroyers, submarines and auxiliary ships were also anchored in the harbor.

The fleet, symbol of America's Pacific might, was at rest. Not a wisp of smoke floated from a ship's stack. One-third of the ships' officers were on shore leave. Sailors sauntered on deck or tended to chores below.

At the nearby Army airfields—Hickam, Wheeler, Bellows—the dozens of fighters and bombers were lined up wing to wing, like toys on a playing board.

At 7:53 a.m., the twenty-nine-year-old Fuchida, in command of the droning swarm of 181 Japanese fighters and bombers, radioed a pre-arranged code —"Tora! Tora! Tora!"—"Tiger! Tiger! Tiger!"— that surprise had been achieved.

The young Japanese flyers, many wearing white "hashimaki" headbands emblematic of their willingness to die, dropped from among the fleecy clouds to carry out what U.S. military manuals would later describe as "one of the most brilliant tactical feats of the war," a long, cruel, global war in which an unready America was about to take center stage.

At that very moment on Makalapa Heights, Kimmel, in his Sunday whites, was on the telephone at his house, receiving a duty officer's follow-up report on the USS *Ward*. The officer suddenly went silent. In a moment he was back on the line. The harbor was under attack, he shouted.

Dive bombers and fighters had peeled off first from the Japanese formation. After Fuchida's signal, they plunged toward the Army and Navy airfields, strafing and loosing 550-pound bombs on the closely parked aircraft, turning the American interceptor arm into fiery scrap.

Meanwhile, the Kate torpedo bombers descended to less than 100-foot altitude, leveled off and bore in on the broadsides of the gray behemoths, the battleships, anchored in the peaceful blue of the harbor.

The airmen knew their targets. Each carried aerial photos of the American fleet at anchor, blowups of simple tourist postcards picked up by a spy in Honolulu.

The Kates turned loose their torpedoes, and the one-ton self-propelled bombs churned through the shallow waters toward the great warships.

Thundering blasts rocked the *California*, the *Oklahoma*, the *West Virginia*. Three torpedoes had found the *Oklahoma*, and the huge hulk gently heeled over, trapping hundreds of men below the capsized decks.

Wrecked patrol planes at Pearl Harbor never got off the ground.

"Air raid Pearl Harbor. This is no drill." View from Japanese plane.

On Battleship Row the vessels were moored side by side just like any other Sunday in peacetime.

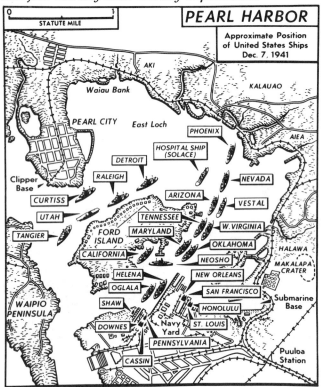

Peace had exploded into the terror of war.

The harbor and airfields quickly became a bedlam of noise and smoke. Screaming dive bombers and whistling bombs fell from the sky. Japanese fighter planes strafed barracks and hangars with deadly stitches of machine-gun bullets. Shattered steel blew across decks and rained down onto the harbor. Desperate men leaped from burning ships into waters turned into lakes of fire by ignited oil.

The seaplane tender USS *Curtiss*, anchored on the far side of Ford Island, took a direct bomb hit on its port side. Seaman Tom Mahoney and his damage-control team forced open a gun-mount door. Inside, Mahoney later recalled, he saw the ''silhouettes'' of five men against the bulkhead—shadows he quickly realized were actually the charred remains of the gun crew.

The battleship *California*, hit by two torpedoes, went straight to the bottom, its smoking upper decks jutting above the surface.

Aboard the stricken *West Virginia*, alert seamen struggled to prevent a capsize.

''We took a lot of heavy hits,'' shipfitter Louis Grabinski later recalled, ''but we counterflooded the ship so we sank slower and most of us got out.''

In one of those hits, a bomb fragment penetrated the bridge and killed the battleship's commander,

Captain Mervyn S. Bennion.

A few hundred yards aft of the *West Virginia* sat the *Arizona*, shielded by a moored repair ship. It escaped the first torpedoes, but not the pinpoint aim of the Japanese dive bombers who followed. A bomb dropped straight down the *Arizona*'s smokestack, exploding first a boiler, then the forward magazine. The battlewagon, ripped asunder, went down with more than 80 percent of its 1,500-man crew, including Rear Admiral Isaac C. Kidd.

James Anderson, a hospital corpsman, watched from another ship.

"I saw that bomb go down through what looked like a stack, and almost instantly it cracked the bottom of the *Arizona*, blowing the whole bow loose. It rose out of the water and settled. I could see flames, fire and smoke coming out of that ship, and I saw two men flying through the air and the fire, screaming as they went. Where they ended-up I'll never know."

On shore, the closely arrayed American aircraft were like practice targets for the Japanese dive bombers and fighter planes.

"Devil's Doom"

Within four minutes of the start of the surprise Japanese assault, American gunners were firing back at the attackers. Above the billowing black smoke from dying ships, the sky over Pearl Harbor was soon dotted with explosive puffs, as anti-aircraft rounds chased the planes along their destructive paths.

The final blows of the Japanese first-wave attack came from forty-nine high-altitude bombers. At 12,000 feet, they passed over the anchorage in single file, 600 feet apart, and unloaded their bombs on the closely massed ships below.

Fuchida, flying a bomber, lay down at the open bay and watched his bombs plummeting toward the ships—"like the devil's doom," he later said.

As doom befell the Pacific Fleet, the leadership in Washington was still trying to puzzle out Japan's intentions. But at 1:50 p.m. EST—8:20 a.m. in Hawaii, twenty-five minutes after the attack began —Admiral Stark burst into Secretary Knox's office with the signal from Hawaii.

The wreck of the Arizona *settles in the mud. One sailor was so frustrated he threw potatoes at the bombers.*

"My God, this can't be true!" said Knox. "This must mean the Philippines."

"No, sir," replied Stark. "This is Pearl."

In Honolulu, disbelief had long before yielded to fear. The trembling voice of a local radio announcer had informed local listeners: "This is the real thing, folks, believe me! Now don't get excited."

Kimmel's proud fleet was devastated by Fuchida's first wave of 181 planes. In forty-five minutes of havoc, all seven battleships moored alongside Ford Island had been damaged. Now, after a lull, a second wave of 170 planes roared in from the east, from beyond Honolulu's Diamond Head landmark, to finish the job.

The brief respite had given American crews time to regroup, and the Japanese paid for it. Anti-aircraft fire brought down fourteen dive bombers and six fighters as they zeroed in on ships that escaped the first attacks.

Meanwhile, another menace had appeared in the harbor. One of a half-dozen midget submarines the Japanese dispatched to infiltrate the harbor surfaced 700 yards from the seaplane tender *Curtis*. Shipboard gunners found the sub's range, but it took a depth charge, dropped by the destroyer *Monaghan*, to sink the seventy-eight-foot, two-man craft.

A short time later, a *Monaghan* depth charge sank another mini-sub as it headed for a U.S. cruiser.

The gray pall was growing thicker over Pearl Harbor. The black of oil and red of flames spread out over water crisscrossed by rescue boats in search of wounded men.

By 9:45 a.m., less than two hours after it began, the attack ended, the Japanese planes flying off in several directions in a final tactic of deception.

The sailors and soldiers of Oahu did not know the Japanese were gone for good, and they stuck by their guns. Nervous ground crews shot down three American planes flying in from the carrier *Enter-*

Sailors take up rifles as submarine **Tautog** *still flies Sunday jack from its bow.*

prise, at sea 200 miles west of Oahu.

The Hawaii military command expected the Japanese next to put infantry ashore, to wrest the territory from the United States.

That fearful night of December 7, Army artilleryman Earl Bangert manned a shore battery and he later recalled his battery mate insisting, "We won't be around to see the 8th, Bangert. We won't be around."

The hospitals ashore could barely cope with the sudden Sunday disaster. At Kaneohe Naval Air Station's hospital, the peacetime sick had to give up their beds to the wartime wounded. Wives of officers and seamen reported to the hospital and

Destroyer **Shaw** *explodes at Pearl Harbor.* **Inset:** *Navy rescuers pull survivors from the waters of Pearl Harbor as battleship* **West Virginia** *burns.*

began tearing up sheets into strips to replace depleted bandages. In Honolulu, Farrington High School was converted into a makeshift hospital.

Day and night, the rescue work went on. Work crews cut through the upended hull of the *Oklahoma* and pulled dozens of men out alive. But some 400 drowned in the capsized battleship.

It was eight days before the American people learned the full extent of the losses: 2,403 Americans killed, half of them when the *Arizona* blew up.

The *Arizona*, the *Oklahoma*, two destroyers, and the target ship *Utah*, a former battleship, were total losses. Six other battleships and eight other vessels were damaged and knocked out of action for at

least several weeks. The attackers also destroyed 188 Army and Navy aircraft, about half of Hawaii's air arm.

In exchange, the Japanese lost just twenty-nine airplanes and six submarines.

Shortly before 1 p.m., as soot-faced sailors collected the human debris of the disaster, a telegraph boy bicycled up to Kimmel's headquarters with the cable from Marshall warning that Hawaii's defenders should be on the alert. Because static had disrupted the Army radio, the message was entrusted to the civilian network. It arrived in Honolulu twenty minutes before the attack, but the messenger, a young Japanese-American, spent much of the next few hours in a ditch ducking the Japanese bombs and waiting to be cleared through roadblocks.

At 2:22 p.m. EST, the "FLASH" had been sent out on Associated Press wires: "WHITE HOUSE SAYS JAPS ATTACK PEARL HARBOR."

Word of the surprise attack rolled across America like a clap of thunder.

In New York, WOR broke into its radio broadcast of the Giants-Dodgers football game with the news. In Dallas, a showing of "Sergeant York" was interrupted at the Majestic Theater with word of the attack. After a moment of stunned silence, the 2,500 moviegoers broke into patriotic applause. Many Americans heard of the Pearl Harbor disaster just before the 3 p.m. (EST) CBS broadcast of a New York Philharmonic concert. And millions learned from friends and neighbors, over the fence, on street corners. After a generation of peace, their nation was again at war.

By evening, hundreds of ordinary Americans had gathered on the sidewalks outside the White House. Inside, Roosevelt brought together Cabinet and congressional leaders to report on the debacle. When he was finished, Senator Tom Connally of Texas sprang angrily to his feet, pounded the Oval Office desk and demanded, "How did they catch us with our pants down, Mr. President?"

The Japanese had, indeed, caught the Americans unprepared.

The Army's antiaircraft gunners in Hawaii had not been issued live ammunition. General Short had ordered his parked planes bunched together, wing to wing, so they could be more easily guarded against any saboteurs on the ground. The warships were dangerously "unbuttoned," too many of their watertight doors left open. And American air patrols over the nearby seas had fallen into a predictable routine.

Military studies had warned that the Japanese might try a carrier-based air attack against Pearl Harbor. But the U.S. commanders could never believe, until December 7, 1941, that Japan would risk such a long-distance strike against the heart of the American Pacific.

Decoded Japanese diplomatic messages showed a growing interest in Pearl Harbor in the months leading up to the attack, but critical intelligence often was not shared with the Hawaii commanders. The messages deciphered the day before the attack convinced key people in Washington that war was imminent. But no new warnings were sent to Hawaii.

Subsequently, nine official investigations into Pearl Harbor allocated blame across the board, although Admiral Kimmel and General Short paid the highest price. Their careers were finished.

Japanese stealth had succeeded brilliantly. The "Kido Butai" task force of thirty-one ships, including six aircraft carriers, had steamed undetected on a little-traveled route across the North Pacific and launched the air attack from a point 200 miles north of Oahu.

But the Japanese success was not total.

When Fuchida landed back on his carrier, he recommended to Rear Admiral Chuichi Nagumo, task force commander, that another attack be mounted on the Hawaii navy base. But the old admiral declined. His flotilla could not risk being spotted; Japan, now at war with a mightier foe, could not afford to lose any ships.

The task force came around to the north and headed home, leaving behind a Pearl Harbor where the repair shops, power plants, gasoline tanks and more than seventy vessels were unscathed in the attack. Perhaps most importantly, the Pacific Fleet's three aircraft carriers, key targets for the Japanese, were either at sea or on the U.S. West Coast during the attack. In the months to come, the three flattops —the *Enterprise*, the *Saratoga* and the *Lexington*— became by necessity the new flagships of the fleet, in a new kind of war.

Last minute briefing for Pearl Harbor pilots. The forecast: clear skies over target.

Japanese plane flies home, its damage done: 2,403 dead, 188 planes destroyed, 19 ships damaged or sunk.

President Roosevelt asks Congress to declare war on Japan the morning after Pearl Harbor, "a day that will live in infamy."

The Japanese hoped the shocking blow at Hawaii would cause America to recoil, to withdraw, to seek some accommodation giving Japan freer rein in the western Pacific. But, instead, the treacherous blow unified a divided and isolationist America.

In Tokyo, eight hours after the attack, an imperial rescript from Emperor Hirohito was published declaring war on the United States and Britain. It accused the Americans and British of prolonging the war in China by aiding Chiang Kai-shek's government. The war declaration "has been truly unavoidable," the emperor said.

Prime Minister Tojo, broadcasting to the nation, declared, "I promise you final victory." But Admiral Isoroku Yamamoto, commander of Japan's Combined Fleet and author of the Pearl Harbor plan, sounded less sure.

"Well, war has begun at last," he wrote his sister. "But, in spite of all the clamor that is going on, we could lose it."

Early Monday afternoon, Roosevelt went before a joint session of Congress. His face lined and drawn, he reviled the Japanese for their attack, on a

"day which will live in infamy," and vowed that "the American people in their righteous might will win through to absolute victory."

The declaration of war was adopted unanimously, except for the negative vote of one House member, Montana pacifist Jeannette Rankin.

Thousands of men packed military recruiting stations across the country. Many stations stayed open at night to handle the overflow. At the new training bases across the South and West, tens of thousands of peacetime draftees, uncomfortable in their new uniforms, already homesick, knew they were now committed "for the duration."

A bickering nation had drawn quickly together. "The only thing to do now," said Senator Burton K. Wheeler, harsh critic of the Roosevelt foreign policy, "is to lick hell out of them!"

Then, on Wednesday, under the terms of their Tripartite Treaty with the Japanese, Germany and Italy declared war on the United States.

Roosevelt, in a second war message, declared that "rapid and united effort by all of the peoples of the world who are determined to remain free will ensure a world victory of the forces of justice and of righteousness over the forces of savagery and of barbarism."

The American people, 130 million strong, were embarked on a period of common hardship and global adventure unprecedented in their history.

For millions of ordinary Americans, Pearl Harbor Sunday became a moment fixed in memory, a borderline between years of hard times at home and days of action and danger abroad. For a handful of military men, too, it was a borderline, marking the passage from the obscurity of peacetime to the headlines of world conflict.

Pearl Harbor was a door from one age to another, a fact most Americans did not recognize as they stepped through it.

The pre-1941 world was gone, blown to bits like the bombers at Clark Field. Three decades later, the historian Richard Polenberg would write that although the war saw the passage of virtually no social legislation, it "radically altered the character of American society and challenged its most durable values."

"Really World War"

As the Japanese planes bore down on Pearl Harbor that peaceful dawn, Vice Admiral William F. Halsey was at sea 200 miles to the west, aboard the aircraft carrier *Enterprise,* in command of a thirteen-ship task force that had just delivered a Marine air squadron to far-off Wake Island.

In sharp contrast with the lack of alertness at his home harbor, Halsey had the *Enterprise's* planes "bombed up" and his fliers under orders to sink any Japanese ship on sight. He knew war would break out at any time.

A descendant of whaling captains and a Cape Cod privateer, Halsey, fifty-nine, was a risk-taker. Naval Academy Class of '04, he had bulled his way through opposition lines as a 175-pound Annapolis fullback. He spent most of his career with destroyers, but in his mid-fifties he learned to fly and became a "carrier man."

Even as the war began, however, the Navy was not totally convinced of the power of carriers. A 1939 Naval War College pamphlet dismissed the idea that air power could defeat a well-organized naval force.

As he steamed back toward shattered Pearl Harbor that day, "Bull" Halsey was setting a course that would dispel those doubts forever.

When word arrived of the attack on Hawaii, Rear Admiral Chester W. Nimitz was in Washington, as chief of the Navy's Bureau of Navigation.

Within nine days, he was chosen to replace Kimmel as commander of the Pacific Fleet.

"You always wanted the Pacific Fleet," his wife said. "You always thought that would be the height of glory."

"Darling, the fleet's at the bottom of the sea," Nimitz replied. "Nobody must know that here, but I've got to tell you."

Nimitz, fifty-six, was a white-haired, scholarly-looking man, deliberate, soft-spoken, incisive, a leader by example. He had a reputation for being able to do much with little, a useful attribute in his new command.

On Christmas morning, eighteen days after the attack, Nimitz flew in to Pearl Harbor to take up that command. Ferried by whaleboat from his Navy seaplane, he could see small craft about the harbor, still searching for the bodies of sailors rising up from the sunken battleships.

Nimitz knew how to wage naval war against Japan. Such a war had been "fought" dozens of times at the Naval War College. But, in the war games, the Americans never began with such a disadvantage.

Franklin Roosevelt's sinuses were bothering him again, so he had skipped a Sunday luncheon hosted by his wife at the White House. The president was sitting in his second-floor office, talking to Harry Hopkins about subjects far removed from the war, when the telephone rang that December 7 afternoon. The president lifted the receiver and his face clouded. Then he shouted: "No!"

Roosevelt's press secretary, Steve Early, arranged a conference call among the three major news services, and read a statement FDR had dictated.

At Griffith Stadium in Washington, Ensign John F. Kennedy and 27,101 other fans had gathered on a clear, brisk afternoon to see the Washington Redskins play the Philadelphia Eagles. Meanwhile, the public address system began carrying one

Investigating commission accused Admiral Husband E. Kimmel (l.) and Lieutenant General Walter C. Short of dereliction of duty.

Sunday, December 7, 1941, started out as Tuffy Leeman's Day honoring the star New York Giants halfback at the Polo Grounds until...

announcement after another, asking various generals, admirals and ambassadors to go to their offices. The crowd was bewildered, but there was no announcement about Pearl Harbor.

At Fort Sam Houston in Texas, Brigadier General Dwight Eisenhower's nap was ended by a ringing telephone. His wife heard him say, "Yes? When? I'll be right down." He, too, ran out the door, dressing as he went and calling over his shoulder that he was off to headquarters and didn't know when he'd be back.

Air Force pilot Paul W. Tibbets was flying between Fort Bragg, North Carolina, and Hunter Field in Georgia. About twenty minutes before he was to land his Douglas A-20, Tibbets tuned in a Savannah radio station. The announcer interrupted a Glenn Miller record with the news.

A motorist in Redwood City, California, who had been listening on his car radio to the increasingly serious reports, died at the wheel of a heart attack—the home front's first casualty.

In Cleveland, eighty Far East experts had gathered to debate ways to resolve the crisis in the region. When the news arrived, wrote one reporter, "There was dead silence for two minutes. In those 120 seconds, eighty different opinions were resolved."

GEORGE S. PATTON

Major General George S. Patton, Jr., was at Fort Benning, in Georgia, when war broke out. His 2nd Armored Division had just completed maneuvers. Soon after Pearl Harbor, Patton called his men together and gave them a credo for the tough years ahead. "Remember," he told them, "the only good enemy is a dead enemy."

Patton, fifty-six, was already an Army celebrity. The next four years would make him a national legend.

In September 1941, at giant war games in Louisiana, Patton's "Hell on Wheels" division "won" the battle by executing an all-night forced drive, with gasoline paid for personally by the general, to outflank the opponent. The move was unauthorized, and pure Patton.

He always wore pearl-handled pistols (against the uniform code), a highly polished helmet, shiny boots and a breastful of campaign ribbons.

The pistols were not just decorative. In 1916 in Mexico, he used them to kill one of Pancho Villa's chief lieutenants in a gunfight. Two years later he served heroically, and was wounded, in the St. Mihiel and Meuse-Argonne offensives in France, where he became General John J. Pershing's aide-de-camp.

Patton's aggressiveness and unpredictability made some of his superiors uneasy. But others knew he was a force to be harnessed in the new war.

As he later wrote before a battle, "It seems that my whole life has been pointed to this moment."

DWIGHT D. EISENHOWER

Lieutenant Colonel Dwight D. Eisenhower (temporary rank, brigadier general) was napping at his quarters at Fort Sam Houston, Texas, that Sunday afternoon when an aide awakened him with the news of Pearl Harbor.

Long days of planning and mobilization followed for the Third Army chief of staff. But on December 12 a call came from Washington. "The chief says for you to hop a plane and get up here right away," Eisenhower was told.

General Marshall wanted Ike to try to map out a plan to help the beleaguered U.S. garrison in the Philippines, where Eisenhower had previously served.

Within weeks, Marshall had named Eisenhower assistant chief of staff for war plans, and soon thereafter chief of operations for the War Department General Staff.

The fifty-one-year-old officer's rapid rise was not surprising to insiders.

Though a 1915 graduate of West Point, he did not serve overseas during World War I. But ever since the spring of 1926, when he graduated first in a class of almost 300 at the Command and General Staff School, he had been high on the promotion lists. Even General John J. Pershing had commended him for "unusual intelligence and constant devotion to duty" after Major Eisenhower, on special assignment, wrote a guidebook to World War I battlefields.

The youthful, athletic-looking Eisenhower also was armed with a sincere, warm personality that enabled him to bring together men, often of opposing views, to work cooperatively.

He was the son of German-descended Mennonites who had settled in Kansas. His pacifistic mother was said to have cried when he was accepted into West Point. Now this son, a warrior who had never seen a battle, was headed into a war greater than any seen before.

Communities staged impromptu blackouts and air-raid drills, and the Office of Civilian Defense began plans to rush 57 million copies of the pamphlet "What to Do in an Air Raid" into print. Telephone calls to Alaska were cancelled. The Navy began censoring cables, the Army, international mail. The government grounded private planes and silenced the nation's 50,000 ham operators.

Some recruiting offices opened on Sunday—"by popular demand," they said—and lines formed outside. In Detroit, a grandfather, his son and his grandson showed up at a Navy recruiting station. In Washington, General John J. "Blackjack" Pershing, long retired and so infirm at eighty-one that he was living at Walter Reed hospital, ordered himself driven to the White House so he could personally offer Roosevelt his services.

That night, in a club somewhere in America, a singer performed the first song written for the war: "We'll Knock the Japs Right into the Laps of the Nazis."

The West Coast was gripped by what the Navy's official history described as "plain, simple, mass hysteria." There were rumors: about enemy planes, spies, Japanese farmers who'd planted crops to form arrows pointing toward military installations. When a University of San Francisco student walked into the living room of his boarding house and flipped on the light, his landlady yelled, "Turn the lights out! The Japs are comin'." The enemy already had bombed the Golden Gate Bridge, she told him. In fact, a woman was shot and wounded because she failed to stop her car at a National Guard checkpoint on the San Francisco-Oakland Bay Bridge.

In Market Square, the flashing electric marquee on the United Artists Theater was pelted with rocks and bricks by a crowd screaming "Blackout!" A man ran up to a streetcar and smashed its headlight with a baseball bat. Up the coast in Seattle, a mob gathered during a blackout to throw rocks and bottles at a huge blue neon sign. Store windows were smashed in the process, which led to looting. Police charged a nineteen-year-old woman with inciting riot. Her comment: "This is war. They don't realize one light in the city may betray us. That's my patriotism."

In Los Angeles, rookie cop Tom Bradley, later to become the city's mayor, heard sirens going off and aircraft guns firing. "It was panic," he would recall. "Here we are in the middle of the night, there was no enemy in sight, but someone thought they saw the enemy. They were shooting at random." On December 9, aviators reported thirty-four Japanese warships between San Francisco and Los Angeles. The military investigated and found the armada

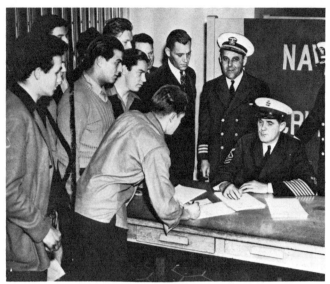

Pearl Harbor still burned as Navy recruits signed up the night of December 7 in San Francisco.

was really fourteen fishing boats. In such a climate, wrote General Joseph Stilwell, "Common sense is thrown to the winds and any absurdity is believed."

There was relatively little hostility toward the region's 125,000 Japanese-Americans. U.S. Attorney General Francis Biddle said there would be no mass roundup, and everyone detained would get a fair hearing. But the FBI ordered air, bus and rail lines to refuse Japanese passengers, and within three days 2,303 Japanese were in custody, including a dozen elegantly dressed Japanese-Americans who were arrested at a Los Angeles wedding reception and taken to the county jail. Japanese-Americans on the West Coast were dismissed from civil service jobs, stripped of licenses to practice law and medicine, and, in some communities, prevented from doing business of any sort.

Although only the West Coast was gripped by hysteria, the entire nation was tense. Boston was "a goddamn madhouse," according to a civil defense leader. Blackout organizers pulled the master switches to the city's power, killing traffic lights and electrically-operated fire station doors in the process.

Washington, D.C., took the news in stride, although several of the 3,000 cherry trees around the Tidal Basin—gifts from Japan three decades earlier—were chopped down.

A crowd saw smoke rise from the Japanese embassy as diplomats burned their papers. Reporters actually walked inside and watched as embassy staffers carried boxes of papers into the garden out back and lit them with kitchen matches. There was a similar scene in New Orleans, where a crowd was

To avoid being mistaken for Japanese, Chinese in Los Angeles wore buttons.

able to watch Japanese consulate officials burning papers in their courtyard. Some blew away before they could burn, however, and diplomats chased them around like chickens while the observers hissed. The Japanese consul in San Francisco was in such a hurry to burn his files that he ended up accidentally setting fire to his home.

Another crowd gathered that evening outside 1600 Pennsylvania Avenue. Although some sang patriotic songs, most stood silently, watching. "People throughout the country seem to have been

In New York's Times Square, Americans listen to FDR announcing war.

looking to the White House and the man who lived there," historian Lee Kennett would write.

That Sunday night, the White House was dark. The great light over the north portico was off for the first time in memory, and the mansion's house-keeper already was taking measurements for black-out curtains. Security—so lax in those days that autograph seekers once wandered in on the president and the first lady—was tightened. Treasury Secretary Henry Morgenthau's order that machine guns be stationed and sandbags piled at all entrances was deemed unnecessary, as was the Army's plan to paint the house black. But the guard was doubled and all staff members were issued gas masks. Roosevelt's hung from the arm of his wheelchair.

In the basement, engineers were marking the opening for a tunnel to the presidential bomb shelter in a vault under the Treasury building across the street. FDR had hinted the shelter might be useful for poker games, with $20 gold pieces for chips.

Soldiers placed antiaircraft guns on the roof of the building where Secretary of State Cordell Hull had confronted the Japanese envoys that afternoon. Machine guns also could be seen on the roof of the Capitol, although they were wood and the soldiers who manned them dummies.

Archibald MacLeish, Librarian of Congress, prepared the Constitution and the Declaration of Independence for their removal to Fort Knox. "I have never been as frightened for the Republic as I was by midnight," he later confessed.

On Monday morning the Secret Service began looking for an armored, bulletproof limousine for the president. They settled on one that had been seized by the Treasury Department in its tax evasion case against mobster Al Capone. "I hope Mr. Capone won't mind," the president said.

Roosevelt was to address a joint session of Congress at 12:30 that afternoon. The New York Stock Exchange suspended trading at noon, and outside people stopped to listen to the speech on a car radio. They and about 60 million other Americans heard the voice of a Hudson Valley patrician begin with these words: "Yesterday, December 7th, 1941—a day which will live in infamy. . . ." The original draft had read "live in world history," but the president crossed out the last two words and substituted "infamy." After the speech there was applause, shouting, even some whistling in the chamber. Every senator voted for war; Representative Jeannette Rankin of Montana, one of several members to vote against war in 1917, was alone this time. After the vote she ran to an anteroom, closed herself in a telephone booth and sat there crying.

At six-and-a-half minutes, Roosevelt's was the shortest declaration of war in American history. There was no attempt to promise a postwar paradise, extensively outline war aims, stir up patriotic fervor or even hate against the Japanese. In his simple description of the provocation and his prescription for a response, the president set the tone for America's business-like war effort.

Americans' first reaction to Pearl Harbor was shock: many regarded the Japanese as small, strange-looking and backward people who could not compete physically or technologically with Americans. However, shock soon gave way to anger. Most Americans had been intellectually resigned to war before the attack, but now they were emotionally committed. Harry Hopkins wrote in his diary that FDR seemed thankful the Japanese "made the decision for him." A week earlier, Roosevelt had said the country was so divided he doubted he could get Congress to declare war if Japan invaded the Philippines. Now, especially with Hitler's declaration of war on December 11, the path was clear. "We are alive, rudely awakened," wrote Jonathan Daniels, a newspaper editor who would later join Roosevelt's staff. "We are men again in America."

For ten years internationalists and isolationists had battled for the soul of American foreign policy. By the end of 1941 the internationalists were winning the debate, but Pearl Harbor ended it. The *Chicago Tribune* changed its masthead's slogan from "Save Our Republic" to "Our Country Right or Wrong."

Patriotic fervor crested in the days after the attack. A union local in Chattanooga voted its own declaration of war on the Japanese empire; Rotarians in Kodiak, Alaska, vowed not to shave until the war was won; a World War I aviator, Arthur Names, wrote to Roosevelt with this offer: "I will personally fly a boatload of high explosives into any Japanese battleship whenever and wherever the C.O. may deem it necessary and expedient. I have had a swell time in this country for fifty years, glad to have been here."

There was much confidence, from Admiral Halsey, who predicted that Japan would be crushed by 1943, to the peanut vendor outside the White House who boasted: "Just three months—we finish them." But the *Nation*'s Washington columnist, I.F. Stone, was less sanguine. "We are going into this war lightly, but I have a feeling that it will weigh heavily upon us before we are through," he wrote. The conflict at hand "makes the last war seem a parochial effort. . . . This is really world war."

Army recruiters in Boston interrupt enlistments to hear Roosevelt ask Congress to declare war.

4 LOW TIDE

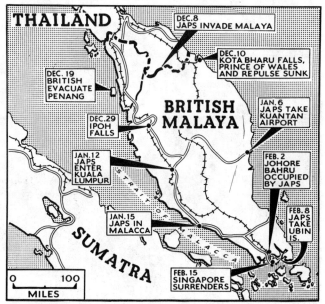

Major General Edward P. King, Jr., (center) surrenders U.S. forces on Bataan to Japanese Colonel Motoo Nakayama. King asked if his men would be well treated. "We are not barbarians," the colonel replied.

One week after Pearl Harbor, Winston Churchill and his military chiefs were headed for Washington aboard the battleship *Duke of York*. After twenty-seven months of setback and lonely struggle, the British prime minister was buoyant. America was in the war.

"Hitler's fate was sealed. Mussolini's fate was sealed. As for the Japanese, they would be ground to powder," Churchill later wrote of his confident mid-Atlantic mood.

But any confidence was fast draining from the Americans and British out in the Pacific.

Pearl Harbor was merely the boldest of a series of coordinated attacks by the Japanese across the Pacific islands and down the face of East Asia, air strikes and troop landings that showed the world. Japan had, indeed, built an agile and potent war machine.

Within hours of the Hawaii attack, as the ocean dawn raced across the blue Pacific, Japanese warplanes roared in from the sea to bomb three other American targets: Guam, Wake, and Clark Airfield in the central Philippines.

Japanese bombers also struck the British colony of Hong Kong that day, already December 8 in the Eastern Hemisphere. Farther up the Chinese coast, Japanese soldiers and sailors swarmed through Shanghai's International Settlement, sinking a British gunboat and forcing an American gunboat to surrender. The "internationalized" core of the Chinese port had until that day been bypassed throughout the long Japanese-Chinese conflict.

The Japanese mounted their biggest attack against the northern coast of the British colony of Malaya. The first units of an army that eventually numbered 200,000 put ashore at Kota Bharu on December 8 and readied for a 350-mile push through the jungles to "impregnable" Singapore, the Royal Navy stronghold at the tip of the Malay Peninsula.

From Singapore that day, two great British capital ships, the new battleship *Prince of Wales* and the heavy cruiser *Repulse*, set out northward in an effort to break up the convoy runs to Malaya from Japanese-occupied Indochina.

In seventy days the Japanese fought 650 miles down the Malay Peninsula to capture 130,000 British Empire troops at Singapore.

THAILAND

DEC. 8
JAPS INVADE MALAYA

DEC. 10
KOTA BHARU FALLS,
PRINCE OF WALES
AND REPULSE SUNK

DEC. 19
BRITISH
EVACUATE
PENANG

JAN. 6
JAPS TAKE
KUANTAN
AIRPORT

DEC. 29
IPOH
FALLS

BRITISH
MALAYA

JAN. 12
JAPS
ENTER
KUALA
LUMPUR

FEB. 2
JOHORE
BAHRU
OCCUPIED
BY JAPS

JAN. 15
JAPS IN
MALACCA

FEB. 8
JAPS
TAKE
UBIN
IS.

SUMATRA

0   100
MILES

FEB. 15
SINGAPORE
SURRENDERS

But the Royal Navy commanders were not prepared for the new lightning war. Without their own air cover, the *Prince of Wales* and *Repulse* were easy targets for Japan's naval air power. In a furious two-hour attack December 10, dozens of high-level and torpedo bombers fatally wounded the two giant ships, sending them to the bottom of the South China Sea, along with about 600 of their 3,000 crew members.

Cecil Brown, a CBS correspondent, was aboard the *Repulse* and later credited the Japanese airmen with "consummate skill and the greatest daring." The shocking loss left the British-American allies with no major naval firepower anywhere in the region.

Hong Kong's 11,000 British and Canadian defenders capitulated on Christmas Day to the Japanese, who had cut off the isolated colony's water reservoirs. Two days later the Japanese landed in oil-rich British Borneo and prepared to invade the Dutch East Indies, an even greater oil prize. Meanwhile, to the west, advance Japanese units were making the first penetration of British Burma through Siam. The helpless Siamese government had surrendered to the Japanese, marching in from Indochina, after only a few hours' resistance December 8.

Earlier in 1941, in global strategy meetings in Washington, American and British military staffs decided that Guam, Wake and the Philippines, U.S. possessions at the distant outer ring of supply and reinforcement lines in the Pacific, probably could

General Tomoyuki Yamashita, "the Tiger of Malaya," took Singapore.

not be held against Japanese assault in the event of war.

Guam, for one, fell quickly.

Just 1,155 miles south of Tokyo, this U.S. naval way station had been deliberately left unfortified, in order not to provoke Japan, as tensions mounted through the 1930s. Japanese bombers pounded the island December 8, and an invasion force swept ashore three days later. Guam's 555-man defense contingent, without antiaircraft guns and coastal defense batteries, surrendered.

But the tiny U.S. Marine garrison on remote Wake and General MacArthur's pocket army in the Philippines did not run down the flag so quickly. In the weeks that followed, their defiance inspired a nation dismayed by the debacle at Pearl Harbor.

A radioman on Wake, 1,800 miles west of Pearl

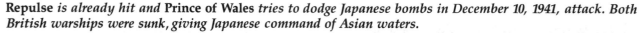

Repulse *is already hit and* **Prince of Wales** *tries to dodge Japanese bombs in December 10, 1941, attack. Both British warships were sunk, giving Japanese command of Asian waters.*

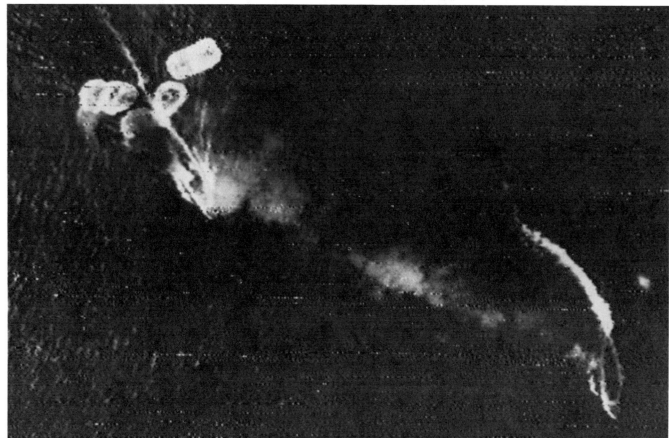

Crew of British battleship **Prince of Wales** *abandon ship. Japanese bombers also sank* **Repulse** *December 10, 1941, crippling British navy in Far East.*

Harbor, caught the distress message from Oahu's Hickam Field an hour after the attack on Hawaii began. Wake's 400 Marines, summoned by a bugler's "Call to Arms," scrambled from their breakfasts to their battle stations.

The war arrived five hours later, from the south. Thirty-six Japanese bombers dropped from a rain squall and bore in on Wake's Marine air squadron, caught on the ground. The Japanese tore apart the parked Wildcats with 100-pound bombs and 20mm incendiary machine-gun fire, killing or wounding thirty-four of the fifty-five men in the squadron. It was the first of the daily air attacks the men on Wake would endure in the two weeks to come.

Wake, a U-shaped atoll of three flat, sun-baked islands, totaled just 2,600 acres of sand, coral and ironwood brush. It had been a trans-Pacific stopover for Pan American Airways' flying boats since 1935, and was now being converted into a military base.

Some 1,100 construction workers, who began arriving on the atoll in January 1941, had already completed a 5,000-foot runway and were building a Navy seaplane base and other facilities. But Wake was not ready to defend itself.

"We weren't prepared at all," one Marine private, Ival Milbourn, later recalled. "We hadn't even filled the first sandbag."

The bombers, from the Japanese-held atoll of Kwajalein, 600 miles to the south, returned daily as the Marines dug in deeper. On the fourth day, the invaders arrived, a thirteen-ship Japanese flotilla bearing a landing force of 450 men.

Marine beach lookouts spotted the ships at 3 a.m. on December 11, murky shapes on a dark horizon. Major James P.S. Devereux, the career Marine in command of the detachment, knew his only chance was to allow the Japanese to penetrate to within range of his shore guns, second-hand five-inchers taken from old battleships.

The ships, led by the light cruiser *Yubari*, approached Wake's southern shore, opened fire and continued firing for forty minutes as they cruised parallel to the beach. When the *Yubari* stood just 4,500 yards offshore, Devereux ordered his batteries to fire. The cruiser was hit twice as it sped away from shore, and a nearby destroyer was hit, exploded and sank. Wake's four remaining Wildcats took off in pursuit of the fleeing Japanese and sank another destroyer. The final toll: two ships destroyed, seven damaged, at least 500 Japanese killed. None of the invasion force was put ashore. The Marines suffered only four men wounded.

The daily, devastating air raids continued. For the Marines and the 300 construction men working closely with them (the rest had scattered to the islands' far corners to avoid the bombings), life turned into an exhausting routine of digging, bombings, repairing. The concussion of the bombs made Wake's ever-present rats wild and trouble-some. Diarrhea debilitated the men, and doubts assailed them. Under the scorching sun and tropi-cal stars, they watched and waited, for reinforce-ments, for the Japanese.

Devereux called it a "foggy blur of days and nights when time stood still."

On December 15, a small naval task force led by the carrier *Saratoga* set out from Pearl Harbor to relieve Wake, carrying a contingent of 200 Marines and a squadron of fighter planes. But the warships were slowed by an accompanying oil tanker that could do only twelve knots.

On December 22, Wake's last two Wildcat fight-ers were lost in action against Zeros from a Japanese aircraft carrier. A carrier over the horizon, Devereux knew, meant an invasion over the hori-zon.

The attack again came against Wake's southern shore. There was no moon the morning of Decem-ber 23; beach lookouts could not see far into the darkness. At about 2 a.m. on December 23, they reported sighting landing barges heading for shore. About 200 defenders were scattered along the four miles of beach, facing 1,000 Japanese naval infan-trymen.

The boats were too close for the five-inch guns to be used. The Japanese streamed ashore and, with fixed bayonets, collided with the Americans in bloody hand-to-hand combat in the darkness and early-morning rain.

One three-inch gun crew found the range on a beached destroyer-transport and set it ablaze as it disgorged landing squads. The fire illuminated the shoreline, and Marine machine-gunners raked the Japanese with deadly fire in the surf and sand.

But the thin and bloodied American line soon bent back. As position after position was overrun, the defenders' telephone link was broken. "They're killing 'em all," a civilian said as he stumbled into Devereux's command post.

At dawn the Americans could see that their atoll was ringed by Japanese warships, and its sandy stretches were dotted with Japanese flags.

They returned. U.S. planes and ships bombard Wake Island in 1943, two years after Japanese capture Pacific outpost.

The Philippines

Japanese propaganda photos of Shanghai POW camp.

The Philippines, 7,000 lush and backward islands strategically situated between Japan and the mineral-rich East Indies, was second homeland to General Douglas MacArthur.

His father, General Arthur MacArthur, had ruled the archipelago as military governor after the United States seized the Spanish colony in the 1898 war. The younger MacArthur served in the Philippines himself, soon after graduating from West Point in 1903.

His career rise was swift and glittering: a heady tour, at age twenty-six, as military aide to President Theodore Roosevelt, his father's friend; promotion to brigadier general in France in World War I; command of the U.S. garrison in the Philippines in 1928-30; appointment as Army Chief of Staff in 1930.

As chief of staff, in 1932, MacArthur personally led the troops who set fire to the tent camps of the "Bonus Marchers." The harsh repression gained MacArthur national notoriety.

The patrician general was never popular with the rank-and-file. He was aloof from his troops, his demeanor haughty, his political views elitist, his public gestures and statements theatrical and bombastic. In the Philippines, he even developed a unique uniform for himself, topped by a gold-encrusted hat.

A British officer who, as a liaison, observed MacArthur closely during the war described him in an intelligence report home as "shrewd, selfish, proud, remote, highly strung and vastly vain."

Shortly after 7 a.m., the island surrendered.

The surviving Americans on Wake, military and civilian alike, were rounded up, stripped and bound, and left sitting on the airstrip, in the open without food, for two days. It was the beginning of long years of brutality in Japanese captivity.

Fifty-two Marines and sailors and seventy civilians had been killed in the defense of Wake. To take the strategic little atoll, the Japanese paid a terrible price, an estimated 1,000 killed.

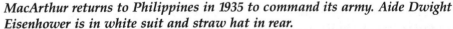

MacArthur returns to Philippines in 1935 to command its army. Aide Dwight Eisenhower is in white suit and straw hat in rear.

A defiant verse in the Philippines jungle: "We're the battling bastards of Bataan / No mama, no papa, no Uncle Sam."

In 1934, as he was being eased toward retirement, MacArthur had been asked by Philippine President Manuel Quezon, an old admirer, to come back to Manila as "field marshal" to build and train the Philippine army, looking toward the day, in 1944, when the United States was scheduled to confer independence on the colony.

MacArthur returned, was ensconced in a plush new penthouse atop the Manila Hotel, and undertook a ten-year plan to produce a home-grown defense force. But the Japanese caught him short.

At 2:30 Monday morning, December 8, 1941, Asiatic Fleet headquarters in Manila monitored the fateful message from Hawaii, "Air raid on Pearl Harbor. . . ."

Ten hours later, the core of the American air arm in the Philippines was sitting on the ground at Clark Airfield, forty miles north of Manila, when fifty-four Japanese bombers arrived overhead, after a 700-mile flight from Japanese-held Formosa.

The Japanese, in a "target shoot" like their rampage through Hickam and Wheeler, destroyed two squadrons of B-17 bombers and a squadron of P-40 fighters. Another squadron of P-40s was wrecked at Iba Airfield, forty miles west of Clark.

This bungled start to the defense of the Philippines was never fully explained. Major General Lewis Brereton, MacArthur's air commander, later said he sought permission to launch a bombing run against Formosa early Monday morning, but MacArthur and his staff chief, Major General Richard K. Sutherland, delayed those orders for hours. Sutherland, for his part, claimed Brereton had failed to comply with earlier orders to disperse his bombers to the southern Philippines. Some planes had taken to the air that day, but their pilots had returned for lunch when the Japanese struck.

The next day, Japanese bombers roared into broad Manila Bay and pounded the navy yard at Cavite, home of the U.S. Asiatic Fleet, a collection of cruisers and destroyers. Admiral Thomas C. Hart, his base facilities in ruins, quickly readied his flotilla for a dash to safety, south to the Dutch East Indies or Australia.

In Washington, the War Department, desperate for good news, found some in the early hours of the Philippine fighting. Captain Colin P. Kelly, Jr., flew his Army bomber against Japanese naval forces gathering off northern Luzon, and "distinguished himself by scoring three direct hits on the Japanese capital battleship *Haruna*." The *Haruna* sank, the War Department claimed. The Army publicists were wrong; the *Haruna* lived on to fight another day. Kelly was shot down and killed. But the American people had their first hero of the new war.

MacArthur, who was reappointed as a U.S. Army general in mid-1941, had under his command 100,000 troops of the Philippine army, 20,000 Americans and 10,000 Scouts, tough Filipino fighters who were integrated in the U.S. Army.

The general earlier had assured the War Department in Washington that his forces could throw back any Japanese invasion force. "The beaches were to be held at all costs," he said.

Planners in Washington were skeptical. They had long dreaded a Japanese thrust against the Philippines, since even an intact fleet at Pearl Harbor would have to sail through 5,600 miles of hostile seas to relieve the besieged commonwealth. But Marshall and Secretary of War Henry Stimson put a longshot bet on MacArthur's analysis. Hopeful that diplomacy might stave off war for another year, they poured weapons and planes into the islands in 1941. Training lagged desperately behind, however. When the Japanese finally did wade ashore, many Filipino soldiers went into action without ever having fired their rifles before.

In the first week of war, small Japanese forces made landing probes in the far north and south of Luzon, the Philippines' main island. On December 22, two weeks after Pearl Harbor, the Imperial Army's central force came ashore, storming the

U.S. Army Engineers prepare pontoon bridge at beginning of Philippines fighting in 1941.

The Japanese Rising Sun flies at entrance to captured Mariveles naval base in Philippines.

beaches of the Lingayen Gulf, a finger of water that pokes into Luzon's midsection and points toward Manila, 110 miles to the south. Lieutenant General Masaharu Homma, commander of the 100,000-man Japanese 14th Army, had been given fifty days to complete the conquest of Luzon.

Two ill-trained Philippine divisions were dug in at the Lingayen shoreline. Under artillery fire and air attack for the first time in their lives, they fell back, and MacArthur's plan to hold the enemy at the beaches crumbled.

An old cavalryman, Major General Jonathan M. Wainwright, was in command of this northern defense. He wanted to mount a counterattack with the Philippine Division, made up of American regulars and Filipino Scouts. But MacArthur, his airpower largely destroyed, his sea link to the east severed, quickly grasped the futility of any offensive operations. Late on December 23, orders went out to the field units to pull back and, under a long-standing contingency plan for "strategic retreat," to concentrate in the rugged Bataan peninsula, across Manila Bay from the capital. At about this time, a second Japanese force was coming ashore in Lamon Bay, sixty miles southeast of Manila.

MacArthur, however, now had no intention of holding the capital. As darkness fell on Christmas

Eve 1941, the general and his staff sped by boat across the bay to "The Rock," heavily fortified Corregidor, a tiny, tadpole-shaped island that was once a Spanish prison and would now become headquarters for one of the most celebrated last stands of modern warfare.

Not all Filipinos were unhappy to see the Americans driven out. As they were doing throughout East Asia, the Japanese showered the Filipino population with leaflets and broadcasts promising that Tokyo's "Co-Prosperity Sphere" would rid them of white Western imperialism and make them free Asians.

One such Filipino was Jose Laurel. "The United States used the lives of the Filipinos to defend purely American interests," said this prominent lawyer and judge, who later became president of a Japanese-sponsored Philippine republic.

The withdrawal into Bataan was a complex operation, carried out under Japanese fire over difficult terrain. Combat losses on both sides were heavy, and thousands of Filipinos deserted the ranks of the retreating army. But by January 7 the American-Filipino forces, fighting holding actions along the way, had streamed in to prepared positions on the hilly, jungle-covered peninsula, twenty miles wide at its base and twenty-five miles long.

The more than 70,000 defenders were exhausted, sick and hungry. Ammunition was plentiful, but food and medical supplies were short. By the end of the first week, rations were cut in half. Only a twenty-day supply of rice was on hand. Men succumbed by the hundreds to malaria, beri-beri and dysentery. Many of the ill-equipped Filipinos had simply worn out their shoes in the long retreat. Many Americans were in tattered, mismatched uniforms.

On Corregidor, two miles offshore from Bataan, MacArthur received a message from Homma: "Your prestige and honor have been upheld. However, in order to avoid needless bloodshed and save your . . . troops, you are advised to surrender."

The American answer was stepped-up artillery fire.

Homma launched his attack down the east shore of the peninsula, the side facing Manila, and ran into stiff resistance and counterattacks by Philippine troops under Major General George M. Parker. One regiment of the Philippine 51st Division lunged too far forward, however, and the Japanese closed in, cut it off and ended up routing the entire division. On the western half of the Bataan defense line, meanwhile, a Japanese battalion threaded its way over the supposedly impassable—and therefore undefended—heights of volcanic Mount Natib and emerged behind Wainwright's lines, blocking a main north-south road. Wainwright's forces finally had to withdraw southward along Bataan's beaches.

By January 26, the defense was re-established on the Philippine Division's fallback line across the peninsula, just twelve miles from its tip.

The Japanese threw artillery, air attacks and infantry against the final defense line, with no success. But the assaults through the steaming jungle were ferocious, in a frightening, fanatical way.

One night in mid-January, American soldiers were stunned to see Japanese troops charging out of a cane field into withering fire, screaming "Banzai!" and hurling their bullet-riddled bodies onto the barbed wire—stepladders for their comrades.

A more chilling episode occurred in late January when the Japanese landed 1,500 troops at Bataan's Quianuan Point, behind the American lines. They were soon trapped and cut down by the defenders, but remnants gathered in a cave at the beach. They could no longer offer effective resistance, but they refused all calls to surrender. They were finally blown to bits by American explosives.

"It had at last dawned on me," wrote Wainwright, "as it was to dawn on so many commanders who followed me in the Pacific war, that a Jap usually prefers death to surrender."

By mid-February, Homma's army was worn down by casualties and tropical disease. While he awaited reinforcements, a lull settled over the Philippines siege.

The rescue of the Philippines was not part of the grand strategy ratified by Roosevelt and Churchill in three weeks of meetings around the Christmas and New Year's holidays in Washington.

As he steamed toward the United States aboard the *Duke of York* in mid-December, the British prime minister's greatest fear was not of the marauding German submarines that made the North Atlantic a killing ground that winter, but of the aroused emotions of the American people. The sneak attack on Pearl Harbor had so enraged politicians, editorial writers and ordinary Americans that Churchill feared the U.S. leadership might abandon the strategy adopted earlier in 1941 in talks with the British on contingency war plans.

"We were conscious of a serious danger that the United States might pursue the war against Japan in the Pacific and leave us to fight Germany and Italy in Europe, Africa and the Middle East," Churchill would write.

But soon after the British leader, with his generals and admirals, arrived in wintry Washington, General Marshall and Admiral Stark reaffirmed the U.S. commitment to Rainbow 5, the basic war plan that proposed a strategic defensive in the Pacific while American forces were sent across the Atlantic "in order to effect the decisive defeat of Germany, Italy, or both." After victory in Europe, American power could be concentrated against Japan.

This meant the sacrifice, in the early months of the war, of U.S. possessions in the far Pacific, including the Philippines.

The Washington strategy meetings, dubbed Arcadia, quickly agreed on trying to close the ring around Germany in 1942 and, hopefully, landing Allied troops on the European continent in 1943. Churchill won Roosevelt over to the idea of joint U.S.-British landings in northwest Africa in 1942, an operation the president thought would boost American morale and give the new U.S. draftee army some early battle experience. But the African plan had major obstacles to clear before it became final.

That Christmastime, a bittersweet season of blackouts and long goodbyes for many Americans, military men were working eighteen-hour days in Washington, laying plans for bases, roads, pipelines, airstrips in such far-off places as Alaska, Australia and Brazil, extending the reach of American power around the globe. The government was setting up the War Production Board to oversee the output of the mighty American economy. And tens of thousands of young men were pouring into military training camps across the country. By the end of the new year, a half-million a month would be called up.

The single-minded Americans were concerned that none of this war effort be wasted. They wanted a streamlined Allied command, and Marshall pushed through the organization of a Combined Chiefs of Staff, a body comprising the four top American and four top British commanders, who would be in daily, almost hourly, touch with each other in Washington and London.

Before the Arcadia meetings ended January 14, a near-showdown developed over the key issue of war materiel, the weapons, aircraft, ships, ammunition, food and other supplies that keep armies and navies going.

Although the United States would produce the bulk of these munitions, the British proposed that they retain responsibility for distribution in the European-Middle Eastern Theater. To Marshall this meant London would retain supreme command of the war in the pivotal region. He rejected the plan and threatened to resign if Roosevelt did not support him. The president backed up his chief of staff, and the British gave in, agreeing to a joint administration that the Americans quickly came to dominate.

The grand strategy was set. But not long after the British embarked for home aboard the *Duke of York*, some of Arcadia's most optimistic scenarios began to evaporate.

In northern Africa, Field Marshal Erwin Rommel's counterattacking Afrika Korps recaptured strategic Benghazi from the British by the end of January. Rommel's parries against the Egypt-based British 8th Army would set back plans for the northwest Africa invasion.

Bataan defender prepares to attack Japanese tank with bottle of flaming gasoline.

Falling Far East

In the Far East, Allied outposts fell one by one, sooner than the planners in Washington and London had feared.

In Malaya, General Tomoyuki Yamashita's 25th Army had cut through the supposedly impenetrable jungle in forced marches through swamps and rice fields, using collapsible boats to cross jungle streams, driving back the British in skirmish after skirmish. By mid-January, the Japanese stood outside the island of Singapore, a "citadel" of the British Empire whose big guns and fortifications faced the sea, not its Malayan backyard.

For a month the Japanese, just across the mile-wide Johore Strait, bombarded the great port from the ground and the air. On February 14 they captured the city's reservoirs. The next day Lieutenant General Sir Arthur Ernest Percival surrendered, with more than 55,000 troops, making a total of 130,000 captured in the campaign.

The conquest of the peninsula gave Japan's war industries access to Malaya's bountiful rubber and tin resources. The Japanese next set their eye on the oil of the Dutch East Indies, whose main island, Java, was defended by an unreliable indigenous force, along with some Dutch warships and remnants of the U.S. Asiatic Fleet that escaped from the Philippines.

By March 1, the Japanese had landed in strength on Java, and within a week its defenses were overwhelmed. Almost 100,000 Dutch and native troops surrendered, along with 5,000 Australians, British and Americans.

That same week, the outgunned British evacuated Burma's capital and main port, Rangoon, lifeline from the West to Chiang Kai-shek's Chinese armies headquartered at Chungking, 1,000 miles to the northeast.

Tens of thousands of tons of U.S. Lend Lease supplies were sitting in Rangoon, awaiting transport north to the primitive Burma Road, the backdoor to China. But unexpected Japanese thrusts from Siam into Burma in late January had stunned the British, and they seemed about to lose another colony.

In mid-March, to shore up the ragged British-Indian defenses in lower Burma, Chinese military units were sent in from the north, under the command of Lieutenant General Joseph W. Stilwell.

"Vinegar Joe" Stilwell, regarded as one of the U.S. Army's most able troop commanders, had just been dispatched from Washington to serve as Chiang's chief of staff and to try to turn China into a true fighting front against the Japanese.

Frank Noel of AP won Pulitzer for photo of survivor from ship that was torpedoed off Sumatra.

Five kills and a live; a Flying Tiger in China.

Colonel Claire Chennault's "Flying Tigers" also flew into the battle for Burma. These American pilots, "on loan" from the U.S. Army and Navy, had put some fire into Chiang's punchless air arm, and their obsolescent Curtis P-40B fighters scored some remarkable successes in Burmese skies against heavy Japanese odds.

But in the 100-degree heat of central Burma, the assorted collection of British, Indian and Chinese troops steadily gave ground northward to Japan's determined jungle fighters.

As the Rising Sun flag fluttered over more and more of Southeast Asia, the 100,000 defenders of Bataan suffered through weeks of deprivation and uncertainty.

"Our perpetual hunger, the steaming heat by day and night, the terrible malaria and the moans of the wounded were terribly hard on the men," Wainwright wrote.

MacArthur, on Corregidor, implored Washington for help. In January, Marshall had sent General Patrick J. Hurley, a former Secretary of War, to Australia to try to assemble a mercenary force of blockade runners to get supplies to the besieged corner of Luzon. But Hurley finally threw up his hands; the Japanese captured or sank almost all of his ships. Only a trickle of supplies was getting through, aboard submarines.

"Sooner or later the relief expedition would have to arrive," wrote Colonel Richard C. Mallonee, an artillery officer.

The troops on Bataan were down to fifteen ounces of food a day, less than one-quarter of the peacetime ration. The Filipino Scouts' 26th Cavalry

Outnumbered American and Filipino troops on Bataan finally yielded to hunger, disease and Japanese invaders on April 9, 1942, after four months of desperate fighting.

had long before killed and eaten their horses. The famished men next devoured the meat of dogs, iguanas, monkeys and snakes. Medical supplies were largely gone, and by early March 500 men a day were reporting to the field hospital with malaria.

Bataan's "battling bastards," who once joked about P-40s swooping to their rescue and who put up road signs pointing to "Tokyo, 3,000 miles," were now blank-faced, desperate men.

They found no inspiration in their leader. Back home, the press showered MacArthur, the "Lion of Luzon," with adulation. The president ordered up a Medal of Honor in recognition of the heroic stand. But his troops noticed that the general had visited the Bataan front only once, early in the campaign. Otherwise he had stayed within the fortifications of Corregidor, issuing press releases and, the men knew, eating well.

"The public has built itself a hero out of its own imagination," Eisenhower, MacArthur's former aide, wrote in his diary.

Roosevelt finally ordered MacArthur to leave the Philippines for Australia. He said it was at the request of the Australian government. On March 11, a PT boat carrying the general, his top staff, his wife and his young son sped from Corregidor through the darkness, past a Japanese naval blockade and on south to the Del Monte pineapple plantation on the island of Mindanao. From the airstrip there, MacArthur flew to Australia, where he proclaimed, "I came through and I shall return."

The weary troops he left behind heard of the pledge on the radio and mocked MacArthur's grandiloquence. Their tiresome joke became, "I am going to the latrine, but I shall return."

News of the general's departure was a blow to the Filipino rank and file. "The heart went out of them," wrote Mallonee.

In early April, MacArthur, still trying to exercise control from Australia, sent a message to Wainwright, now in command on Corregidor: "When the supply situation becomes impossible there must be no thought of surrender. You must attack."

But when Homma's reinforced troops launched an all-out offensive on the Bataan line April 3, the issue was never in doubt. About 80 percent of the American and Filipino front-line troops had malaria. All were weak with hunger. One artillery unit depended on men who could barely walk to carry every round of ammunition three miles.

The fresh Japanese 4th Division broke through the front on the night of April 6 and pushed the defenders back until three days later, trapped just a mile or two from the sea, Major General Edward P. King, Jr., in command on the peninsula, gave the order to surrender.

Seventy-six thousand prisoners, 12,000 of them Americans, fell into Japanese hands. For them an even grimmer chapter of the war was about to begin.

Some of the Bataan force managed to escape to Corregidor, further crowding the bunkers and tunnels, further depleting the scarce water and rations of the holdout island.

In Corregidor's hot, humid Malinta Tunnel, his headquarters, Wainwright could hear the moans of the sick and wounded who filled the 1,000-bed underground hospital. He could hear the incessant thunder of Japanese shelling.

Soon after they captured the Bataan heights facing Corregidor, the invaders began a bombardment that, for such a small target, was probably unequaled in the war.

The punishing barrages would begin at dawn, ease up in early afternoon, then resume and last until about midnight. On one day, May 4, a Japanese shell landed every five seconds. The cost was high: Corregidor's big batteries in open pits were destroyed, and in three weeks the beach defense units were reduced from 4,000 to 3,000 men.

All the bone-weary defenders of The Rock could do was to dig in deeper and wait for the inevitable Japanese landings. They came late on May 5.

Japanese boats streamed toward the beaches near the island's North Point, and the U.S. 4th Marine Regiment put up a wall of fire, killing half the attackers before they reached shore. But more and more units followed, and tanks and light artillery were brought ashore. By dawn the defenders were pulling back toward the central tunnel.

In the early morning hours, Wainwright received a final message from Roosevelt, in which the president praised the defenders of Bataan and Corregidor as "the living symbols of our war aims."

Several hours later, as the Japanese pushed to within a quarter-mile of the tunnel, Wainwright ordered white flags run up. He sent a message to Washington: "There is a limit to human endurance. . . . Without prospect of relief I feel it is my duty to my country and to my gallant troops to end this useless effusion of blood and human sacrifice."

The Corregidor station then radioed in uncoded English: "Going off the air now. Goodbye and good luck. Callahan and McCoy."

The Philippines were now Japan's.

After a remarkable five months of uninterrupted conquest, the Imperial Army and Navy now held 12.5 million square miles of the Asian continent, East Asian islands and the western Pacific Ocean under the Japanese flag. Japan's enemies were impressed, and uneasy.

"The violence, fury, skill and might of Japan far exceeded anything we had been led to expect," Churchill conceded.

The Japanese were threatening to extend their conquests even farther to the south and west.

From a base in the Japanese-held sector of New Guinea, Japanese bombers on February 19 had

Besieged Corregidor from Japanese viewfinder.

Captured Japanese photo shows Jonathan Wainwright surrendering forces in Philippines in 1942.

struck Australia itself, attacking the far northern port of Darwin and causing major damage.

A month later, in a thrust at the heart of the British Empire, a five-carrier naval force under Admiral Nagumo, commander of the Pearl Harbor attack group, cruised into the Indian Ocean. The carrier aircraft bombed the British naval base at Trincomalee in Ceylon and the Ceylonese capital of Colombo. Out at sea, they sank two British heavy cruisers and an aircraft carrier. The Royal Navy's outgunned Eastern Fleet eventually withdrew to East Africa.

In upcountry Burma, Stilwell's Chinese divisions and Sir Harold Alexander's British and Indian troops were beaten back step by step by the determined Japanese, who pushed northward up Burma's three major river valleys.

Outflanked and finally cut off from the Burma Road, the exit to China, the Chinese forces disintegrated into disorderly flight in late April. Stilwell led a core group of 114, including his own staff, on a treacherous twenty-one-day retreat westward through mountainous jungle, emerging May 20 in eastern India, where the British Imperial forces had also fled.

"We got run out of Burma and it's humiliating as hell," the dispirited American general told reporters in New Delhi.

Japan's jungle fighters, who had tasted nothing but victory, now stood on the doorstep of India, jewel in the British imperial crown. As in much of East Asia, many Burmese cooperated enthusiastically with the Japanese, fellow Asians, in driving the white colonizer out of their land. The British now had to strengthen their political hand in India, placating Indian nationalists while, with American military help, readying for a possible Japanese invasion.

In the spring of 1942, U.S. strategists surveying the global map could find a worldful of worries.

In the Battle of the Atlantic, the U-boats, Germany's submarines, were wreaking havoc with early U.S. efforts to resupply Britain and to maintain its own commerce. In February alone, Admiral Karl Doenitz's subs sank seventy-one Allied ships in the Atlantic, many of them oil tankers bound for U.S. ports from the petroleum fields of Latin America.

On the Russian front, where a Soviet winter offensive had pushed the Nazi army back from the approaches to Moscow, a summer counteroffensive was expected to advance the German line again, perhaps into the oil-rich Caucasus.

In North Africa, too, Rommel was preparing to renew his offensive, in another bid to seize British Egypt and drive into Palestine and Arabia.

A doomsday scenario took shape: a link-up of Japanese forces coming through India with German armies racing through the Middle East from North Africa or the Soviet Union. The horizons looked limitless to Hitler, who soon after Pearl Harbor had taken personal command of the German Armed Forces High Command.

For Americans, the grim news grew even blacker in the weeks following the fall of Bataan when first word began filtering out, from escapees and Philippine sources, of the fate of the Bataan prisoners.

Six days after the surrender, the 76,000 Filipino and American soldiers, sick and starving, were

CHINA-BURMA-INDIA THEATER

The China-Burma-India Theater was a blood-guts-mud-disease struggle often in defense of a paper tiger.

To the Japanese, their grasp at the very limits of their reach, their goal was to wrest India from the British with the aid of dissident recruits from the raj's empire. To the British it was a last ditch defense of the jewel in their crown. To the Americans it was to keep open a supply lane to Chiang Kai-shek whose poorly-trained, poorly-led armies were nonetheless holding down 1 million Japanese invaders in the vastness of mainland China. Chiang's army was almost a fiction, a hodge-podge of peasants recruited by corrupt and feuding local warlords. Chiang's principal aim, American propaganda notwithstanding, was not to fight the Japanese so much as to hold in check the communists of Mao Tse-tung, slowly gathering strength and popular support in the remoteness of northern China.

Early in 1942 the Japanese cut the supply link to Chiang in Chungking, the Burma Road. To keep Lend Lease aid coming, Chiang agreed to appoint an American as his chief of staff. On February 2, 1942, Washington assigned one of its best troop commanders, Lieutenant General Joseph W. Stilwell, to the post. They called him Vinegar Joe and the CBI soon learned why. Stilwell developed a hatred of Chiang as soon as he laid eyes on him, using his code name of Peanut (Stalin was Glyptic, Roosevelt Victor, Churchill Former Naval Person, Eisenhower Duckpin) with unveiled contempt. Stilwell was also soon feuding with Major General Claire Chennault as to the use of his irregular air force with Chiang, the Flying Tigers.

The Japanese routed Stilwell's Chinese troops in Burma, and the American led his staff on a remarkable trek through the jungles to India. "I claim we got a hell of a beating," he told reporters when he got out. To keep Chiang supplied for military as well as political purposes, Major General Lewis A. Pick started construction with native labor of a parallel road, the Ledo Road nicknamed Pick's Pike. Meanwhile, American pilots braved the Himalayas flying supplies to Chungking over the 15,000-foot Hump.

While the British fought off a Japanese invasion of India, Stilwell organized a jungle regiment of commandos under Brigadier General Frank Merrill who became known as Merrill's Marauders. Fighting disease and the jungle as well as the Japanese, they finally captured Myikyina in northern Burma August 3, 1944, shortening flights over the Hump.

Chiang finally prevailed on Roosevelt to replace Stilwell, but his armies were incapable of stopping the Japanese from overrunning Chennault's air fields in eastern China. Towards the end of 1944 Chennault, now commander of the 14th Air Force, began bombing targets in Southeast Asia and Japan proper with the new, bug-prone B-29 that even their boss, Major General Curtis LeMay, conceded had not yet made "much of a splash in the war."

But besides tying down troops, the CBI was to have a longer range effect. The Japanese had shown the natives of Southeast Asia that the white man was not invincible after all. And the war had left arms in their hands to do something about it once it was ended.

General Stilwell, "Vinegar Joe," led survivors out of Burma. "We took a hell of a beating."

*Ledo Road over the Himalayas into China was an engineering miracle. **Inset:** After his Burma walkout, General Stilwell took command of U.S. troops in the China-Burma-India sector, the CBI.*

General Jonathan Wainwright and fellow U.S. prisoners in Japanese camp. Americans were forced to eat own excrement and many were beheaded by captors.

On the Death March Japanese conquerers tied their prisoners' hands.

Picture stolen by a Filipino from the Japanese shows Bataan and Corregidor survivors.

Americans did not forget the Bataan Death March; of the 76,000 who began it, 54,000 finished it.

herded off on a sixty-mile forced march, an ordeal during which many of their Japanese guards proved murderously sadistic, perhaps influenced by the Japanese warrior code, "bushido," that viewed soldiers who surrendered as beneath contempt.

Prisoners who fell out of the march, exhausted, were bayoneted or shot to death. Thirst-crazed men who drank from roadside ditches were beaten or killed. Prisoners with dysentery who stopped to relieve themselves were forced by the Japanese to eat their own excrement, or be shot. The line of march was littered with scores of headless corpses, decapitated by swords.

At the San Fernando railhead, the remaining prisoners were jammed into unventilated boxcars and transported northward. They then had to make a final seven-mile march, under the tropical sun, to a prison camp.

An estimated 10,000 prisoners, including 2,000 Americans, died on the Bataan Death March. Another 10,000 were unaccounted for. These atrocities, the enemy's capacity for inhumanity, shocked the American people. And, like Pearl Harbor, they aroused in Americans an even more profound hatred and a deep-seated determination to destroy the Japanese Empire.

On the day Corregidor was overrun, May 6, 1942, in a stretch of ocean called the Coral Sea, 2,500 miles southeast of Manila Bay, the U.S. Navy started on that long road back.

MacArthur and his chief of staff, Major General Richard K. Sutherland (r.), son of Supreme Court justice, prepare to escape from Corregidor.

5 HOME FRONT: ARSENAL

On April 27, 1942, Alvin York put on his suit, tie and hat and went down to the general store in Pall Mall, Tennessee, where he had registered for the military draft a quarter of a century earlier. The Selective Service System was holding its fourth wartime registration, and York and about 13 million other men between the ages of forty-five and sixty-four had to sign up. The last time York went off to war he had killed twenty-five Germans, singlehandedly captured 132 others and won the Congressional Medal of Honor. Now he was fifty-four, but he said he was ready to fight again.

No one over the age of thirty-six was ever called, but the message of the fourth registration was clear: this was a war in which almost everyone was liable to serve, including Sergeant York. Even the president got a draft card, which he kept in his wallet for the rest of his life. Lieutenant Franklin D. Roosevelt, Jr., commanded a destroyer in the Pacific and Lieutenant Colonel Henry Cabot Lodge, Jr., commanded tanks in Africa. Baseball stars Joe DiMaggio, Ted Williams and Hank Greenberg served, as did less celebrated young men such as John Kennedy, Lyndon Johnson, Richard Nixon and Gerald Ford. Walter Winchell was a naval officer, and Paul Douglas, a fifty-year-old University of Chicago economist, joined the Marines as a private. Major Glenn Miller died when his plane went down en route to a concert. Novelist Sinclair Lewis lost a son, as did Governors Herbert Lehman of New York and Leverett Saltonstall of Massachusetts. Joseph P. Kennedy lost his oldest boy, Harry Hopkins his youngest.

In all, nearly 16 million people served in the military during World War II, three times as many as during World War I. One in every eleven Americans was in uniform at any given time, and almost everyone who wasn't knew someone who was.

The demands of the first truly global war transformed the Army. In 1942 alone, 4 million men—about two-thirds of them draftees—joined the service, most for the first time. They called themselves GIs, after the general issue uniforms they wore. They fought well, but regarded the service as a decidedly temporary obligation. With their disdain for routine, authority, and military life in general, the GIs provided the war with its essentially anti-heroic flavor.

Their first contact with the military was the local draft board, such as the one in Fentress County, Tennessee, which Alvin York chaired. These boards classified men in more than a dozen categories, from 1-A, fit for service, to 4-F, unfit. The military's manpower needs were so great that the draft age steadily widened and deferments shrank. Eventually everyone from eighteen to sixty-five had to register, and by the end of 1944 only 80,000 men still held deferments as fathers.

Nearly 50 million men registered, and about 10 million were ordered to report for induction. More than 5 million registrants were rejected because of physical, mental or educational deficiencies, and the rest were deferred because of job, dependents or age.

Almost 43,000 men were classified as conscientious objectors: 25,000 served as medics or in other non-arms bearing roles; 12,000 did non-military tasks in 151 Civilian Public Service Camps; 6,000 refused to serve in any capacity and were sent to federal prison. Most were Jehovah's Witnesses, Quakers, Mennonites and members of the Church of the Brethren.

Military life usually began with a tearful good-bye, followed by a long trip on a crowded train or bus to a camp for forty-four weeks of basic training. There, the new soldiers entered a world of blaring bugles, painful innoculations, sadistic drill sergeants, ill-fitting uniforms, and bad haircuts.

They were in the Army now—but it wasn't 1917, and they didn't have to like it. A poll of new recruits at Fort Bragg, North Carolina, in late 1941 found that about half felt they shouldn't even have been inducted into the Army, and blamed their draft boards for not giving them deferments. These men objected to the Army's dull, apparently meaningless training exercises, and cared little for spit and polish. They also were unimpressed with their equipment. One man was issued a cartridge belt in which he found a pack of cigarettes from 1917. Many others complained that they had never seen a tank.

The new men did things differently, as Chief of Staff Marshall learned. A soldier stranded in a bus station and about to be AWOL phoned Marshall at home to ask what to do. The general told him. Another soldier, served a piece of meat at a training camp in Louisiana that he considered inedible, mailed it to Marshall.

As the war went on, soldiers got older. The average age of draftees in the 77th Infantry was close to thirty-two—they were men with their own homes, families and careers, and their own way of doing things. The regimental historian described the inductees as "bewildered, uncomfortable, somewhat resentful, but resigned."

Soldiers from the North hated drill sergeants from the South; soldiers from the South hated the weather in the North. Everyone hated wherever their base was located. Heroes back in their home towns, soldiers were socially unacceptable in their base towns—especially to the parents of young women.

Some communities were simply overwhelmed by the military buildup. The construction of Camp Blanding changed life forever in Starke, Florida. The 20,000 men who built the camp in six months overran the quiet town of 1,500. "People were sleeping in the streets, in the churches, in the trees," one resident said. The local grocer had to work eighteen to twenty hours a day because he couldn't find help—everyone was working for better wages building the camp. Starke soon became the state's fourth largest community.

An infusion of sailors and workers increased San

The famous Stage Door Canteen in New York, a home away from home for men in uniform.

Diego's population 44 percent. When the Navy dug a huge hole for a dry dock, one old-timer described it as "a hole that you could have dumped most of this town into when I first saw it." In 1940 six families a day were moving to Norfolk, Virginia, Atlantic fleet headquarters; by June 1942, a welfare agency found six buildings in which 161 people were living—and a bathroom shared by fourteen families.

Red-light districts inevitably flourished in these settings, further straining relations. An alternative to such entertainments was provided by the USO, which opened 3,000 centers across the country. Churches and volunteer groups ran hundreds of servicemen's canteens, the most famous of which was the Stage Door Canteen in New York. Located in the basement of the 44th Street Theater, it offered GIs free food and drink, pretty dancing partners, and a chance to chat with the stars who checked coats, poured coffee and cleaned up.

Civil Defense

On Tuesday, December 9, 1941, the United States had been at war for two days, but its largest city was as prepared for attack by the Axis powers as it was for invasion from Mars. Mayor Fiorello LaGuardia was director of the national civilian defense effort, but New York City had no air raid sirens, and its air raid wardens had no helmets, armbands, flashlights or gas masks. Many bought their own whistles, some of which bore the inscription "Made in Japan."

That morning the Army base on Governors Island received a call asking about a report that bombers had been sighted off the East Coast. An Army man called the Air Corps on Long Island to inquire, apparently giving the impression that he was not asking if, but reporting that, planes had been sighted.

The alert was sounded at 1:25 p.m. by police and fire sirens alternating long and short blasts. There was no panic; on the contrary, many people stood in the street, looking or pointing up at the sky. Schools were let out, but instead of going home and climbing under their beds, many of the million students played or hung out in the street. But the stock market, which held steady the day before despite Sunday's attack on Pearl Harbor, took a dive.

Finally the Army admitted that it had never received a confirmed report of enemy planes, and the whole thing was called off.

"City Nonchalant as Sirens Wail" was the headline in Wednesday's *New York Times,* but at 8 a.m. a call went out again—the Air Corps said unidentified planes were approaching the coast. Again the sirens wailed, long and short. Again, New Yorkers glanced at the sky and proceeded to work. Again, the alarm was false. The planes were ours.

First lady Eleanor Roosevelt begins work in 1941 as deputy director of Civil Defense for New York Mayor Fiorello LaGuardia.

Doin' the Lindy at the Stage Door in New York.

The mayor, fortunately, was on the West Coast. "Am I embarrassed. Am I humiliated," he said upon learning of the fiascos back home. "Here I go around the country telling people they must stay inside during air raid alarms. And right in my own city—this happens!"

Asked if the problem was general, he said, "Nowhere in the country is civilian defense operating to my satisfaction."

The Battle of Britain and the butchery on Europe's eastern front had proved that in total war the home front was as vulnerable as it was crucial. As weapons became more important than soldiers, the civilians who made the weapons became the most important targets of all. But while Americans had talked about civil defense since the fall of France, the federal government had done very little.

In May 1941, Roosevelt created the Office of Civilian Defense (OCD) and named LaGuardia as director. When the Japanese attacked Pearl Harbor he raced around the city in a police car, siren blaring, crying, "Calm! Calm!" His deputy was the president's wife, Eleanor Roosevelt, who had the rather broad goal of improving civilians' morale and physical fitness. The New Yorkers were an odd couple; the tall, refined first lady noted diplomatically that the director seemed more interested in "the dramatic aspects of civilian defense;" the feisty, diminutive mayor dismissed her concerns as "sissy stuff."

After Pearl Harbor, women report for duty as airplane spotters in San Pedro, California.

Air raid wardens provide escort service through blackouts.

Youngster learns where school air raid shelter is.

By December 1941, each state and almost 6,000 communities had civil defense councils which were supposed to work with OCD. But since the agency's authority was about as strong as an air warden's armband, the councils often did as they pleased. What they really needed was equipment—the state of Illinois had only two gas masks—but OCD was unable to provide them with little besides encouragement.

Pearl Harbor galvanized the civil defense movement without doing anything to give it national direction. By January, 5.6 million Americans had volunteered for civil defense work, but the years of neglect could not be overcome with a few weeks of enthusiasm.

Washington held its first air raid drill December 21, but those who were waiting for a mighty warning blast were disappointed. The city's only air raid siren, a World War I relic that sat atop a building downtown, emitted a barely audible sound described variously as a croak, a squawk and a wheeze. A blackout nine days later was more successful, but only because officials spent days publicizing the hour when it was to begin.

When Treasury Secretary Morgenthau phoned LaGuardia to complain about the inept Washington drill, the OCD head agreed that such exercises were failing in the capital "and in every other city. It's the acoustics. . . . There are no sirens anywhere in the United States that are any good." In cities and towns across the nation, worried civil defenders tried to cope. Lacking real air raid sirens, they resorted to police and fire sirens. Most people couldn't hear them, and those who could were hard pressed to distinguish air raids from other emergencies. Once, when the fire siren wailed in Smithville, Georgia, the town blacked out and volunteer firemen rushed to civil defense stations. Meanwhile, a warehouse burned down.

"Get those lights out!" became a familiar cry, and for a while, at least, the nation took blackout drills seriously. At the Virgin Holy Family Church in Chicago, altar lights that had burned steadily since the Great Fire of 1871 were extinguished in symbolic compliance. In Sheridan, Wyoming, blackouts were facilitated by the fact that the civil defense director headed the local electric company.

Blackout products hit the market. Kresge's department store in Newark, New Jersey, opened its "blackout shop" two days after Pearl Harbor, offering "50 items from black sateen and heavy black crepe paper to black out windows, candles, flashlights, tape to protect windows, sandbags, buckets and axes, oil stoves, canned goods and bottled water . . . white raincoats, white umbrellas and white overshoes." Not to be outdone, Bamberger's announced it would have official civil defense uniforms on sale in time for Christmas.

If Americans took all this seriously, it was because, for the first time since the War of 1812, the threat of an attack on the mainland seemed serious. Historian Samuel Eliot Morison noted that Americans went from saying, "It can't happen here," to "Anything can happen now." A Gallup poll in late December reported that 45 percent of East Coast residents expected their cities to be bombed. Military lawyers, trying to justify the expulsion of Japanese-Americans from the West Coast, told the Supreme Court that if the Japanese army chose to land it could take everything west of the Rockies. Of the 700 cannons guarding the nation's coastlines, more than half dated from before 1910.

In early 1942, German submarines were seen regularly off the East Coast, and by May they had sunk eighty-seven ships. People heard explosions, and they saw bodies, lifeboats, oil and ship debris wash up on shore.

Roosevelt took to the radio on the evening of February 23, 1942, to reassure the nation. As he was speaking, a Japanese submarine surfaced off Santa Barbara and fired more than twenty shells at an oil complex, causing minor damage. In June another sub surfaced and fired at the Oregon coast, and five months later a Japanese pilot became the first enemy ever to drop bombs on American soil. Although he managed to scatter incendiary bombs on Oregon forests and return to the sub from whence his plane was launched, no major fires developed.

One night after the shelling off Santa Barbara came "The Battle of Los Angeles," in which the sleep of more than 3 million people was interrupted by an hour of air raid blasts and cannon fire. Dozens of people were injured by falling artillery shell fragments. The War Department later conceded there had been no Japanese planes.

There was much talk of espionage and sabatoge. The large Japanese population in Hawaii was widely (and incorrectly) blamed for aiding the Pearl Harbor attack. On the mainland, people began to see a pattern in various events: several trees on a high cliff suddenly burst into flame in a Santa Cruz beach area occupied by Japanese farmers; twenty-eight insulators were mysteriously shattered near the Bonneville Dam; a series of fires in Washington state were said to form arrows pointed toward Seattle. A Mississippi Gulf town was plagued by a "phantom hair cutter" who would break into homes at night and snip the locks of sleeping occupants. The police chief, unable to catch the intruder, concluded that since the town was a center for defense work, the hair snipping was "an insidious form of sabotage."

There was at least one attempt at the real thing.

On June 13, 1942, a German sub dropped off four trained saboteurs in a rubber raft off Amagansett Beach on Long Island; a few days later, four others landed at Ponte Vedra Beach in Florida. Both parties had forged identification, plans of railroad terminals, bridges and factories, and lots of explosives. But a Coast Guardsman came upon the agents who landed on Long Island shortly after they put ashore. The Germans, all of whom had lived in America and spoke fluent English, said they were fishermen but offered the Coast Guardsman $300 to forget he ever saw them. He pretended to go along, but called the FBI. One saboteur— George Dasch, a naturalized U.S. citizen—was arrested, and his confession led to the roundup of the seven others by June 27. All were convicted by a military tribunal; six were executed. Dasch and another man were given long prison sentences, but released after five years.

The FBI investigated almost 20,000 reports of domestic sabotage—Americans were encouraged to report anything suspicious—but found nothing.

The Office of Civilian Defense, meanwhile, had become a joke. In Washington, fifteen air wardens assigned to the area where the agency was headquartered quit to protest a lack of equipment. The OCD office lights blazed throughout one citywide blackout. When the head of the local OCD effort was told that instructions he gave conflicted with others that had been issued, he admitted: "These

Air raid drill at New York's LaGuardia Airport in last peacetime summer of 1941.

Pennsylvania schoolboy gets instruction on spotting enemy planes.

are the directions you are getting today. It is only fair to tell you, however, they may be changed tomorrow. I would not be surprised if they were changed again a week from tomorrow. And ten days later they may be changed back to the directions you are getting now."

Given the grass-roots concern for civil defense, even OCD was bound to succeed eventually in mobilizing the country. By summer the number of civil defense volunteers had doubled to 10 million, and by mid-1943 more than 12 million Americans were registered—almost as many as served in the armed forces.

But in early January the House voted to strip LaGuardia's powers and give the War Department responsibility for civil defense. Instead, Roosevelt installed James Landis, dean of the Harvard Law School, to run the office as the Little Flower's deputy. Having saved face, the mayor resigned February 10, and Landis became director.

An experienced administrator who had worked in the New England civil defense program, Landis boasted of having removed fifteen mayors from their positions at the head of local civil defense councils in one night. Under his guidance, things seemed to get better: dozens of new publications were issued; Illinois's two masks grew to 22,000; Bell Labs developed the Victory siren, so powerful that the Army considered using it as a weapon, so loud that some communities considered not using it at all.

Pilots of the Civil Air Patrol scanned the seas for German subs, and actually dropped bombs on fifty-seven of them. Members of the Ground Observer Corps searched the skies, reporting aircraft of any kind to the military. At its peak, the corps included 600,000 volunteers, some of them blind. (Observers were not required to identify aircraft, merely report their existence.) The work was lonely and often uncomfortable, but the observers helped the war effort by reducing the rumors and false reports that had nerves on edge.

The ultimate significance of the nation's civil defense effort was undercut by the fact that it answered a massive false alarm—and tardily, at that. Ill-prepared to defend anything when the war began, civilian defense gained some coherence only after the threat of attack had passed. By the time a general "dim-out" was achieved along the East Coast, for instance, the German submarine campaign was well past its peak, and a plan to evacuate the West Coast in case of attack was not agreed upon until six months after Pearl Harbor. The threat, at any rate, was not real. Neither the Germans nor the Japanese seriously planned to invade the U.S. mainland, and even one-way bombing runs from the nearest enemy-occupied territory would have been difficult, though Hitler for a time considered the effort.

Still, civil defense served a need. It gave people a way to help win a war being fought by a far-off husband, father, son or brother. In the unity and discipline of the blackout, said a Chicago air raid warden, "The war is no longer in far-off London or Chungking." Historian Lee Kennett has written that "the triangular OCD emblems had become badges of involvement in an unusual partnership between government and people. For the millions who wore those badges, the war became less remote."

Civil defense was home front America's gut response to the challenge of war. People wanted to do something, and they often didn't wait for Washington or the state capital to do it for them. Untested and possibly unnecessary, their preparations for an attack that never came marked the progress of the nation's mood: first fearful, then confident, and finally weary.

War Bonds

In November 1941, the U.S. Department of Agriculture issued a warning against "emergency" or "defense" gardens like the ones that sprouted during World War I. The nation already had big food surpluses, and if more was needed the farmers could grow it. On December 6, in case anyone had missed the point, the USDA press office warned against "converting backyards, parks, playgrounds or other land unsuited for the purpose into gardens, as in the last war."

Naturally, Americans began planning or planting such gardens within a few hours of Pearl Harbor. "Victory gardens," which ranged from 100-acre spreads maintained by munitions complexes to tiny plots in city backyards, were the most popular expression of the home front's volunteer spirit. Many of those who dutifully paid their taxes or worked in war plants wanted to do something more to feel part of the war effort. So they bought war bonds, saved kitchen fats, used V-mail, and collected scrap metal.

And they grew their own food. Within a few months, there were 10 million Victory gardens, on Ellis Island and Alcatraz and just about everywhere in between, including vacant lots, parks, village greens, roofs and fire escapes. A New Orleans parking lot emptied by gasoline rationing was put into cultivation, as was Boston's Copley Square. In Chicago, gardens were planted at the county jail and Arlington Race Track.

By 1943, a year in which the nation's truck farmers and market gardeners produced 10 million tons of food, 20 million Victory gardens were producing 8 million tons. The Victory gardeners' instincts had been vindicated; snarled transportation and farm labor shortages produced spot fruit and vegetable shortages. The amateurs, the Secretary of Agriculture admitted, "surprised a lot of people."

As jobs became more plentiful and materials more scarce, too many new dollars were chasing too few products and services, and prices began to rise. Most advisers to Roosevelt and Treasury Secretary Henry Morgenthau said a compulsory savings program, in which money would be withheld from paychecks, was the best way to fight the inflation. It also would guarantee a stream of income to finance the war and avoid the jingoistic bullying that had marked voluntary fund raising in World War I, when some people who declined to buy war bonds had their houses painted yellow.

In Portland, residents till Victory garden right up to the road.

But Roosevelt and Morgenthau decided to ignore the experts and launch a campaign to get Americans to buy war bonds. There were many ways to raise money, but bond drives could build popular support for a distant war, the Treasury Secretary argued; he wanted to use the bonds to sell the war, not vice versa. It was a way, he said, to give people an opportunity to join the war effort and to "make the country more war-minded." He received an approving letter from a man in Oregon: "We are a queer bunch, we Americans. Try to take anything away from us and you get a bust in the snoot; ask for it, and you get the shirt."

In this war there was no bond bullying, but Morgenthau's reliance on what one historian has called "Madison Avenue hard-sell and Hollywood

Backyard farmer plows garden in Richmond.

hoopla" made the campaign something more than a polite, reasoned request.

Movie stars and bond drives were a natural marriage. In September 1942, Hollywood launched a "Stars over America" cavalcade with 337 actors and actresses. Dorothy Lamour was credited with selling $350 million in bonds, and Loretta Young once sold $40,000 worth at a single Kiwanis lunch. Hedy Lamarr offered a kiss to anyone who bought a $25,000 bond; one excited purchaser reportedly fainted before he could collect. A pair of Betty Grable's nylons were auctioned off for $40,000, a high price even considering the scarcity of nylon.

Hollywood raised $838.5 million—$63 million over its target—on the first tour. In all, seven Hollywood bond cavalcades visited about 300 communities, some of which had never seen a star before. It was hard work, and sometimes dangerous. Carole Lombard died in an airplane crash in early 1942 during a bond tour, Greer Garson collapsed from exhaustion, and Rita Hayworth had to quit in mid-tour for the same reason. Bette Davis completed her schedule, but had to rest afterward.

Screen goddess Dorothy Lamour aids the effort to sell war bonds.

BUY A SHARE IN AMERICA

DEFENSE SAVINGS BONDS AND STAMPS

Sow the seeds of Victory!

plant & raise your own vegetables

WRITE TO THE NATIONAL WAR GARDEN COMMISSION— WASHINGTON, D.C. for free books on gardening, canning & drying

"Every Garden a Munition Plant"
Charles Lathrop Pack, President

Seed power sowed the path to victory in the nation's backyards.

Bond drives also enlisted celebrities such as violinist Yehudi Menuhin, who played Mendelssohn's Concerto in E minor on the Treasury Department's weekly radio program, and Superman (who was classified 4-F because Clark Kent accidentally used his X-ray vision to read the wrong vision chart—the one in the next room).

New York City's baseball teams staged a three-way benefit exhibition game in which the Yankees, Giants and Dodgers each came to bat six times over nine innings against rotating opponents in the field. The price of admission was a war bond. Final score: Dodgers 5, Yanks 1, Giants 0. Babe Ruth came out of retirement to trot around the bases at a bond rally at Washington's Griffith Stadium. Standing on the pitcher's mound, Bing Crosby sang "White Christmas," a song that was less topical but more popular than custom-written tunes such as "Swing That Quota" and "Get Aboard the Bond Wagon."

Radio was a powerful medium for bond sales. Phil Baker, emcee of the popular program "Take It or Leave It," always signed off, "Bye-bye, buy bonds." Singer Kate Smith presided over a bond sales marathon on CBS radio in 1943, speaking sixty-five times over an eighteen-hour period and raising a stunning $39 million.

Hollywood and Broadway got the glory, but Madison Avenue set the tone of the government bond campaign. Morgenthau relied increasingly on advertising agencies, especially after sales turned sluggish in 1942. Reminders to buy bonds appeared on milk bottle tops, matchbook covers and diaper wrappers. No ad was too obscure because no person was too obscure. For both morale building and inflation fighting, the target was the little man. The $25 bond was designed for him, and for that reason, Morgenthau once chose gritty 14th Street in Manhattan over fashionable Rockefeller Center as the location of a bond sale booth.

Some ads played on an underlying home front guilt. One featured a photo of a haggard young soldier with the caption: "He gives his life. You only lend your money." Others appealed to racial prejudice, especially in the case of the Japanese, and stirred fear and hatred of "Hitler's hordes."

If Madison Avenue directed the bond drives, there still was plenty of selling on Main Street. Local movie theaters had days on which anyone who bought a bond got free admission. Schools raised $2 million; students bought 10-cent and 25-cent defense stamps which could be traded in for a $25 bond when they filled a book. Stamps were sold by beauticians, theater cashiers, grocers and Boy Scout troops. Soon, Morgenthau commanded an army larger than Eisenhower's.

No stunt was too absurd. Thirteen chorus girls in bathing suits rode a train between Washington and Richmond, Virginia, their bodies covered with defense stamps. They walked up and down the aisles, inviting passengers to buy stamps and peel them off; $500 was raised in nine minutes. The Sunset Victory Pig Club in Jonesboro, Arkansas, held the first Victory pig sale, and seven men set themselves adrift on a raft in the Willamette River in Oregon, refusing to come ashore until the city of Portland met its quota.

On one level, war bonds were a success. Americans bought about $135 billion worth, and in 1944 sales of $25 bonds alone absorbed 7 percent of personal income after taxes. Patriotic bond advertising reached millions of Americans, including those in the most remote regions of the country.

However colorful, the bond drives were largely ineffectual and irrelevant. Sales of $25 and $50 bonds—the ones designed for the "little man" on whom Morgenthau hoped to sell the war—were disappointing; most bonds were bought by institutions. Nor did bond sales come close to financing the war or stopping inflation.

The first of the great home front scrap drives began inauspiciously. Interior Secretary Harold Ickes believed that enough rubber could be scrounged from the nation's attics, basements and garages to help relieve the serious shortage. But when Ickes began by scooping up doormats around the Interior Department building, the Public Buildings Administration objected; without mats, people would slip on the marble. Undaunted, Ickes grabbed one from the White House. He also got a contribution from one of the residents; the president's dog Fala gave up his rubber bones.

The drive sometimes seemed like one huge publicity stunt. In New York, a carload of Broadway chorus girls pulled up to a collection center and wriggled out of their girdles. In Seattle, a shoemaker contributed six tons of rubber heels. A Southern senator gave the rubber mat under his spittoon and Cecil B. DeMille donated the rubber squid used in the film "Reap the Wind." Everyone seemed to have a scheme for conserving, salvaging or producing rubber. A Los Angeles dentist thought a significant amount could be salvaged from road surfaces, particularly at stops and curves. Price administrator Leon Henderson suggested using less rubber in condoms.

Besides rubber, there were drives for almost everything else: aluminum, tin cans, waste paper, toothpaste tubes. Milkweed floss—600,000 pounds of it—was collected for life preservers. Blood was the most valuable donation of all. The 13 million pints collected, combined with technological developments that allowed transfusions on the battlefield, saved many lives.

Children, who were told the most humble substances could beat Hitler, rummaged through attics, emptied garages and collected door-to-door. Over a two-year period, eighth graders in Gary, Indiana, collected 500,000 pounds of wastepaper. (They also sold an average of $40,000 in war stamps a month; delivered Community Chest material to every home in the city; distributed anti-black market pledge cards and "War Workers Sleeping" signs; taught young girls infant care; and collected library books for servicemen.)

Junk dealers urged Americans to "get in the scrap." "Junk ain't junk no more," went the song, "cause your junk will win the war." In Virginia, men raised the iron wreckage of sunken ships from the James River; in Wyoming, a group dismantled an old steam engine and built several miles of road to get it to a collection center. An old jalopy rolled off toward the scrap heap with a sign reading "Praise the Lord, I'll Soon Be Ammunition."

There also were conservation drives. An anti-inflation feature entitled "Use It Up, Wear It Out, Make It Do or Do Without" was a monthly, full-page feature in hundreds of magazines. Advertising, for a change, urged people to resist their consumptive impulses. New York Telephone reversed its slogan, "Don't Write—Telephone," because long distance lines were needed for the military. The Post Office urged civilians writing to soldiers to use "V-Mail," tissue-thin letters designed to save cargo space. Microfilm of letters was shipped overseas, where it was blown up back to regular size.

The drives may have raised morale, but they rarely raised enough of anything else. One problem was the sheer voracity of mass production, and another was that by the second half of the war there had been so many drives that many people stopped listening. Volunteerism had limits, as even Harold Ickes found out. He had predicted his drive

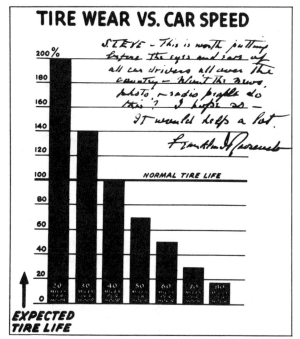

FDR noted slower speeds saved rubber.

would garner a million tons of scrap rubber; he got less than half.

Volunteerism may have made the volunteers feel better, and rendered many real services, but it was no substitute for centralized government authority and industrial mass production. However precious the memories of small town scrap drives or neighborhood Victory gardens, the war was won by weapons made in Detroit and decisions made in Washington. Volunteerism's spirit, individualism and decentralization—and its ultimate irrelevance—contrasted sharply with the other great movement of the home front: the conversion to a war economy.

The Warfare State

Wendell Willkie went to see the president a week after America's entry into the war. Much of the Pacific Fleet lay on the bottom of Pearl Harbor and Detroit was still making many more cars than tanks, but the 1940 Republican presidential candidate told reporters he was confident.

"It's a war of production," Willkie said on his way into the Oval Office, "and I think American productive capacity can outproduce any country or any combination of countries."

But it was a staggering challenge: an economy that had never produced more than $80 billion in a single year was being asked to fill a $100 billion weapons order—immediately. "For the first time in the history of war, battles were as much tussles between competing factories as between contending armies," wrote the British general, J.F.C. Fuller.

"God now marched with the biggest industries rather than with the biggest battalions."

The nation had been so ill-prepared for World War I that its armies had to rely on European factories for many weapons even after the American entry into the conflict. But this time "the great arsenal of democracy" Roosevelt had promised was taking shape before Pearl Harbor. Fifteen percent of industrial capacity had been given over to military products, and munitions production had tripled in 1941.

But it was not enough. Much of what had been produced since the fall of France was exported. Some Army units had to train with trucks marked "tank" in war games just before Pearl Harbor, and U.S. forces were scheduled to receive less than a fourth of the tanks produced by their own factories in early 1942. Spare tank parts were in such short supply that General George Patton ordered some from Sears and paid the bill himself. The Army, meanwhile, was ordering 20,000 new horses.

The weapons the services did have often were World War I leftovers, poorly designed, or both. The Army, for instance, placed a large order for a Chrysler tank that would not have been out of place at Verdun. Its air-cooled engine couldn't be used in the desert, and its treads could only be used on smooth roads.

A month after Pearl Harbor, General Marshall estimated that only ten of the Army's thirty-five divisions would be fully equipped by the end of March 1942. The rest, he said, would have half the equipment they needed. Still, the Army would be activating three or four new divisions a month.

Industry had been slow to convert to war production. With sales booming, car makers were in no hurry to devote themselves to planes and tanks, and they increased production of autos by a fifth in 1941. Although they promised to make more weapons and fewer cars in 1942, that year's models were still to be trimmed with chromium, an increasingly scarce material needed for war work.

Some manufacturers' reluctance to extend themselves was a legacy of the Great Depression. Others simply held out for a better deal: if the government wants us to make weapons, let the government build us weapons factories. Whatever the reason, no company wanted to be forgotten by customers, lose a hard-won market share, or go through the costly process of retooling without knowing how long weapons would be needed.

The armed services, meanwhile, swamped manufacturers with excessive or competing demands. The Army ordered enough typewriters for every third member of the service; the Navy sought the nation's entire diesel fuel production—including

Donald M. Nelson gets ready to take over as head of U.S. war production in early 1942.

that for the railroads that would deliver it.

The government itself bore much of the blame for the slow pace of industrial mobilization. The late 1930s and early 1940s had seen a series of largely impotent war production agencies, including the Council of National Defense, the National Defense Advisory Committee, the Office of Production Management and the Supply Priorities and Allocation Board. Some opened and closed before most Americans learned what their initials stood for. (The SPAB was sometimes confused with Spam, the luncheon meat.) Each new agency would assume many of the same functions and personnel as its predecessor, reminding one observer of the primitive belief that a sick man could be cured by changing his name.

Agency officials usually lacked the power to compel manufacturers to increase weapons production and decrease production of civilian products. Nor could they resolve the increasingly frequent clashes between manufacturers over scarce materials. There were bureaucratic tangles, as well. One agency supposedly had seven different bosses, although in the whole government there was only one boss that mattered. "Bring it to Papa," Franklin Roosevelt used to tell his aides. When officials

*James F. Byrnes, director of war mobilization, tells
Americans that new U.S. campaigns are imminent.*

asked the president, "Who is our boss?" he replied.
"Well, I guess I am." That went, in the early days
especially, for the entire mobilization effort.

But Roosevelt could not run the home front by
himself, and the government had no system for
resolving the disputes over materials and production that the war economy was spitting out faster
than tanks.

Pearl Harbor should have resolved the mobilization crisis. But now the generals and admirals
demanded "astronomical quantities of almost
everything, and to hell with civilian needs," according to reporter Henry Pringle. Meanwhile,
business executives' preparations for war production quickened only from glacial to slow.

Although some businesses began to convert
even before they signed a contract, many others
hesitated—notably the automakers. More than
200,000 auto workers stood to lose their jobs
because their factories had not begun to convert.
After a delegation of automakers visited Washington in early January and left without agreeing to cut
car production, the historian Bruce Catton—then a
bureaucrat—complained that conversion was being "bitched, botched and buggered from start to
finish."

Despite the confidence he had expressed on his
way to see Roosevelt in December, Wendell Willkie
was worried when he returned to the White House
in mid-January. He told FDR that he had called for
appointment of a single director, or "czar," of the
war production effort eighty-seven times during
the 1940 campaign and thirty-seven times since.
That night, Willkie said, he would make his 125th
appeal in a speech to the U.S. Conference of
Mayors.

He did not have to. Later that afternoon Roosevelt announced he was creating a new mobilization
agency, the War Production Board, and naming
Donald Nelson its chairman.

Nelson, who had joined the government several
years earlier after a career at Sears, seemed energet-
ic and perceptive to some, weak and indecisive to
others. At any rate, he probably was chosen as
much for his acceptability to both businessmen and
New Dealers as for his talents, which included
knowing the best place to buy 100,000 different
items of merchandise.

Nelson was a czar in neither temperament nor
power. He preferred persuasion, especially in his
dealings with the military, and he lacked control
over areas such as agriculture, petroleum and manpower. The result was bureaucratic infighting that
continued at least until May 1943, when Roosevelt
finally delegated his home front authority to James
F. Byrnes, who became rather an assistant president.

The idea was to have a referee, other than the
overburdened Roosevelt, to settle intragov-
ernmental disputes and prevent news leaks. The
WPB did not award military contracts—the armed
services continued to do that—or operate factories.
Instead, its mission was to coordinate the war
economy by acting as a sort of referee among the
various manufacturers and military services. It
allocated scarce materials by issuing preference
ratings, or "priorities," to companies producing
munitions or civilian essentials; set production
quotas for war goods (in consultation with the
military); and formulated production schedules far
in advance so that components made by subcontractors would be ready for final assembly.

Less than a week after his appointment, Nelson
called a meeting with auto executives which he
began by announcing, "Gentlemen, we have a
problem." It was theirs. The world's greatest industry would have to shut down, and its leaders had
three choices: make weapons, make cars out of
wood, or close up for the rest of the war. In
mid-February, the last civilian autos rolled off the
assembly lines, including Ford's 30,337,509th car.
Two months after Pearl Harbor, the nation finally
had begun to act like it was at war.

In the next four months Nelson halted production of items ranging from commercial trucks and metal office furniture to spittoons and asparagus tongs. Home construction was frozen. May 31 saw the end of civilian production of fifty appliances, including radios, phonographs, refrigerators, vacuum cleaners, washing machines, griddles and waffle irons. Nelson banned vests for double-breasted wool suits, and banished the two-pants suit and trouser cuffs. Even girdles were out—at least those with elastic in them.

Although the government could not force manufacturers to make munitions or civilian essentials, it could, through its control of "critical, essential and strategic" materials, stop them from making just about anything else of value. The WPB determined what was "critical, essential and strategic." The obvious, such as aluminum and copper, were joined by the likes of stramonium leaves and pig bristles. The latter, most of which had come from China, went into brushes used by ship painters.

To decide which cosmetics were essential to home front morale, the WPB commissioned a survey of American women, which resulted in a nice distinction: bath oil was essential, bath salts non-essential. Other morale essentials included tobacco (all those who harvested it were entitled to draft deferments), Coca-Cola and chewing gum.

Such sweeping government control of production "marks the end of laissez-faire," wrote I.F. Stone. That was only the half of it.

Congress gave Roosevelt and his WPB virtually unlimited power to mobilize the home front. But how? A "command economy" was one option: draft whole industries and tell them what to produce. Instead, the government decided to combine the stick of compulsion with the carrot of "cost-plus."

Cost-plus meant that the Army could negotiate a contract with a manufacturer for 500 tanks without

Plants like this Firestone tire factory in Akron, Ohio, made United States "the arsenal of democracy."

"VICTORY" GOODS

The war machine's appetite for materials forced changes in many goods—not, in most cases, for the better. They were called "Victory" products, but many were losers. Shoes had less leather, glasses less glass. Faucets were made with cast iron instead of brass and chrome. No bicycle could weigh more than thirty-one pounds, and the government planned an entire line of smaller, lighter Victory appliances if the war continued long enough.

The flimsy Victory fly swatter, made of wood and paper, saved metal screen, not to mention the lives of untold flies. Victory erasers left smudges, and the rubber in Victory inner tubes was useless for sling-shots. There was less iron, steel and zinc in kitchen utensils, and none in caskets. The dead were encased in wood.

A shortage of fabric inspired the home front's most notorious fashion failure, the Victory suit. It had no collar, no lapels, no cuffs, no belt, and, as it turned out, no market.

Makers of women's girdles switched from rubber to whalebone or piano wire. The latter was a critical material, but the War Production Board ruled girdles essential to women's health. Hosiery makers also lurched from shortage to shortage. First silk, then nylon were requisitioned for parachutes; that left rayon, which was needed for tires, and cotton lisle, which became scarce, too. "We could figure a way to knit (stockings) out of grass one day and the next day there would be a priority on grass," complained one manufacturer. Some women simply painted seams on their legs, and others wore slacks. Turbans and bandanas also became popular, partly because they kept factory workers' hair out of the equipment, partly because of the shortage of felt for hats, and partly because Americans no longer had anyone in Paris telling them what to wear.

If customers didn't like a Victory product, sales clerks all had the same reply: "Don'tcha know there's a war on?"

having to seek competitive bids; in addition to the contract price, the government would cover any of the manufacturer's unexpected costs.

This, delighted businessmen soon realized, was close to profit without risk. In addition, there were low-interest federal loans and grants for plant construction or expansion; tax breaks for private construction related to war production; and immunity from anti-trust laws. It all added up to what economist Elliot Janeway has called "the biggest and most resilient cushion in the history of public finance. . . . Roosevelt was counting on money, not leadership, to prime the production pump."

Secretary of War Stimson, a former Wall Street lawyer, outlined the rationale in his diary: "If you are going to try to go to war in a capitalist country, you have got to let business make money out of the process, or business won't work."

Business, at any rate, was ready to work. It had, out of necessity, increased its productivity 40 percent since the beginning of the Depression. Freed now from the worry of over-extending themselves, businessmen could go all out. The system would mean some waste, but it also would yield the most weapons in the least time. With the Pacific a Japanese lake and Europe a Nazi fortress, that was all that really mattered. As Donald Nelson put it, "The only gauge . . . is this: What method will most quickly give us the greatest volume."

In the year after Pearl Harbor, about 200,000 companies converted to war production. They switched from making ladies' compacts to delaying mechanisms for shell fuses; from merry-go-rounds to gun mounts; from model trains to bomb fuses; from kitchen sinks to cartridge cases. A grower and shipper of furs learned to make bomb chutes, and a soft drink bottler put gunpowder into shells.

Except for some problems—for instance, the difficulty of reconciling assembly lines to the Air Force's constant desire to refine plane designs—conversion was a relatively simple technical challenge for large manufacturers. But for many small businesses, the war was hell.

The Army and Navy were used to working with large companies, and were not eager to deal with a medium-sized maker of washing machines that now wanted to start making guns. The services would rather wait for the large operators to convert and give them all the business.

Small businesses faced other obstacles: many could not afford representatives in Washington, where the contracts and regulations were made; the time and money for retooling sometimes proved lethal for those with tighter profit margins; the WPB system for allocating materials required so much paperwork that some small operators couldn't keep up with it. As a result, industrial capacity expanded not by increasing the number of companies, but by the big getting bigger. In 1943 companies employing fewer than 100 people got less than one-twentieth of Army contracts, and those with fewer than 500 got an eighth. When the defense build-up began, the nation's 100 biggest companies were doing 30 percent of all manufacturing. By May 1943, even though twice as much was being produced, they did all but 70 percent.

The casualties included the American Bantam Automobile Co., which had led in the development of the jeep. The Army decided it needed more than

In two years Firestone's former tire plant in Akron rolled out 25,000 antiaircraft guns.

600,000 of the vehicles and could not wait for the relatively small company to gear up. The bulk of the business went to larger firms, including Ford.

Some businesses had nowhere to go, among them 2,500 signmakers who were driven under by limits on metals, blackout rules and a slump in advertising. In 1942 alone an estimated 300,000 retailers closed their doors; by the end of the war, more than 500,000 small businesses had failed.

The nation's 44,000 auto dealers were stuck when the government froze the half-million unsold 1942 models. A North Carolina dealer added gardening and poultry departments; one in Peekskill, New York, turned his place into a roller skating rink. The Goebbels Beer company took out ads offering distributorships to auto dealers, arguing that empty showrooms were ideal places to store beer. A few dealers accepted the inevitable and went to work for the government that had put them out of business.

Some industries were revived by the war. Mica mines in New Hampshire and North Carolina, which had been put out of business by competition from abroad, reopened. Companies that had made wood automobile frames, for which there was not much call, provided the Army with gliders. The hemp industry had to be revived because of the fiber shortage, and vast fields of marijuana were planted in Kentucky under government auspices. Some unlikely materials also joined the war effort. Castor beans, source of the odious castor oil, were used in an engine lubricant. Spider web thread saw duty as cross hairs in gunsights.

The war production campaign produced thousands of success stories, symbolized by the Army-Navy E (for Excellent) pennants that flew over plants with good records. One of the best was Jack and Heinz of Cleveland, which made airplane starters and automatic pilots. The plant had an absentee rate below 1 percent, virtually no turnover, and a waiting list of 35,000 worker candidates. Co-owner Bill Jack, a former machinist and union organizer, ran the operation. Several thousand production line workers, whom Jack called "associates," worked eighty-four-hour weeks composed of seven twelve-hour shifts. (Anything after forty hours was time-and-a-half.) Jack himself worked an eighteen-hour day, sometimes sleeping in his office. The plant's work was so good, and Jack's own inspectors so thorough, that the Army stopped bothering to inspect the starters itself. When a Navy contract was brought in under cost, the profits were shared with the workers—or, rather, the associates.

THE STORY OF WAR PRODUCTION

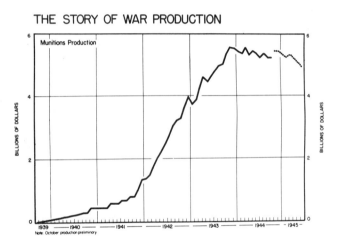

Production peaked in 1943.

Once industry was committed to conversion, the question was whether the government could give it the materials. The military placed so many orders for so many goods requiring so many critical materials that the WPB priorities system, in which companies applied directly to the WPB for permission to obtain a critical material, broke down.

By mid-1942, the WPB still had no comprehensive production plan, and it was clear Roosevelt's production goals—60,000 planes and 45,000 tanks by January 1, 1943, would not be met.

There was no precedent for converting such a huge and complex economy, let alone expanding it at the same time. If the war was the storm of Churchill's rhetoric, those running the home front were flying blind in its eye without a compass. At the end of April, a WPB division head suggested another metaphor: "We are going down a road

which we have never traveled before, and which we are traveling much faster than have either our enemies or our allies." Nelson later wrote: "To be seriously wrong at any point might have meant disaster on the battlefield or on the home front."

At times the system seemed about to collapse from sheer paperwork. There were not enough bureaucrats to answer the mail from thousands of factories around the country seeking priority orders, and no way to monitor who had what. Mail simply piled up in Washington, uncollected and unopened, filling up space in the increasingly crowded capital. Some priority orders were mislaid, and some critical materials continued to wind up in the hands of producers of non-critical products.

The intricacies of production schedules complicated the WPB's problems. If a tank had to be ready by March 1943, for instance, the ore had to be mined a year beforehand, and the steel plants needed the specifications by November 1942. The tank would be assembled from thousands of parts manufactured at hundreds of different plants. Each part had to be available in the right amount at the right time in the right place. And if, once the first tank was delivered, the Army demanded a design change—say, more head room in the turret—assembly lines would have to stop before more could be made.

In July 1943 the WPB finally implemented a solution, more or less, to the materials problem—the Controlled Materials Plan. It worked this way: Chrysler, having contracted with the Army to make tanks, told the WPB how much steel it needed to

In 1943, the United States outproduced Germany and Japan combined. Martin PBMs on line in Baltimore, Maryland.

WILLOW RUN

Willow Run was the world's largest, most sophisticated aircraft plant, and its best publicized. The architects, who had used five miles of blueprint paper a day, described it as "a vast precision tool." The newspapers called it "the most enormous room in the history of man." But for more than a year after it opened, Willow Run offered daily proof that Americans were winning the production war in spite of themselves.

The federal government paid for Willow Run, but the Ford Motor Company built it, breaking ground in spring 1941. The site was a rural region of eastern Michigan named after a stream that meandered through en route to Lake Huron. Ford planned to consolidate, under one huge roof, all the men and machinery needed to build a B-24 bomber. The raw stuff of flight—steel, copper, aluminum—would flow in one door, and a thirty-ton plane would roll out the other. In between, parts would be made and pieced together on four assembly lines. They, in turn, would feed a final assembly line—the world's longest.

Almost immediately, however, it become obvious that while Willow Run might be the most enormous room in history, it certainly was not the most efficient. The problems started at the top. Henry Ford—increasingly crotchety and cantankerous at seventy-nine—insisted the floor plan be changed so that no part of the plant would fall in a neighboring township that was controlled by the Democrats. So the planned mile-long building was cut in half, although errands still had to be run by motorcycle or car.

The plant was located twenty-seven miles west of Detroit, a city in which Ford declined to build his factory because it was too pro-labor. There was a reason for that: thousands of workers lived there. Willow Run didn't have unions, but it didn't have workers, either. It had even less housing, so most of those who worked in the new plant faced a long and costly commute from Detroit.

It was a trip many chose not to make, especially with plenty of good jobs available in the city. By the end of 1943 the plant had been able to fill only 35,000 of its 58,000 jobs, and turnover and absenteeism made even the 35,000 a sometime thing. In 1942 an assembly line worker could have looked at the man next to him (Ford was slow to hire women) and reasonably expect that in a month one of them would have moved on. Almost a fifth of the work force was out on any given day, a rate three times higher than the national average. By the end of 1943 the plant was turning out only one bomber a day, and discouraged workers began calling their factory "Willit Run?"

The government wanted to build permanent housing for 30,000—Bomber City, it would have been called—but that was opposed by Ford, who was afraid it would become a union town, and by local residents, who were afraid it would become a ghost town. Instead, the government built temporary housing for about 14,000, including a third of the Willow Run work force.

Ford's huge Willow Run plant could turn out a B-24 bomber every seventy minutes.

The government issue wasn't much unless compared to the alternative. Many of the 32,000 people who moved to the area had to live in trailers and dwellings without indoor plumbing. One house had five people in the basement, a family of five on the first floor, four more people on the second floor and nine people out in the garage. Four families lived in trailers in the backyard.

There were production problems as well. The plant used costly, long-lasting hard steel dies, instead of the cheaper, soft steel dies that were more conducive to production changes. There were lots of those: in the first year alone, the Air Force made 575 design changes on the B-24.

Finally, Ford production wizard Charles Sorensen scaled down his original plan, farming out production of parts to subcontractors back in Detroit, and making Willow Run strictly an assembly line. By August 1944, Willow Run was producing a B-24 every sixty-three minutes—more in a month than all Japan's factories put together.

The man who launched a thousand ships: Henry J. Kaiser.

Kaiser's yards built a ship in four days from prefabricated sections.

HENRY KAISER

In 1941, with German U-boats in control of the Atlantic, the U.S. Maritime Commission announced a crash program to build a new type of basic cargo ship. If all went well, the commission hoped, then perhaps a shipyard could produce one of the new Liberty class ships every six months. That would be a major improvement over World War I, when a similar emergency drive produced a nationwide total of less than a dozen cargo ships before the armistice.

This was the crisis that made a hero of Henry J. Kaiser. Balding, bespectacled, paunchy and jowly, the 260-pound Californian didn't look heroic. He didn't even look like a shipbuilder. A landlubber who called a ship's bow the front end, Kaiser had been in a shipyard only once before he bought one. But no businessman was better suited to the produce-at-any-cost economics of the home front.

Soon Kaiser and his partners were making a Liberty ship not every six months, but every twelve days. In 1943 Kaiser's ten shipyards built almost a third of the nation's ships, including destroyer escorts, small aircraft carriers, troop ships and tankers—the kinds of vessels the big, established shipyards did not have time for. By 1945, Kaiser yards were producing more than a ship a day.

In the materials-starved war economy, Kaiser always got what he needed. When steel mills failed to provide enough plate for his ships, he convinced the government to loan him $105 million and used it to build his own steel mill in nine months. (He named the blast furnace ''Big Bess,'' after his wife.) He also had expeditors to make sure things were delivered on time. They were given only two basic instructions: Never give up and no bullying. If parts or materials were late, expeditors might make the delivery themselves. Some would label a boxcar and follow it to its destination. Once, when an order of cranes was late, one of Kaiser's men visited the factory and found it had all the pieces but no room to assemble them. So he rented a lot, rounded up some workers, and put the cranes together himself.

Kaiser's can-do style made him a real-life, management version of Rosie the Riveter. Americans were awed by his $250,000 annual telephone bill and his suites in Washington and Manhattan hotels where no one else could get a room. They talked about how Kaiser did everything at top speed. When he decided to build himself a vacation house at Lake Tahoe, he brought in a huge crew and completed the whole estate in less than a month. One of his executives likened Kaiser to an elephant: "He just leans on you, smiles, and you move." Another was more direct: "He pounds you." But Kaiser expected no less of himself.

Kaiser did for shipbuilding what Ford had done for automobile manufacturing. The key was prefabrication. Instead of laying a keel in a shipway and slowly building the ship around it, Kaiser and his partners built large sections of the vessel—bows, deckhouses—on dry land nearby. Huge cranes would then swing these pieces onto the shipway as soon as the keel was laid. Almost everything was welded instead of riveted, because welding was faster and stronger. Also, welding could be broken down into a series of tasks, any one of which could be mastered by inexperienced workers—of which Kaiser had many. Less than two dozen of the 96,000 workers at the Richmond, California, complex had been experienced shipfitters.

That many of Kaiser's workers were as gung-ho as he was became apparent in November 1942, when Richmond assembled and launched a cargo ship, the *Robert E. Peary*, in just over four days.

The *Peary* record grew out of a rivalry between Kaiser shipyard workers in Richmond and Portland, Oregon, many of whom had worked for Kaiser before and knew each other. In September, the Portland yard had launched a cargo ship ten days after the keel went down. Not long after that, the Richmond complex manager came across a prefabricated bulkhead in yard No. 2 that didn't belong there. He found a supervisor, who told him a group of workers had started preparing to break Portland's record.

More than half the riveting and welding was done before any pieces of the *Peary*'s keel appeared on the shipway. The clock started running just after midnight on November 8, and by noon the engine was in place. By the second day the hull was completed up to the deck, and the engine was running. The deckhouse was lifted onto the ship on the fourth day, complete with electric clocks, mirrors and life belts. Four days and fifteen hours later, the ship slid down into the water and left for sea trials three days later. Thanks to lessons learned in the construction of the *Peary*—workers contributed hundreds of suggestions to speed up building—the complex was able to reduce by a fourth the average time ships spent on its shipways.

This was heady stuff, and there is no evidence Kaiser was unaffected by it. He saw himself, *Fortune* reported, as "at least the joint savior of the free enterprise system." Whatever Kaiser was doing, however, it was not free enterprise. He was as much a federal creation as the Boulder Dam. Although his son boasted, "We are building an empire," it was an empire built on government largesse and wartime expediency.

make the tanks. The Army then joined the Navy and other agencies with claims on essential materials in reporting their contractors' steel needs for the next quarter. Meanwhile, the steel companies sent the WPB their production estimates for the next quarter. The WPB then would divide up the pie, parceling out a portion of the available steel to the Army and the other agencies. The Army, in turn, passed along part of its steel allotment to Chrysler. The plan was not perfect, but it at least acknowledged that there was not enough steel, copper and aluminum to go around, and that everyone had to make choices.

Rubber was the most acute need at the beginning of the war, because the government had not begun stockpiling it until 1940. When Southeast Asia, source of most of the rubber, was overrun by the Japanese in 1941, the United States had about 500,000 tons. Since each tank took a ton of rubber, and each battleship seventy-five tons, that amounted to a seven months' supply. The Army had to drop plans for a Mickey Mouse-face gas mask for children because the ears would have required too much rubber.

Although some genius invented a tire made of bedsprings, the WPB thought a more likely course would be to develop synthetic rubber. The government spent $700 million to build fifty-one plants, which it leased to rubber companies for a nominal fee. They included a seventy-seven-acre facility at Institute, West Virginia, that could produce 90,000 tons a year, as much as could be collected from 20 million rubber trees. By 1944, more than 80 percent of the nation's rubber was synthetic, compared to 1 percent in 1941.

Meanwhile, the nation built the world's longest pipeline—"Big Inch," a 1,250-mile oil line from Texas to the Northeast—and the world's most spacious office building. The Pentagon was the War Department's new headquarters across the Potomac River from Washington. It was a great, five-sided pile, a mile in circumference, with three times more room than the Empire State Building. It could accommodate 40,000 workers.

There also was a lot of construction for purposes that remained mysterious. In Oak Ridge, Tennessee, workers cleared a hillside and laid building foundations without knowing why or for what. Asked what he was making, a worker said, "a dollar-thirty-five an hour." Oddly, two German spies were picked up nearby in the autumn of 1942. In the desert of eastern Washington state, the entire town of Hanford was moved to make way for a huge industrial complex. Workers asked, What are we building? Wheels for miscarriages, they were told. The boss himself didn't know.

The nation's science labs also were mobilized. Annual federal spending on research and development increased more than twenty times during the war. The Office of Scientific Research and Development, directed by mathematician Vannevar Bush, organized the scientists and engineers who developed many valuable weapons, including the bazooka and the radio proximity fuse. The latter, which detonated any antiaircraft shell which even came near the target, was such a breakthrough that it was used only over water to prevent a dud from falling into enemy hands. Innovation was constant; by the end of the war it was said that no battle was won with the same weapons that won the last.

Medical researchers produced a class of pharmaceuticals whose nickname—wonder drugs—pretty much summed up their importance. Other developments included quinine substitutes to fight malaria, and numerous repellants and insecticides, including DDT, which were used against the pests causing epidemics of typhus and malaria. Penicillin, which had been discovered in 1928, was mass produced during the war to treat blood poisoning and battle wounds. Dried blood plasma allowed battlefield transfusions. All these combined to allow the U.S. armed forces to save the lives of 97 percent of the wounded.

Wartime Labor

As many as 20 million Americans left home during World War II to seek work, often at factories almost as new in town as they were. Four million of them (and five million of their relatives) left specifically to join war plants. Many went west; California alone attracted 1.4 million. Although the state had only 6.2 percent of the nation's population, its factories and shipyards attracted 9.7 percent of war spending. Two years after the war, a survey found that a third of the residents of Los Angeles had moved there since 1940.

John Brauckmiller and his family left Iowa in 1942 heading for industrialist Henry Kaiser's Swan Island shipyard in Portland, Oregon. Before long he and fourteen of his relatives had landed jobs on the graveyard shift. Brauckmiller, eight of his sons and his son-in-law worked as shipfitters, while a daughter and four daughters-in-law worked as welders' helpers and shipfitters' helpers. "The shipbuildingest family in America" earned enough to invest up to half of its weekly pay in war bonds.

High school enrollment plummeted as students dropped out to go to work. Lockheed Aircraft hired 1,500 boys in their mid-teens as riveters, draftsmen, electricians and sheet metal workers, and found that two boys working four-hour shifts could accomplish more than an adult did in eight hours. Some states experimented with a six-day school week to get their students into the work force faster.

At the same time, wizened ship's carpenters in Maine were hired out of retirement to work on wooden mine sweepers. Aircraft factory recruiters in Los Angeles scouted nursing homes. Their finds included Spanish-American War veterans who were put to work sorting nuts and bolts. In Marietta, Georgia, the widow of Confederate General James Longstreet, who gave her age as "fifty plus," joined the morning shift at the Bell Aircraft factory as a riveter.

Almost everyone got a chance to work, especially if they could not be drafted. Almost 200,000 of the handicapped were working in 1943, compared to 27,700 in 1940. The blind salvaged rivets from sweepings in aircraft plants, and the deaf worked in some of the noisiest jobs. Midgets inspected the insides of plane wings. The War Production Board found jobs for 200,000 prisoners, including San Quentin inmates who produced camouflage strips and Victory sirens, and local police rounded up skid row inhabitants to see if they had any skills. Many did, and were offered jobs. The president of a national hoboes group said that virtually all its members had left the road and gone to work or war. There was even a place for a woman who believed she was the queen of England. "As long as she was addressed in a manner which she considered befitting her dignity, she did an excellent job at her machine," reported the War Manpower Commission.

Many of the new workers were people who had given up hope of ever finding a job during the Depression. The number of unemployed dropped from 8 million in 1940 to less than 1 million in 1944. The unemployment rate dropped to 1.2 percent, the lowest before or since.

Most of the new workers were unskilled; some couldn't write their names. But assembly line production allowed the manufacturing process to be broken down into a series of tasks, one of which could be mastered fairly quickly by an inexperienced worker. At Chrysler, assembly line workers—some of whom had been picking cotton a year earlier—were taking ten hours to turn out machine guns that took the Swedes 450 hours to handcraft. Because welders in Henry Kaiser's shipyards had fewer, more repetitive tasks, the training period could be shortened from three months to ten days.

Labor became a precious commodity, sometimes too precious for the good of the war effort. "Manpower pirating" threatened to stall production in Detroit in the spring of 1942. On the West Coast,

Westinghouse president Frank Reed raises Navy citation at New Jersey plant. **E** *is for* **Excellence.**

aircraft plants and shipyards reported that four of every ten employees stayed less than a year. The War Manpower Commission tried to encourage voluntary cooperation among war contractors, but by the end of 1942 labor reserves were dry, and absenteeism and turnover rates up. There simply were not enough workers. The government, which had spent the last decade trying to find jobs for people, now had to find people for jobs.

In December 1942, in an attempt to prevent further losses of skilled labor, the president ended Navy enlistments. In January 1943, the Manpower Commission issued a "work or fight" order, which essentially forced workers to choose between the factory and the infantry. Even men with children would be drafted if they held non-essential jobs. (Eleven months later Congress countermanded the order by making it impossible to take a father ahead of a man without children, regardless of the importance of either's job.)

In summer 1943, the government began to solve the manpower problem by giving contracts to firms only if there were enough workers in an area. It also barred defense workers from switching from one government contractor to another at will.

Housing these workers was even more difficult.

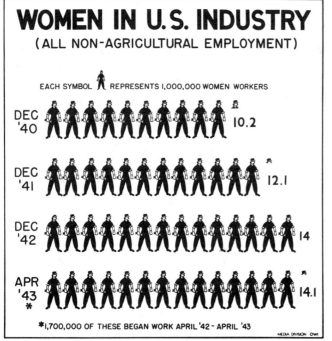

WOMEN IN U.S. INDUSTRY
(ALL NON-AGRICULTURAL EMPLOYMENT)

EACH SYMBOL ⚊ REPRESENTS 1,000,000 WOMEN WORKERS

DEC '40   10.2

DEC '41   12.1

DEC '42   14

APR '43   14.1
*

*1,700,000 OF THESE BEGAN WORK APRIL '42 - APRIL '43

MEDIA DIVISION OWI

the newcomers were not. A teacher in Mobile, Alabama, where the population increased 65 percent during the war, described workers who flocked in from the backwoods as "the lowest type of poor whites. . . . They prefer to live in shacks and go barefoot, even when two or three workers in a single family earn as much as $500 a month. . . . I only hope we can get rid of them after the war."

And there was jealousy. A Detroit resident told novelist John Dos Passos: "There's a restaurant here a gang of us has patronized for some time. . . . Well, I'll be damned if four of them (war workers) didn't come in there one evening and sit down at a table and ask for a bill of fare. . . . The fellow who runs it, he has a special bill of fare for people he doesn't like, about twice the usual price. Well, these guys never batted an eyelash. They ordered up all the most expensive wines, the guy ran his finger down the card until he found what cost most and paid for it out of [a] paycheck on one of the automotive concerns for $126."

Production Miracle

"The arsenal of democracy is making good," Roosevelt boasted in early 1943. By the end of the year he was proven right.

Production peaked in October; factories were turning out more medium tanks, for instance, than anyone could use, and cutbacks began in December. Since 1941 military production had increased eightfold, even though the labor force had increased only modestly. Probably for the first time in the nation's history, its factories' productivity was limited only by the number of hours in the day.

Although it took a year and a half to mobilize the war economy, the result was recognized by everyone from U.S. production czar Donald Nelson to Josef Stalin as a production miracle. A nation, which in 1938 made almost no weapons, was by 1943 making more than twice as many as all its combined enemies. Overall production of civilian goods, meanwhile, barely faltered. In the aircraft industry, manufacturing space expanded from 14 million square feet to 170 million, employment from 100,000 to over 2 million, and production increased tenfold, for a total of 300,000 warplanes.

For all conversion's pitfalls—bureaucratic tangles, industrial reluctance, inter-service competition —the outcome probably was never in doubt. "Before we had been in the war a year, our war production was the wonder of the world," Nelson wrote later. FDR did not get all the planes he asked for in 1942, but the 47,000 he did get were still twice as many as the United States was able to make when the war began. In World War I not one

No city had enough single family houses to meet the demand, and most did not have enough apartments. This housing shortage had been guaranteed by the ban on new residential construction, but it was hugely exacerbated by war work. New factories created settlements where none had existed, turned sleepy villages into boom towns, and filled large cities to capacity.

The government estimated that 9 million migrant workers needed housing; but even after it spent $7 billion on new housing, much of it temporary, at least 2 million people had to look for their own lodging. Often, there wasn't any. Thousands lived in trailers, converted garages, tents, shacks, and overpriced single rooms. Some spent the night in 25-cent "hot beds," so called because they accommodated two or three shifts of sleepers. A social worker spotted a twelve-year-old girl in a beer hall late at night, sitting alone in a corner. Asked what she was doing there, she replied, "I'm just waiting for 12 o'clock. My bed isn't empty until then."

Like soldiers in camp towns, the new workers sometimes overwhelmed their communities. A reporter for *Daily Variety* described Detroit as "the hottest town in America, Baghdad on Lake Michigan," a place where people stood in line for a glass of beer and couldn't get a good steak, even on the black market. It was a city "with more hillbillies than Arkansas" and people "who previously lived in whistle stops, four corners, and fur pieces down the road."

The new money usually was welcome, but often

"Rosie the Riveters" became heroines of war production.

armistice; now, factories were turning one out every five minutes.

The production war turned into a mismatch. In 1943, the United States built twice as many planes as Germany and Japan combined, which helped give the Allies a three-and-a-half-to-one advantage in aircraft production. On D Day, June 6, 1944, the Germans mustered 319 aircraft against the Allies' 12,837; in the months that followed, Allied forces in France held a twenty-to-one advantage in tanks.

In a war where a battle's outcome often was determined by the number of ships sunk or tanks destroyed, the United States could replace weapons and equipment faster than the enemy could destroy them. The Germans sank an awesome 12 million tons of Allied shipping in the Atlantic in 1942-43, but over the same two years the Allies launched 16 million tons. The United States alone produced a ship a day.

America not only made more weapons than its enemies, it kept making new ones and better ones. Radar, improved depth charges and long-range bombers turned the tide against the U-boats; the long-range Mustang fighter protected bomber for-

mations over Europe after 1943; the B-29 Superfortress allowed the Air Force to pulverize Japan with virtual impunity by 1945. In retrospect, even allowing for the enormous importance of military skills, it is hard to see how the Axis could have overcome the gap in sheer firepower.

The production effort, one historian has said, was the equivalent of digging more than two Panama Canals a day. WPB chief Nelson called the conversion "almost magical" and no less than "the biggest economic undertaking in history. . . . It was like nothing else the nation had ever felt or witnessed," he wrote. "It was not so much industrial conversion as industrial revolution, with months and years condensed into days."

"Never before had war demanded such technological experimentation and business organization," historian Allen Nevins observed. "The genius of the country of Whitney, Morse, and Edison precisely fitted such a war." Even Stalin had to acknowledge the obvious. At the Tehran conference in late 1943, he proposed a toast: "To American production, without which this war would have been lost."

War had been an art to Europeans, but it was a business to Americans. They knew technology and material would win. An artillery officer at Tunis, about to unleash an artillery barrage, said, "I'm letting the taxpayer take this bill." Eisenhower said the four weapons that proved decisive in North Africa were the bulldozer, the jeep, the two-and-a-half-ton truck and the C-47 transport airplane.

The war, Nevins wrote, was "a relentless massing of resources in the right place at the right time" in order to achieve victory as quickly, and with as few lives lost, as possible. It was no crusade, and Americans did not want or need martyrs. By 1945, tired of shortages and casualties and confronted with an obstinate enemy, they would embrace the ultimate technological solution.

The New World

It was cool, a good afternoon for squash that afternoon in Chicago in the fall of 1942. When Dick Adams and his three friends shut the door behind them, they were the last players that day to use the court under the stands of Stagg Field at the University of Chicago. And the last ever.

The next day the court was closed. Government business, was the terse explanation. That was enough. There was a war on. People didn't ask too many questions around the campus. Some days later, Adams, who had his own key, let himself into a storeroom to get something. That was odd. There were a number of containers marked "Uranium." Why uranium? You don't suppose . . . ?

Adams, a knowledgeable chemistry student well read in scientific journals, had guessed the squash court's secret.

What was to happen in the squash court on December 2, 1942, was the world's first nuclear chain reaction. It produced only as much power as a lit match, ran for only a few brief minutes. But it changed the world, probably forever.

The road to December 2 was as bizarre as any science has traveled, a chain reaction in itself of accident, coincidence, teamwork and the minds of many scientists increasingly interacting and bumping into each other. The road went by way of an accidentally exposed film in Paris, a stoplight in London, a goldfish pond in Italy, a visionary novel in Britain, labs in Germany and California, a snow-covered path in Sweden, and Adolf Hitler. It was the German dictator who was to make refugees of so many of the best minds in European physics who were come to America and in time help make the atomic bomb.

Gertrude Kram of New York was first to join Gold Star Mothers of World War II after her son Leonard was lost in North Atlantic torpedoing.

Radiation was discovered in 1896 in Paris when Henri Becquerel inadvertently stored some uranium salts on top of a photographic plate he stored in a desk drawer. Pierre Curie, the French scientist, and his Polish-born wife, Marie, expanded research into radiation. In Britain the New Zealand-born Ernest Rutherford outlined the structure of the atom. German Albert Einstein posited that the energy potential of a substance was its mass times the speed of light squared, the fateful $E=mc_2$. The atom became a scientific artichoke, many hands peeling away its secrets.

In 1914 the Englishman H.G. Wells wrote a novel entitled *The World Set Free* which forecast "the unquenchable crimson conflagration of the atomic bombs." Rutherford was to harumph that talk of energy from the atom was "moonshine." But on September 12, 1933, a brilliant, pushy Hungarian physicist named Leo Szilard, who had read Wells' book, was to have a flash of inspiration while waiting for a red light to turn green across from the British Museum in London. He envisioned a chain reaction of neutrons knocked off an atom and colliding with other atoms to shoot off further neutrons and on and on. Rutherford subsequently dismissed the idea, but Szilard saw a potential of unlimited energy. To make electricity. Or a Wellsian bomb.

Meanwhile in Italy, Enrico Fermi was bombarding elements using a goldfish pond as a damper. When he bombarded uranium, odd things happened. But science said the atom could not be split. Two years later in 1936 Swiss scientists saw immense energy releases from bombarded uranium. They thought their machine was broken.

With Hitler in power, Fermi, whose wife was Jewish, left Italy for America. Szilard came to the United States, too. And Hungarian Edward Teller. And Hans Bethe. And John von Neumann. And Eugene Wigner. And George Kistiakowsky. More than a brain drain. A hemorrhage. One of the lesser of the emigres was a German named Klaus Fuchs.

One of the important researchers at the Kaiser Wilhelm Institute in Germany had been Lise Meitner who, being Jewish, had fled Germany for Sweden. Otto Hahn, a fellow researcher, nonetheless continued to write her about his experiments with Fritz Strassmann. When they bombarded uranium, they seemed to get two elements of about half the weight. Meitner was talking this over with her nephew, Otto Frisch, as they walked the snowy countryside outside of Gotteborg, Sweden, during Christmastime 1938. They held back from a conclusion, but when Frisch visited the great Danish physicist Niels Bohr a few days later with the details, Bohr clapped his forehead with his hand and exclaimed:

"Oh, what idiots we all have been! This is just as it must be!"

The atom had been split.

This was electrifying news in the close world of science. But it was also sobering. It had happened in Hitler's Germany.

At the University of California in Berkeley a physics professor named J. Robert Oppenheimer wrote a friend: "The (uranium) business is unbelievable." To Leo Szilard, then at Columbia in New York, it was ominous. His noisy, aggressive behavior was an abrupt contrast to the quiet, methodical Fermi who was also at Columbia. So Szilard asked an intermediary, Dr. Isidor I. Rabi, to get Fermi's opinion on whether fissioning uranium could produce the neutrons to set off a chain reaction.

"Nuts," the great researcher replied. Szilard took Rabi along to ask the Italian just what that meant. That neutron emission was only "a remote possibility," perhaps a 10 percent chance, Fermi explained.

"Ten percent is not a remote possibility if it means we may die of it," said Rabi.

Szilard and then Fermi did experiments that showed the neutrons would be there. On March 17, 1939, the day after Hitler occupied the rest of the Czechoslovakia he had already dismembered, Fermi told the Navy in Washington of the possibili-

Enrico Fermi abandoned Italy for America after getting his Nobel Prize. His wife was Jewish.

Lise Meitner (center) *with physicist Max Born and his wife in 1954.*

ty of an atomic weapon of undreamed-of power. The officers listened politely and asked to be kept informed. That was that. But not for Leo Szilard. That summer he tracked down Einstein at his summer home in Long Island, New York, and began drafting a letter to President Roosevelt himself. The letter was conservatively worded but said it was "conceivable" to build "extremely powerful bombs of a new type."

Through contacts Szilard decided on Dr. Alexander Sachs, a Wall Street economist who had served in the Roosevelt administration, to deliver the letter in person. Sachs arrived at the White House October 11, five weeks after World War II had begun. "Alex, what you are after is to see that the Nazis don't blow us up," said Roosevelt.

"Precisely," said Sachs.

Roosevelt handed the letter to his secretary, Brigadier General Edwin M. "Pa" Watson. "Pa, this requires action." But it wasn't until the following February that the government gave Fermi $6,000 to buy some graphite. Fermi had found, first with his goldfish pond and then with graphite, that neutron bombardment was far more effective if first slowed with a moderator. But how much graphite would be needed? How much uranium? Would the whole thing run out of control and explode?

Fermi, with the help of some muscle from the Columbia football team, began piling graphite to find out. "We were reasonably strong, but we were, after all, thinkers," Fermi later recalled.

Elsewhere the pieces that were to make the bomb were falling into place more by chance than design. In December and January of 1940-41 a team at the University of California under Glen Seaborg discovered that bombardment of uranium 238 produced a new man-made element, plutonium. Six months later Seaborg determined that plutonium was fissionable and thus could be material for a bomb. In July 1941 British scientists came to the United States and reported their research indicated a bomb could be made within two years from between eleven and twenty-two pounds of uranium 235. The process of separating U235 from the more common U238 would be by gaseous diffusion, an incredibly intricate atom by atom process. Meanwhile in September 1940 the government had advanced Fermi another $40,000—and balked at paying a $6.67 phone and mail bill Columbia had submitted. It was eventually to pay $2 billion to build a weapon no one was certain would work.

In October 1941 Roosevelt authorized Dr. Vannevar Bush, the nation's science coordinator, to proceed full speed on atomic research. A month later Arthur Compton of the University of Chicago summarized progress saying a bomb of "superlatively destructive power" could be made from between four and 220 pounds of U235. Then came Pearl Harbor and a month later Fermi was sent to Chicago with a team to try and achieve a chain reaction. Space being at a premium at the university, Fermi's group was assigned the squash court.

Gus Knuth, a master carpenter, directed the actual construction of the pile. "It was just another job to me. You know how universities are, always making one thing or another." George Maronde, one of the security guards, sometimes wondered what the big black blocks of graphite were. "For all I knew those guys were building a little house. If I'd have known, I'd have run 800 miles north without stopping."

Almost everybody who was anybody in American physics mysteriously showed up at Chicago and as mysteriously disappeared again. There were strange men with briefcases manacled to their wrists. Gossip, which thrives like ivy on a university campus, flourished.

"When we told Washington we were going to build a pile in the West Stands, we damn near didn't need a bomb," Dr. Norman Hillberry, a physicist on the project, now known as the Metallurgical Laboratory, later remembered. "Ears were scorched. They took our word (nothing would explode), but they were very unhappy."

Youngsters were recruited from Chicago vocational high schools to mill graphite blocks to one five-hundredth of an inch tolerances. The graphite dust was treacherously slippery underfoot. "It would have made a wonderful dance floor," recalled Leona Woods, a physicist and the only woman present December 2, 1942, when Fermi decided his 40,000-block pile was ready to go critical.

"There were so many wheels the cogs couldn't get close," said Bob Nobles, a junior member of the team crowded around the meters. Hillberry was assigned to swing an axe at a rope holding a control rod if things ran away. He felt "damn silly, but the thing that really made the hair rise on my neck was wondering when the Germans would have their first reaction."

The pile behaved just as Fermi's slide rule said it would as the Italian matter of factly directed George Weil to gradually withdraw the last control rod. At 3:25 p.m. Fermi said: "Pull it another foot, George. This is going to do it. Now it will become self-sustaining. The (graph) will climb and continue to climb. It will not level off."

"To me it was a philosophical moment," said Dr. William Sturm, a recent graduate of the university. "For the first time man had obtained energy not from the sun."

After a few minutes, Fermi ordered the pile closed down. Those that remained shared a swig from a $1.39 bottle of Chianti Wigner had brought. Except for carpenter Knuth. He didn't drink.

Later that day Compton, head of the Metallurgical Lab, phoned Dr. James B. Conant, president of Harvard and a leading scientist in the war effort.

"Jim, you'll be interested to know that the Italian navigator has just landed in the new world."

"Is that so," Conant replied. "Were the natives friendly?"

"Everyone landed safe and happy."

6 STOPPING THE THRUST

The Allies were sticking to their Europe-oriented global strategy. In January 1942, token U.S. Army forces were sent to Iceland and Northern Ireland.

But first, even before the Germany First policy, Japan's relentless drive had to be stalled, and the great bulk of American troops sent overseas in the first half of 1942 embarked not eastward, but westward, to the Pacific.

The Americans were building up Australia as a base for future offensives against the Japanese, and were keeping open the sea lanes southwestward from the U.S. West Coast and Hawaii by garrisoning the Samoa and Fiji Islands and New Caledonia with Army units.

Admiral Halsey and the carrier *Enterprise* shepherded some of these troop transports to Samoa in January. On a wide detour on the way home, Halsey's carrier planes and warships bombarded Kwajalein and other Japanese bases in the northern Marshall Islands. Moving farther north, Halsey later attacked the Japanese contingent that had taken over Wake Island.

The raids did little serious damage, but Bull Halsey's aggressiveness boosted American morale and showed how the swift, versatile "carrier task forces," the survivors of Pearl Harbor, could pin down the enemy's front line in a vast ocean war.

Pacific commander Nimitz, waiting for Washington's strategists and mainland shipyards to strengthen his hand, believed that American personnel, "superior . . . in resourcefulness and initiative," could turn the war against the Japanese. And in early March, in the skies over the distant island

of New Guinea, Navy carrier pilots did take the initiative.

On March 8, 1942, Japanese troops had landed at Lae and Salamaua on the north coast of eastern New Guinea, an Australian protectorate. From there, they were to push up and over the jungle-clad Owen Stanley Mountains to capture Port Moresby on the south coast, a potential base for air attacks and eventually an invasion of northern Australia.

But on the morning of March 10, swarms of American aircraft swooped down from the mountain peaks and attacked the Japanese at Lae and Salamaua, where convoys were still unloading soldiers and cargo.

The air strike caught the invaders by surprise. The U.S. dive bombers and torpedo planes must have come from airfields near Port Moresby, the Japanese commanders assumed. But in fact the raid represented the first time one naval force attacked another over a mountain range.

The carriers *Yorktown* and *Lexington* had steamed into the Coral Sea, south of New Guinea, to try to blunt the Japanese advances in the Southeast Area, as Tokyo's war planners dubbed the loop of wild tropical islands that stood off Australia's northeastern shoulder.

When task force commander Vice Admiral Wilson E. Brown learned of the Japanese landings in northern New Guinea, he pulled in toward the

Above: *Japanese cruiser somehow survived fearsome battering at Midway, but was sunk two years later at Leyte Gulf.*

island coast and launched more than 100 planes from the two carriers.

As the Americans descended on the north coast, one large Japanese convoy was unloading and another was coming into port. In the attack, the Devastators had little success; their torpedoes, like many early in the war, were faulty, misfiring or churning beneath the enemy ships. But the accompanying Dauntless dive bombers scored hit after hit, and when the Americans headed back south they left behind five troop transports and cargo ships sunk, and a light cruiser and two destroyers damaged. The cost to the Americans: one plane.

The lightning strike in New Guinea, launched as Bataan's defenders still clung desperately to that battered peninsula, hinted at a new American aggressiveness in the Pacific. The next step brought the American boldness home to the Japanese.

Doolittle's Raid

Nine days after the New Guinea raid, a cryptic message went out from Pearl Harbor to Washington: "Tell Jimmy to get on his horse."

Lieutenant Colonel James H. Doolittle was awaiting that signal. He quickly gathered up his First Special Aviation Project, seventy-nine fellow Army aviators, and took off from Eglin Field, Florida, in sixteen B-25 bombers bound for California.

The airmen and their commander, a flamboyant former stunt pilot, had been at Eglin for a month, practicing short takeoffs under the tutelage of a veteran Navy carrier pilot, Lieutenant Hank Miller.

Miller had never seen a B-25 before arriving at Eglin. But he had a feel for it, and on his first takeoff with the Army men he lifted one of the twin-engined medium bombers into the air at just sixty-five miles an hour.

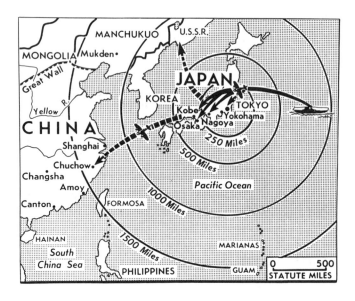

"That's impossible. You can't do that," one told Miller. But before long he had taught all the Army pilots how to take off at slow speed, not their usual 110 mph, and within 500 feet.

At California's Alameda Naval Air Station, the B-25s were lifted by crane aboard the USS *Hornet*, and the Navy's newest carrier steamed out of San Francisco Bay, heading for the western Pacific.

The Army fliers had never taken off from a heaving carrier deck, but they knew that was what they had trained for. Once at sea, they were told why: they were going to bomb Tokyo. Four months after Pearl Harbor, America was striking back.

Jimmy Doolittle plans his Tokyo raid with Captain Marc A. Mitscher, skipper of the carrier **Hornet**.

Long days of poker playing and intelligence briefings followed. On April 13, the *Hornet* rendezvoused with its escort, Halsey's *Enterprise* task force, and headed straight for Japan.

The meticulous bombing plan called for launching the planes just before dark, at a point 500 miles from the Japanese coast. But on the morning of April 18, while still 650 miles from the target, the Navy flotilla encountered Japanese patrol boats. Halsey, fearing that surprise had been lost, ordered the B-25s to take off at once.

It was a wet, rough morning. Stripped of some of their guns and other heavy equipment, and fitted with extra fuel tanks, the bombers revved up for takeoff. Captain Marc A. "Pete" Mitscher, the *Hornet*'s commander, turned the carrier into the raw wind. And at 8:20 a.m. the cool-handed Doolittle, the man who once piloted the world's fastest airplane, took his awkward B-25 down the rolling deck and up and out into the gray skies.

"He did it just like the book says," an admiring Miller later recalled.

Once all the bombers were off safely, the *Hornet* and *Enterprise* came about and headed back toward Pearl Harbor at top speed. Their loss to Japanese land-based bombers would have been a crippling blow to the Pacific Fleet.

Doolittle's raiders skimmed the waves to Japan, approached Tokyo at treetop level, then climbed to 1,500 feet to drop their bombs. The bombers sought out military and industrial targets in Tokyo, in the nearby naval ports of Yokohama and Yokosuka, and in three other cities in the Japanese heartland.

The midday raid stunned the Japanese. At 1:10 p.m., Tokyo radio excitedly reported that planes were bombing the capital and then abruptly went off the air. One crew reported flying over a baseball field where players and spectators, paralyzed by the sight, didn't scatter until the plane was long past. The Americans encountered only ineffective fire from interceptor planes and antiaircraft batteries.

After the raid, Doolittle's daring aviators were to fly on west to land at airfields in China. But the early takeoff, coupled with strong headwinds, depleted their gasoline reserves, and almost all had to abandon their planes and bail out.

Five men drowned or were killed when they parachuted. Eight landed in Japanese-held China and were imprisoned, three later to be executed as war criminals and a fourth to die in prison. But Doolittle and sixty-six others came down in free China or the Soviet Far East, and eventually made their way back to U.S. forces.

The Doolittle raid inflicted no major damage on Japan. A later Naval War College study could find "no serious strategical reason" for the attack. But it stirred American morale and put the Japanese people on notice that their cities were in reach of U.S. air power.

For the U.S. Navy, however, the bold approach to the Japanese coastline had been a risky venture. Still hobbled from the Pearl Harbor attack, American fleet commanders were anxious to avoid a great sea battle with a Japanese navy whose battleships were thus far unscathed and whose intentions had been puzzled out only sporadically by American codebreakers.

The surprise American air attack against the Japanese on New Guinea's north coast in March had set the stage for the crucial naval clash now shaping up for early May. When the Dauntless dive bombers wrecked the Japanese cargo ships at Lae and Salamaua, the loss of supplies scuttled the Imperial army's plans for an overland assault on Port Moresby. Tokyo's planners instead looked to the ocean, an amphibious assault through the Coral Sea, as the roundabout route to the conquest of all New Guinea and control of the approaches to northern Australia. And they devised an intricate plan for this southward thrust, launched from the sprawling new Japanese naval base at Rabaul, on New Britain island. It was code-named MO.

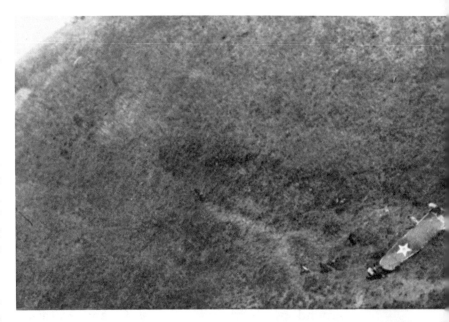

Doolittle crash-landed in China as did twelve other U.S. bombers from the Tokyo raid. The Japanese caught and beheaded three of the airmen.

Coral Sea

First, a small task force of troop transports and destroyers would protect the left flank of Operation MO by capturing the strategically placed island of Tulagi, an excellent fleet anchorage in the Solomons group east of New Guinea.

Then an invasion force of a dozen troop transports, supported by cruisers, destroyers and the small aircraft carrier *Shoho,* would steam around the eastern tip of New Guinea into the Coral Sea and head for landing beaches at Port Moresby, which was defended by a small Australian-American contingent.

At the same time, a powerful striking force built around two new carriers, *Shokaku* and *Zuikaku,* 25,000-ton showpieces that took part in the Pearl Harbor attack, would dash around the far end of the Solomons group and take up position in the eastern stretches of the Coral Sea. Attacking from the rear, the carriers' 120 planes would pounce on any Allied warships trying to block the invasion.

The Japanese were not worried. They didn't expect heavy opposition from the carrier-short Americans, since two U.S. flattops reportedly had just taken part in the Tokyo air raid, far to the north. Besides, Imperial Navy strategists knew, surprise was on their side.

But Nimitz, armed with information from a broken Japanese code, had a surprise waiting for the Japanese. In mid-April, as the *Hornet* and *Enterprise* plowed through the North Pacific waves to meet Doolittle's appointment in Tokyo, Nimitz dispatched the *Lexington,* another of his four precious carriers, southward from Pearl Harbor to link up with the fourth, the *Yorktown,* already in the area, for a showdown in the Coral Sea.

The *Lexington* and *Yorktown* task forces rendezvoused on May 1 outside the rim of islands ringing the Coral Sea in 1.4 million square miles of brilliant blue, unusually calm waters. The next day, Rear Admiral Frank Jack Fletcher, a quick-tempered, quick-thinking seaman, led the way into the sea with his *Yorktown* task force. The codebreakers had put U.S. seapower in the right vicinity. The admirals now had to find the action.

Late on May 3, Fletcher learned that Australia-

Pilot Robert Dixon radioed as the light carrier **Shoho** *went down in the Battle of the Coral Sea: "Scratch one flattop!"*

based planes had spotted Japanese forces landing at Tulagi, whose small Australian garrison had pulled out just hours before. Fletcher headed north at top speed, and just before sunrise on May 4 launched the *Yorktown's* planes against the island.

The torpedo and dive bombers found no air shield over Tulagi; the Japanese striking force carriers were too far away. The American airmen, attacking through heavy antiaircraft fire, wrecked a Japanese destroyer, a cargo ship, and some auxiliary vessels and drove the remnants of the flotilla back toward Rabaul.

Recovering his planes, Fletcher returned to the central Coral Sea, where he took command of Task Force 17, combining the *Yorktown* and *Lexington* groups with a third force of American and Australian cruisers and destroyers sent from Australia by MacArthur.

On that day, May 6, the *Yorktown's* radiomen intercepted the final American sign-off from Corregidor. Now, from Hokkaido down to the edge of the Coral Sea, the Japanese raised their flag unchallenged over the western Pacific. And now it was up to Fletcher, the man who four months earlier commanded a relief force that turned away

in Wake Island's final bitter hours, to stop them.

By the night of May 6, reports from reconnaissance planes convinced the American admiral that the Port Moresby invasion group was on its way. Assuming all three Japanese carriers were accompanying the invaders, he headed northwest to draw within air-strike range by the next dawn. In fact, however, the two big Japanese carriers were to his northeast, 150 miles away, having looped around the Solomon Islands to lay their ambush. But Japanese carrier commander Takeo Takagi also was groping through the soft tropical night, unaware of the Americans' position.

A day of blunders followed, as two armadas searched for each other and for the chance to strike the first powerful blow.

At first light on Thursday, May 7, both Fletcher and Takagi sent out scout planes. The Japanese made the first sighting, radioing back that an American carrier and cruiser had been found far to the south. The Japanese launched an all-out attack, sixty planes in three waves descending on the U.S. vessels. But the targets turned out to be the oiler USS *Neosho* and the destroyer USS *Sims*, waiting at a fueling rendezvous point.

The Japanese bombed the two small ships relentlessly. The *Sims* exploded and sank in a huge tower of flame, killing almost her entire crew. The *Neosho*, fatally crippled, somehow stayed afloat, but dozens of men drowned when they panicked and leaped overboard.

To the north, Fletcher's aviators were making mistakes of their own. A scout plane's message reported two Japanese carriers and two heavy cruisers near New Guinea's eastern tip. Fletcher immediately launched waves of attackers from the *Yorktown* and *Lexington*. But he soon learned that the message had been coded incorrectly; the scout spotted only two light cruisers and two destroyers. Fletcher let his bombers fly on nonetheless, gambling that they might still find a worthier target. And an hour later, the news arrived: a reconnaissance plane had found a small carrier, the 12,000-ton *Shoho*, in the same area.

Ninety-three American planes swarmed over the hapless *Shoho*.

Lieutenant Commander Bob Dixon, leader of an attack wing, radioed back triumphantly to the *Lexington*:

"Dixon to carrier: Scratch one flattop!"

"It amounted to an overkill," Captain Paul D. Stroop, the *Lexington's* flag secretary, later concluded. "It was our first battle of this kind, so everybody went after the big prize and sank her very quickly."

The destruction of the *Shoho*, first of many Japanese carriers to be lost in the Pacific war, led the Port Moresby invasion force to turn back.

But Admiral Takagi still wanted the American carriers. And misfortune continued to plague him that long day.

In late afternoon, he sent twenty-seven bombers and torpedo planes off to find the American carriers. But they made no sightings, flew into bad weather and then were themselves picked up on the *Lexington's* radar—a device with which the Japanese carriers were not yet equipped. Fighters roared off from the *Lexington* and *Yorktown* and intercepted the wandering attack planes, shooting down nine. Some of the surviving Japanese, disoriented, then mistook the *Yorktown* for their own carrier, attempted landings and were blown out of the sky. In the quickening darkness, others crashed into the sea. Only six of twenty-seven returned to Takagi's carriers.

The next morning, Friday, May 8, the carrier forces finally found each other, 150 miles apart in the northern Coral Sea.

Dixon's bombers spotted the *Shokaku* and *Zuikaku*, and Dixon himself, darting among the clouds, shadowed the carriers until other American planes could reach the area.

By then the *Zuikaku* had disappeared into a rain squall, but the attackers still had the *Shokaku* in their sights. Wave after wave descended on the 844-foot-long carrier. It dodged the slow U.S. torpedoes, but the dive bombers scored three hits, one of them setting gasoline stores afire and damaging the flight deck.

"She's going down with her head up, a lady to the last," said an officer as the **Lexington** *sank beneath the Coral Sea.*

About twenty minutes after the Navy airmen began their attack, seventy Japanese torpedo planes and dive bombers, launched earlier from the *Shokaku* and *Zuikaku*, reached the *Lexington* and *Yorktown*.

The American carriers, with only fifteen fighters to protect them, had to rely on maneuver and antiaircraft fire against the Japanese. The *Yorktown* dodged eight torpedoes and took only one bomb hit. But the longer, less maneuverable *Lexington* was helpless against the well-coordinated attack.

From 1,000 yards away, the wave-skimming Japanese aviators laid down a crisscross pattern of torpedoes against the *Lexington's* bow. Two scored hits on the port side, and a bomb damaged the main deck.

As the last attackers departed, the *Lexington* was ablaze and listing to port. Damage-control crews rapidly extinguished the fires and corrected the list through counterflooding, and the great ship was able to receive its own planes back from their mission.

But in early afternoon, as the carrier steamed south toward Australia, wounded but doing a good twenty-seven knots, a thunderous explosion rocked her interior. An electric motor's sparks had ignited fumes from a broken fuel line. Other explosions followed, and shortly after 5 p.m. the order to abandon ship was given. More than 2,000 sailors went over the side, down hawser ropes and into the warm Coral Sea, to be taken aboard small boats. Some 150 of their shipmates had died in the attack and explosions.

Stroop, one of the last off, watched from another vessel and later recounted the death throes of the "Lady Lex":

"It was getting quite dark and . . . there was a tremendous explosion and a whole elevator, No. 2, was lifted out of the ship and followed by a solid mass of flames which went as high as the mast of the ship. Then the whole bridge area broke out in flames. It was quite spectacular, silhouetted against the night sky."

The destroyer USS *Phelps* finished the *Lexington* off with four torpedoes, sending it to the bottom.

The Battle of the Coral Sea, the "Battle of Naval Errors," as historian Samuel Eliot Morison dubbed it, was the first naval clash in history in which warships battled without firing a single salvo at each other. It established the aircraft carrier as the queen of the seas.

For the Japanese, it was a tactical victory. The destruction of the 30,000-ton *Lexington* more than offset the Japanese loss of the *Shoho* and some smaller vessels. But strategically it was a setback.

Fletcher's resistance forced the Japanese to postpone, forever as it turned out, the amphibious assault on Port Moresby. The U.S. Navy had finally drawn the line in the Pacific. MacArthur would later use Port Moresby as a base for his promised return to the Philippines.

But Coral Sea pointed up potential problems in America's waging of the Pacific war. Just a month before the battle, the newly organized U.S. Joint Chiefs of Staff, disregarding a cardinal tenet of warfare, split the command of the Pacific Theater: MacArthur, in Australia, was given command of the southwest Pacific, an area from the Philippines and Solomons westward, and Nimitz was given command of the rest of the ocean area.

This division of leadership guaranteed an often uneasy partnership and a sometimes open rivalry between two huge military organizations, one dominated by the Army, the other by the Navy.

During the Coral Sea fighting, these parallel lines of command meant that Nimitz's navy depended on land-based aircraft over which it had no control, and MacArthur's air arm was called on to support naval movements over which he had no influence.

One incident dangerously underscored the friction. On May 7, in the midst of the Coral Sea battle, a U.S. destroyer came under attack from three Australia-based U.S. B-26s whose crews mistook it for a Japanese vessel. MacArthur later not only refused to acknowledge the error, but he also rejected a Navy proposal to better train his pilots in warship recognition.

In the end, the most telling blows dealt at Coral Sea may have been the superficial wounds suffered by the two prize Japanese carriers. The repairs needed by the *Shokaku* and the heavy loss of planes and air crews by the *Zuikaku* kept these two modern giants out of the next battle, a fateful mid-Pacific encounter on which Japan's Combined Fleet commander, the poker-loving Admiral Yamamoto, was about to place all his chips, and for which the Americans' Commander Joseph Rochefort, the tireless American cryptanalyst, was even then, in his airless code-breakers' cellar in Honolulu, preparing a marked deck.

Crewmen ate up **Lexington's** *ice cream stores waiting to abandon the doomed carrier.*

Midway

Yamamoto had opposed going to war with the United States. He knew the American adversary well, having studied at Harvard and served as Japanese naval attache in Washington. He knew that in any conflict U.S. industrial might would eventually crush Japan.

But if war was inevitable, the admiral had reasoned, an early, deadly blow would have to be struck against the U.S. Pacific Fleet. Then the Japanese could sue for a quick peace on favorable terms.

Yamamoto's first blow was Pearl Harbor, an attack that bought Japan some time but left the American Navy with a potent arm, its aircraft carriers.

Now the emperor's naval commander sought to lure the Americans into an all-out "fleet action" at sea. He chose his spot: the Midway Islands.

A tiny, two-island atoll at the western end of the Hawaiian chain, 1,135 miles from Honolulu, Midway had been developed into a key mid-Pacific sentry post by the Americans, with a large airfield, seaplane base and artificial harbor.

To Tokyo's strategists, U.S. control of Midway and the Aleutian islands, far to the north, opened a dangerous gap in Japan's outer defensive perimeter, a gap through which they assumed, correctly, the Doolittle carrier had penetrated.

Yamamoto's battle plan was complex:

One naval force would assault the small U.S. base at Dutch Harbor in the Aleutians. A day later, a big carrier force would launch air strikes against Marine and Navy defenses on Midway. A third group would follow up with troop landings on Midway. A fourth group, the Main Body, would lie in wait west of Midway, ready to pounce on the U.S. fleet expected to sail from Pearl Harbor to Midway's assistance. Finally, to cover all contingencies, a fifth force would be stationed between Midway and the Aleutians, in case American ships moved toward the Aleutians instead.

For this master stroke, Yamamoto was assembling more than 200 ships, almost his entire navy, an overwhelming force the Americans could not possibly match. He himself would command the Main Body from the newly launched flagship *Yamato*, the greatest battleship the world had ever seen, a 72,000-ton dreadnought whose eighteen-inch guns fired 3,200-pound shells.

A winning hand, thought Yamamoto. But Nimitz was already reading his cards.

By May, U.S. code-breakers, helped by intelligence units in Washington and Australia, were deciphering about 90 percent of the average Japanese message. They intercepted a series of signals that reported on the assembling of ships and supplies for "the forthcoming campaign." The codebreaker deduced that the target, code-named AF, was Midway.

Skeptics demanded that Rochefort produce positive confirmation that Midway was the target. He got the Japanese to do it for him.

He arranged for the Navy's Midway installation to transmit an uncoded radio message reporting a shortage of fresh water on the atoll. Soon afterward, Japanese radio monitors relayed that "AF" was reporting a water shortage.

Nimitz readied for battle, gathering forty-eight vessels to sail out against an enemy fleet more than four times that size.

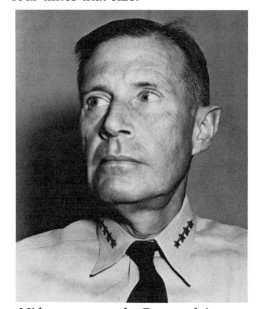

Midway commander Raymond A. Spruance could see the enemy's cards thanks to the wizards who broke the Japanese codes.

He had Admiral Halsey's carriers *Enterprise* and *Hornet*, commanded by Rear Admiral Raymond A. Spruance while Halsey was hospitalized with a skin infection. He also had, through the extraordinary efforts of repair crews, Admiral Fletcher's *Yorktown*.

As that carrier limped home from the Coral Sea, specialists estimated it would take three months to repair its battle damage. Nimitz said he needed it in three days.

When the *Yorktown* entered a Pearl Harbor dry dock May 27, some 1,400 skilled workmen immediately clambered over it and began working day and night to put it back in shape. Two days later, the *Yorktown* eased out into the harbor to take on fuel, with the repair work still under way, and on May 30 it embarked for Midway.

By then, any questions Nimitz still had about the

timetable and makeup of the Japanese attack force had been answered by Yamamoto himself, in a transmission from his Combined Fleet headquarters that carried the entire lengthy Midway operations order, in JN25b code—already broken by U.S. cryptographers.

His plans complete and his ships under way, Nimitz now could only stand by at the Pearl Harbor headquarters and await the battle reports.

Aboard the warships, steaming westward at flank speed, thousands of sailors and airmen sensed the danger ahead.

"Obviously there was a big battle coming up in the middle of the Pacific," recalled fighter pilot John S. Thach.

Spruance sent a visual signal from the *Enterprise* to his other ships, summing up matter-of-factly their historic mission: "The successful conclusion of the operation now commencing will be of great value to our country."

Unlike Halsey, this admiral's style was low-key and unassuming. But in the coming days he was to show himself to be, in the words of an Annapolis classmate, "a cold-blooded fighting fool."

The Americans were headed for a position northeast of Midway, where they would be beyond easy Japanese detection but able to launch air attacks against the enemy force.

They cleared their first hurdle by passing a planned Japanese submarine picket line off Hawaii before June 1, when the subs took up position. The underwater pickets were supposed to alert Yamamoto to ship movements out of Pearl Harbor. But it was already too late.

On the morning of June 3, 1942, the huge Japanese force, sailing into the rising sun, had no idea it was falling into a trap.

At a little before 9 that Wednesday morning, the first sighting was reported. A Navy Catalina flying boat spotted the convoy carrying Japanese invasion troops toward Midway, 700 miles away. Two bombing runs by Midway-based planes did little damage to the task force.

Meanwhile, some 2,000 miles to the north, the Japanese Northern Force raided the U.S. base at Dutch Harbor.

In the early morning darkness of June 4, a Japanese carrier force approached to within 240 miles of Midway from the northwest. The carriers *Akagi, Kaga, Soryu* and *Hiryu* and their commander Admiral Nagumo had stealthily navigated north Pacific waters before, six months earlier, when they launched the planes that devastated Pearl Harbor.

On this morning, at 4:30 a.m., Nagumo ordered another attack, sending 108 planes against the ground installations at Midway. The "softening up" had begun.

The Japanese bombers wrecked the Marine command post and other facilities on Midway. But the flight leader reported back to Nagumo that a second wave would be necessary.

By now, American patrol planes had spotted the Japanese carriers. Midway's land-based bombers had flown off toward this new-found target in the northwest, and Spruance's *Enterprise* and *Hornet,* about 200 miles away from Nagumo, were closing from the northeast.

Nagumo's fighter and antiaircraft screen easily handled the Marine and Army torpedo planes and bombers that bore in on the carriers. One by one, the inexperienced American fliers were shot out of the sky, plunging in flames into the deep blue Pacific. Of sixteen Marine dive bombers commanded by Major Lofton Henderson, eight were lost, including Henderson's. Of the planes that survived, none scored hits on the Japanese vessels.

Nagumo meanwhile was being pressed to make a second attack on Midway. It would mean removing anti-ship torpedos and armor-piercing bombs from his reserve planes and rearming them with ground-attack ordnance. The four carriers would be unprepared to deal with American naval forces. But as far as the Japanese knew, the American carriers were still back in Pearl Harbor.

Nagumo, in one of those rare individual decisions that shape history, gave the order to rearm.

Fifteen minutes later, a Japanese scout reported an enemy naval group to the northeast. The admiral, now facing a dilemma of targets, halted the rearming and awaited further information, while his task force dodged and downed the Midway-based planes.

It wasn't until fifty minutes later that the scout reported the chilling news: the U.S. group included a carrier. A timely attack was now vital, Nagumo knew, but his Midway bomber force was just then returning to the carriers. He cleared the deck of ready planes to receive the bombers.

By this time, the first of 152 planes from the *Enterprise, Hornet* and *Yorktown* were speeding toward the Japanese carriers. The coolly calculating Spruance had launched his aircraft from the limit of their combat radius, risking his airmen's lives in a bid to catch the Japanese in the confusion of recovering their Midway attackers.

The American torpedo squadrons were the first to find Nagumo's carriers. They dropped down into attack approaches at 9:25 a.m., and what followed was thirty-five minutes of raw flying courage and wholesale death.

The first wave consisted of fifteen lumbering Devastators of the *Hornet's* Torpedo Squadron Eight, led by Commander John C. Waldron, who wiggled his wings and led them into clouds of bursting shells and streams of machine gun fire from Japanese Zeros. Every one was blasted into the sea, with no damage done to the carriers.

Next came fourteen torpedo planes from the *Enterprise*. Ten were shot down; none scored any hits. Finally, eleven torpedo planes from the *Yorktown* bore in on the carriers. Commander Thach led a fighter group trying to fend the Zeros off from the *Yorktown* Devastators.

"The air was just like a beehive," he recalled. "The Japs kept coming in . . . and more of our torpedo planes were falling, but so were some Zeros. And we thought, 'At least we're keeping a lot of them engaged.'"

The self-destructive runs by the torpedo pilots kept the Japanese from launching their own strike aircraft, and kept the Zero interceptors and antiaircraft gunners tied down near sea level. Three miles above the furious battle, meanwhile, more than

fifty dive bombers from the *Enterprise* and *Yorktown* arrived overhead.

"I saw a glint in the sun that looked like a beautiful silver waterfall," Thach later said. "It was the dive bombers coming in."

The *Enterprise* squadrons shrieked down toward the *Kaga* and *Akagi*, Nagumo's flagship, and the *Yorktown's* went after the *Soryu*.

They scored hit after hit on decks crowded with men, with planes being fueled, with torpedoes removed during the rearming. Fires and explosions turned the 800-foot-long carriers into infernos.

Mitsuo Fuchida, lead pilot of the Pearl Harbor attack, had been below decks aboard the *Akagi*, suffering from appendicitis, but he came up to witness the battle.

"Looking about," he later wrote, "I was horrified at the destruction that had been wrought in a matter of seconds."

Despite barrage of ack-ack, Japanese bomber scores fatal hit on carrier **Yorktown** *at Midway.*

The glory of Japan's triumphant navy was being incinerated—and Pearl Harbor avenged.

The carrier *Hiryu*, some miles off, escaped this ferocious attack, and launched twenty-eight torpedo planes and dive bombers against the Americans. At midday the dive bombers bore in on the *Yorktown*. Its formidable fighter screen eliminated most of the attackers, but three bombs hit the American carrier, killing dozens of men and leaving it dead in the water.

The damage was temporarily repaired and the *Yorktown* was under way again an hour later when the torpedo planes attacked. Two torpedoes ripped into its port side, and the battered veteran of Coral Sea began to list severely. The "abandon ship" order went out. Admiral Fletcher, senior officer in the Midway operation, had to transfer his flag to a cruiser and overall command to Spruance, who still had carriers.

Off to the southwest, meanwhile, the *Yorktown's* own scouts had located the *Hiryu*. *Enterprise* dive bombers closed in on the last of the Japanese flattops, delivering four bombs that started fatal fires.

That evening, June 4, the seas north of Midway glowed with giant flames and echoed with the faint cries of lost and wounded men. Ensign George H. Gay, a torpedo-plane pilot shot down early in the action, was among them.

The lone survivor from the *Hornet's* doomed Devastator squadron, Gay floated through the middle of the battle for a full day, clinging to a seat cushion. He watched the Japanese carriers explode in towering flames and saw the often futile efforts of other vessels to save the carriers' crewmen.

"Overhead, Japanese planes appeared to be circling in a vain attempt to land on the smashed carrier," according to an Associated Press account of Gay's experience. "They would pass above her, then soar out of sight and return."

Gay, rescued the next day by a Navy seaplane, never saw them, but many of the homeless Japanese planes simply crashed into the sea.

Over the horizon, far to the west, Yamamoto grimly received word of the disaster: not one or two carriers lost, but all four. He quickly ordered his Main Body warships, along with units from the other task forces, to converge on a point closer to Midway. He hoped to catch the enemy fleet at night, when the U.S. air advantage would be neutralized and Yamamoto's powerful guns could tear the Americans apart at will.

But Spruance was well briefed on Yamamoto's strengths. He did not want to run into any battleships in the dark. He withdrew eastward.

In the early morning hours of June 5, realizing he would not catch the Americans, Yamamoto ordered a general withdrawal toward Japan. Daylight, he knew, might bring American dive bombers down on his mighty capital ships.

But the losses did not cease. The heavy cruisers *Mikuma* and *Mogami*, two of the Japanese navy's finest ships, collided in the darkness early on June 5 as they tried to avoid attack by the American submarine *Tambor*. Later that day and the next, U.S. carrier bombers and Marine bombers from Midway found the damaged and slow-moving cruisers, sinking the *Mikuma* and leaving the *Mogami* a floating wreck.

The burning carriers *Kaga* and *Soryu* sank on the evening of June 4. *Hiryu* and *Akagi* were finished off by torpedoes from their own destroyers early the next morning.

The *Yorktown* seemed salvageable. It was taken under tow and was proceeding slowly toward Hawaii June 6 when a Japanese submarine slipped inside its destroyer screen, blew the escorting destroyer *Hammann* in two with a torpedo and finally sank the crippled *Yorktown* with two more.

The Battle of Midway was costly in more than ships. The Japanese also lost 322 airplanes, almost all of them caught aboard their carriers, and at least 3,500 men, including some of their best aviators.

American losses were put at 307 dead and 147 planes destroyed.

Military historians would later conclude that Yamamoto's complex plan had made a fundamental error: if he had simply concentrated his overwhelming force on a single objective, the capture of Midway, he would have succeeded.

But first credit for outwitting a far stronger Japanese force belonged to the sleepless landlubbers who broke the Japanese code.

Without the code-breakers' advance information, Nimitz later said, "the Battle of Midway would have ended differently."

But their work could not be acknowledged publicly. The Japanese still did not realize their security had been deeply compromised.

For a while it looked like stricken Yorktown *would survive Midway. Then a Japanese sub found it.*

As his shattered armada steamed westward into the setting sun June 5, Yamamoto knew he was conceding the first major Japanese defeat in battle in more than three centuries. The debacle at Midway, the loss of four of Japan's six first-line aircraft carriers, meant that the initiative was now with the Americans in the Pacific War, a war in which naval aviation was playing an increasingly critical role, and for which U.S. shipyards would soon be producing flattops at a rate of almost one a month. After Midway, Japan's imperial forces would necessarily turn to the defensive, to cling to what they held.

Japan's premier seaman was bewildered by the Americans' uncanny luck in their mid-ocean encounter. Ten months later, in the skies over the Solomon Islands, Pearl Harbor's lucky code-breakers would deal Yamamoto his last hand.

Strategy for Victory

Word of the Midway triumph elated an American home front that in six months of war had heard considerable bad news from the Pacific and very little of any news from the Atlantic.

The American economy—the industries that Yamamoto told his comrades were "much more developed than ours"—was now firmly on a war footing.

The two-ocean Navy was taking shape in eleven government shipyards. Giant defense plants were rising in California orchards, Indiana cornfields, Long Island potato patches. In April, the new War Manpower Commission froze 27 million workers in their jobs, and the president froze prices and wages. Millions of men were in Army tans or Navy blues in training camps across the country, and the complex workings of a modern economy were entirely under the central control of Washington.

But Allied strategy necessarily was the child of Allied production, and nothing could be produced overnight.

By June 1942, the American press was echoing the Soviet cry for a "second front" against the Germans. Eisenhower, the Army's chief planner, lamented that the impatient public merely showed "a complete lack of appreciation of the problems involved."

American and British commanders knew, for example, that landing craft, newly contrived amphibious vessels, would be essential for the major invasions contemplated in both theaters. But in June 1942, Eisenhower later wrote, "some of the landing craft were not yet in the blueprint stage."

Production limitations on a broad range of naval,

George Marshall meets with chiefs of staff in 1942.

air and ground equipment "ruled out any possibility of a full-scale invasion in 1942 or early 1943," he wrote.

In the early weeks of 1942, Eisenhower and his staff studied the "second front" possibilities from all angles. Their two overriding goals: keeping Britain and the Soviet Union in the war.

The War Department planners looked at the possible use of American forces to attack Germany through the Soviet Union. They considered striking through Norway, or through neutral Portugal and Spain. They weighed the merits of relying solely on naval firepower and airpower, with no invasion force.

In the end, Eisenhower said, it was clear that the approach offering the quickest, most efficient access to the heart of the enemy was a buildup of American forces in England followed by an invasion of northwest Europe.

On April 1, 1942, General Marshall presented a memorandum to Roosevelt, based on Eisenhower's calculations, calling for "an attack, by combined forces of approximately 5,800 combat airplanes and forty-eight divisions against western Europe as soon as the necessary means can be accumulated in England." The target date was estimated at April 1, 1943.

The plan also envisioned a limited assault across the English Channel in September 1942 if it appeared the hard-pressed Soviets were about to collapse on the eastern front.

The president immediately endorsed the proposal, and sent Marshall and Harry Hopkins off to London to secure British agreement. The Army chief and presidential aide returned convinced they had it. But the British harbored misgivings, particularly about the possible 1942 assault, code-named Sledgehammer.

The chief of the Imperial General Staff, Sir Alan Field Marshal Brooke, confided his concerns about

Sledgehammer to his diary:

"The plans are fraught with the gravest dangers. . . . The prospects of success are small and dependent on a mass of unknowns, whilst the chances of disaster are great and dependent on a mass of well-established facts."

Brooke knew the iron power of the German army. He had led four British divisions in the bitter retreat from Dunkirk, and in the two years since he had watched from afar the building of Hitler's "Fortress Europe."

The British field marshal, who would spar repeatedly with Marshall until the end of the war, felt that the American chief of staff had not begun "to visualize the problems that would face any army after landing."

While the Americans and British debated long-term strategy, the Soviets' short-term outlook grew more desperate by the day.

Their winter counteroffensive against the Germans, launched in December 1941, had been only partly successful.

They retook one-fifth of the 500,000 square miles of Soviet territory seized by Hitler's Wehrmacht the previous five months, driving the Germans back from the outskirts of Moscow. The coldest winter in 150 years was Stalin's greatest ally. Ill-clad and ill-shod, many German troops were found frozen in the snow at the front lines.

But by April, when the Russian offensive stopped, the invaders still had Leningrad and the southern port of Sevastapol besieged, and Hitler's generals were planning a powerful spring-summer campaign along the entire 1,800-mile front to knock their eastern enemy out for good.

British Chief of Staff Sir Alan Brooke (r.) *almost came to blows with King, and thought Eisenhower "incapable of running a land battle."*

Well-rested panzer divisions scored the first victory May 23, seizing the southern city of Kerch, a gateway to the oil-rich Caucasus region, and capturing 170,000 Red Army soldiers. The Germans then took aim at the Soviets' critical Volga River lifeline and the industrial city of Stalingrad.

The Soviet foreign minister, Vyacheslav Molotov, arrived in Washington at about this time for urgent discussions with Roosevelt on getting more American Lend Lease supplies to the Soviets. Molotov again pressed the Soviet case for a second front to force the Germans to withdraw some of their 180 divisions from the Soviet Union. Stalin suspected the anti-communist British and Americans of standing aside purposely to allow the Nazis to bleed the Soviet Union.

Molotov left the White House pleased; the president told him to expect a second front in 1942. And, a short time later, Roosevelt mentioned it again to a second visitor, the British Admiral Lord Louis Mountbatten, to whom the president commented that a sacrifice attack might have to be made across the Channel to relieve the burden on the Soviets. Informed of this, Churchill and his military counselors were troubled anew.

On June 6, 1942, when Washington received first word from Nimitz of the great Midway victory, Hopkins dashed off a letter to Churchill, suggesting another face-to-face conference to discuss global strategy now that the pressure in the Pacific appeared to have eased, pressure that might otherwise have forced a reappraisal of the Germany First policy.

On June 21, Churchill and Brooke strode into the Oval Office of the White House, intent on making clear Britain's serious reservations about any 1942 cross-Channel operation.

Within minutes a cable arrived. Roosevelt read it and handed it to his visitors: Rommel had captured the key Libyan port and garrison of Tobruk, with its 33,000 British and Imperial soldiers.

The news stunned Churchill. The year before, Australian troops had withstood an eight-month German siege at Tobruk. Now the garrison had surrendered in a one-day battle. It was "one of the heaviest blows I can recall during the war," Churchill later said.

In three days of discussions, Churchill urged the Americans to consider an invasion of North Africa in 1942. The idea, raised previously by the British, had intrigued Roosevelt as a relatively quick way to boost American morale and give green U.S. troops some battle experience. Churchill argued that driving the Germans and Italians from North Africa would not only remove the Axis threat to seize Middle East oil, but also clear the Mediterranean for supply shipments to the Soviet Union and to Asian war theaters.

But Marshall resisted, believing that such a diversionary campaign would drain resources away from preparations for the major 1943 invasion of Europe.

The Washington talks ended on vague and ambiguous notes, although Marshall felt the Allies had agreed firmly on going ahead with the invasion buildup in England and with preparations for Sledgehammer, the 1942 cross-Channel action, on a contingency basis.

On July 8, however, word came from London that the British War Cabinet had definitively decided not to mount Sledgehammer, which would have been a largely British operation, and was asking the United States to agree to a North African invasion.

In those steamy July days beside the Potomac, historic decisions would have to be made.

Marshall, who had just sent Eisenhower to London as commanding general of all American forces in Europe, was furious with the British move, which he interpreted to mean that Churchill and his generals were also not clearly committed to a full-scale 1943 invasion of northwest Europe. He brought together the Joint Chiefs of Staff and produced a new proposal: that the United States adopt a defensive stance in the Atlantic Theater and shift all available resources instead to the Pacific, an idea particularly pleasing to Admiral Ernest J. King, chief of naval operations.

Roosevelt took just a day to consider and reject the Pacific proposal. The commander-in-chief stuck to Germany First, and again dispatched Marshall and Hopkins to London, this time with Admiral King along, to work out firm plans once and for all. They carried with them instructions from Roosevelt to make the immediate objective "U.S. ground forces fighting against Germans in 1942."

By the end of July, after more direct intercession by Roosevelt in the squabbling among military men, the Allies settled on a timetable calling for an invasion of northwest Africa by November 1942.

Eisenhower was given command of what was to be a largely American operation in North Africa, a campaign that would tie up Allied resources for months to come and, as Eisenhower later wrote, "almost certainly . . . eliminate the possibility of a major cross-Channel venture in 1943."

Instead, for now, the lead on the European front would have to be taken by the British and American air forces.

Flying Lancasters, their new four-engine heavy bomber, the British had opened an air campaign in March and April 1942 with raids on the historic German cities of Luebeck and Rostock on the Baltic Sea.

The RAF Bomber Command soon was launching massive strikes. On the night of May 30-31, it staged its first 1,000-plane attack, on the city of Cologne, dropping blockbuster bombs up to two tons. The steady pounding indirectly helped the Russians, since the German Luftwaffe had to pull back hundreds of Messerschmitts and other fighters from the eastern front to face the enemy in the skies over the homeland.

On July 4, 1942, while strategists in Washington and London still mulled their next moves, a handful of U.S. Army aviators celebrated Independence Day by taking the American war to the Germans for the first time, raiding German airfields in the Netherlands. But they had to borrow six RAF twin-engine Boston bombers to do it, and two never returned.

The U.S. Army Air Forces eventually would fly thousands of B-17 Flying Fortresses and B-24 Liberator bombers over Europe. But in mid-1942 this air armada was still largely on the drawing boards, and the British bombing raids were doing little to stop the continent-wide economy that was feeding the German war machine.

As almost an afterthought to Midway, it was reported on June 6 that the Japanese Northern Force had seized the unpopulated islands of Attu and Kiska at the western tip of the U.S. Aleutian chain. The move, establishing a Japanese presence on a distant appendage of North America, troubled some in Washington. But over time these desolate and remote spots would prove of no importance in the U.S.-British global offensive that would soon unfold.

North Africa

Horizon to horizon, the gray steel of ships covered the sea, an army in transit to war.

Two great convoys, packed with 84,000 American and 23,000 British troops, had set out for northwest Africa in late October 1942, one sailing south from Britain, the other east from the U.S. East Coast.

For the untested U.S. Army "dogfaces," these were days of boredom, seasickness and apprehension. Zigzagging endlessly, blacked-out at night, stacked four high in bunks or canvas hammocks, the GIs could only reread letters and worn-out books, play blackjack, shoot dice, spread rumors: they were headed for Egypt, for Senegal, for Norway.

By early October 1942, 300 American M-4 Sherman tanks had arrived in Egypt, by convoy around the Cape of Good Hope, to reinforce the battered armored units of the British 8th Army, a patchwork force of English and Scotsmen, Indians, Australians, New Zealanders and South Africans.

The standoff in North Africa pitted two of the war's outstanding generals, Desert Fox Rommel and British Lieutenant General Bernard L. Montgomery, newly named commander of the 8th Army. But both men knew the eventual battle would be about logistics more than leadership. It was estimated, for example, that the 8th Army required 70,000 gallons of gasoline a day for full operations.

Replenished with American tanks, trucks, jeeps and guns, and backed up by squadrons of American bombers and fighters, Monty built up a decisive edge over the German-Italian forces that had been facing the 8th Army since July along a north-south front anchored at the coastal rail station of El Alamein, sixty miles west of Alexandria. Although the Axis army had a relatively short supply line across the Mediterranean from Italy, three-quarters of its supply ships were being sunk along the way by the British navy and air force.

In September, Rommel met with Hitler at the fuehrer's Wolf's Lair headquarters in East Prussia to appeal for more help from the Luftwaffe, whose planes were then heavily committed to the Russian front.

Goering, the Luftwaffe chief, ridiculed Rommel's contention that British planes had knocked out German tanks with 40mm shells sent from the United States.

"All the Americans can make are razor blades and refrigerators," Goering insisted.

Rommel, producing some shell samples, retorted, "I only wish, Herr Reichsmarschall, that we were issued similar razor blades!"

By the time the great battle began, with a skirl of bagpipes from Montgomery's Highlanders and the roar of 1,000 big guns, the British forces numbered 200,000 to the 100,000 Germans and Italians, and fielded 1,000 tanks to 500 for the Axis. The German African command knew its job would be not to roll back the 8th Army, but to hold losses to a minimum and carry out an orderly withdrawal of their own.

After the initial barrage on the night of October 23, a World War I-style bombardment that rent the desert night with lightning and thunder for four hours, Montgomery's infantry advanced to clear pathways for his tanks through defensive minefields miles deep.

The fighting was fierce, but the Axis forces were outgunned and short on fuel. Some of the 300 obsolete Italian tanks that joined in the battle shook themselves apart when they fired their guns.

The first morning, General Georg Stumme, tem-

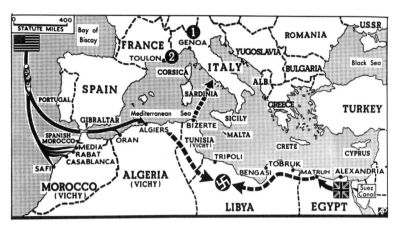

The Torch landings in Africa were half of a vise that gradually squeezed Rommel's Afrika Korps.

porarily replacing the ailing Rommel as African commander, died of a heart attack under heavy shelling. Rommel rushed back from Germany, reaching the front on October 25. Six days later, he mounted a desperation counterattack and was repulsed.

As the British artillery and air attacks turned Afrika Korps tanks into burning hulks, Hitler messaged Rommel, "You can show your troops no other way than that which leads to victory or death."

But by November 4, Rommel's troops were in full retreat on the clogged road to Tunisia, having lost 20,000 dead and 30,000 prisoners, to some 13,000 dead for the British. And within four days, as slower units fell captive to the advancing British and as a rear guard sought desperately to protect the German withdrawal westward, word came that the vise now had two jaws: the Americans had landed to the west at three points in northwest Africa.

For their leaders, Operation Torch was a gamble.

The surf on the Moroccan coast, one of three landing zones, was unpredictable in November. If the seas were rough, the Moroccan operation might be scuttled.

And beyond that, as soldiers jammed shipboard religious services the night before the landings, a central question remained unanswered: Would the fourteen French army divisions in North Africa resist the invaders?

The amphibious forces would be pouring ashore in territories—Morocco and Algeria—governed by the French regime in Vichy, a technically neutral government that controlled southern France and some French colonies in collaboration with the Axis.

The Allies had worked for months to try to line up French cooperation in Africa. In one secretive mission two weeks before the landings, Eisenhower's deputy, Major General Mark Clark, was landed from a British submarine onto an isolated spot along the Algerian coast, where he conferred with a French general who supplied vital information about the deployment of French forces in North Africa. At one point, Clark had to hide in a wine cellar from French police, and then barely made it back safely to the submarine.

The Allies, meanwhile, had enlisted General Henri Giraud, a maverick French officer recently escaped from a German prison camp, as a figurehead around whom the liberated French of North Africa could rally.

Fearful that French-British antagonisms might threaten the operation, the Allies sought to give Torch a thoroughly American look. The soldiers were issued American flag armbands, and an American, Eisenhower, was put in command of the invasion.

On November 5, skimming the waves aboard a B-17 Flying Fortress, Ike flew from London to Gibraltar and established his headquarters in the dank, dark corridors within the famous British Rock.

But even by that night, as he watched some of the 850 Allied warships, transports and cargo vessels pass into the Mediterranean, dark shapes on a phosphorescent Gibraltar Strait, Eisenhower could not be sure how the French defense forces would react.

It was "a most peculiar venture," he later wrote. ". . . We were invading a neutral country to create a friend."

Security had been extremely tight. Although German agents in Spain saw the convoy enter the Mediterranean, Axis intelligence decided it was reinforcements bound for the British-held island of Malta, or possibly a Sicily invasion force. Axis defenses were mobilized far to the east to meet the threat.

Aboard the ships, where the troops were informed of their objective during the journey, months of training came down to the small hours of the morning of November 8, D Day for Operation Torch.

Some men approached the hour with dread. Corporal John Moglia of the 1st Infantry Division later recalled that a friend, Smitty, handed him two cigars.

"Tomorrow I die," he told Moglia. "Promise me that when things quiet down you'll smoke one for me."

In the dim pre-dawn hours, in thousands of squads and platoons, GIs sat among their gear—the new Garand M-1 rifle, bandoliers of ammunition, canteens, trench knives, gas masks, steel helmets—and waited for the loudspeaker to call their unit number.

Some French troops fiercely resisted the U.S. African landings; some French-Africans willingly surrendered.

"Serial 123, muster at sally port No. 1."

Then out, down into their landing boats, and off toward the shadowy hulk in the distance, Africa. Soon Smitty and hundreds of others would be dead.

For Eisenhower, the Atlantic surf off Morocco remained a deep concern until the end. The weather report on November 7 was bleak, but when the hour came for the landing the seas were reported satisfactory, and the Western Task Force, commanded by his old friend Patton, headed for the beaches at three spots south and north of Casablanca.

Torch was the greatest amphibious assault to that point in the greatest war in history, staged over almost 1,000 miles of coastline. Both American performance and French resistance varied from landing zone to landing zone.

At 4:30 a.m., two American destroyers cruised into the Moroccan port of Safi, carrying a small Army vanguard entrusted with seizing the important harbor. But one destroyer promptly ran aground and the other smashed into a pier. The two rifle companies, shaken up, scrambled ashore to begin long hours of fighting against French army positions.

Near Oran, Algeria, where the Center Task Force under Major General Lloyd R. Fredendall came ashore, a landing barge disembarked a general's jeep too early, into eight feet of water. A paratrooper unit, meanwhile, missed its objective, a French airfield, by thirty-five miles.

But most of the landings took place according to plan, and the Americans encountered some stiff resistance from the French, although the outdated French equipment and poorly trained troops soon began to fall before the invaders.

Divided French feelings were obvious at Oran, where a French motor launch roamed the harbor firing a machine gun at wounded Americans in the water, while other Frenchmen in rowboats were trying to rescue the GIs.

The Allied task proved easiest in the easternmost area, around Algiers, where the U.S. 34th Infantry Division and the British 1st Army came ashore. The French surrendered on the first day.

At Oran, where the Big Red One, the 1st Infantry Division, got its first taste of battle, the Americans gained control of the city within two days.

The resistance was toughest in Morocco. Up and down that coast, French shore batteries opened up on the invaders. The French battleship *Jean Bart*, immobile in Casablanca harbor, dueled with the battleship USS *Massachusetts,* and lost. At Port Lyautey, north of Casablanca, the French held out at the Kasba fortress and even launched an armored counterattack against the Americans.

Giraud was brought to Algiers to order the French to cease fire across North Africa, but he was ignored. The French generals let it be known that they would respect only a legal order from Vichy.

Eisenhower had put his money on the wrong horse. But by chance the right one, Vichy armed forces chief Admiral Jean Darlan, was trapped by the invasion in Algeria, where he was visiting his ill son.

Clark, Eisenhower's emissary, quickly negotiated with the opportunistic Darlan, who on November 10 ordered the French military to cooperate with the invaders, in exchange for an Allied pledge not to interfere with the Vichyites' internal administration of the territories. In the end, Darlan did not administer long. He was assassinated by a French patriot on December 24 and replaced by Giraud.

The French in Casablanca agreed to the armistice November 11, just as Patton was readying an all-out assault on the city by his 2nd Armored Division. Elsewhere in Algeria and Morocco, the last fighting subsided November 12.

In four days of sporadic combat, the Allies had lost 860 men killed or missing.

The Darlan deal, an Allied accommodation with fascist collaborationists, touched off bitter political debates in London and Washington. But Eisenhower and his generals believed they had done the right thing militarily by bargaining with Darlan. The Allies could now turn and face the real enemy: the German and Italian armies in North Africa.

Within a day of the Torch landings, the Germans began airlifting troops from Sicily into Tunisia to transform that French colony into an Axis bastion. Up to 1,500 men a day poured in from across the Mediterranean.

Hitler, doublecrossed by Vichyites, also ordered his Wehrmacht to occupy southern France. Most of the French fleet had sat at Toulon, uncommitted, for more than two years. Now, on November 27, as German troops occupied the Mediterranean port, fleet commander Admiral Jean de Laborde ordered the more than seventy ships and boats scuttled, to keep them from falling into German hands.

Tunisia was good defensive ground for the Axis forces. Mountains along the western border with Algeria were a natural barrier protecting the Tunisian ports. To Tunisia's east, in Libya, Rommel's Afrika Korps faced Montgomery's 8th Army.

The swift French capitulation left the Torch commanders with a dilemma. The way was now open to Tunisia, but they would have to race eastward before the Germans could build up their forces there. And the Allied supply lines, dependent on clogged North African ports, probably could not keep up.

Lieutenant General Kenneth Anderson, commander of the British 1st Army, which came ashore at Algiers, struck out for Tunisia even before the Darlan deal was closed. British Tommies leapfrogged by sea to land at Bougie, east of Algiers, and airborne troops descended on Bone, another port farther east, just west of the Tunisian border. On the ground, meanwhile, Anderson drove ahead with the bulk of his force.

The 1st Army first clashed with German patrols sixty miles west of Tunis. The British pushed on, advancing through towns littered with concrete anti-tank obstructions and heavily salted with land mines. By November 28 they stood just twelve miles from Tunis. But then winter intervened.

The primitive road and rail system of supply, already overwhelmed, was further choked off by rain and mud. Anderson lost much of his air cover when the conditions shut down the forward Allied airfields. The Germans, meanwhile, had taken over two all-weather French airfields in Tunisia. In early December, the Germans counterattacked with tanks and Stuka dive bombers, and forced the British back from their positions before Tunis.

Eisenhower and Anderson planned one final push before winter took full hold. But after touring the front, and observing a motorcycle become hopelessly mired in the mud, the American commander called off the planned attack on Christmas Eve. The Allies would go on the defensive for the winter.

Rommel, whose beleaguered Afrika Korps was then 350 miles east of the Tunisia border, near Sirte in Libya, flew back to Germany for an emergency consultation with Hitler. Rommel favored an immediate German pullout from North Africa. But an angry Hitler refused and sent Rommel back to his command, and to inevitable debacle in Africa.

On other fronts, too, the tide was running against the Axis.

The Wehrmacht had given up its efforts to relieve the encircled 6th Army at Stalingrad, where a terrible winter was setting in. The U.S. Army's American Division had taken over from the bloodied 1st Marine Division on Guadalcanal and was hammering the battered Japanese back toward the island's western shores.

And Italian emigre scientist Enrico Fermi and his assistants, under the watchful eye of Arthur Compton at the University of Chicago, had just completed an experiment that led mankind into a new world.

Casablanca

On January 14, 1943, as Axis and Allied units probed and parried on the muddy North African front, Roosevelt and Churchill came together for the third time since America's entry into the war. And this time, in a move symbolic of Allied success, they met on "liberated" territory, at the hilltop Anfa Hotel, overlooking the dazzling blue Atlantic just outside Casablanca.

They had wanted Josef Stalin to join them in mapping out the next steps in the war against the Axis. But the Kremlin leader refused, explaining that the Soviet counteroffensive, centered on Stalingrad, demanded his presence at home.

The British came to Casablanca well prepared to push their plan: a thrust into what Churchill called the Axis "soft underbelly," southern Europe. A 6,000-ton ocean liner had brought Imperial Army and Royal Navy staff specialists from London to Casablanca to supply the documentary material to back up their plan.

The Americans, though not nearly so meticu-

At stormy Casablanca conference Roosevelt surprised Churchill with fateful declaration of unconditional surrender for Axis while brass heatedly argued war's direction: (l. to r.) Arnold, King, Marshall and British service chiefs Pound, Brooke and Portal.

lously prepared, felt just as strongly that an attack on southern Europe would drain Allied resources needed for the more critical invasion of northern Europe. Privately, they also questioned the British commitment to this attack across the English Channel, an operation whose code name, Roundup, would soon be transformed to Overlord.

But even the impatient American generals, led by Marshall, recognized that Roundup was impossible in 1943. The Allies had not mustered the necessary men and equipment in England. Instead, the Americans favored going on the defensive in the European Theater after the expected conquest of Tunisia, and mounting a major offensive against the Japanese.

The British-American debates among the bougainvillaea and begonias of the Anfa Hotel left Brooke, the overall British commander, exasperated by King's Pacific focus.

"The European war was just a great nuisance that kept him from waging his Pacific war undisturbed," the British field marshal later said.

But General Sir John Dill, chief British liaison to the Americans, helped piece together a compromise. He had a hand from the absent Stalin, since the Americans had to respond to the unending Soviet pressure for a second front on the European continent.

The final agreement called for an invasion of Sicily in the summer of 1943, Operation Husky. It also called for a continued Allied buildup of men and equipment in England for a cross-Channel invasion, probably in 1944. It left it to the American chiefs of staff to decide the next steps against Japan, although they were expected to be limited.

The strategy set at Casablanca was political as well as military.

Roosevelt and Churchill pressured Brigadier

Matchmaker Roosevelt arranged an uneasy marriage at Casablanca conference between Giraud (l.) and DeGaulle.

General Charles de Gaulle, the haughty and strong-willed commander of the Free French movement based in London, to come to Casablanca to accept Giraud's leadership in French North Africa.

De Gaulle's flight to Britain as France collapsed in June 1940 made him an unpopular figure among many French officers in North Africa and elsewhere. Because of this, and because of Allied fears his organization had been leaking confidential information, he had been kept uninformed of the plans for the Torch invasion. He resented that deeply, and later was infuriated by the Allied accommodation with the Vichyites. But the proud De Gaulle, almost totally dependent on the British and Americans, swallowed his pride as the Casablanca conference wound up on Sunday, January 24. Cajoled by Roosevelt, the two rival French generals, De Gaulle and Giraud, shook hands before a platoon of photographers on the steps of the Anfa Hotel. On the surface at least, a Gallic unity had been forged.

Then Roosevelt, the French question aside for the moment, uttered a few words that abruptly changed the complexion of the war.

"Peace can come to the world only by the total elimination of German and Japanese war power," he told the assembled reporters.

". . . The elimination of German, Japanese and Italian war power means the unconditional surrender of Germany, Italy and Japan."

"Unconditional surrender" meant the Allies would not end the war through negotiation with the Axis powers. It meant that the future political life of Germany, Japan and Italy, after an Allied victory, would be decided upon by the victors. It also meant, many analysts said, that Germany and Japan would now fight on to a bitter, deadly end.

Churchill later wrote that he was surprised by Roosevelt's statement. The British and Americans had not formally agreed upon such language. In fact, however, the issue had been discussed among American policy-makers in Washington for months. One key reason for such a declaration: it would reassure Stalin that the Western Allies would not seek a separate peace with Hitler, allowing the Nazi fuehrer to then turn his full force on the communist giant to the east.

But the secret military-political program that emerged from the ten-day summit on the Moroccan coast did not lead off with the long-range goal of total Allied conquest, or the Sicily invasion, or French unity, but with the desperate need to break the stranglehold that Admiral Doenitz's U-boats had on Atlantic shipping. The Allies would not win until more American ships could get through to Britain, North Africa and the Soviet Union, carrying the wherewithal of war.

It is mid-February 1943. In the chill and flare-light of the Tunisian night, in the stark winter sun of the desert day, the U.S. 2nd Armored Division is taking a beating at Kasserine Pass.

A tank captain, heading out into the teeth of battle in a hopeless bid to slow the German advance, is bitter as he talks with Associated Press reporter Hal Boyle.

"Why don't you tell the people at home the truth," he says. ". . . They haven't given us enough men or weapons here to hold the Nazis."

The outgunned and outguessed Americans are in retreat.

Rommel, who by early February had withdrawn from the east and linked up in Tunisia with Colonel-General Juergen von Arnim's forces, had decided to strike against the British-American units in the west before they were built up any further.

He aimed the blow at the weak southern end of the Allied line in the Tunisian hills, the II Corps area under Major General Fredendall's command. A mixture of less experienced U.S. units and French troops held the heights and passes there, while the slow buildup of men and equipment continued for a spring offensive. Allied planners expected a pre-emptive German attack, but farther to the north.

"Desert Fox" Rommel peers from tank in North Africa.

Eisenhower, on an inspection tour from his Algiers headquarters February 13, found the defensive positions in the southern area poorly prepared. It was too late. The next morning, Valentine's Day, scores of German tanks poured through Faid Pass, overrunning the defenders and sending the survivors reeling back forty miles toward the next line of defense, the Kasserine Pass.

The new German Mark VI Tiger tanks, armed with 88 mm guns, outperformed the new American tank, the Sherman. The panzers opened their deadly fire long before they came within range of the Shermans' 75-mm guns. The Americans tried to counterattack but it was suicidal. In one battalion, the 2nd of the 1st Armored Regiment, only four tanks of fifty survived a battle at Sidi Bou Zid. Scores of Americans were killed and hundreds captured. They were no match for the battle-hardened Afrika Korps and the Tigers.

AP's Hal Boyle, a Pulitzer Prize-winning war correspondent, at the front.

The Germans, supported by dive bombers, broke through the rugged Kasserine Pass on February 20 and, with the Desert Fox himself leading the advancing columns, headed northwest and north toward the towns of Tebessa and Thala. A successful drive to the coast might have cut the Allied army in two.

But Allied reinforcements finally began to arrive. South of Thala, as retreating troops and vehicles streamed past, artillery of the U.S. 9th Infantry Division took up defensive positions with British infantrymen, after a four-day forced drive of 777 miles across the Algerian desert. The panzers and German infantry were just 2,500 yards away when the Americans lowered their 105-mm howitzers to almost flat trajectories and fired, opening a day-long duel with the German tankers and their 88s, a battle that ended with a German withdrawal. At

Tebessa, too, the attack was stopped short. The Americans had found in their 105 an answer to Germany's excellent 88.

The Germans had not fully exploited the early rout at Faid and Kasserine, and Rommel now pulled back to better consolidate his overextended forces to face new pressure from Montgomery's 8th Army in the east.

Although the Allies held in the end, the initial Kasserine defeat shook British confidence in the fighting ability of the American forces.

But the Germans, after their first major encounter with the Americans, were impressed by one thing—the U.S. arsenal.

Rommel later commented that the Americans were "fantastically well equipped." German generals particularly admired the deuce-and-a-half, the two-and-one-half-ton trucks that by the hundreds rushed fresh units up to block the February advance.

In the east, Montgomery's sun-browned Desert Rats had chased the Afrika Korps and its Italian allies 1,400 miles westward across the sands since October 1942 and El Alamein, sometimes advancing forty miles a day. On January 23, they rolled into Tripoli, capital of Italian Libya, finally crushing Mussolini's dream of a new Roman Empire.

Monty and his troops were supported by U.S. air squadrons and by a mechanized column of Free French forces, under General Jacques Leclerc, that had trekked 1,700 miles northward across the Sahara from Chad, knocking out Italian positions in Libya along the way. By February 18, as the Kasserine battles raged, Rommel's easternmost units had pulled back to the French-built Mareth Line, a defensive complex just inside the Tunisian border stretching southward twenty-two miles from the Mediterranean coast.

After Kasserine, the two sides settled into weeks of reorganization. More trucks and planes poured in from America. Allied airfields were built in days. U.S. Army engineers tripled the capacity of the decrepit old French railroad that led to the front, transforming it into a system that could carry 3,000 tons of supplies a day.

Eisenhower, meanwhile, ordered the discredited Fredendall back to a training command in the States and put Patton in command of II Corps. A new offensive was planned, and on March 15 Blood and Guts called together his division commanders.

"Gentlemen, tomorrow we attack," Patton told them. "If we are not victorious, let no one come back alive."

Traveling in nighttime truck convoys to avoid the strafing German Messerschmitts of daylight, the Americans made steady progress eastward. Mont-

Field Marshal Rommel (l.) *began to think Hitler was the enemy for not reinforcing his African forces.*

Fuehrer congratulates Rommel for desert victories.

gomery, who with a tipoff from British intelligence, had repulsed a major Rommel counterattack on March 6, opened an all-out assault on the Mareth Line on March 21. By then Rommel, his health weakened, had again flown back to Germany, never to return to the desert.

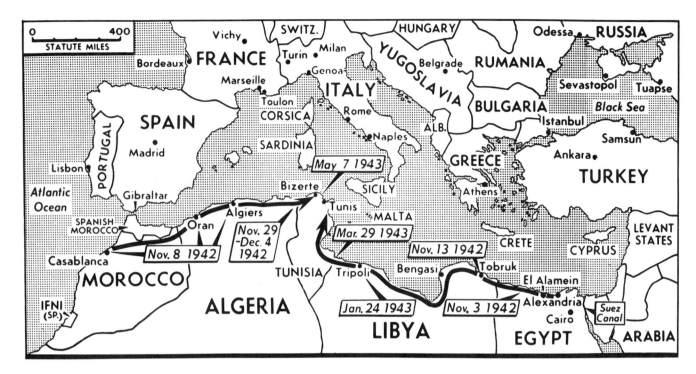

In the long road across Africa the GIs and their generals began to master their trade.

Advancing in a two-pronged attack through the khamsin, the searing African wind that stirred up sandstorms, the 8th Army pushed the Afrika Korps northward toward a pocket in the northeastern corner of Tunisia, and linked up at last with the Allied forces driving in from the west.

American B-25 bombers, their noses painted with the white silhouettes of 500-pounders betokening their growing number of missions, battered the German and Italian troops day after day. The buildup, which put lightning-swift P-38 fighters—Fork-Tailed Devils, the Germans called them—in the Tunisian skies, had given the Americans clear air superiority. At one German airfield, patrolling American fighters kept every German plane from taking off one afternoon.

And again, as throughout the North African campaign, British submarines, Spitfires and destroyers based in Malta had turned Axis efforts to ferry supplies across the Mediterranean into a deadly gamble, one the German and Italian ships often lost.

The American troops, driving down from the mountains past sweet-scented almond trees and brilliant red poppy fields, could smell victory. But the fighting was fierce.

Much of it was done at night, by infantrymen slithering in single file along hillside goat paths, on guard for German machine gun nests and land mines, especially the dreaded "bouncing Bettys," which sprang three feet into the air when stepped on and exploded in a hail of shrapnel.

For the 1st and 34th Infantry Divisions and the 1st Armored Division, Tunisia was a battleground

without let-up in those April days. The men slept on the ground and ate only cold canned rations. The tankers spent hours inside their buttoned-up machines, where the daytime temperature would cook up to 130 degrees.

Men of once-victorious Afrika Korps were only too glad to step forward in surrender as Allies brought Tunisian campaign to climax.

The Germans fought desperately from hill to hill. Relentless American artillery fire chewed up enemy positions on the reverse slopes, and American infantry would then sweep around the flanks. But the fighting was often hand-to-hand.

The AP's Boyle reported finding a private from Brooklyn suffering from hysterical paralysis of his right arm. He had bayoneted two Germans. "One of the men fell in the mud and cried in German for his mother," the soldier recounted. He hated killing so much his arm would no longer work.

The final push came in the last week of April. The 8th Army had been stopped by strong German defenses along the eastern Tunisian coast. Eisenhower and his chief deputy, British General Sir Harold R.L.G. Alexander, realizing that German commander Juergen von Arnim would expect the knockout punch to be delivered by Montgomery, concentrated forces instead in the northwest.

The job fell to the British 1st Army and to the U.S. II Corps, now under the command of Eisenhower's old friend Major General Omar N. Bradley, "the soldier's general." Patton had been assigned to plan the invasion of Sicily.

In a crucial action, the 34th Division captured a formidable German position, Hill 609, that blocked the Allied path. This, Eisenhower later wrote, "was final proof that the American ground forces had come fully of age."

Emerging at last from the hills, dirty, tired, unshaven, the Allied troops now dashed across the Tunisian plain and captured the two key port cities the same afternoon, May 7. Anderson's 1st Army rolled into Tunis at 3:40 p.m., and II Corps elements were in Bizerte at 4:15. On May 12, the last Axis forces in Africa surrendered.

Von Arnim and 240,000 Axis prisoners, half German, half Italian, were marched into captivity, choking the roads of Tunisia. The Axis had suffered more than 340,000 men killed, wounded or cap-

Italians began deserting Rommel's Afrika Korps in droves to surrender to Allies.

After the uprising of Jews in the Warsaw ghetto nothing remained but rubble.

tured in the Tunisian campaign, compared with 70,000 Allied casualties.

But beyond that, the overwhelming victory in their first campaign against the mighty Wehrmacht boosted the Americans' morale and steeled their fighting spirit.

Eisenhower's aides suggested that he receive the defeated Von Arnim in the time-honored custom of military leaders. But the Allied general refused.

He later wrote: "The forces that stood for human good and men's rights were this time confronted by a completely evil conspiracy with which no compromise could be tolerated. . . . The war became for me a crusade."

But for many in Europe, the crusade would arrive too late.

Four days after the surrender in Africa, the German SS commander in Poland's capital city reported that "the former Jewish quarter of Warsaw is no longer in existence."

For four weeks, the remaining 60,000 Jews of the Warsaw Ghetto, those not already shipped to the Nazi death camps, had struggled with pistols, rifles, machine guns and Molotov cocktails against a Nazi army sweep. The SS finally set the tiny district ablaze, block by block. Many Jews chose to die in the flames rather than be captured.

The Anglo-American nutcracker took 240,000 prisoners in Tunisia, more than surrendered at Stalingrad.

7 HOME FRONT: CRIMPED LIFESTYLE

The worst single violation of the civil rights of Americans began shortly after dawn on March 23, 1942, as soldiers of the U.S. Army fanned out across peaceful Bainbridge Island in Puget Sound. They posted copies of Civilian Order No. 1, which informed the island's 272 residents "of Japanese ancestry" that they had a week to turn themselves in at the local civilian defense station. So began the mass incarceration, on false evidence and racial grounds, of more than 120,000 West Coast Japanese-Americans—two-thirds of them U.S. citizens.

When the shock of Pearl Harbor wore off, and the war continued to go poorly, the search for a scapegoat began. The West Coast was wild with rumors of Japanese saboteurs and spies, of "arrows" cut in fields and forests that pointed toward military targets, of a Japanese "fifth column" in Hawaii.

The FBI investigated the reports thoroughly and found no evidence to support them. No West Coast Japanese was ever charged with sabotage. But that hardly mattered.

As Lieutenant General John DeWitt, head of the Western Defense Command, put it: "A Jap is a Jap. . . . It makes no difference whether he is an American citizen or not. . . . I don't want any of them. . . . There is no way to determine their loyalty." To skeptics, he offered this logic: "The very fact that no sabotage has taken place to date is a disturbing and confirming indication that such action will be taken."

Wartime paranoia made pariahs of Japanese-Americans, but prejudice against Asians in the West dated back a century. After a 1924 law barred Japanese immigrants from becoming citizens, many withdrew into their own community and culture. Meanwhile, their agricultural success aroused the envy of their white competitors. DeWitt could report accurately to Washington that action against the Japanese was supported not only by know-nothings, "but by the best people of California."

The best people of California: the governor, Culbert Olson, who reported as fact unsubstantiated allegations of subversive activity; state Attorney General Earl Warren, who echoed DeWitt, calling the absence of sabotage "the most ominous sign in our whole situation;" the editorialist of *The Los Angeles Times* who wrote of Japanese-Americans born in the United States, "A viper is nonetheless a viper wherever the egg is hatched. . . .''; and *San*

Francisco Examiner columnist Henry McLemore, who urged the Army to "Herd 'em up, pack 'em off. Let 'em be pinched, hurt, hungry and dead up against it."

The best people of America took up the cry. "Their racial characteristics are such that we cannot understand or trust even the citizen Japanese," said Henry Stimson, a distinguished lawyer before becoming Secretary of War. Columnist Walter Lippmann, probably the nation's most respected journalist, wrote that since the West Coast was a potential battlefield, like the deck of a warship, "everyone should be compelled to prove that he has a good reason for being there." There was no civil liberties problem, he added, since "under this system all persons are, in principle, treated alike," including Americans of German and Italian ancestry. This argument, which Lippmann biographer Ronald Steel has termed "a deft bit of sophistry," ignored the fact that the order was applied only to the Japanese and that no one was given the chance to show "a good reason for being there."

Attorney General Francis Biddle's mail ran four-to-one in favor of evicting the Japanese. In Congress, Senator Robert Taft, a conservative, was the only one to speak against legislation supporting evacuation. On February 19, 1942, Roosevelt signed Executive Order 9066, which authorized commanders to "prescribe military areas . . . from which any or all persons shall be excluded."

Japanese-Americans, two-thirds of them citizens, being interned at Manzanar, California.

At first there was no plan for internment, only evacuation. In early March thousands of Japanese, many fearful for their safety, pulled up stakes and headed east. Their reception proved that prejudice did not stop at the Sierra Nevada or the Cascades. The governor of Arizona said his state was not going to be "a dumping ground for enemy aliens" and recommended placing them in "concentration camps." The governor of Idaho said, "The Japs live like rats, breed like rats, and act like rats. We don't want them." Neither did anyone else. When five Japanese who had fled the West Coast were hired by a farmer in New Jersey, vigilantes set the man's barn afire and threatened to kill his youngest child.

The Japanese had nowhere to hide. The man charged with relocating them, Milton Eisenhower, Ike's brother, later told Roosevelt the Japanese had been put in camps because no one would take them. "Voluntary evacuation was not a feasible solution," he wrote. "Public opinion . . . was bitterly antagonistic to the influx of Japanese."

The "feasible solution"—internment—had, as a War Department report blandly observed, "no precedents . . . in American life." There was no mention of German life, and no attempt to distinguish between the loyal and disloyal, the dangerous and the harmless.

Harry Sumida, seventy, was a veteran who had been wounded during the Battle of Santiago Bay in the Spanish-American War. He was moved from a sanitarium in Los Angeles, where he had been pensioned by the Navy, to an internment camp hospital. Also caught in the net was ten-year-old Norman Mineta, a future California congressman, whose family was taken from their San Jose home at gunpoint. Meanwhile, Japanese-Americans in Hawaii—far more influential than their mainland counterparts—were left alone.

The West Coast Japanese were told to take only what they could carry, but no pets, liquor or razor blades. Nothing could be shipped ahead. They were given anything from a few days to a few weeks to turn themselves in. People sold their land, their businesses and their possessions at ridiculously low prices. One man said: "It is difficult to describe the feeling of despair and humiliation experienced by all of us as we watched the Caucasians coming to look over our possessions and offering such amounts, knowing we had no recourse but to accept whatever they were offering because we did not know what the future held for us."

In all, a government commission later estimated, the Japanese lost property worth between $810 million and $2 billion in 1982 dollars.

First the Japanese were taken to interim holding facilities, such as the Rose Bowl and the Santa Anita race track. Some families at the latter slept in

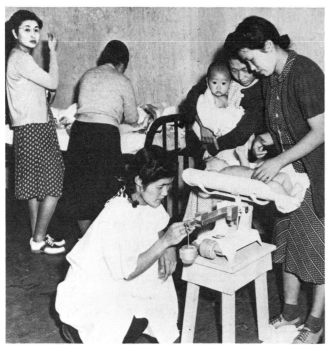

Baby clinic at the internment center for Japanese-Americans at Santa Anita race track.

white-washed horse stalls and bathed in former horse showers. Yuriko Hohri was twelve then; years later she would remember filling a bag with straw to sleep on the asphalt floor, and shudder at the thought of the huge cockroaches. She also kept the document with the details of her internment. "Keep Freedom in Your Future with U.S. Savings Bonds" was printed at the bottom.

Next, the prisoners were taken to ten camps located in five Western states and Arkansas that had been established by a new agency, the War Relocation Authority. Roosevelt once referred to them as "concentration camps," which was accurate. Located for the most part on unused federal land in barren, arid areas—some of the worst land in the nation—the camps were surrounded by barbed wire. Armed guards stood in watchtowers. At night, searchlights swept across the camps.

The prisoners lived in tarpaper-covered wooden barracks broken into twenty-by-twenty-five foot rooms for families or groups. The barracks had oil-burning furnaces and bare light bulbs hanging from the ceiling, but no stoves or running water. There were communal toilets and eating facilities. Japanese women sometimes had to bathe in full view of sentries.

The barracks were only slightly more comfortable than tents. Army regulations listed such buildings as suitable housing only temporarily, and only for combat-trained troops, let alone civilians of all ages and sexes for a period up to four years. The prisoners froze in winter, when the wind whipped them with snow, and sweltered in summer, when

the snow was replaced by dust. Temperature extremes ranged from 130 degrees at the camp at Poston, Arizona, to minus-30 at Heart Mountain, Wyoming, where inmates had to bank the earth against the barracks walls as a windbreak.

Life was hard, but it went on to the rhythm of 2,120 marriages, 5,981 baptisms and 1,862 funerals. At Camp Manzanar, in the desert of east-central California, there were neither funds nor materials for individual tombstones; instead, a single white obelisk was built with Japanese characters that said "Memorial to the Dead."

Manzanar's prisoners established a cooperative store and a newspaper, and built a stage, a baseball field and a Japanese "pleasure garden" around a little creek that ran through the middle of the camp. They elected block leaders and formed a system for arbitrating disputes. There was even a branch of the Bank of America.

Camp life had many of the trappings of small town America. Prisoners assembled each morning to raise the Stars and Stripes while the Boy Scout drum and bugle corps played the national anthem. On July 4, 1942, Manzanar celebrated Independence Day with public ceremonies, band concerts, picnics, a baseball game, a beauty contest and no apparent sense of irony.

Plans to make all the camps economically self-sufficient failed because of climate and isolation. Manzanar, however, grew enough to feed itself and ship surplus food to other camps. "From the harsh soil they have extracted fine crops," wrote photographer Ansel Adams, who visited the camp in 1943. "They have made gardens glow in the firebreaks and between the barracks." Meanwhile, California suffered a vegetable shortage: Japanese farmers had produced a third of the state's crops, and the government was spending millions to subsidize the less efficient operators who took over their land.

But Manzanar was no paradise. A riot erupted in December 1942, after a prisoner was arrested for beating up a suspected informer. When a large crowd demanded his release and taunted soldiers, two Japanese youths were shot to death. Similar incidents occurred at the camp at Tule Lake, California, part of which was reserved for those suspected of disloyalty. There, poor food, crowded barracks and petty authority prompted a series of increasingly vehement protests. Some inmates even adopted traditional Japanese warrior manners and dress. Eventually several thousand Japanese, some of whom renounced their American citizenship, were allowed to leave the camps and go to Japan.

No matter how well the Japanese coped, the fact remained they were prisoners in their own land.

The War Relocation Authority's intentions were good, but, as historian John Morton Blum has concluded, "a principled internment . . . was no more possible than a principled genocide."

Even so, the camps were periodically criticized for coddling their inmates. Senator E.V. Robertson of Wyoming rose in the Senate to deplore the "pampering" of Japanese at Heart Mountain, and later hinted that all Japanese-Americans should be deported to Japan after the war, including citizens.

In January 1943, the Army announced it would accept U.S. citizens of Japanese descent as volunteers if they renounced the emperor. Thousands took the loyalty oath behind barbed wire and went off to fight; others were drafted. They joined the combined 100th Infantry and the 442nd Infantry. The unit's casualty toll was more than twice its official strength of 4,000, and its members were awarded almost 10,000 Purple Hearts. Man for man, no American fighting unit in any war suffered more casualties or earned more honors.

Where was Roosevelt? When he agreed to the evacuation, the president urged it be handled as humanely as possible. After that, it appears he forgot about his prisoners. When Interior Secretary Ickes wrote to complain about camp conditions in April 1943, FDR referred the letter to Milton Eisenhower for a reply—apparently unaware Eisenhower had resigned his relocation-authority post nine months earlier.

And what of the Supreme Court? Evacuation of civilians during war clearly was a military prerogative, but could it be limited to a specific ethnic group? Twice the court said yes. In the case of a University of Washington student who refused to obey a curfew for Japanese-Americans that predated the evacuation order, the court unanimously ruled that the military acted legally, saying that

Japanese-Americans could still smile in California internment camp, even pin up MacArthur on wall.

"residents having ethnic affiliations with an invading army may be a greater source of danger than those of different ancestry." The military did not have to prove a danger, or explore alternatives.

Behind the facade of unanimity was bitter division, however. Justice Frank Murphy drafted and circulated a dissent that said the treatment of Japanese-Americans in this country bore "a melancholy resemblance" to that of Jews in Germany. But he was persuaded by Justice Felix Frankfurter to vote with the majority so the court could show a solid front.

In December 1944, the court specifically upheld the exclusion of Japanese-Americans from the West Coast as a reasonable military precaution. This time Murphy dissented, however, labeling the majority's decision "a legalization of racism." He was joined by Justice Robert Jackson, who called the ruling "a loaded gun."

On that same day the court handed the Japanese their only legal victory, ruling that although the government might exclude citizens from a war zone, it could not detain them after they had been ascertained to be loyal. Accordingly, the court ordered the release of Mitsuye Endo—two-and-a-half years after she had filed a petition of habeas corpus.

In fact, a day earlier the government had revoked its order banning Japanese-Americans from the West Coast. The prisoners were told they could return home; the threat of invasion was long past and the election was over. Each was given $25 and train fare.

Many who went back learned that goods they stored had been stolen or illegally sold; mortgages had been foreclosed; land had been sold to pay taxes; cars had been requisitioned by the government. Tetsu Saito's family had stored sixty-four crates of possessions and six trucks, all of which vanished. Yoshio Ekimoto found his forty-acre farm in northern Los Angeles County mortgaged to the limit, and he had to sell. Although he kept a list of all the personal property he lost while interned, the government paid him only $692 against a claim of $23,824. In all, the Japanese submitted $148 million in property claims and received $37 million. In 1988, Congress apologized for internment and agreed to pay $20,000 to every camp survivor.

Eventually about three-quarters of the prisoners, or 90,000 people, returned to the West Coast. Despite a severe labor shortage, many establishments posted signs saying "NO JAPS WANTED." In Oregon, the Hood River American Legion Post removed from its rolls the names of all local Japanese-Americans who had fought in the war. By New Year's Day, about sixty attacks against returning Japanese had been reported.

Rationing

The day after Pearl Harbor, a housewife was spotted at the market with a mountain of canned goods in her shopping cart. "Just stocking up before the hoarders get here," she explained.

It had been clear for two years that war would mean shortages or inflation or both. The government was pumping money into the economy at the same time that raw materials and manufactured goods were being diverted to the military, so more dollars were chasing fewer products. Gas and sugar became scarce in some areas in the summer of 1941. Some merchants had imposed their own makeshift rationing systems, and a few even printed ration cards.

A way had to be found to allocate scarce goods and fight inflation. But the government had been as slow to prepare the consumer economy for war as it had been to mobilize industry. The Office of Price Administration was created in April 1941, but lacked the power to hold down price and wage increases.

To deal with the emergency, Roosevelt settled on two schemes far more radical than any component of the New Deal: rationing, to distribute hard-to-get items fairly, and price controls, to resist the inflationary spiral. Ideally, price controls ensured that scarce goods would not go to the highest bidder; rationing ensured they would not go to those with a friend in the butcher shop, the time to stand in line or enough cash for hoarding.

Rationing was foreign to America except for a brief experiment in World War I. "No form of regulation," historian Richard Polenberg has written, "conflicted more sharply with traditional American values." Poor amidst plenty during the Depression, Americans now had plenty of money but little to buy.

The War Price and Rationing Program was only slightly less popular than Hitler, and the thankless task of administering it fell to the Office of Price Administration (OPA). As price controller, the agency set prices on, and standards for, thousands of products. As rationer, it supervised the printing and distribution of stickers, cards, stamps and certificates that entitled every American to a certain ration of about twenty essential items. Retailers usually had to report their inventories at the beginning of a rationing program, and pass along ration coupons they collected from their customers in order to get new supplies. As coupons moved up the production-distribution pyramid, goods moved down. As many as 3 billion coupons a month changed hands.

Although OPA's 60,000 employees issued reams of rules and regulations—including prices for 1,800 oils and fats—the price and rationing system was essentially an adventure in administration by amateurs. A network of thousands of local boards was staffed by hundreds of thousands of regular volunteers who held hearings and meetings in post office lobbies, schoolrooms, country stores and courthouses, guided only by OPA regulations and their own sense of equity. When the paperwork became too overwhelming, some boards stacked forms and instruction sheets in the corner and forgot about them. When rules conflicted with reason, boards often came down on the side of fair play. In one small Western town, for example, the parents of a crippled child were caught with a set of worn-out tires when rationing began. There was no bus service, and they could not afford to take the child to school in a taxi. Legally, the local board could not allow them to buy new tires, but it did anyway.

Although the local rationing board was an expression of popular sentiment, the OPA in Washington was a popular target. The personification of the new bureaucratic power, and the object of much of the resentment against it, was Leon Henderson, the brilliant, arrogant, cigar-chomping economist who headed OPA. Henderson under-

New York couple learn about rationing and how to do without coffee and sugar.

stood the value of public relations: he was photographed riding to work on a bicycle, his secretary in a basket on the handlebars, and he applied for the lowest gas ration. But he predicted at the outset that he would become the most unpopular man in America, and, as usual, he was right. By the time Henderson resigned at the end of 1942, he was one of Roosevelt's biggest political liabilities.

Rationing began shortly after Pearl Harbor when Roosevelt froze sales of cars and tires, which were doled out to physicians and other civilians with essential tasks. OPA made its first hard choices: trucks that delivered bee hives could get new tires; those that delivered beer could not. Police departments could buy cars only if their old ones were at least five years old and had 100,000 miles on them. Even then, the cops had to take what they were given. One state highway patrol got stylish Chrysler Town and Country models, including wood-paneled coupes and convertibles.

Rationing began in earnest May 4, 1942, with the issuance of 131 million copies of War Ration Book No. 1—the sugar book, filled with a year's supply of ration coupons, each about half the size of a postage stamp. More than 100,000 volunteers, many of them teachers, distributed the books at schools across the nation. Nine out of ten Americans showed up to collect, although many were confused by the forms and nervous about having to declare the amount of sugar they had at home. (A New Jersey man was later found to have a 557-year supply.) Rationing, worried one observer, was liable to induce mass perjury.

There was the usual assortment of crackpots and characters, including a farmer who demanded a ration book for a mule who supposedly would not work unless rewarded with sugar. Some people saw humor in their predicament. There was the joke about the burglar who stuck his hand into the cookie jar and complained, "Nothing here but money." Columnist Walter Winchell was moved to verse: "Roses are red, violets are blue. Sugar is sweet . . . remember?"

Gasoline virtually disappeared from the East Coast in the summer of 1942. Many truckers and some motorists were stranded, and tanker-trailers bringing new deliveries to gas stations attracted lines of drivers who hoped to fill up so they could follow more trucks to more gas stations. The Labor Day weekend highway death toll was 169 compared to 423 a year earlier. "You could have fired a bazooka down any Main Street in the country without hitting a vehicle," according to the writer Paul Gallico.

Although many of his advisers felt national gasoline rationing was inevitable, FDR knew how unpopular it would be with 30 million car owners.

Even Fala's doggy bags were rationed.

So, early in 1942, he appointed a commission headed by financier Bernard Baruch to study the problem. In September the commission called for gas rationing to save rubber, and in December—after the congressional elections—FDR imposed it, along with a ban on recapping tires, a national speed limit of 35 mph and a prohibition on pleasure driving.

Under gas rationing, each driver received a windshield sticker. "A" drivers, which included roughly half the motoring public, had no essential driving to do and could only purchase about three gallons a week. "B" drivers had some essential driving to do (such as commuting to a war production job) and "C" drivers used their cars to perform essential jobs.

The ban on pleasure driving extended even to "A" card holders, who had assumed they'd be able to use their paltry three gallons however they wanted. It was one of the most sweeping orders ever issued by the U.S. government, and one of the least enforceable. But until it was revoked nine months later, the OPA tried. Agents began hanging around horse race tracks, ballparks and nightclubs, taking down license plate numbers. In Rochester,

Restaurants turned vegetarian twice a week (fish excepted) to help cut meat consumption 21 percent.

Joy riding was over as 100,000 service stations on East Coast shut down at night to save gas.

New York, motorists who drove to a symphony concert had their ration cards taken away.

Other rationing programs limited Americans to less than a cup of coffee a day, three pairs of shoes a year, and enough fuel oil to keep a home at 65 degrees. The Philadelphia rationing office was forced to close because it forgot to authorize a fuel oil ration for itself.

Meat began to disappear in late 1942, because the military and Lend Lease were taking a fourth of the nation's production. Soon there wasn't even hamburger in the East. Shoppers trudged from market to market, lucky and happy if they could find frankfurters—which were being stretched with various fillers. In most large cities, Tuesday and Friday were meatless days. One restaurant menu listed ox tongues, ox tails, and "nothing in between."

Meat rationing, imposed in March 1943, was the last major rationing program, and the least popular. Civilian meat demand was estimated at 164 pounds per person a year; rationing allowed 140, or about two-and-a-half pounds a week.

Rationing became more complicated with the issuance of War Ration Book No. 2, which contained blue stamps for processed food and red ones for meat, cheese and fats. Before, rationing had been on a single-item basis. Now different values were assigned to different products; the rarer the product, the more points it cost.

Shoppers had to keep an eye on two prices, one in dollars, the other in ration points. Not only did the OPA keep changing point values as items became more or less scarce, but the stamps had expiration dates. Shoppers followed both in the newspaper like stock prices or baseball standings.

In attempting to fix meat prices the OPA met its regulatory Waterloo. OPA assigned different point values to various cuts of meat, but butchers could evade the price controls by upgrading poorer cuts of meat and selling them at higher prices, or by simply selling meat with excess fat or bone. So OPA decided to precisely define each cut, down to the last incision—it decided to tell butchers how to cut meat.

Eventually many of the rules were rescinded.

Price control gave rise to other follies. Agriculture Secretary Claude Wickard briefly banned sales of sliced bread to hold down prices, outraging housewives and giving birth to the expression "The greatest thing since sliced bread."

Like rationing, price control started slowly. At first, the agency tried to fix prices piecemeal, imposing a ceiling when it seemed the price of a commodity was beginning to shoot up. The attack on inflation was not expanded and systematized until the end of April 1942, when the General Maximum Price Regulation was issued. "General Max," as the regulation came to be known, froze most manufacturing, wholesale and retail prices.

But General Max did not control wages or farm prices. When food costs rose, workers demanded higher wages, and the inflationary spiral ascended. Finally, in April 1943, Roosevelt issued a "hold the line" order freezing wages, prices and salaries, and followed up with a campaign to roll back food prices. Prices remained fairly stable during the rest of the war.

The OPA did not have the staff to enforce its own rules, so it relied to a large extent on Americans' honesty—and their guilt.

Fortunately for the OPA, most big retailers were relatively conservative, law-abiding and public-relations conscious. If they broke the rules, they usually did not do so routinely or blatantly. And the agency found that if it kept the big operators in line, inflation remained under control.

The OPA itself had only 3,100 investigators, one for about every 1,000 businesses. Even when it had the evidence, the agency lacked the resources to prosecute most violators; usually it had to be content with a court injunction. Fewer than 2 percent of OPA criminal cases resulted in a prison sentence. One merchant convicted of overcharging $400,000 was fined $30,000.

When both buyer and seller wanted to break the price and rationing law, there was virtually nothing the OPA could do. If you wanted a pair of $5 shoes but didn't have the necessary coupons, you could often get them anyway by paying a couple of extra bucks. Between 20 and 25 percent of Americans told pollsters that sometimes this sort of transaction was OK—in other words, sometimes the black market was OK.

The black market was as American during World War II as Rosie the Riveter and Victory gardens. A black market transaction was any one in which the price was over the official ceiling, or in which required ration coupons did not change hands. The black market was the neighborhood butcher shop and the corner gas station. "Mr. Black" was the bellboy who could supply cigarettes; the landlord who required a side payment to rent an apartment; the criminal who dealt stolen or counterfeit ration coupons. There was a black market in everything from grand pianos to penny candy.

A study found that one in fifteen businesses was charged with illegal transactions during the war,

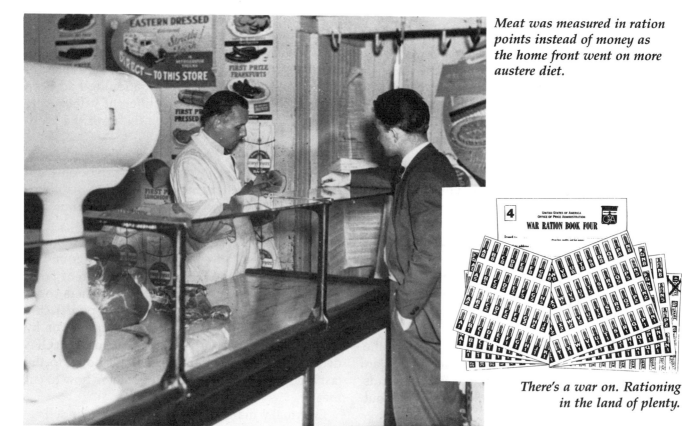

Meat was measured in ration points instead of money as the home front went on more austere diet.

There's a war on. Rationing in the land of plenty.

and one in five received a warning. An OPA probe of 1,000 sugar wholesalers found that about three-fourths were violating price regulations. By the summer of 1944, 1,300 people had been convicted of black marketeering in gasoline; 4,000 gas stations had lost their licenses; and 32,500 motorists had ration books revoked for using counterfeit or stolen coupons. As many as a quarter of all sales may have violated OPA regulations.

Given the lack of enforcement, black marketeers didn't have to be excessively crafty. Many meat wholesalers simply ignored rationing; a newspaper reporter doing a story on the black market was able to buy a ton of meat with $2,000—and not one coupon. Unlicensed or uninspected slaughterhouses increased their business after rationing began, and many farmers slaughtered their own beef and sold it at illicit prices. As much as a fifth of all meat may have been sold on the black market; after the military took its cut, there wasn't much left for the law-abiding meat eater.

For gangsters, the war offered some of the most lucrative opportunities since Prohibition. They printed vast numbers of counterfeit gas coupons and sold them for up to 50 cents each to motorists or gas station owners, who used them to cover up sales at illegally high prices. In 1944, a racketeer was found with counterfeit coupons worth 38,000 gallons of gas and 437 pairs of shoes. Some criminals simply stole coupons, and OPA was the logical place to start. Burglars took gas coupons worth 5 million gallons from the Cleveland office, and ones worth four times as much from the Washington office.

Estimates of illegally purchased gasoline ranged as high as 2.5 million gallons a day. About 15 percent of "C" cards were fakes, although the ratio was twice as high in some big cities, including Chicago, Baltimore and Newark.

After the completion of the government's anti-inflationary arsenal in mid-1943, prices advanced less than 2 percent during the next two years. In World War I, prices had risen 62 percent between 1914 and 1918, and doubled between 1914 and 1920; this time prices rose only about 30 percent, even though the government was spending five times as much as it had during the first war. Historian Arthur M. Schlesinger, Jr., has called OPA "one of the war's brilliant successes," and some economists took its performance as evidence that wage and price controls could work in peacetime.

Consumers sacrificed but rarely suffered; they did not even feel the pinch on most goods until well into 1943. They drove a third fewer miles in 1943 than 1941. They consumed about 70 percent as much sugar as before the war, and half as much tea. Butter consumption dropped from seventeen pounds a person a year in the late 1930s to eleven pounds a year during the war.

In his study of home front life, *Don't You Know There's a War On?*, Richard R. Lingeman described the price and rationing system as a hastily-erected, temporary dam. Though riddled with leaks, it held. Americans, he concluded, "grumbled, connived, sacrificed and, for the most part, complied."

Life at Home

On the first Christmas Eve of the war, President Roosevelt went to the South Lawn of the White House to light the national Christmas tree. This year, he told the audience, he had a special guest—Winston Churchill.

The British prime minister spoke to the crowd about Christmas, but his words would describe the home front that was taking shape in the land of his mother's birth: "Here, in the midst of war, raging and roaring over all the lands and seas, creeping near to our hearts and our homes, here, amid all the tumult, we have tonight the peace of the spirit in each cottage home and in each generous heart . . . happiness in a world of storm."

World War II was a plague on almost every nation that fought it. But for Americans it was

Wartime spending by U.S. kayoed the Depression.

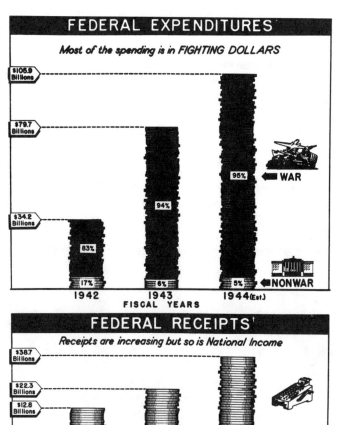

much more complex: people earned more than ever, but were also taxed more than ever. The government controlled everything from war news to skirt lengths, but many of its citizens enjoyed unprecedented personal freedom. U.S. soldiers died in Pacific heat and European mud, but their relatives back home were relatively comfortable.

When the war began, Harry Hopkins feared that the conflict's demands for manpower and material would drive the nation's standard of living below the depths reached even during the Great Depression. Instead of deepening the Depression, however, the war ended it. What the New Deal had done with a cup was now being done with a bucket: the government was spending about $300 million a day. The war validated Keynes' theory that government spending could prevent a depression, and that economies did not have to endure the cyclical extremes of boom and bust. Even full employment now seemed possible.

Starting virtually from scratch, America built an army and a navy to fight two mighty empires, spent $2 billion to develop the atomic bomb, and held consumer production steady. Civilians spent a fifth more than they had before the war, and the average factory worker's weekly pay almost doubled. Observed one: "It's a pretty good war if you don't get shot at."

Even the poor got richer. While income among the top fifth of wage earners increased 20 percent, it soared by almost 70 percent among the bottom fifth. And the wealth was more evenly distributed. In the five years after 1939, the share of national wealth held by the richest 5 percent of the population declined from 24 percent to 17 percent. The Women's Christian Temperance Union in Illinois could not find a single family in need of a Christmas basket in 1943.

A nation supposedly stripped down for the supreme sacrifice of war instead seemed to be reliving the Jazz Age. Hotels, restaurants and nightclubs were jammed. Jewelry sales rose 12 percent in 1942. On December 7, 1944, Macy's reported its busiest day ever. "You just bought everything," recalled one war worker. "You'd make more in a day than you had in a week." She and others like her were commemorated in a song: "Minnie's in the Money." Since there was a shortage of things to buy, services boomed, particularly those that catered to soldiers, including tattoo parlors and brothels. Sales of greeting cards and prophylactics also soared.

As women went to work, factories became social centers. Swing shift workers would finish up, change clothes and head out at midnight for dancing, bowling or carousing. North American Aircraft even had its own dating service.

"There is not a class or a group in this country which has not benefited by the war, which is not eating better—yes, eating better—and living better than it did before," I.F. Stone wrote in the *Nation*. Of all the world's home fronts, he added, America's "has suffered least and benefited most, and occupies the softest spot in the greatest war of human history."

Since there were never enough goods and services to accommodate the booming demand, the spending spree was necessarily complemented by a saving spree: personal savings rose from $6 billion in 1939 to $39 billion in 1944.

The foundation of what economist John Kenneth Galbraith would call "the affluent society" was laid between 1939 and 1945, when the gross national product—the total value of all the goods made and services rendered by the people of the United States—rose from $90 billion to $215 billion. In

Despite the war, U.S. income soared to record levels. So did taxes.

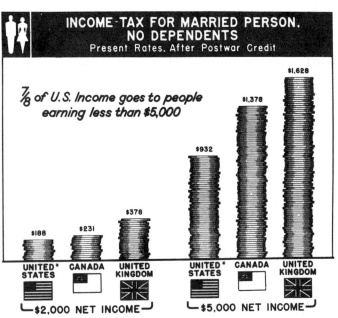

INCOME-TAX FOR MARRIED PERSON, NO DEPENDENTS
Present Rates, After Postwar Credit

⅞ of U.S. Income goes to people earning less than $5,000

$188 $231 $378 $932 $1,378 $1,628

UNITED STATES*   CANADA   UNITED KINGDOM   UNITED STATES*   CANADA   UNITED KINGDOM

└─$2,000 NET INCOME─┘   └─$5,000 NET INCOME─┘

* U.S. includes net victory tax and N.Y. State income tax

these years the economy's ability to produce goods increased about 50 percent. So rapid an increase had never been seen in a developing nation, let alone the most industrialized on the planet.

The war also foreshadowed what the new wealth might buy. Government scientists refined products such as television and air conditioning and something called a computer. A model introduced at the Massachusetts Institute of Technology in 1942 weighed 100 tons and had 2,000 electronic tubes, 150 electric motors and 200 miles of wire. And wartime shortages and restrictions gave rise to some products whose greatest days lay ahead, including plastics (to replace precious metals), frozen foods (to save trips to the store), and microfilm (to ship V-mail overseas).

If the war brought new affluence, though, it also required new taxes. In April 1942, Congress approved a law raising personal and corporate income taxes and levying a flat 5 percent tax on all income in excess of $624. In addition, FDR limited salaries to $25,000 net after taxes. By the end of the war, surtaxes were taking 94 percent of net income in the highest brackets.

"People at every level were paying taxes that would have seemed inconceivable a short time before," historian Schlesinger wrote. Many workers were paying income taxes for the first time. Before the war, between 3 million and 4 million Americans earned enough to pay the tax; by 1945, that number had grown to 50 million. In 1941, for example, a married man with two dependents paid no tax unless his income was $2,500; then he paid $6. If his income was $5,000 he still paid only $271. In 1943, however, he paid $179 on $2,500, and $773 on $5,000.

He paid, but he did not like it. Indeed, Congress did not approve the war tax for five months after Pearl Harbor because of political opposition to higher taxes. It didn't matter that U.S. taxes were far lower than those imposed on the citizens of any other belligerent. As historian John Morton Blum has noted, opposition to taxes showed "the degree to which World War II was a foreign war for Americans."

The ease of American life formed a surreal contrast to the hardship and danger almost everywhere else. "We live in the light, in relative comfort and complete security," said Edward R. Murrow, who knew firsthand the harrowing sacrifices of shell-shocked England. "We are not tired, as all Europe is tired."

By one estimate, World War II killed almost twice as many civilians as soldiers; civilian casualties outnumbered military casualties in Europe for the first time since the Thirty Years War. The fast-moving battlefront, a result of the development of

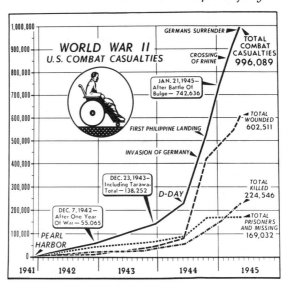

The war's cost in blood.

the tank and the dive bomber, condemned wide swaths of Europe to dust. In the western Soviet Union 6 million to 8 million civilians were killed, and the physical devastation was almost unimaginable. Seven million of the region's 12 million horses were killed or taken away, as were 20 million of its 23 million pigs. About half of all the homes in cities and towns were destroyed.

One of the thousands of victims was Belgorod, a city of 34,000 on the Black Sea when the Eastern Front moved through for the first time in October 1941. After it passed through the fourth time, in August 1943, only 140 residents were left. The rest were dead, conscripted, or refugees, and the city was ruins. Belgorod had no military importance, as journalist Gwynne Dyer has noted. It just got in the way.

The Asian home fronts were equally hellish. China was torn in half by Japan, and Japan itself was devastated by U.S. bombers.

American GIs died as well. Each day the battlefield casualty lists in the newspapers grew longer as the death toll mounted toward the final count of some 300,000 dead, nearly six times the number of American soldiers killed in World War I. Three hundred thousand wasn't a lot in a war which would kill an estimated 50 million people, but that didn't make it any easier. American boys were dying so fast that George Marshall had to abandon his practice of writing personally to the families of those killed in battle; now word was sent via Western Union.

"The class just ahead of me in college was virtually wiped out," novelist William Styron later recalled. "Beautiful fellows who had won basketball championships and Phi Beta Kappa keys died like ants in the Normandy invasion. Others only slightly older than I . . . stormed ashore at Tarawa and Iwo Jima and met ugly and horrible deaths on the hot coral and sands."

There were more mundane problems as well. All radio stations on the West Coast went off the air after dark, except for KIRO in Seattle. A ban on beach fires was enforced by mounted police, and bridges were patrolled by armed guards. Sentries killed one duck hunter and wounded another when their boat came too close to a Coast Guard cutter on Lake Michigan.

Even sports were devalued. About 4,000 of the nation's 5,700 pro baseball players went into the service, leaving the game to players with flat feet or punctured eardrums, as well as overage fathers, Latin Americans, old-timers, and Pete Gray.

Gray made the baseball St. Louis Browns in 1945 despite the fact he had one arm—his left. He played in seventy-seven games and batted only .218, but he was an excellent outfielder. He would catch the ball in the glove on his left hand, and toss the ball above his head while he tucked the glove under the stump of his right arm; then he would

Big leagues still played ball but war-thinned rosters made a starter of St. Louis Browns' one-armed outfielder Pete Gray.

grab the ball out of the air with his now bare hand and fire it to the infield.

The Cleveland Rams of the National Football League suspended operations after the team's owner and coach entered the service; the Philadelphia Eagles and the Pittsburgh Steelers combined to form one team, the Steagles. The already-legendary Bronko Nagurski emerged from a six-year retirement to lead the Chicago Bears to the championship in 1943.

Boxing was expected to suffer most from the war, because anyone able to fight presumably should have been doing so for his country. Most of the top boxers were in the service, but "promoters soon found that anyone who could lace on a boxing glove and climb into the ring under his own power would make an acceptable substitute," according to *New York Mirror* sports editor Dan Parker. After the War Department restricted soldiers' participation in pro bouts, boxing commissions created duration champions. The contenders included the lame, the halt, and Luther "Slugger" White. When the California commission examined White before a bout in 1945, it discovered he had a glass eye—and had passed several other inspections.

The 1942 Rose Bowl was moved from Pasadena, California, to Durham, North Carolina, where Oregon State beat Duke, 20-16. Travel restrictions made the 1944 game a strictly West Coast affair in which Southern Cal beat Washington, 29-0. Other wartime casualties included the Henley Regatta and the Indianapolis 500, a Memorial Day fixture since 1916.

Information and Propaganda

The government warned constantly of sabotage, espionage and air raids, but most Americans never learned about the only enemy attack that ever killed anyone on the mainland.

In late 1944, the increasingly desperate Japanese began lofting large paper balloons east across the Pacific. The balloons, 9,300 of which eventually were launched, carried thirty-pound bombs with timers. The strategy was to start fires in dry forests on the West Coast. Although one balloon made it as far east as Iowa, only about 300 reached land. Some bombs were spotted and defused before they went off, and others were duds. Some went off and started fires, but the forests were not dangerously dry.

One, however, landed on Mount Gearhart in Oregon, where the Reverend Archie Mitchell and his wife had taken five children from their parish on an outing in the summer of 1945. While the minister parked the car, his wife and the children searched for a campsite. They came on the bomb just as it exploded, killing all six.

It was a sensational story, but one almost no one ever heard. After a newspaper in Wyoming reported the discovery of a similar bomb there in 1944, the government had clamped a lid on the news to keep the Japanese in the dark. The full story was not told until years after the war.

The story of the intercontinental balloon bombs illustrates a basic fact of home front life: the government regulated information as surely as it regulated sugar and steel. Like everything else in the war, it began with Pearl Harbor.

Two days after the attack, Roosevelt met with three advisers to plan his first wartime fireside radio chat. The issue: how much to tell the national audience about U.S. losses. One aide argued that they should be revealed in grim detail, but Roosevelt sided with the others: if the Japanese did not know what they had wrought at Pearl Harbor, he didn't want to be the one to tell them. Instead, the president told the nation that although the losses were serious, he did not have enough information "to state the exact damage." Secretary of the Navy Frank Knox, meanwhile, misled reporters into thinking that five battleships which had been sunk or disabled at Pearl were at sea, seeking out the enemy.

The Japanese, as it turned out, knew the damage before Roosevelt did. It was in all the Tokyo papers. "Our people are the only ones who don't realize just what has happened," Agriculture Secretary Claude Wickard wrote in his diary. It was months before most Americans learned details of the battle; not until the war was over did the government release the names of the sunken battleships.

For better or worse, Roosevelt's decision on December 9 set a pattern for the rest of the war. The key test for releasing information was whether the enemy might profit; if so, it was withheld. Little or no attempt was made to measure how the truth might affect home front morale.

As a result, war news was often old news. Ships were sunk, battles won and lost, the course of the war changed, and it might be weeks or months before anyone on the home front was any wiser. The carrier *Langley* was lost in February 1942, but the Navy did not announce it until April; the sinking of the *Yorktown* at Midway in early June was not disclosed until mid-September. The war was a year old before casualty lists were printed, and not until 1943 did the military allow the release of pictures of American dead.

Often the truth was suppressed entirely. In 1943 the United States shot down the plane of Admiral

Isoroku Yamamoto, planner of the attack on Pearl Harbor. It was never disclosed for fear the Japanese might realize the Americans learned the plane's location because they had broken the Japanese code. When the atomic bomb was tested near Los Alamos, New Mexico, officials told local reporters it was an ammunition dump explosion; when the bomb was dropped on Hiroshima, no account of the destruction it had caused or the effects of radiation poisoning reached the public for almost a month.

The Navy was notoriously close-mouthed. Admiral King, chief of operations, may not have been joking when he said his idea of good wartime press relations was to call one news conference to announce the war had been won. Admiral Nimitz accurately called Midway "a stupendous naval victory." But because of the absence of U.S. reporters and the military's tendency to describe everything as a stupendous victory, it was months before the battle was recognized as a turning point in the war. George Marshall told King to call a news conference and give details, but the admiral never got around to it.

Some censorship was designed solely to bolster the armed services' image at home. Allied atrocities never were reported, and one of World War II's contributions to the art of warfare—the mass bombing of cities—was not adequately covered, either. Although Air Force communiques said American planes bombed only military objectives in Tokyo, and then with pinpoint accuracy, not indiscriminate fire bombings. Only after the fire bombing of Dresden in 1945 did Allied commanders in Europe admit they had decided to engage in "deliberate terror bombings of German population centers as a ruthless expedient of hastening Hitler's doom." In fact, such bombing by the British had been going on for three years.

Some of the Japanese balloon bombs reached the United States.

While military censors overseas concentrated primarily on withholding information, those on the home front had the authority to open and read every piece of mail that entered or left the country, to scan every cable, to screen every phone call. A letter from a soldier overseas often arrived with a few words, a sentence or an entire paragraph snipped out, and the envelope resealed with a bit of tape bearing the label "Opened by Censor."

Roosevelt established the Office of Censorship under Byron Price, a former Associated Press editor who instituted a voluntary code for publishers and broadcasters. They were asked not to report on subjects like production figures, troop movements, ship landings and battle casualties. If there was a close call, the office's censors were on duty twenty-four hours a day. Price interpreted his role narrowly—"What does not concern the war does not concern censorship," he said. There would be no prior censorship of text or copy, not even penalties for violating the code. Nor were they necessary. It was a popular war, and journalists cooperated. They even agreed to drop man-on-the-street interviews and live call-in talk radio shows. The former allegedly risked the spilling of a military secret; the latter supposedly offered spies a way to transmit information in code.

In September 1942, FDR embarked on a two-week, 8,800-mile tour of war plants. He took along three reporters, one from each of the major news agencies, but the whole trip was censored—not one word could be sent out until Roosevelt was back in the White House. Roosevelt said the reason was secrecy and the object his personal safety, although he may have wanted to avoid the appearance of pre-election politicking. In Portland, Oregon, the president told an audience of shipyard workers: "You know, I am not supposed to be here today. So you are the possessors of a secret that even the newspapers of the United States don't know."

Roosevelt personally found propaganda distasteful, and was well aware it had stirred up so much fear and hate during World War I that it impeded postwar foreign policy. So he founded the Office of Facts and Figures in 1941 to provide even-handed accounts. The director, Librarian of Congress Archibald MacLeish, promised an information policy based on "a strategy of truth," but the agencies and services with the facts and figures were loathe to share them.

In June 1942, Roosevelt replaced the agency with the Office of War Information (OWI), which had a broader mission and the authority to match. Unlike MacLeish's demure operation, OWI tried to sell the war and boost the war effort. Much of its propaganda was devoted to tighter domestic security. There

Loose talk cost lives: censors' scissors snipped ceaselessly at mail from GIs overseas.

Byron Price, the nation's censor.

was motivatation by slogan: "Pay Your Taxes, Beat the Axis," or "Loose Lips Sink Ships." It also sought to polish the image of America's allies, a rigorous challenge in the case of China and the Soviet Union. In American propaganda, Chiang Kai-shek was fighting a lonely, courageous battle. In fact, he was a corrupt, inept dictator motivated more by hatred of Chinese communists than the Japanese. Similarly, Stalin, who probably killed more innocent people than Hitler, was pictured as a benevolent reformer.

Ernie Pyle of Scripps-Howard shared mud and blood with GIs and won Pulitzer for telling it like it was.

General Stilwell, who clashed with Chiang and eventually was relieved of his command in China, was allowed to meet reporters after his return to the United States . . . but not alone. A censor sat beside Stilwell, deciding which questions the general would be allowed to answer. The reporters were not even allowed to report which questions the censor had ruled out.

Dwight Eisenhower understood publicity. "Public opinion wins wars," he told a group of newspaper editors. "I have always considered as quasi-staff officers (those) correspondents accredited to my headquarters."

Because of the many barriers to accurate reporting of the war's more complex stories, some of the best journalism stuck to the lives and experiences of average troops, and in this way conveyed some sense of the war's drudgery, savagery, fatigue and insanity. The best at this was Ernie Pyle of Scripps-Howard newspapers.

Pyle was no hero himself, and he wasn't looking for ones. Instead, he wrote about what the ordinary GI thought and felt, saw and heard, ate and drank. He discovered his calling in North Africa when he and a soldier jumped into a ditch to avoid strafing. After the plane had passed, he turned to the soldier next to him and said, "Whew! That was close, eh?" The man was dead.

Pyle walked in a daze to a press conference he had been assigned to cover. Unable to focus on that, he instead wrote about the soldier who had died next to him. He had discovered his point of view, which was that of the infantryman.

When Jane Russell talked, shipyard workers were all eyes.

Although newspapers were still the dominant daily news medium—they had more than 700 reporters overseas, 400 covering the Normandy invasion alone—radio came of age during the war. Almost a third of CBS's programming was war news, and by 1944 NBC was devoting 20 percent of its air time to news, compared to 4 percent when the war began.

Hollywood also adjusted to the production demands of war. The government wanted upbeat films about the conflict, the studios wanted to make them and, for a while at least, audiences wanted to see them. Between July and October in 1942, thirty-eight of eighty-six studio films released dealt with war themes.

The government made propaganda and information films of its own, including documentaries such as Frank Capra's "Prelude to War," and told Hollywood how movies could best serve the war effort. Its Bureau of Motion Pictures urged directors to ask themselves: "Will this picture help win the war?" They were encouraged to insert a casual war message whenever possible. The bureau received synopses of films before they were released and sometimes suggested changes. Although this smacked of prior restraint, most studios went along. Their basic cooperation was never in doubt, because the government controlled everything from set building materials (limited to $5,000 per picture) to unprocessed film—the basic stuff of the industry. Hollywood, in fact, overdid it: there were so many espionage films in 1942 that the government feared a serious case of war jitters. By 1944 people were sick of the war, and Hollywood abandoned martial dramas for escapist fare.

Tin Pan Alley also joined the war effort. "What America needs today is a good five-cent war song," Representative J. Parnell Thomas said after Pearl Harbor, and tunesmiths across the land tried to provide it. The problem was it already had been written—George M. Cohan's World War I song "Over There." In World War II no one was able to come up with anything better. The more memorable attempts included "Praise the Lord and Pass the Ammunition," by Frank Loesser, based loosely on the exploits of a chaplain at Pearl Harbor; Irving Berlin's "Any Bonds Today?;" "The Boogie-Woogie Bugle Boy of Company B;" and "Rosie the Riveter."

There were many, many more failures. Though the tunes are long forgotten, their titles remain: "Goodbye, Mama, I'm Off to Yokohama;" "Slap the Jap Right Off the Map;" and "To Be Specific, It's Our Pacific."

The biggest recording of the war was Bing Crosby's rendition of "White Christmas." With nary a word about Japs or Nazis or war bonds, its bittersweet nostalgia said all there was to say about the nation's mood.

Women

Women were the hidden army in the production war. Eventually 5 million women, more than half of them married, would go to work loading shells, operating cranes, painting ships, driving rivets and running lathes. They became welders, bus drivers, train conductors, bellhops, cowpunchers and mechanics. While Germany preferred to keep its women outside munitions plants, American women comprised a third of the wartime work force.

But it didn't start out that way.

In 1941, most American women lived as their mothers had. The vast majority of the 12 million who worked did so out of necessity; the career girl depicted by Katharine Hepburn in the movies actually represented less than an eighth of the female work force. Most women worked in service jobs—as domestics, clerks, waitresses—or in lower-paying manufacturing jobs. When they did work in the same sorts of jobs as men, they were paid less.

Women were supposed to have jobs only until they married, and wives and mothers who worked were regarded with a mixture of pity and scorn. A poll taken five years before the war began found that 82 percent of Americans believed a wife should not work if her husband did; a majority favored a law to prohibit it. But home life was no idyll. In 1941 one-third of housewives still cooked with wood or coal, and half did laundry by hand or with a hand-cranked washing machine. Both farm and city women spent about fifty hours a week on household chores.

But, when the war began it was apparent more workers would be needed, even though women were among the last hired. In the six months after Pearl Harbor, about 750,000 women applied for war work; only 80,000 were hired. Factory managers said women would have too little interest in machines and too much interest in male workers.

But soon all the men who could work were. There was no alternative but to hire women. Factories tried to lure women by likening their tasks to a housewife's. Differences between welding and sewing were minimized. If you can operate a washing machine, women were told, you can operate a lathe. "If you've followed recipes in making cakes, you can learn to load a shell," one billboard proclaimed.

The propaganda didn't have to emphasize war work's greatest attraction—$35 to $50 a week, plus overtime. Sarah Killingsworth, who worked for Douglas Aircraft in Los Angeles, said most of her co-workers "weren't interested in the war. Most of them were only interested in the money. Most of us

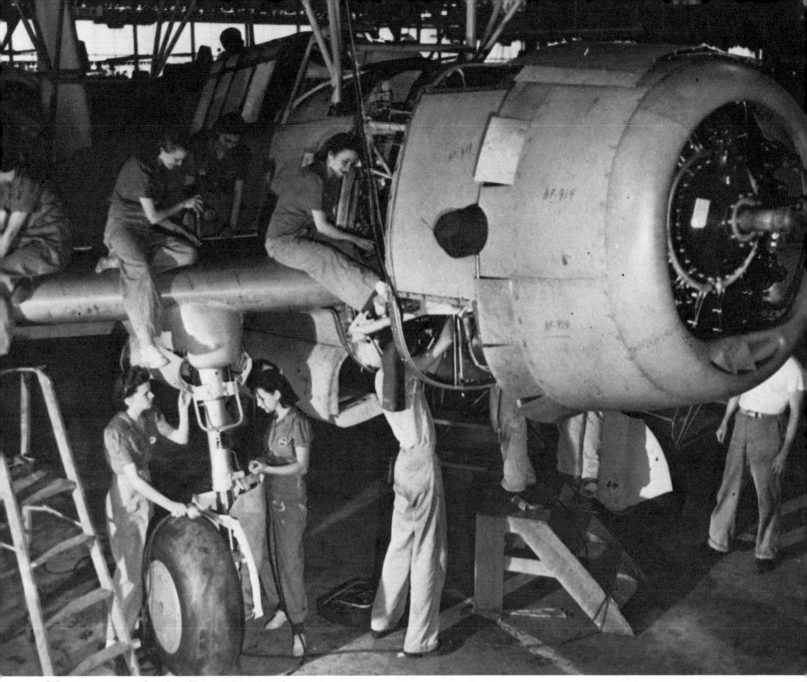

Women man production line at Boeing plant.

were young and we really didn't know. All we were after was that buck.''

At first, most of the women war workers were single. But the demand for labor was so great that soon the factories needed housewives, too. Lockheed had its married employees go door-to-door in their neighborhoods to recruit full-time homemakers for war work. By 1943, married women workers outnumbered single ones for the first time in U.S. history, and almost one in three female defense workers was a former homemaker.

Women accounted for a third of aircraft plant workers and 10 percent of the employees of shipyards and steel mills, where they did some of the toughest, dirtiest jobs. In all, about 3 million more women went to work during the war than would have in peacetime; in those six years the percentage

of women in the work force grew as much as it had from 1900 to 1940.

But women still were not treated equally. Their wages averaged 60 percent of men's, even though the government ruled they should receive equal pay for equal work. Companies circumvented that regulation by reclassifying the jobs they had women do.

Not all the war work was in factories. The War Department sent recruiters around the country, encouraging young women to come to Washington as clerks and secretaries. A quarter of the girls graduating from high school in Alma, Arkansas, signed up; and several of their teachers quit and joined them on the train to the capital. The pay was about $1,500 a year, which didn't go far in the crowded, increasingly expensive city. But the cause was good. As one young typist put it, "The men may have started this war, but the women are running it."

More than 200,000 women also entered special branches of the military services, including the WACs (Women's Army Corps), WAVES (Women Accepted for Volunteer Emergency Service) and WAFS (Women's Auxiliary Ferrying Squadron). The women did a variety of tasks that freed male soldiers for combat, but they were not allowed to handle weapons or fight. The WAVES, in fact, were not allowed to go overseas until late in the war, and WAFS—technically civil servants and not in the armed forces at all—were restricted to shuttling planes from factories to air bases.

Many women had their own home front to worry about, because the number of families headed by a married woman jumped from 770,000 in 1940 to 2.8 million in 1945. Many couples wed hurriedly in the weeks and months after Pearl Harbor (the sale of wedding rings increased 300 percent in the first three months of 1942), and conceived children before the husbands went overseas. Called "good-bye babies," these infants pushed the 1943 birth rate to its highest level in two decades.

Contact! WAC spins prop at Wright Field.

Working life was hard for these women. After eight to ten hours at the plant, often on a night or overnight shift, there was the long bus ride home. (Transportation was such a problem that etiquette arbiter Emily Post ruled it permissible for women to hitch a ride.) Then there was a wait in line to buy rationed beef or other products; home delivery was a victim of gasoline rationing. At home, there were few electrical appliances to help with cooking and cleaning, and the children to look after.

The stress was reflected in high absenteeism and turnover rates. Boeing's turnover was so high that over four years it had to hire 250,000 women to maintain a work force of 39,000. Asked why more women did not go to work, one snapped, "Because they don't have wives."

The war also saw an increase in juvenile delinquency, presumably because there were fewer controls on children. Juvenile arrests increased 20 percent in 1943, even though crime in general declined. One of the biggest forms of teen crime was prostitution, a category in which arrests increased 68 percent in 1943. A step short of prostitution was the teen-aged "V-girl," a military groupie who hung around bus stations and military bases to meet soldiers. In Detroit, the Navy had to erect a fence around its property to keep them out.

Because of the need for workers, child labor standards were routinely violated. Reports of illegal employment of minors more than doubled in 1942. In New York, the number of illegally em-

Sailors leave for sea duty as WAVES take their place ashore in San Diego.

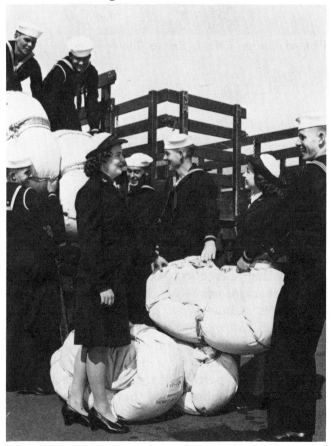

ployed children rose nearly 400 percent, and a study of bowling alley pinsetters revealed that boys as young as nine went to work immediately after school and worked until midnight on school nights.

But for many families, the greatest strain of home front life was the waiting: for news from overseas, for shortages to end, for the men to come home. A poll of young wives in 1943 found nearly half believed their husbands were being unfaithful to them. Two years later, the divorce rate was almost double the pre-war figure.

The war gave women a patriotic license to leave home, but when the war ended, so did that sanction. Although a poll by the Department of Labor found that 85 percent of the female members of the United Auto Workers union hoped to keep their jobs after the war, women soon became targets of a broad campaign by government, industry and advertising.

Massive layoffs followed the war's end; the last hired were the first fired. More than 1.3 million women were released in the second half of 1945. Within a year of V-J Day women's share of the work force had dropped from 36 percent to 29 percent.

In the Los Angeles aircraft industry, the proportion of women plummeted from more than 40 percent to less than 18 percent by 1946 and to 12 percent by 1948. Many of those who stayed were forced into lower-paying, traditionally female posts.

Despite the exodus, about two-thirds of the women who went to work during the war stayed there, and about 4.6 million more women were working after the war than before it.

Angry protest by union head A. Phillip Randolph in 1941 caused Roosevelt to end racial discrimination in defense plants.

Blacks

One day during the war, Lloyd Brown and several other black servicemen walked into a restaurant on the main street of Salina, Kansas. The counterman rushed to the rear to get the owner, who hurried out front to intercept them. "You boys know we don't serve colored here," he said.

"We ignored him," Brown wrote years later, "and just stood there inside the door, staring at what we had come to see—the German prisoners of war who were having lunch at the counter.

"If we were *untermenschen* in Germany they would break our bones," Brown reflected. "As 'colored' men in Salina, they only break our hearts."

No group gained more on the home front than America's 13 million blacks, but the war brought many a heartbreak. For every new opportunity

there was also a reminder that the Allies' ringing rhetoric of freedom and equality often did not apply to them. Out of this tension sprung a new defiance—blacks would no longer acquiesce in their own subjugation. "A wind is rising throughout the world of free men," wrote Eleanor Roosevelt, "and they will not be kept in bondage."

Blacks won their biggest victory before the war began. In May 1941, A. Philip Randolph, head of the Brotherhood of Sleeping Car Porters, threatened to organize a mass march on Washington unless the federal government stopped discrimination against blacks at the new weapons plants. The defense boom had done little to reduce black unemployment. Of 100,000 aircraft factory workers, only 240 were black, and most of them were janitors. Randolph said the marchers would have this cry: "We loyal Negro American citizens demand the right to work and fight for our country!"

The prospect of such a march alarmed Roosevelt. Five days before it was scheduled to take place he headed it off by signing Executive Order 8802, which forbade racial discrimination by federal defense contractors and created the Fair Employment Practices Committee to enforce the edict.

But the committee never had the authority or the staff it needed. It could only investigate complaints and recommend—not impose—a solution. Eventually it was able to resolve just a third of the 8,000 complaints it received. Many blacks were unwilling to complain or unaware of their right to do so.

White Southerners were the only ones who acted as if the committee had any power. Roosevelt received a letter in 1942 from Eugene (Bull) Connor, commissioner of public safety in Birmingham, Alabama. "There is no doubt that federal agencies have adopted policies to break down and destroy the segregation laws of . . . the entire South," he wrote. The Fair Employment Practices Committee, added the man who twenty years later would personify white resistance to black civil rights, was "causing plenty of trouble when there ought to be unity." In fact, the committee was charged only with fighting discrimination in hiring, not segregation itself. A munitions plant in Indiana, constructed entirely with federal money, was segregated down to its air raid shelter.

Still, Order 8802 was a breakthrough on two counts: it marked the first federal intercession on behalf of black civil rights since Reconstruction, and it showed that militant, black-organized demonstrations—or the threat thereof—could get results.

The most important black gains on the home front, however, stemmed from the war's demand for strong hands and lofty ideals.

Most blacks were hired not because of federal pressure but because there was no one else. In the summer of 1942—a year after FDR's order but before the manpower crunch—blacks accounted for just 3 percent of war workers; three years later they constituted 8 percent of a larger work force. One million blacks, two-thirds of them women, took jobs during the war. The number of skilled black workers doubled and the number of blacks holding federal jobs rose from 60,000 to 200,000. Still, by war's end the average black family income was half of that for white families, and the hot, hard and heavy jobs still fell disproportionately to blacks.

Blacks also benefited from the wild disparity between American rhetoric and reality on the subject of race. An innocuous Office of War Information pamphlet which described blacks' contributions to the war effort was attacked by Southern Democrats who said it was too complimentary and "filled with Negro pictures."

In 1943 the shadow between rhetoric and reality fell on Detroit, a city inundated by white and black Southerners seeking work in war plants. The city's critical housing shortage exacerbated animosities. In May 1941, plans were approved for a housing project for blacks, the Sojourner Truth Homes. Polish-Americans in the area protested, and congressional pressure forced federal housing officials to reverse their plans and schedule it for whites only. When that reversal was itself reversed, and the first twenty black families tried to move in February 28, 1942, they were confronted by a mob of several hundred whites armed with stones and clubs. Several days of fighting ensued, and the Ku Klux Klan picketed the project. The black families finally moved in in April, protected by several hundred members of the state militia.

But the real trouble started on a hot Sunday more than a year later: June 20, 1943. After a series of relatively minor racial fights broke out in and around a crowded park on an island in the Detroit River, rumors began to spread. Soon large groups of whites and blacks were running amok. A white milkman and a white doctor making a house call were beaten to death by a black mob, while white mobs attacked blacks who strayed across Woodward Avenue, a racial dividing line. Before federal troops quelled the fighting thirty-six hours later, thirty-four people were dead—nine whites and twenty-five blacks. Eight hundred had been injured and property damage was estimated at more than $2 million. It was the worst race riot in the nation's history.

Rioting also occurred in several other communities—Harlem exploded in August, with six deaths, 543 injuries and $6 million in damage—forcing whites to take a new look at race relations. In 1942, a year before the riots, nearly two-thirds of whites interviewed in a national survey said blacks were "pretty well satisfied" with their lot. In 1944, however, only a quarter admitted harboring such impressions.

For black soldiers, racism was as much a part of

Blacks got menial jobs in segregated U.S. Army.

General Truscott inspects still-segregated black troops in Italy.

Racial riots in Detroit in 1943 left thirty-four dead.

service life as reveille and taps. Not only were the races strictly segregated when the war began, but the Navy still took blacks only as messmen, and the Army funneled many blacks into manual labor. Segregation on Southern trains and buses particularly irritated Northerners and Westerners. Lieutenant Jackie Robinson, later the first black to break major league baseball's color line, was court-martialed after he refused to sit in the back of a bus at

Camp Hood, Texas. There also were problems in the North. The commanding officer of the 25th Infantry, stationed near Walla Walla, Washington, bowed to the wishes of the local businessmen who refused to serve black servicemen.

There were battles between white and black soldiers at Fort Dix, New Jersey, and eight other training camps, most of them in the South. In one incident, a black sergeant became the first man ever shot to death with the new M-1 rifle. In another, at Camp Stewart, Georgia, blacks who believed white soldiers had raped a black woman seized submachine guns. A military policeman was killed and four soldiers were wounded in the battle that followed.

In rigidly segregated Alexandria, Louisiana, the arrest of a black soldier from a nearby training camp by a white military policeman turned into a pitched battle on the main street between black GIs and white police and MPs. When it was over, thirty black soldiers had to be hospitalized, three for serious gunshot wounds to the back. Proclaimed the *Baltimore Afro-American:* "The rest of the country might be fighting against Germany, Italy and Japan, but the little prejudice-ridden town dipped in the deep dye of the Old South is still fighting the Civil War."

Black discontent was not the only kind that spilled over into violence. In Los Angeles, Mexican-American youths clashed with sailors in the "zoot suit" riots of 1942, which were named after the flashy outfits worn by the youths. A year later, upon hearing a rumor that some zoot suiters had beaten up a sailor, a mob of several thousand soldiers and sailors went on a rampage and beat up anyone wearing a zoot suit. The city of Los Angeles responded by banning zoot suits.

By the war's end, however, blacks were a far more coherent and active pressure group. Membership in the NAACP increased ninefold, and new, more militant groups such as the Congress of Racial Equality were born, along with the tactics, ideals and leaders of the post-war civil rights movement. The war saw the armed services begin to move toward integration, and in 1944 the Supreme Court outlawed the all-white party primary, a first step in breaking the white hammerlock on Southern politics. The migration to the North that the war encouraged also enhanced black political power.

Finally, the war helped make civil rights a national issue—and a cause for progressive whites. In the 1930s, a senator like George Norris could oppose anti-lynching legislation and still be considered a liberal. But by 1945 support for civil rights was a progressive acid test, and within two decades it had become standard for virtually any serious contender for national office.

Cloth shortage trimmed zoot suits but government relented to allow "drape shape" in Hollywood gangster film. Real thing caused riot in Los Angeles.

8
ON THE
OFFENSIVE

Since the German panzers swept through Eastern and Western Europe in 1939-40, Hitler's Reich had established a patchwork of annexed, occupied and controlled satellite states.

Germany drew foodstuffs from Denmark, oil from Romania, coal and grain from Poland, and slave labor from almost everywhere. In March 1942, Hitler ordered the drafting of forced labor from occupied countries to free Germans to fight on the war fronts. In the next three years, almost 5 million people, including 1 million Poles, were imported into Germany to work in munitions and other factories, and to live in often inhuman conditions.

The heavy-handed, often brutal Nazi occupation stirred up its own nemesis. Called the "Maquis" in France, the "Partisans" in Yugoslavia, the "Milorg" in Norway, the resistance movements in occupied lands kept the Germans off balance and the British and Americans well informed about developments on the continent.

Resistance took many forms. Armed bands sniped at Germans from the hills, derailed trains and blew up bridges at night, knifed German officers in city alleyways. The underground also slowed production or sabotaged equipment in factories, helped rescue downed Allied airmen, and spread anti-Nazi propaganda through widely circulated underground publications.

In occupied Yugoslavia in 1942, Communist leader Josip Broz, war-named Tito, was building a Partisan army of tens of thousands that later would keep the Germans engaged in a full-fledged guerrilla war. But the Yugoslav resistance was fractured:

the anti-communist Chetniks fought the Partisans as much as they fought the Germans. A similar split in the resistance developed in German-occupied Greece. But in France, the Netherlands, Belgium, Norway and elsewhere, patriots put aside political differences to undermine the Nazi regime. They, and their countrymen, often paid a cruel price.

On June 9, 1942, as Americans cheered the Midway victory and Germans the new Rommel desert offensive, a convoy of SS troopers rolled into the tiny Czech village of Lidice and sealed it off from the outside world.

Five days earlier, Reinhard Heydrich, "Reich Protector" of the occupied Czech lands and one of the most notorious of SS officers, died of wounds suffered at the hands of Czech assassins. The Germans decided to teach the Czechs a lesson and chose Lidice, apparently because two men from the village were serving in the British RAF.

The Germans methodically rounded up all 172 male villagers over age sixteen and shot them. The women and children were shipped off to concentration camps. The village itself was dynamited and leveled.

Lidice came to symbolize the resistance to tyranny in Europe. But it was not unique. Such ferocity was repeated time and again across the occupied lands, and the worst ferocity came in pursuit of Adolf Hitler's pathological hatred of Jews.

Above: *On Guadalcanal, Marine tanks overran fanatic Japanese in their foxholes until treads "looked like meat grinders."*

As Germany's grasp on conquered Europe weakened, communist partisans arose, nowhere more fiercely than in Yugoslavia under Josip Broz—war name Tito (r.).

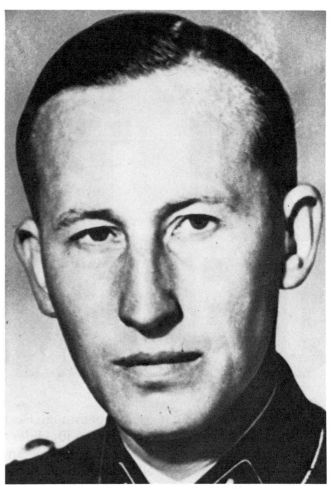

Until assassination by Czech agents in 1942, Reinhard Heydrich, sinister SS general, was charged with "final solution" of "Jewish problems."

Colonel Adolf Eichmann of the Gestapo's Jewish Evacuation Office told a friend: "I will obey, obey, obey."

ence in the Berlin suburb of Wannsee to discuss what they called an "Endloesung" for the Jews, a final solution. Eichmann was put in charge. And by April, as U.S. defense plants were rolling out tanks, airplanes and ammunition for what American leaders knew would be a years-long war, German technicians at a Polish camp called Auschwitz were making final checks on a new system of gas chambers.

Fortress Europe

The outside world had heard only hints and fearful rumors of what was happening inside the Nazi realm. It was known that for years the Nazis had targeted Jews, in both Germany and the conquered lands, for relentless persecution, and that thousands had been sent by train to concentration camps in Poland. To Hitler's Nazi lieutenants, the Jewish problem was a bureaucratic and technological problem. On January 20, 1942, Heydrich of the SS and aide Adolf Eichmann summoned officials of other government agencies to an important confer-

In the summer of 1942, after three years of war, the German military still looked daunting: between 260 and 300 divisions, including twenty-five armored divisions, more than 5,000 warplanes, at least 7 million men under arms, many of them well-trained and battle-hardened veterans.

Hitler's forces were making strides again in Russia, capturing Sevastapol on July 2. Rommel had the British on the defensive in North Africa. German U-boats had sunk 400,000 tons of Allied shipping in the Atlantic in just one week in July, an unprecedented rate.

British and Canadian prisoners after 1942 Dieppe raid.

Few people then knew, General Marshall later wrote, "how close Germany and Japan were to complete domination of the world."

Fortress Europe looked impregnable. But at dawn on August 19, 1942, a force of 5,100 Canadian infantrymen and 1,000 British Commandos and American Rangers went ashore near the French port of Dieppe in a surprise raid aimed at testing the defenses of the fortress.

The operation was a tactical disaster. The German defenders hit back hard. Only one-third of the Canadians returned alive, and the RAF lost ninety-eight planes flying air support for the mission.

"HANDS OFF EUROPE!" the Nazi Party newspaper *Volkischer Beobachter* proclaimed in reporting the Allied rout on the French coast.

Dieppe was a debacle. But twelve days before, on another beach halfway around the world, another relatively small detachment had waded ashore to take the offensive against the Axis. And the U.S. Marines who were now dug in on this obscure South Pacific island, an island whose name, Guadalcanal, would soon become a synonym for hell, were somehow holding their own.

Sketch of disastrous but instructive Commando-Canadian raid on Dieppe.

Long road back begins in Solomons as Navy bombs Tanambogo Island preparatory to Marine landing on Guadalcanal.

"Where are the United States Marines hiding?" a Japanese propaganda broadcast asked sarcastically on August 5. "The Marines are supposed to be the finest soldiers in the world, but no one has seen them yet."

At that moment, the 1st Marine Division and a regiment of the 2nd Marine Division, packed aboard transports in a seventy-six-ship U.S. and Australian armada, were plowing through the Pacific, headed for an encounter that would answer the Japanese question forever.

Guadalcanal, a mountainous, jungle-covered island near the southern end of the Solomons chain, 1,000 miles northeast of the Australian coast, gained the attention of American planners by mid-July 1942, after reconnaissance flights and radio intercepts determined that the Japanese were building an airfield on the island's northern coast.

Blunted in their eastward drive at Midway, the Japanese were again trying to extend southward. Control of the Solomons, together with New Guinea, would enable them to threaten the U.S. supply lifeline to Australia, and to threaten Australia itself from both the north and the northeast.

Guadalcanal

In Washington, the Joint Chiefs of Staff authorized a new operation, codenamed Watchtower, by which U.S. forces would drive the Japanese from Guadalcanal and the previously established base at nearby Tulagi, push through Japanese-held areas of the Solomons and New Guinea, and finally destroy the main Japanese base at Rabaul.

The first job fell to green, half-trained Marines just arrived in the southwest Pacific from camps in

North Carolina and California. They were both excited and fearful.

One Marine lieutenant, Paul Moore, Jr., later recalled looking out at the huge fleet of gray steel that surrounded his transport. "It felt like the Greeks going to Troy or something. . . . You felt totally invincible."

When they finally stormed ashore on Guadalcanal on the morning of August 7, 1942, opening the first U.S. offensive of the war and embarking on a bloody six-month battle, the Marines met no resistance. Japanese construction troops, caught by surprise by the American landings, had simply fled into the jungle, leaving behind half-eaten meals. By the second day, the Marines had control of the almost completed airstrip.

Twenty-two miles across Sealark Channel, on the smaller islands of Tulagi, Gavutu and Tanambogo, it was a different story. The Japanese marines holding those islands had radioed out, "Enemy forces overwhelming, we will defend our posts to the death," and put up a brief but furious resistance. In two days, dozens of Americans and hundreds of Japanese were killed, many of them holdouts in the islands' coral caves.

The deadliest clash of those first hours exploded offshore, in the black waters of Sealark Channel in the early morning of August 9.

Seven Imperial Navy cruisers had steamed 600 miles from Rabaul and slipped into the channel undetected, south of the small island of Savo. They maneuvered between a group of Allied warships

In New Guinea sudden death and crippling disease lurked in the jungle.

and the shore of Guadalcanal, a background of 7,000-foot mountains that foiled any American radar scanning. The Japanese then illuminated the Allied ships with star shells and opened fire.

The surprised American and Australian seamen had little chance. In less than an hour, Japanese shells and torpedoes sank the Australian cruiser *Canberra* and the American cruisers *Astoria, Quincy* and *Vincennes.* The Japanese flotilla, having suffered little damage, then withdrew northward, its commander fearful that American carriers lurked in the area and their dive bombers would find him in the daylight. In pulling back, the Japanese left the defenseless U.S. landing ships untouched.

The Battle of Savo Island was the worst American naval defeat since the War of 1812. And now the U.S. armada that accompanied the Marines into these perilous waters was breaking up.

The American aircraft carriers were no longer on the scene. Just hours before the Japanese attack, Vice Admiral Fletcher, wary of Japanese airpower, had withdrawn his three carriers from the Guadalcanal area. Hours after the attack all but wiped out his shield of warships, Rear Admiral Richmond Kelly Turner ordered his convoy of supply vessels also to head back south, before all the Marines' cargo was unloaded.

The ground commander, Major General Alexander A. Vandegrift, now had 6,805 Marines on the smaller islands and 11,145 on Guadalcanal, where they were cutting through the jungle and setting up a perimeter around a seven-by-four-mile coastal strip, centered on the airfield, now named Henderson Field, after Major Lofton Henderson, the Ma-

Japanese waited just beyond the treeline from these machine gunners near Buna in New Guinea.

rine dive bomber killed at Midway. The Marines held just 1 percent of the land area of a forbidding island where the Japanese now could largely operate at will.

As vulnerable as they were, the Marines' strength was still somehow underestimated by the enemy. On August 18, a Japanese vanguard of 1,000 men came ashore east of the Marine perimeter, and within three days they were on the attack, probing the American line where Alligator Creek ran into the sea.

In the early morning darkness August 21, sometimes in bayonet-to-bayonet combat, the Marine defenders along the western bank of the creek held against the determined Japanese, members of an elite force led by Colonel Kiyono Ichiki. After dawn, Marine reinforcements swept across the creek upstream, trapped the Japanese in a coconut grove between the creek and the sea, and slaughtered them. The estuary was littered with Japanese bodies, many quickly half-buried by the tide-driven sands. The final toll: 871 Japanese dead and only fifteen captured, and thirty-four American dead. Colonel Ichiki buried the regimental colors and committed hara-kiri, ritual suicide.

The day before, the first American fighters and dive bombers arrived to make their base at Henderson Field, helping to even the odds against Japanese forces that dominated the nearby seas.

On August 24, Fletcher's carriers intercepted a Japanese task force headed for Guadalcanal and fought an inconclusive battle with enemy carriers. The next day, Marine dive bombers from Henderson and B-17 bombers from an American airfield at Espiritu Santo, 600 miles to the southeast, found the large troop transport the carriers were escorting and sank it, killing hundreds of Japanese and foiling a planned landing.

Japanese commanders then fell into a pattern of building up troop strength on Guadalcanal through nighttime convoys that came in at the island's northwest tip. To throw off U.S. aircraft and submarines, these troopships were sometimes blanketed with palms and other vegetation, so that they looked like lush offshore islets. By November, this Tokyo Express route, as journalists quickly dubbed it, had landed 20,000 Japanese troops on Guadalcanal. But even before then, General Kiyotake Kawaguchi, ground commander on the island, decided to throw his 6,000 men against the American positions south and west of Henderson Field, in what proved to be one of the crucial ground battles of the campaign.

On the night of September 12, the Japanese struck against a T-shaped ridge that guarded the southern approach to Henderson Field. Artillery and the guns of three Japanese warships offshore pounded the Marine positions as Kawaguchi's soldiers, screaming "Banzai!" surged forward out of the jungle.

The Marine Raiders and paratroopers holding the ridge, under the command of Lieutenant Colonel Merritt Edson, a somber, redheaded Vermonter, were stunned and driven back by the violent attack. But, through twelve assaults into the morning hours, Edson's men held the final knoll blocking the Japanese from the airfield, just a mile away.

The Japanese came back at them the next night, in vicious fighting from foxhole to foxhole, in jungle blackness. The Marines fired wildly at flashes and sounds in the dark. The Battle of Bloody Ridge tested their fiber as no fighting had before on Guadalcanal.

Marine howitzers lobbing shells over the ridge methodically chewed up the Japanese. After daybreak on the 14th, when Kawaguchi rallied his exhausted troops for one last charge, two fighter planes from Henderson Field joined the defense, further devastating the Japanese line. Finally, Kawaguchi led his battered force back into the jungle westward. The Americans counted more than 600 Japanese bodies around Bloody Ridge, and hundreds more were to later die of their wounds in the jungle. More than 100 Marines were killed.

Weeks and months followed of attack and pursuit in the dense rain forests, of dodging sniper fire, of air and naval bombardment of Henderson Field. The Marines, soon to be joined by Army troops, were settling in to a hellish routine on the steamy, mud-coated and insect-filled landscape of far-off Guadalcanal, where they rifled Japanese rations to supplement their own, and where malaria was beginning to claim more victims than the Japanese. Eventually a leatherneck would have to register a temperature of 105 degrees before he could be pulled out of the ranks.

Guadalcanal was more than a battle for crucial territory. It also was the first major collision of citizen armies that had been built almost overnight from the untested youth of two nations.

In October 1942, Americans were still focused on Guadalcanal, the Marines' foothold in Japan's Pacific empire. Lieutenant Colonel "Red Mike" Edson's Raiders had routed the Japanese in mid-September, but Imperial Army reinforcements had been pouring into the island since then aboard transports of the nocturnal Tokyo Express.

About midnight on October 11, a flotilla of U.S. Navy cruisers and destroyers under Rear Admiral Norman Scott surprised a Japanese task force off northwest Guadalcanal's Cape Esperance and sank a cruiser and destroyer. Two days later, 3,000 men of the Americal Division disembarked at Guadalcanal, the first U.S. Army reinforcements for the hard-pressed Marines. The GIs brought with them the new standard-issue M-1 semi-automatic rifles, which were replacing the 1903 bolt-action Springfield rifles with which the Marines had been holding Guadalcanal.

The Army men arrived just in time for the heaviest shelling yet of Henderson Field, three nights of nonstop bombardment by Japanese battleships and cruisers out in Sealark Channel, shelling that left the U.S. air arm on the island gravely damaged.

From his headquarters in New Caledonia, 1,000 miles south of Guadalcanal, South Pacific commander Rear Admiral Robert L. Ghormley

Armchair admirals preferred the dependable Spruance to Halsey. But the swabbies loved "Bull's" simple credo: STRIKE! REPEAT, STRIKE!"

messaged Nimitz that the Japanese were about to launch an all-out offensive and his forces were totally inadequate to stop them.

Nimitz's first action was to replace Ghormley. News of the appointment of "Bull" Halsey to lead the fight in the South Pacific galvanized the men on Guadalcanal. In the war's early months, Halsey had won a reputation as a man of action. He told Vandegrift, the Marine commander, that he would help him with "everything I've got." And soon every leatherneck and GI on Guadalcanal learned Halsey's motto: "Kill Japs, kill Japs, kill more Japs."

By late October, the killing was wholesale.

On October 23, the Japanese, after a grueling march through the wet jungle, mounted a confused attack from the west and the south against the Henderson Field perimeter. The first assault, from the west, was easily repulsed. The later attack, from the south in a driving rain near midnight, threatened to overrun the American defenders, who were dug in better than ever on Bloody Ridge. Line after line of charging Japanese fell before the machine guns of the Marines and the Americals 164th Infantry. In two bloody nights of repeated attacks, an estimated 3,500 Japanese were killed, before the ragged survivors retreated into the forest.

New Jersey Marine Sergeant John Basilone won Medal of Honor for killing thirty-eight Japanese on Guadalcanal.

Bravery was an everyday virtue on Guadalcanal. In this second Battle of Bloody Ridge, for example, Platoon Sergeant John Basilone was a one-man weapons squad, positioning, repairing, feeding ammunition to machine gun positions at key points in the Marine line all through the murderous night. For his daring actions, he became the first Marine enlisted man in World War II to win the Medal of Honor.

But selfless bravery also could produce terrible waste. In one attack against the Japanese across the Matanikau River, beyond the Marines' western perimeter, Lieutenant Colonel Lewis "Chesty" Puller sent one Marine platoon after another running down a sandspit where the river reached the sea, and then across the river against entrenched opposition.

Recalled Lieutenant Paul Moore: "One platoon went over and got annihilated. Another platoon went over and got annihilated. Then another. . . . Ours was the fifth platoon to go over, and you know, we all realized it was insane. . . . But if you're a Marine, you're ordered across the goddamn beach and you go."

Moore's platoon took heavy casualties and pulled back. The young lieutenant, who went on to become Episcopal bishop of New York, remembers thinking that "if I get out of this, maybe it means I should do something special."

After the second Japanese defeat at Bloody Ridge, a series of naval clashes in nearby waters turned the tide for good against the Japanese on Guadalcanal.

The first, the Battle of the Santa Cruz Islands, on October 26, was a carrier duel like Midway. The U.S. flattop *Hornet* was sent to the bottom, and the *Enterprise* was damaged, but two Japanese carriers also suffered damage, and the Japanese naval force withdrew.

Five torpedos missed but last killed stricken carrier **Hornet,** *here during Tokyo raid, in Battle of Santa Cruz Islands, October 1942.*

Five Sullivan brothers of Waterloo, Iowa, served together and died together when cruiser **Juneau** *went down off Guadalcanal in November 1942.*

Almost three weeks later, as the U.S. Navy delivered another Americal regiment to Guadalcanal, a powerful Japanese naval force was intercepted nearby by American cruisers and destroyers. The outgunned American vessels, under Rear Admiral Daniel Callaghan, steamed straight into the circle of Japanese ships and opened fire from close range. The Americans took heavy hits in the furious night fighting. The cruisers *Atlanta* and *Juneau* were sunk, the *Juneau* exploding and going down with all but ten of its 700-man crew, including the five Sullivan brothers of Waterloo, Iowa, a family tragedy soon translated into a Hollywood script. And Admiral Callaghan was killed. But the Japanese were forced to retire, and the task force's damaged flagship, the battleship *Hiei,* was sunk the next day by American warplanes.

On November 15, planes from Henderson Field found eleven transports off Guadalcanal ferrying troops to the Japanese side, and sank six of them, along with an escorting cruiser. That night, American and Japanese battleships met off Guadalcanal. The new battleship *Washington* locked onto the Japanese battleship *Kirishima* with fire-control radar and blasted it with dozens of shells, leaving it sinking.

The next day, November 16, in a desperation move, a final four Japanese transports were beached near Guadalcanal's northwestern corner, but planes from Henderson and from the *Enterprise* caught the enemy troops as they disembarked. A massacre followed.

The battle for Guadalcanal would go on until February 1943, when the harried Japanese managed to secretly evacuate their last 11,000 men from the island. But the victory was sealed in those furious sea and air battles of November 1942.

Japan lost an estimated 25,000 men in the campaign for the little-known island, and the Americans lost 1,500 lives.

Soviet Winter

In the fall of 1942, as the German army hammered its way into the Caucasus region of the southern Soviet Union, and Rommel's Afrika Korps stood on the doorstep of British Egypt, it appeared that Hitler's Wehrmacht might close a giant pincers on the oilfields of the Middle East, from Russia to the north and from Egypt to the west. The Axis partners, Germany and Japan, might then link hands across south Asia.

But in a few fateful weeks of November 1942, the course of the global war changed, not just in the turquoise waters off Guadalcanal, waters now fouled with the oil of sunken ships, but also in the windy Soviet steppes between the Volga and the Don, and on the endless sands of North Africa.

The Third Reich had reached too far.

In July and August, rebounding from the treacherous Russian winter of 1941-42, the Germans punched forward at the southern end of their 1,800-mile-long Soviet front and drove into the mountainous Caucasus region. A 330,000-man army under General Friedrich Paulus then turned north and, on August 22, launched an all-out attack on Stalingrad, a city of tractor factories and armaments plants sprawled on the west side of the mile-wide Volga River. Seizing this strongpoint on the Volga would enable the Germans to choke off a vital artery linking the Soviet heartland with the southern oilfields.

"We are attacking Stalingrad and we shall take it," Hitler proclaimed in Berlin.

The first day's German bombardment flattened three-quarters of the city. But the Soviets would neither surrender nor retreat. Through September and October, German panzers and infantry pushed forward block by block through the ruins of Stalingrad, but they were held up, pinned down and

War flowed and ebbed through Belgorod in the Soviet Union four times. In the beginning it was home for 34,000; at the end 140.

bloodied by a Soviet army, aided by civilians, that had transformed itself into a deadly urban guerrilla force.

The fighting was often hand to hand, in the shells of apartment houses, in the rubble of factories. Thousands died every day. Soviet children hurled Molotov cocktails at the Germans. Women sniped at them with old rifles. Elderly men carted supplies across the Volga on bridges strung just beneath the river surface to avoid German air detection.

The Soviets fought like "swamp animals," Hitler complained. But the fuehrer rejected his generals' recommendation that Paulus' 6th Army be withdrawn from the mire of Stalingrad before the onset of winter.

On November 19, three days after American warplanes devastated the Japanese landing force at Guadalcanal, Soviet troops under General Georgi Zhukov opened a great counteroffensive at Stalingrad.

The reserves of Soviet strength repeatedly surprised the aggressors. Despite their vast conquests in Russia, the Germans had been unable to hobble Soviet industry. In a monumental effort in the face of advancing armies, the Soviets had moved their machinery eastward and built new factories in the Ural Mountains, Siberia and Central Asia, producing the tanks, artillery pieces and ammunition they would need to drive Hitler's legions from their soil.

High tide of Nazi invasion of Russia began to ebb at the bitter battle of Stalingrad, major turning point of the war in Europe.

By 1943, Hitler had learned the lesson Russia taught Napoleon: the land and its manpower are inexhaustible.

By tens, hundreds, then thousands, soldiers of Hitler's "master race" gave up at Stalingrad.

On the first day of Zhukov's Stalingrad counter-attack, the Soviet artillery, lined up 300 to 400 pieces to a mile, fired 689,000 shells. A great enveloping movement from the northeast and southeast caught Paulus' forces in an ever-tightening wedge. Finally, twenty German and two Romanian divisions, up to 350,000 men, settled in for a grim, hopeless winter in a pocket twenty-five miles long and twelve miles from north to south.

Their rations shrinking, the Germans ate horses, dogs and cats. An attempt by a panzer division to relieve them was crushed by the Soviets.

"Everything around us is collapsing," a German soldier wrote in a last letter home. "A whole army is dying, and night and day are aflame."

Week by week, the ring was tightened, and more Germans perished in combat or by starvation. In the last twenty days of January 1943, more than 100,000 German officers and men were annihilated. Finally, on January 31, in the basement of a department store, Paulus and his staff surrendered to a twenty-seven-year-old Russian lieutenant.

Stalingrad was a monumental turning point in the three-and-a-half-year-old war. Hitler's divisions would thereafter be on the defensive on their vast eastern front. And, as Zhukov readied his November push at Stalingrad, the Axis had already suffered another critical defeat in North Africa, near a dusty way station called El Alamein.

At Stalingrad, Hitler ordered his troops to stand or die. They did.

9 ROAD TO VICTORY

The writer Nicholas Monsarrat called it the cruel sea. It was all of that, the North Atlantic. In winter it was an inhuman seascape of ice and furious storms that flayed the freezing waters into sixty-foot waves. Survival in such water was measured in minutes. And yet for the second time in twenty-five years the North Atlantic was to be the artery between the abundant fields and factories of the New World and its embattled partners of the Old. Without it the one free light left in Europe would have dimmed, then gone out.

Adolf Hitler was not unaware that German U-boats almost severed the Allies' lifeline to America in World War I. But the panzer blitzkrieg was uppermost in his plans for World War II. His fleet commander Admiral Erich Raeder had programmed a Nazi navy of 200 submarines by 1942 plus four aircraft carriers and six battleships. But Hitler marched to a different tempo. Raeder had only forty-six U-boats in hand when the war began in September 1939.

The shortage did not become a strategic factor until 1941 when Britain stood alone in the West and Russia teetered on defeat in the East. Their one hope was the arsenals, the mines and the granaries of the United States. By then Raeder had 200 submarines on hand. They were sinking British ships in the Atlantic three times faster than they could be replaced. Knowing this but knowing, too, he faced a strong isolationist sentiment, Roosevelt played as strong a hand as he felt political considerations and a facade of neutrality would allow. He devised a strategem he called Lend Lease, by which a financially strapped Britain would be supplied by

the United States to pay for it at war's end. Congress voted the plan March 11, 1941. The U.S. traded fifty World War I mothballed destroyers for bases in the Caribbean and Bermuda. In August of that year Roosevelt met with Churchill in Argentia, Newfoundland, where the two issued the Atlantic Charter. It declared the two English-speaking powers had no territorial ambitions, that the world's peoples should be free to choose their own governments and that international differences would not be resolved by war. In addition, the president agreed to help escort British freighters as far as Iceland where U.S. Marines had just landed to set up air and naval bases. It was a precocious stance for an alleged neutral to take, and the results were predictable.

On September 4, 1941, the American destroyer *Greer* traded fire with a German U-boat. On October 17 the destroyer *Kearny* was torpedoed. Eleven sailors were killed, the first American casualties of the war. After the *Greer* incident, Roosevelt had ordered American ships to fire at U-boats on sight. Then on October 31 the destroyer *Reuben James* was sunk by a submarine with a loss of 115 lives. Conflict on the Atlantic, which had drawn the United States into war in 1798, 1812 and 1917, was threatening to do it again. Pearl Harbor made the matter moot.

Submarine warfare had changed more by degree than substance in between the wars. The British had developed sonar, a system of detecting submerged U-boats by electronic pulses, the "ping"

Above: *True to his pledge, MacArthur returns to the Philippines at Leyte.*

167

Doenitz gets Hitler's blessing for U-boat campaign.

U-boat crew abandons ship as patrol bombers help turn tide in Atlantic.

famliar to any viewer of submarine movies. But sonar did not detect surfaced vessels. So the German U-boats concentrated their attacks at night while surfaced. Britain had also developed radio direction finders by which receivers in England, Greenland and Canada intercepted U-boat communications back to Germany and located the source of the radio by triangulation. The U-boat commanders luckily were careless about radio silence. Then in 1941 the British captured intact U-110 near Greenland and cracked the German radio codes found aboard. British scientists had also been experimenting with radar since 1936. By 1940 radar stations along England's southeast coast were key to winning the Battle of Britain. By 1941 a technological breakthrough made radar small enough to be mounted in ships, even planes. It was precise enough to pick up surfaced U-boats which took a part of the ocean surface from them. On the surface, the U-boats could use their air-breathing diesels and make seventeen knots, enough to maneuver around plodding convoys. Submerged, the U-boats were reduced to seven or eight knots on batteries. To make up for this handicap Admiral Karl Doenitz, head of the submarine service, ordered his captains to hunt in wolf packs. The U-boat commanders referred to those days as "the happy times." One of them, Otto Kretschmer, sank forty-four ships.

When the United States entered the war, the U-boats—only six of them—fell on American shipping along the East Coast. Restocked by supply subs called milch cows, the U-boats of Operation Paukenschlag made a murderous shooting gallery of the U.S. vessels which unwisely still were not traveling in convoys. By May 1942 the U-boats had sunk eighty-seven ships off the coast. On June 15 bathers at Virginia Beach watched in horror as a submarine sank two freighters off the beach right around the corner from Atlantic naval headquarters in Norfolk. Another submarine torpedoed a U.S. freighter, then radioed in English to a second vessel that he was a lightship and the American should approach closer. The captain obliged and was torpedoed. The American ships were sitting ducks illuminated against the coastal skyline. When a blackout was ordered, Miami balked at turning off its neon for fear of ruining the tourist season. When the Americans, who had had only twenty-four escort vessels available along the coast when the war started, began convoying with everything available including lavish private yachts now painted battleship gray, the Germans took on more fuel from the milch cows and headed for the Caribbean. U-boats sank 750,000 tons there in three months, many of them tankers.

Naval commander King, a man so tough, Roosevelt said, he shaved with a blowtorch, was slow to convoy American coastal shipping despite British urging and despite the loss of 10,000 tons a day. Eventually as escorts became available, U.S. ships were shepherded into groups and guided by Navy and Coast Guard vessels to the main trans-Atlantic jumping off port of Halifax, Nova Scotia. Convoys left every eight or ten days bound for the British Isles.

Hitler, preoccupied with the invasion of the Soviet Union, refused to give U-boat construction highest priority even though German's U-boat campaign in World War I had almost shut down the Allies. Britain depended on the U.S. and Canada for one-quarter of its food alone. The British Isles needed 30 million tons of supplies a year and were getting only 25 million. As the submarine blockade went, so went rationing in Britain. And so went rearming after Dunkirk and preparing for the invasion of France. England's fate, as ever, was the sea. "The only thing that ever really frightened me during the war was the U-boat peril," Churchill was to write.

By 1942 Germany was launching twenty submarines a month including 1,100-tonners that could range halfway around the world. Doenitz directed the wolf packs to ambush south of Greenland beyond the reach of air patrols. In November the U-boats sank 637,000 tons alone and a total of 8 million tons for all of 1942. Some of the most lethal attacks were on the runs above the top of Norway to the Soviet ports of Murmansk and Archangel. Convoys there were prey to submarines, land bombers and the threat of the battleship *Tirpitz*, lurking in a Norwegian cove. Just a report that *Tirpitz* had sortied in July 1942 caused the cruiser escorts of convoy PQ-17 to abandon the convoy to stalk the battleship. PQ-17's thirty-five merchantmen were ordered to get to Archangel on their own. Only eleven made port. The Germans sank the rest with the loss of 431 tanks, 210 planes and 99,316 tons of other supplies. The U-boats had sunk a high of 144 Allied ships in June 1942, 119 in December and 108 the following March.

SCRATCH THE BISMARCK

In the early days of the war, German surface raiders, some battle cruisers, some disguised as merchantmen, marauded the seas of the world.

One of the most feared was the *Bismarck*, deemed an almost invulnerable super battleship. It came out into the Atlantic from occupied Norway in May 1941 to blow up the battleship *Hood*, the jewel of the British fleet, with an unlucky hit on its magazine. After a furious hunt, it was spotted. Two days later an antique cloth-covered Swordfish biplane that looked like it belonged in an air museum instead of battle put a torpedo into the *Bismarck*'s steering gear. After two days of pounding from the air and by two British battleships, the *Bismarck* went down, some said scuttled by its captain. It took 1,900 of its 2,000-man crew with it.

A sister, the *Tirpitz*, remained hidden in Norway. It was such a threat, however, that the British launched sixteen air strikes against it. The last one in late 1944 succeeded. *Tirpitz* capsized, never having fired a shot in anger.

Sink the Bismarck! was the order. The British did.

The winter of 1942–3 was the worst in fifty years in the North Atlantic. Incessant storms raged over the waters southeast of Greenland, called The Gap because it was beyond reach of Allied patrol bombers from either continent. Both sides had broken the other's naval codes. Warfare became a chess game of trying moves away from and toward where each knew the other side would be. The wolf packs took an almost strangling toll. Allied losses in the fall of 1942 outpaced ships being built by 700,000 tons. Torpedoed sailors had a fifty-fifty chance of survival in the cruel sea. Eight thousand British seaman died in 1942.

In March 1943 the battle reached a crescendo. The U-boats sank ninety-six ships in only three weeks. Twenty-one of them went down in a convoy attacked by forty submarines. Only one U-boat was lost. But B-24 Liberators, sacrificing depth charges for extra fuel, could now reach The Gap. An improved radar could pick up surfaced subs, even periscopes. The naval escorts had been hampered by the sonar which lost contact when a target got within point blank range. As more escorts came out of American, Canadian and British shipyards, escorts could team up, one keeping the target on sonar while its teammate made the depth charge run. New detection gear that picked up submerged U-boats from its magnetic field were in the works. By May the Germans got only fifty ships. And forty-one U-boats were sunk. In time a U-boat could average only three patrols before being sunk.

For the submariners, all volunteers, U-boat duty alternated between grim tedium—relieved by group singing, chess, books, shark fishing—and terror, the "tin-can neurosis" of a depth charge attack. By war's end, 28,000 of the 40,000-man U-boat service had died, many of them only teenagers serving a fuehrer who often failed them.

Unlike these survivors, 70 percent of U-boat crews were lost.

With Allied losses at a peak, Hitler ordered large numbers of U-boats to run the narrow gauntlet of Gibraltar into the Mediterranean to keep open the supply line to the Afrika Korps. Sixty-two of the U-boats never made it back out into the Atlantic. He balked until too late at a crash program to build a new U-boat with an air-breathing snorkel that permitted the submarine's diesels to outspeed most merchant ships while submerged. By the time Hitler approved the program, Doenitz considered the Battle of the Atlantic had been won—by the Allies.

Close studies of losses proved to the Allies the value of convoys. A convoyed ship had four times the chances of survival over one sailing alone. Merchantmen converted to escort carriers that could hold thirty planes added portable air cover. Smaller destroyer escorts and corvettes—Monsarrat said they'd even roll in wet grass—began flanking the convoys along with the destroyers. Convoys were spread out widthwise to minimize easy broadside attacks. Tankers, ammo carriers and troop ships were kept in the center of the pack shielded on the flanks by less crucial grain and ore carriers. Longer range aircraft with the improved radar made surfacing a U-boat to charge batteries and replenish oxygen a hazard.

In May of 1943 a pack of fifty to sixty U-boats attacked a westbound convoy and sank a third of it. But in earlier days such a force would expect to destroy the entire convoy. "The German submarine campaign was wrecked by the introduction of the convoy system," Doenitz was to say. By that May, he said: "In the Atlantic the destruction of every 10,000 tons was paid for by the loss of one U-boat. . . . The losses have therefore reached an unbearable height." He himself was to lose two sons and a son-in-law in the submarine service.

By mid-'43 American and Canadian shipyards had turned out enough escort craft to form hunter-killer packs that scanned the seas far beyond the convoys. American yards were turning out 140 Liberty ships a month. They only made eleven knots but carried 10,800 tons of cargo. Henry J. Kaiser's yard in California built one from keel laying to launch in eighty hours and thirty minutes.

But the bloodied North Atlantic remained one of the most dangerous fronts of the war. Endless hours on watch in fog, storm, snow, nerves constantly on end, jumping at the sound of a dropped wrench. Steaming in zero visibility trying to steer clear of other vessels, particularly the ammo carriers, in a tightly packed convoy. Suddenly blown into that cruel sea, made even crueler by choking oil or engulfing fire. Possibly adrift in a lifeboat never to be found. It was a life where the sailor reversed his normal inclination and prayed for

Crew of British destroyer prepare to rescue survivors of U-boat they sank in Mediterranean.

U.S. Coast Guard cutter picks up crew of U-boat it sank.

storms to neutralize the menace of the U-boat waiting just below the surface.

That cruel sea took its toll of brave men. Thirty-two thousand British seamen lost their lives in the Atlantic, a quarter of the total who served. The American merchant marine lost about 6,000 lives. All told 4,600 ships went down. And 785 U-boats.

Alexander Werth, an English journalist, described his feelings on the Murmansk run after a sister ship to his freighter had gone down in the arctic seas:

"They also had their captain, and their steward . . . and a smoke-room like ours, and cigarettes, and bottles of rum, and pictures of the king and queen, and tea cups and saucers, and lavatories, and a great big deep engine room like ours, and a refrigerator with a lot of cheese and ham. And now it was all smashed, at the bottom of the sea, or some of it still floating—and it was horrible to think of parts of human bodies floating about the ocean in life jackets."

New Guinea

When Douglas MacArthur finally reached Adelaide in Australia on his odyssey from Bataan, he gave his famous promise: "I shall return." He did so in a campaign of brilliance, bravery and braggadocio, all hallmarks of probably the most controversial of the Allied commanders.

He would do so through one of the least known, hostile parts of the world, the mountainous jungles of New Guinea, second largest island on Earth.

Within days of his arrival Down Under, MacArthur closeted himself with maps. He spent weeks memorizing the terrain. He had almost no troops, few planes. The U.S. 41st Division didn't begin embarking in Australia until April 6, 1942. The 32nd Division arrived nine days later. Churchill grudgingly agreed to send Australia's three divisions home from Africa. But then what?

Two key concepts drove MacArthur. As a youth he had toured the Orient with his father and wrote after the trip, which included a visit to Japan: ". . . the very existence of America [is] irrevocably entwined with Asia and its island outposts . . ." He had also sat on the court-martial of General Billy Mitchell, an old friend who was an early and spurned apostle of air power. MacArthur had come to agree with Mitchell's prediction: "Any offensive . . . against Japan will have to be made under the cover of our own air power . . . Campaigning across the sea will be carried on from land base to land base under the protection of our aircraft."

MacArthur **(fourth from left)** *sat on court-martial of his friend, air power prophet Billy Mitchell, in 1925.*

Scorned as "Dugout Doug" at Bataan, MacArthur was front-line regular in New Guinea, here watching parachute attack.

General Kenney didn't think MacArthur's staff knew about airpower.

Yet MacArthur was to protest unendingly that his southwest Pacific theater was shortchanged by the high command. "To make something out of nothing seems to be my military fate. I have led one lost cause and am trying desperately not to have it two." Yet the general had little use for the Navy, deeming it reckless of lives in a "damn the torpedoes" attitude instead of one of deft movement. He was also highly suspicious of the Army Air Corps which he thought incompetent if not disloyal, obedience to higher command being one thing he insisted on. The Navy for its part didn't think generals like MacArthur understood the first thing about water. When Major General George Churchill Kenney arrived in Australia on July 28, 1942, to assume command of the slowly gathering 5th Air Force, MacArthur chewed his ear at length. But when Kenney found MacArthur's chief of staff, Major General Sutherland, vain son of a Supreme Court justice, drawing up air plans, he took a pencil and stubbed a dot on a sheet of paper. "That's what you know about air power," said Kenney. "The rest of the sheet is what I know." He told MacArthur his bags were packed if he were ever deemed anything but steadfast. MacArthur-Kenney henceforth became like hand-glove. That was because Kenney performed. When he told a dubious MacArthur he could fly trucks to New Guinea, he did so by cutting them in half, loading them into C-47s (the civilian DC-3) and welding them back together on arrival.

MacArthur was also a man of Olympian vanity and a master of public relations and favorable press releases.

But Dugout Doug, as some of the less fond GIs came to call him, unfairly, was a genuine hero. He won the Medal of Honor as well as seven Distinguished Service Crosses, the last rallying troops outside Manila in 1945. He gave his staff fits by walking into battle areas scorning a helmet in favor of his tarnished gold braid hat from Bataan and armed with nothing but a walking stick. MacArthur made a point of wading ashore the same day his troops landed, and, when he finally did return to the Philippines, did it twice for the benefit of photographers who missed it the first time.

He did not immediately seize upon the strategy his campaign ultimately took. But the lessons of air power were soon borne in on him. New Guinea was an exotic, equatorial hell for the soldiers: 16,000-foot mountains, Stone Age cannibals, jungles that took an hour to hack a few feet through, swamps, insects and savannas where seven-foot-tall grass cut like razors. No one was considered sick until his temperature reached 102. The Japanese slithered single file over the Owen Stanley Mountains towards Port Moresby on New Guinea's south coast before being turned back by disease, starvation and Australian jungle fighters. It was to be the southern most extent of the instant Japanese empire. Americans and Australian soldiers hacked their way back across the mountains towards Japanese strong points at Buna and Gona on the north coast under Eichelberger of whom the determined MacArthur said: "I want him to die if he doesn't get Buna." He didn't, but Americans took 8,546 casualties before the villages were taken. By then a strategy had evolved to save lives, time and distance. While the Japanese, anticipating MacArthur would fight by traditional methods of warfare,

Orders for General Eichelberger: capture Buna in New Guinea "or don't come back alive."

girded for a goal line stand with 200,000 troops in Rabaul on the island of New Britain off New Guinea's northeast coast, MacArthur began a series of quarterback keeper end sweeps instead. His troops leapfrogged westwards along the New Guinea coast, bypassing Japanese strongholds. The idea was to secure a foothold and build airstrips for Kenney's bombers and fighters to soften up the next invasion point. Rabaul's troops never fired a shot except at bombers who methodically fulfilled Admiral Halsey's aim to "bomb Rabaul into rubble." The American plan was for MacArthur to command a left wing relentlessly curving towards the ultimate goal of the Philippines. Meanwhile the right arm under Nimitz, a resolute Texan, island hopped westward across the Pacific.

Air power was the key. The goal was eventually to cut the Japanese supply lines to Indonesia and its crucial oil, the essential fuel of war. The American pilots were as colorful as any comic strip heroes. There was Major Gregory "Pappy" Boyington and his Black Sheep Squadron. And Major Richard Bong, America's all-time ace with forty kills who had come to Kenney's attention in San Francisco when he flew his P-38 so low a housewife complained his prop wash blew her laundry off the clothesline. And Captain William Shomo who shot down six fighters and a bomber on his very first mission and said he couldn't get more because "I ran out of bullets."

War's top U.S. ace Richard Bong shot down fifteen more in his P-38 before dying in 1945 crash of new jet.

A Japanese threatened to shoot "Black Sheep" Squadron's Boyington (arrow), downed after twenty-eight kills. "Well, ain't you the cheerful son of a bitch," said "Pappy."

Japanese bodies strewn about a blasted pillbox after U.S. Marine invasion of Tarawa. AP's Frank Filan earned Pulitzer Prize for the dramatic photo.

By the spring of 1944 the Japanese high command was debating withdrawing from New Guinea, and the Bismarck, Solomon, Gilbert and Marshall Islands and concentrating within "an absolute national defense sphere." A few considered the war already lost. By the summer of 1944 with the capture of Morotai, MacArthur was at the gates of the Philippines. Looking north, the general said: "They are waiting for me there. It has been a long time."

In two years his forces, in what Churchill called a "triphibious" war, had advanced 2,000 miles, farther than the marches of Alexander the Great. His men had made eighty-seven landings, all successful. His casualties were only 27,684 men. Military analyst Mark A. Watson called MacArthur's thrusts "ingenious and dazzling." The British historian B.H. Liddell Hart was to write: "MacArthur was supreme among the generals. He outshone [them all] including Montgomery."

William Manchester titled his outstanding biography of MacArthur *American Caesar* for all the imperial self-glorification and genius it implies. The toga fits.

Island Hopping

MacArthur's engineers carved airstrips out of jungle in a matter of weeks. Nimitz's admirals brought theirs with them.

To unlock the Pacific door to Japan the carrier was the key. Massed Navy planes first cleared the air of Japanese aircraft. Then ships moved in closer

U.S. recaptured Attu and Kiska in Aleutians in 1943.

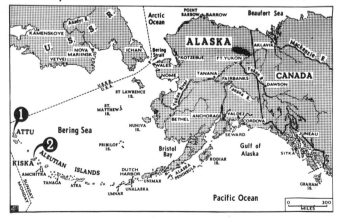

to join the aerial bombardment with cannon fire. Then the landing craft moved to the beaches. Once again the strategy was to hop-scotch from one island to the next within range of land-based planes. The Japanese bastion at Truk some 3,000 miles southeast of Tokyo in the Carolines was ignored, for instance, once its planes had been destroyed. When Kwajalein was bombarded on February 1, 1944, one sailor said, "It looked like it had been picked up to 20,000 feet and then dropped." By then even War Minister Tojo, the hard disciplinarian they called The Razor, was having second thoughts. He asked Saburo Kurusu, the Pearl Harbor Day diplomat who had been exchanged for Ambassador Grew, to see if he could arrange for peace. "It's easier to start a war than end one," Kurusu replied.

The first U.S. advance into the Pacific occurred May 11, 1943, the day before Rommel's Afrika Korps surrendered in North Africa, and the 7th Division landed on Attu in the distant Aleutians. When the fighting ended almost three weeks later, nearly all of the 2,350-man Japanese garrison were dead. The Americans suffered 512 casualties. On August 15 a U.S.-Canadian force of 34,000 men landed on Kiska unaware that the Japanese had evacuated their Aleutian toehold eighteen days before. The invaders were met by three dogs which produced the poem:

> It took three days before we learnt
> That more than dogs there simply weren't.

The Aleutians also produced one of the most concise messages since the Gettysburg Address. After Captain Fred M. Smith sank a Japanese mine-sweeper from his P-38, he radioed: "Saw steamer, strafed same, sank same, some sight, signed Smith."

On November 20, 1943, soldiers of the 27th Division landed on Makin, an atoll some 2,500 miles southwest of Hawaii, and four days later secured the island against moderate resistance by 800 defenders. Tarawa, 105 miles to the south, was another story for the 2nd Marine Division. Rear Admiral Keiji Shibasaki, who commanded the 2,600 first-line troops on the atoll, said, "A million men cannot take Tarawa in a hundred years." Tarawa's tiny islet of Betio, about half the size of New York's Central Park, had been battered by a combined force of seventeen carriers, eight battleships and twelve cruisers. Then the Marines, whose tactics were full ahead where the Army preached more methodical fighting, stormed ashore over the reefs and up against a coconut-log seawall. Betio had been softened up with ten tons of explosives per acre, but the Japanese were cleverly dug in beneath domed bunkers that deflected direct hits.

PT-109

One of the more dashing forces in the island fighting of the southwest Pacific was the PT boat, useful for night scouting and swift hit-and-run raids on shipping. A standing order was never to turn off their powerful but hard-to-start engines while on patrol.

On the night of August 2, 1943, PT-109 was on patrol in the Solomons under command of Lieutenant John F. Kennedy, son of the prewar American ambassador to Great Britain, Joseph P. Kennedy. The torpedo boat, dead in the water, was rammed by a Japanese destroyer. Kennedy, hurt himself, heroically swam to a nearby island towing an injured shipmate with him. Kennedy scratched a message on a coconut shell that friendly coast watchers eventually relayed back to his base. He and ten of his crewmen were rescued.

Red Marsden, a Marine combat correspondent who was to have gone along on the patrol but didn't due to a last minute cancellation, said at first Kennedy was going to have to face a court-martial for turning off his engines. Instead, he was awarded the Navy Cross.

The coast watchers were scarcely less heroic. They were usually friendly natives or planters and beachcombers, usually Australian, who reported on Japanese ship and plane movements by concealed radios.

PT-109, Lieutenant Kennedy commanding (r.), helped launch a president. Kennedy committed a no-no by turning off his engines.

One hundred machine guns were aimed over the seawall.

Half of a battalion of 700 men were killed or wounded in the reddening water. It took seventy-six hours and 1,056 lives before the tiny island and its fighter airstrip were conquered. Only seventeen Japanese surrendered. It was a sobering lesson but instructive. After Tarawa the amphibious amtracs were more heavily armed and armored. The Navy learned that high trajectory fire was more effective against blockhouses. Assault commanders learned to wait for the smoke and dust of bombardment to clear to better assess the damage before sending in the troops.

At Tehran in November 1943, Big Three met for first time. Stalin was noncommittal about future of Poland.

Meanwhile on November 28, 1943, half a world away in the Persian capital of Tehran, Roosevelt, Churchill and Stalin met for the first time. The Soviets reaffirmed their intention to fight Japan once Germany was beaten. The Allies agreed to set a date the next May for the invasion of Europe, to be code-named Overlord. At dinner one night the Soviet dictator teased Churchill by saying 50,000 Germans must be shot as part of the invasion. Churchill flamed he would rather be shot himself than "sully my own and my country's honor by such infamy."

"I have a compromise," offered Roosevelt, a peacemaker with tongue in cheek. "Not 50,000 but only 49,000 should be shot."

On the way to Tehran, Roosevelt and Churchill had stopped in Cairo to meet with Chiang Kai-shek. The British had proposed an invasion of Burma as well as the Balkans, long a favorite of Churchill who likened the Balkans to "the soft underbelly of Europe." At a subsequent meeting in Cairo on the way home from Tehran, the Allies agreed to drop both invasions. Europe was to continue as the main focus of the war. In the Pacific, justifying some of MacArthur's paranoia, Nimitz was to get the larger slice of the armament pie than the general.

Nimitz swiftly put his weapons to work. On February 1, 1944, his Marines and Army soldiers invaded Kwajalein in the Marshall Islands, 1,000 miles nearer Japan, from Tarawa. Later that month the Americans moved 350 miles closer with the capture of Eniwetok. At the same time, nine carriers of Rear Admiral Marc A. Mitscher's fleet, now based in the huge lagoon of the undefended Majuro Atoll, hit Truk, destroying 200 planes on the ground and sinking forty-one ships. Saipan in the Marianas, within bombing distance of Japan proper, was invaded June 15, 1944. The 3rd Marine Division and the Army's 77th Division landed on Guam on July 21 and secured the island the next month.

Nimitz' watery campaign next moved to close the pincers on the Philippines with the invasion September 15, 1944, of the island of Peleliu, only 450 miles from Mindanao. Halsey had wanted to bypass the island fearing, correctly as it turned out, another Tarawa. Nimitz, however, overruled him. Marines of the 1st Division, some singing "Give My Regards to Broadway," charged ashore into a month of some of the heaviest fighting of the Pacific war. The 6,500 Japanese defenders practiced a new tactic of defense in depth which claimed 1,252 Marine dead and 277 from the Army's 81st Division which later joined the fighting. The Americans calculated it took an average of 1,589 rounds of ammunition to kill each Japanese soldier to capture the five-mile long island.

As always, hardly had the smoke cleared than the Navy's Construction Battalion, the famous Seabees, moved in to turn the rubble into a base. With their motto of "Can Do," they could turn a jungle into an airstrip in eight days. On Guam they built

"Bull" Halsey: "The bugaboo of many sailors, the fear of losing ships, was completely alien to him."

Texan Chester Nimitz loved dogs, risque jokes, classical music; excelled at horseshoes, thinking (Midway), coordinating egos and running the war in the Pacific.

and paved one hundred miles of road in ninety days. They even worked under fire, using the blades of their bulldozers as a shield.

On October 20, 1944, the pincers finally reached home when 132,000 soldiers of Eichelberger's 6th Army came ashore on Leyte in the central Philippines. Right behind them, wading knee deep because his landing craft had grounded on a rock, strode MacArthur, wearing his old Bataan hat and smoking his corncob. He said, as he had promised two-and-a-half years before: "I have returned."

For Nimitz and his fleet, their next point of return loomed some 1,500 miles to the north where lay two islands. One, tiny, was named Iwo Jima. The other, large, was called Okinawa.

Sicily

Of the invasion of Sicily, Omar Bradley said: "Seldom in war has a major operation been undertaken in such a fog of indecision, confusion and conflicting plans."

Sicily was an obvious stepping stone from North Africa for an invasion of southern Europe. "Anybody but a damn fool would know it is Sicily," said Churchill. The British intentionally gave false signals to hide their hand. Marshall, who favored a buildup in Britain for a cross-Channel invasion of France, only grudgingly gave his consent. Ike was to be in overall command. General Alexander would lead some 450,000 Allied ground troops, the Americans under Patton and the British 8th Army veterans under Montgomery. It was a recipe for trouble all the more because the various commands were spread over 500 miles from Tunis and Malta to Algiers.

The island was defended by 30,000 Germans in two divisions and about 200,000 of their uncertain Italian allies. Most of the Italians wanted out of war. "It was a curious position," said Roman

journalist Romano Giachetti. "Men still armed were forced to fire at an enemy that was actually their friend. The enemy was among them: Fascists and Germans." Morale was almost nonexistent. Officers dined on multi-course meals while their men did without even field kitchens. Officers went to town leaving no one in charge. "Wherever I go I see commanders behaving like cinema actors," said an Italian corps commander. Sentries slept, officers ducked combat. After the invasion started, a British Tommy engaged in vicious fighting against the Germans angrily told a company of Italians trying to surrender to him to "Get Lost!" Mike Chinigo of the International News Service was in a captured bunker with the first Americans ashore when a phone rang. It was an Italian general inquiring if an invasion was going on. "Say it isn't so," he entreated. Chinigo, who spoke Italian, told the general it wasn't so, so he rang off.

D Day, July 10, 1943, was preceded by an airborne landing that was completely fouled up. Gliders crashed into the sea, drowning their men. Paratroopers dropped miles from their landing zones. Subsequent airborne operations were disrupted by friendly naval antiaircraft shooting down their own Allied planes.

Within two days, 80,000 troops, 7,000 vehicles and 900 guns were successfully ashore, carried by newly designed LSTs, LCIs and smaller craft. Leading the Americans was the 1st Division, the Big Red One, the oldest active division in the Army. Two of its artillery regiments dated to the American Revolution. It was commanded by Major General Terry de la Mesa Allen, a carousing fighter who got overseas in World War I by sneaking into a line of Europe-bound graduates from a stateside combat school. His battle philosophy: "A soldier doesn't fight to save suffering humanity or any other goddam nonsense. He fights to prove his unit is the best in the Army and that he has as much guts as anybody else in the unit."

Guam, one of many "Can Do" bases built by Navy Seabees.

It soon became clear, to Patton's increasing outrage, that Alexander did not trust the fighting capability of the Americans. Patton's 7th Army was assigned to protect Montgomery's left flank while the 8th Army advanced to Messina, the key objective just two-and-a-half miles across the strait from the Italian mainland. Historians have harshly criticized Alexander, nonetheless one of Eisenhower's favorite British generals, for not having a determined plan once the Allies got ashore such as having Patton's men swing around Mount Etna, an active volcano, in a flanking drive on Messina. Instead, Patton got mad and marched in search of publicity and Palermo way to the west and irrelevant to the central campaign. Patton said: "The

Patton (l.) *and Bradley* (center) *would threaten to quit over Monty* (r.).

MAJOR MARTIN

One of the cleverest tricks of the war, or any war, was "The Man Who Never Was."

Largely the brainchild of Lieutenant Commander Ewen Montagu, a lawyer in civilian life now with British Naval Intelligence, Operation Mincemeat was designed to mislead the Germans that the Allies would invade Sardinia or Greece, anywhere but their intended object, Sicily. With the permission of the family, Montagu obtained the body of a man in his thirties who had just died of pneumonia. He would be outfitted as British Marine Major William Martin who had died in a plane crash while carrying top secret invasion papers from England to Gibraltar.

To make him credible, he was equipped with love letters from his fiancee and a snapshot of her, a stern letter from his father frowning on the engagement, two theater ticket stubs and an overdraft notice from his bank. The body was cast adrift from a submarine off the Spanish port of Huelva where Montagu gambled local officials would find the body and turn the papers over to a German agent the British knew to be active in the area. Montagu's gamble worked. Copies of Major Martin's documents made it all the way to Hitler. A whole parachute division was transferred from France to Greece. For critical days the Germans believed the Sicily invasion was only a diversion from an imminent invasion elsewhere in the Mediterranean. The British cabled Churchill conferring in Washington: "MINCEMEAT SWALLOWED WHOLE."

Montagu kept his word to the family that Major Martin's identity would never be disclosed. All he ever said was that he was "a bit of a ne'er-do-well and the only worthwhile thing he ever did he did after his death."

Major Martin lies today under his headstone in a cemetery in Huelva.

Allies must fight in separate theaters or they hate each other more than they do the enemy." Patton emerged as a master of movement while Eisenhower became critical of Montgomery who he thought lost initiative by not attacking until everything was in place. Major General Lucian K. Truscott's 3rd Division, trained to hike up to five miles an hour instead of the standard two-and-a-half in what became known as The Truscott Trot, typified the American mobility by marching 100 miles through intense heat in just three days.

Allied air superiority was never utilized to the maximum by coordinating close support with the ground troops. Naval gunnery, decisive when called upon, was also not fully integrated. Personalities conflicted. The Allied naval commander, Admiral Sir Andrew Cunningham, thought his countryman Montgomery so obstinate he wouldn't have his countryman's name mentioned in his presence. "In dealing with [Monty]," said one British commander, "one must remember that he is not quite a gentleman." Patton was quietly furious because his old friend Eisenhower seemed to be supporting the British view: "This is what you get when your commander in chief ceases to be an American and becomes an ally," he fumed.

Patton captured Palermo and headlines with ease, then turned east to Messina. Several times he landed troops by sea ahead of his advancing army, a tactic better conceived than executed. On one landing the first troops the Americans encountered were their fellow GIs.

Montgomery, meanwhile, was facing off with Germans reinforced by paratroopers who were some of the world's best fighting men. They were brilliant extemporizers of battle, fought with exem-

ARRIVEDERCI, DUCE

Mussolini, puffing like a pouter pigeon, boasted his soldiers would hurl the Allies back from Sicily "right at the water's edge." He got thrown out instead.

His operatic posturings had already struck a sour note with the mass surrenders of Italian troops in Africa. There was yet more discord when the Allies, expecting a bitter struggle to capture the island of Pantelleria prior to the Sicily invasion, took it without a shot when the 11,390-man garrison surrendered. The only casualty was a Tommy who was bitten by a mule.

With Sicily seemingly to follow, the Italian Grand Council met July 24 for the first time in three-and-a-half years. They poured scorn on the once strutting Il Duce. "You believed yourself a soldier," said the scathing Council president Dino Grandi. "Let me tell you, Italy was lost the very day you put the gold braid of a marshal on your cap. . . . In this war we have already a hundred thousand mothers who cry: 'Mussolini assassinated my son!' "

The next day Mussolini appeared before his king, Victor Emmanuel. "Il gioco e finito," the king said. "The game is over, Mussolini. . . . You'll have to go."

"Sire," said the fallen dictator, "this is the end of fascism." He got that right.

Mussolini was arrested, hustled off in a Red Cross ambulance and sent to the island of Ponza off Naples. He was replaced by Field Marshal Pietro Badoglio, an aging soldier of common sense and peasant realism who pledged: "The war goes on."

Hitler's reaction was immediate. "I cannot and will not leave Italy's greatest son in the lurch. I

Italy's king told Mussolini, "The game is over."

Colonel Otto Skorzeny, Hitler's master of the impossible, rescued Il Duce.

will keep faith with my old ally and friend." He was fearful the Italians would turn Mussolini over to the Allies. Hitler assigned commando daredevil Colonel Otto Skorzeny to the rescue. Skorzeny searched high and low for Mussolini's whereabouts without success until a radio intercept spoke of security precautions at a ski resort high in the Appenines.

Skorzeny led a glider assault team on the inaccessible hotel where Mussolini's guards surrendered without a struggle. "I knew my friend Adolf Hitler would not leave me in the lurch," said Mussolini to Skorzeny. "Thank you for my life."

What remained of it was to be as a puppet for Hitler.

---

plary ferocity and knew when to retreat leaving behind an intricate cover of land mines.

Patton thought Bradley, a corps commander under him, was timid, called him Omar the Tentmaker. Bradley thought Patton bombastic and impetuous. Somehow their alleged shortcomings coalesced. For all his pearl-handled Colts at his hip and burnished helmet, Patton was hounded by uncertainties as to his own courage. He was an anomaly, a lover of poetry, a dyslexic, and had been a hero in charging a machine gun nest in World War I. Lord Alan Brooke, the British chief of staff, thought Patton was "good for operations requiring thrust and push but at a loss in any operation requiring skill and judgment."

Patton conceded he took "calculated risks. That

is quite different from being rash. My personal belief is that if you have a 50 percent chance take it because the superior fighting qualities of the American soldier led by me will surely give you the extra 1 percent necessary." The Germans came to rank Patton as the most formidable of the Allied generals.

Bradley was a direct counterpoint of the patrician Patton, a Midwesterner with all the homely virtues and simplicity. He didn't taste alcohol until he was thirty-three.

About this time Lord Louis Mountbatten, who was assigned to lead Allied forces in India and Burma, wrote Eisenhower for his views on the requirements for a commander of combined forces. "He is in a very definite sense the chairman of a board," Ike replied. "He must execute those duties firmly, wisely and without any question as to his own authority . . . .take full blame for anything that goes wrong . . . .whether or not it results from his mistake." He must be self-effacing, resist the human need for personal praise, quick to give credit to others. "Patience, tolerance, frankness, absolute honesty . . . .and never permit any problem to be approached in your staff on the basis of national interest." Holding the alliance together, Eisenhower concluded, came first at the expense of overall direction of the battlefield.

This was accentuated by Eisenhower's remoteness from Sicily at his headquarters in Algiers. Sicily was a forerunner of troubles with Montgomery. The desert warrior, who the first time he met Ike curtly told him to put out his cigarette as he couldn't abide smoke, thought the American "is probably quite good on the political side. But I can also say, quite definitely, that he knows nothing whatever about how to make war." For his part, Eisenhower believed Montgomery "is so proud of his successes to date that he will never willingly make a single move until he is absolutely certain of success."

But there was an unshared memory behind this. Monty, fifty-five, could well remember his World War I service in France where, for instance, 60,000 Englishmen fell at the Somme in a single day in the absurd belief that the flower of the nation could somehow overcome machine guns simply by the mass of its flesh. This memory was always present when the British considered the casualties of a direct assault across the Channel.

Relations with the Allies was one concern. When Patton slapped two GIs who had sought refuge from battle nerves in field hospitals filled with wounded, Eisenhower faced a crisis with his own countryman. Bradley, who was amazed at a man who could harangue his men with the coarsest obscenities yet converse with great erudtiion at dinner, said he "would have relieved [Patton] on the spot." Eisenhower, however, valued Patton as a fighter and convinced three correspondents of as much when they threatened to break the story which was hushed up for ten months.

The disarray among the Allies and the respective services was nowhere better illustrated than when the Germans evacuated 60,000 troops and most of their equipment across the Messina Strait. Much of it was accomplished in broad daylight in spite of Allied air and naval superiority. The escape, more successful than the Dunkirk evacuation though on a smaller scale, marked a bitter end of thirty-eight days of fighting. The Germans boldly ferried troops even at high noon knowing the Allied pilots habitually broke for lunch.

MAFIA AT WAR

What role the Mafia played, if any, in the invasion of Sicily and later Italy is, as usual, obscure.

Organized crime was approached by the U.S. Navy to enlist for the duration by keeping peace on the mob-ridden New York waterfront, a major port of embarkation. Rumors that the OSS (Office of Strategic Services), the American intelligence arm, used Mafia connections to set up a military government in Sicily after the invasion have never been substantiated. Vito Genovese, a mob ruler, did serve as an interpreter for the Americans in Naples, but whether he had other duties has never been proven.

Mussolini had been an avowed enemy of the Sicilian hoodlums, but his removal and the lucrative lure of black marketeering in the chaotic aftermath of the battle plus the looting of American supplies at dockside in Naples (up to a third of what was landed) contributed to a rebirth of the Sicilian gangs.

In Sicily, Patton was almost sent home for slapping GIs.

It had been a hard victory, as well. The 60,000 Germans had stood off 450,000 Allied soldiers for more than a month, taking 19,600 casualties while suffering 29,000 themselves. Some of it had been ugly. Germans tied a captured American to a tree and shot him. Two Americans were court-martialed for shooting seventy-three German and Italian prisoners.

If nothing else, the largest invasion of history demonstrated that there was homework to be done.

Salerno to Rome

To the British, an invasion of Italy was a not-to-be-missed opportunity to suck German divisions away from the Soviet Union and the French invasion coast and hasten victory there. To the Americans, an Italian campaign would become a stalemate chewing up men and material better used elsewhere.

Both were right. By the end of the war Hitler had sent thirty-six divisions to fight in Italy. And limited Allied objectives originally became open-ended.

Ever since the extension of the British Empire to India in the 18th century and the digging of the Suez Canal in the next, the Mediterranean became a vital artery for England. Furthermore, centuries of combat in Europe had taught the island British the advantages of a warfare of the unexpected. Wellington, for instance, had attacked Napoleon via Spain. Churchill as First Lord of the Admiralty in World War I had attempted a decisive and in the end disastrous strike at Germany through Turkey. A war later, the British prime minister still had an overwhelming attraction to "the soft underbelly of Europe." His armies were already in the Mediterranean in great strength. Sources of further manpower were near their limits. But its almost unlimited resources in men and industrial capacity had made the United States the senior partner.

Said a rueful Air Chief Marshal Sir Charles Portal of the RAF: "We are in the position of a testator who wishes to leave the bulk of his fortune to his mistress. He must, however, leave something to his wife." The fond mistress was the soft underbelly. The wife was the United States.

The Americans had yielded on invading Sicily so long as it did not detract from the main landing to come in France. George Marshall was adamant on that point while the Americans were generally suspicious of Britain's ultimate intentions. At the Trident meetings of the Joint Chiefs of Staff in Washington in May 1943, Brooke confided in his diary: ". . . the Americans are taking up the attitude that we led them down the garden path by taking them into North Africa. That at Casablanca

we again misled them by inducing them to attack Sicily. And now they do not intend to be led astray again." The Trident conferees decided to make no hard plans beyond Operation Husky, the Sicily invasion. The decision was left to the commander on the spot, Eisenhower.

With that in mind, Churchill came to Algiers later that month to unleash his powers of persuasion on Ike. The prime minister kept Ike up far into the night over brandy depicting a "glorious campaign" up the Italian boot culminating in the occupation of Rome, target of so many invasions throughout history. Eisenhower was ever mindful of Roosevelt's assurances to Stalin that the Allies would open a second front as soon as possible. Supplying an occupied Italy would take, just for starters, ten million tons of coal a year. Landing craft were in critically short supply and were being husbanded for France and urgently needed in the Pacific. Without bombers, which were pounding Germany from British bases, Eisenhower's staff predicted an Italian invasion would fail. Ike would wait and see how Sicily went before making any promises.

Only once had an invader captured Rome from the South. The reason: mountains.

It went acceptably well. The grandiloquent Churchill cooed to his staff in July: "It is true, I suppose, that the Americans consider that we have led them up the garden path in the Mediterranean—but what a beautiful path it has proved to be. They have picked up peaches here, nectarines there. How grateful they should be." On July 17 Eisenhower agreed to an Italian landing. This was affirmed by Roosevelt the following month at the Quadrant conference in Quebec with Churchill. In return, the British agreed to an invasion of France the following spring any time from May 1 on. Had they not done so, Marshall had threatened to cut back on the American effort in Europe to concentrate on the Pacific. Roosevelt acquiesced to a campaign that would take Naples and the airfields at Foggia near the Adriatic coast but stop short of Rome.

The invasion already had taken on the duality that was to mark the war in Italy. In July Hitler had called off the battle of Kursk in Russia, where 4,000 tanks had fought the greatest armored battle in history, to reinforce Sicily and begin occupying his wavering Italian ally. Operating with limited resources, Alexander, named to head the Allied ground forces, said the invasion set for September 9 at Salerno would be "a dangerous gamble." The Allies were counting on surprise, so did not schedule a softening-up bombardment. The military historian J.F.C. Fuller was to call the plan to take Naples and Foggia "reasonable," Rome "political" and the rest "daft." Only one invader in history had ever taken Rome from the south.

A major question mark was what role the 1.3 million soldiers of the Italian army would play. With Sicily taken and Mussolini fallen, Marshal Badoglio approached the Allies. If they would make a show of force in Rome, Italy would surrender. Major General Maxwell Taylor snuck into Rome to negotiate. When Badoglio learned only Taylor's 82nd Airborne Division was available to occupy Rome, he backed down, to the Allies' intense anger. The invasion fleet was already at sea. A parachute drop by the 82nd was scrubbed at the last minute. Meanwhile, Hitler had sent nineteen divisions already into Italy with more coming. They were under the command of Field Marshal Albert Kesselring, dubbed "Smiling Albert" by correspondents for his always sunny countenance in photographs. Smiling Albert, who was to prove a master of defensive warfare, had talked his fuehrer into defending Italy south of Rome no matter what the Italians did. The idea of giving up any soil of his brand new empire without a fight gave Hitler even more fits than customary. On September 8 Italy surrendered, officially to the Allies, in fact to the Germans who had orders to shoot them if they didn't, lest they turn on Kesselring's occupiers. Roosevelt had hoped the Italians would resist the hated Germans, but, as Ike had predicted, they turned in their weapons with hardly a fight and melted into the countryside

Allies took gamble at Salerno by landing without softening-up barrage.

"Smiling Albert" Kesselring, here relaxing at Hitler's Berchtesgaden, was a master of defensive warfare.

towards home, delighted to be out of it.

When Eisenhower announced the surrender, one of the soldiers aboard the invasion transports exulted: "We dock in Naples unopposed with an olive branch in one hand and an opera ticket in the other." It was not to be.

Montgomery had, indeed, landed on the toe of Italy September 3 almost without opposition. Other 8th Army airborne troops quickly took the naval base at Taranto as the Italian fleet steamed off to join the Allies. The Germans correctly took these landings as diversions. Hitler thought the real target would be Yugoslavia and Kesselring, Rome. But his able and tenacious ground commander, Colonel General Heinrich Vietinghoff, correctly guessed Salerno.

Marshall himself had wanted a secondary landing towards Rome, but Eisenhower had neither the men nor landing craft, and Salerno was at the outer range of fighter air cover. Nature had shaped Salerno along the lines of an ancient Greek amphitheater, the stage being a flat plane overlooked by a ring of hills where 17,000 German troops were keen spectators as two American and two British divisions came ashore. They were tempting targets for artillery as were the huge LSTs, nicknamed Large Stationary Targets by their nervous occupants, lined up along the beach. By nightfall, however, the 36th Division, a Texas National Guard unit and the first Americans to set foot on continental Europe, had pushed four miles inland to the foothills of the mountain.

Resistance was moderate, fortunately, for the beachhead was a sandy gridlock as everything imaginable was unloaded including a piano for the future sergeants' mess. Alexander was no stranger to beaches. He had been the last man off the beach at Dunkirk. In Britain's best stiff upper lip tradition, he had told an aide who said it looked like they would have to surrender: "So it does. But I don't know the form for surrendering. So it seems we can't." The American commander of what was the 5th Army was forty-seven-year-old Mark Clark, the youngest lieutenant general in American history. Salerno was his first combat since World War I. Codenamed Avalanche, the operation suffered from last minute planning. The landing armada had been packed as hastily as a suitcase with too little time to get to the airport. Nonetheless, early objectives were taken by hand-picked American Rangers and British Commandos who numbered among them Colonel "Mad Jack" Churchill, a true exotic and ex-film bit player who went to war playing his bagpipes and wielding a claymore, the fighting sword of his ancestral Scottish clansmen. Churchill was a Brit the Yanks could understand. GIs in general were mystified by the British regimental system and its privates asking officers "Permission to speak, sir." For their part, the Brits thought Yanks sloppy and far too familiar with their own officers.

National quirks were forgotten September 13

GIs wait for expected German counterattack on Salerno beachhead.

GIs land at Salerno on the double under German fire.

when Kesselring struck with his swiftly-mobilized forces precisely at the gap between the two armies. The Germans penetrated to within a few miles of the beach. Clark ordered cooks, orderlies, truck drivers and anyone who could hold a rifle into the line. Lieutenant Colonel Hal Muldrow of the 189th Field Artillery clambered up the tiled roof of a barn to shout down firing instructions to his 155mm howitzers, now shooting point blank at German panzers. Safety regulations were thrown to the winds as the cannoneers stuffed their weapons with furious speed to get off a round every twenty seconds. In the British sector, the Duke of Wellington, a fifth generation descendant of the hero of Waterloo, died in a counterattack. Mad Jack, swinging his claymore alongside an aide with a tommy gun, brought in a dozen German prisoners. The Germans were so close Clark considered moving his headquarters offshore. One GI began lobbing mortar shells by hand, arming them by slamming them on a barn floor. Getting a loaded landing craft off a beach made evacuation an unlikely option. Major General Troy Middleton of the U.S. 45th Division didn't consider it. "We are going to stay here," he told his men at the peak of the crisis. On the worst night, 1,200 men of the 82nd Airborne parachuted onto the beachhead while naval gunners blasted the Germans from just offshore. Half of a company of Germans approached soldiers of the 45th waving a white flag. Suddenly they dropped it as the GIs stood up and began firing. The Americans shot down forty of them. Bombers pasted the Germans with 3,020 tons of explosives in a single day. But the Nazi enemy was unyielding. Private Ike Franklin was captured along with some wounded Americans and some plasma bottles. The Germans refused to use any of it for their wounded. "You're doctors. You know better than this," Franklin said. "Our orders are clear," replied a German physician. "It might be Jewish or Negro blood."

Eisenhower ordered Montgomery to hurry on with his 8th Army which had only covered forty-five miles in a week moving up the toe of Italy. Said Monty: "I have not been told of any plan, and I must therefore assume that there was none." Clark said later: "[Monty] landed first and he was coming up, well, I won't say leisurely, but it sure wasn't as fast as I had hoped. I kept getting messages 'Hold up—we've joined hands.' I sent a message back: 'If we've joined hands, I haven't felt a thing yet.'"

With reports that some troops had broken under the stress of battle, Eisenhower paced the floor: "By God, the 5th Army ought to emulate the Russians at Stalingrad and stand and fight." Many did and with a superior force of 170,000 now facing him at Salerno, Kesselring drew back. As he did so, the 8th Army finally linked up with the 5th Army on

Hill circling Salerno made ideal gun platform for German 88s.

September 17. The Allies were in Europe for good.

A German officer belittled the Allies for "ineptitude and cowardice spreading down from the command and this resulted in chaos." Sergeant Joe Gill of the 36th saw the battle's successful conclusion another way. "We just thought that was the way war was and we didn't know any better. If we had known any better, we might not have made it."

The nine days of Salerno had cost the Allies 9,000 casualties. It was only a beginning.

Naples was liberated October 1. There was no opera in the bombed-out city. The port was a wreckage of 130 ships sunk in the harbor. Yet within three days of miracles by Army engineers the first Liberty ship began to unload. All over the city Germans had left mines timed to explode weeks later. On October 11 Foggia and its airports fell. The reasonable goals had been achieved, but on September 26 Eisenhower had issued orders to keep fighting up the peninsula to Rome. But by mid-October the Germans had nine more divisions in Italy than the Allies. The stalemate had begun.

Terrain created it. The Italian boot is actually a tortuous spine of stony mountains with no room to maneuver, only places to dig in. "God's gift to gunners," Kesselring called it, looking at the unbroken horizon of peaks, cliffs and crags of the Abruzzi range. He improved on nature. Using forced Italian labor, the Germans built a series of defensive lines across the peninsula. Deadly 88s were built into mountains and zeroed in on the few roads that traversed them. Machine guns were sited for sweeping crossfire. Portable bunkers of steel five inches thick were hauled by tractors to key points and cemented into the crags. Tanks were buried to their turrets or hidden in the stone houses to make hundreds of little forts. An attacker had to either try the impossible and struggle over the mountains or dare the few valleys in full view of the emplaced batteries. Mines, millions of them, were everywhere. Antitank mines. Mines in wooden boxes to foil magnetic detectors. Mines that blew off a foot at even a tip-toe touch. Mines that sprung up to waist height and then exploded. Mines all over the mountains that were so steep it took four hours to hand carry cans of water up them and six hours to bring a wounded soldier down. A hurried call went back to the States for mules, harnesses and mule skinners. When mules couldn't make it, human beasts of burden took over. Foxholes were impossible to dig, so soldiers hid by day behind homemade parapets of stones that were as lethal as shrapnel when they exploded

under artillery fire. Soldiers waited until nightfall to relieve themselves. Snipers would get them literally with their pants down by day. Sometimes the enemies were so close they threw rocks at each other or hurled their slops. Men huddled three to a blanket in holes filled with icy water in the sleet, snow and rain that made sunny Italy a bitter joke. Pinpoint German fire could cost a unit 20 percent casualties in just one day. A mule would clamber up a mountain with ammo, food and water and mail—and come back down with the wounded and some mail. The addressee had died. Water was too short to wash bearded faces, even brush teeth. Some units were up in the hills for twenty-seven days without a hot meal. Of one caravan of thirty mules, only two reached the top. Snipers got the rest.

"Our troops were living in almost inconceivable misery," wrote Ernie Pyle. "They lived like men of prehistoric times, and a club would have become them more than a machine gun."

In some of the Italian battlelines, mules, only supply vehicles that could make it, took six hours to reach GIs.

In Italy GIs were fighting in mountains where only supply mules could tread.

U.S. Rangers quickly took Salerno-Rome Road and after German atrocity, took no prisoners.

UP FRONT WITH MAULDIN

"Fresh, spirited American troops, flushed with victory, are bringing in thousands of hungry, ragged, battle weary prisoners." (News item.)

U.S. 5th Army landing at Salerno was meant to stop at Naples, but instead became long mountain battle without end.

Pictorially, the scene was best captured by the acerb cartoonist Sergeant Bill Mauldin. His GIs Willie and Joe were unshaven, slumped, sardonic men who seemed to have no age and had never existed except in the mud and rain and rocks; men of no yesterday and no tomorrow.

The Germans main defense was the Gustav Line centered on 1,700-foot Monte Cassino, a glowering almost unscalable bastion that Italian military schools taught was the perfect fort. Instead it had a monastery, a living lighthouse of art and culture since it was founded by St. Benedict in 529 A.D.

It was obstacles like this the 5th and 8th Armies were ordered to capture. It could be done. The 1st Special Service Force, a U.S.-Canadian group of handpicked soldiers, took the 3,000-foot peak of La Difinsa one night after 600 soldiers scaled a 1,000-

foot cliff by rope to surprise the German garrison. One defender advanced hands up in surrender, then drew a gun and shot a captain through the head. After that the Special Forces took no prisoners.

Sergeant Bill Mauldin's Willie and Joe won Pulitzer for cartoonist.

SGT. BILL MAULDIN

The war's best known GIs, Willie and Joe, joined the Army when twenty-two-year-old Sergeant Bill Mauldin begin drawing cartoons in Sicily for the 45th Division's weekly newspaper.

Mauldin, a New Mexican, had joined the Army at eighteen after a year at the Academy of Fine Arts in Chicago. In the fashion of his inimitable antiheroes, he spent sixty-four days of KP duty in his first four months of military life. In Sicily, Patton thought Willie and Joe "damned unsoldierly" and ordered Major General Troy Middleton, the 45th's commander, "to get rid of Mauldin and his cartoons." Middleton replied: "Put your order in writing, George," and nothing more was heard of the matter.

In Italy, where he received a Purple Heart, Mauldin would spend three days at the front, then return to the *Stars and Stripes* office in Naples to draw.

At Anzio, Truscott told him: "When you start drawing pictures that don't get a few complaints, then you'd better quit because you won't be doing anybody any good."

Other efforts at breakout were less subtle. One of the most notorious was the effort by the 36th Division to cross the Rapido River west of Cassino. It was to be a night attack January 20, 1944, across a freezing cold, fast-flowing river ten feet deep in places, almost into the muzzles of the German defenders. Wrote Major General Fred Walker, the division commander, in his diary: "We might succeed but I don't see how we can." His men tried again and again, attacking by rubber boat and finally across a foot bridge heroic engineers managed to build under fire. A sergeant of the 36th remembered:

"It was the only scene that I'd seen in the war that lived up to what you see in the movies. I had never seen so many bodies. I remember this kid being hit by a machine gun: the bullets hitting him pushed his body along like a tin can." Another sergeant, wounded: "I could hear my bones cracking every time I moved. My right leg was so badly mangled I couldn't get my boot off on account of it was pointed to the rear."

Both sides called a truce to clear the dead and wounded. Then the battle resumed, the Americans finally withdrawing. The Germans captured a carrier pigeon and let it go with a note: "Your captured syphillitic comrades have shown us the quality of American soldiers. . . . Your troops south of Rome are getting a kick in the nuts—you poor nosepickers."

An American major said: "I had 184 men . . . forty-eight hours later I had seventeen. If that's not mass murder, I don't know what is." A congressional inquiry was later to clear Clark and his staff for ordering the repeated assault.

But such head-on attacks caused Brooke to confide in his diary: "To my mind it is quite clear that there is no real plan for the capture of Rome. . . . [Clark] seems to be planning nothing but penny pocket attacks." Before leaving the 8th Army to prepare for the landing in France, Montgomery, whose ego was even larger than Clark's appetite for public relations, said: "Clark would be only too delighted to be given quiet advice as to how to fight his army." Clark thought no more of his alleged ally whom he regarded as a slow mover with an inflated reputation.

The Briton's complaint was more of a Montgomeryism than fact. Italy's unyielding geography cramped a strategy of movement and encirclement. Clark did not have the men or landing craft to bypass the mountains even if it didn't. His army had taken 40,000 casualties by the end of 1943. Another 50,000 had become sick. He kept battering, particularly against Monte Cassino.

The defenses were manned by the German 1st Parachute Division, an elite of the elite. When Alexander visited a hospital where some captured paratroopers were being treated, a German sergeant hollered: "Achtung! Herr General!" Despite their wounds, his men snapped rigidly to attention in their beds. The commander of the Cassino front was Lieutenant General Frido von Senger und Etterlin. He was an intellectual who had spent stimulating years in France, was a Rhodes scholar, hated Hitler and his Nazis but decided to stand by his people and had concluded the war was lost when his troops failed to relieve Von Paulus' doomed army at Stalingrad. He was also, ironically, a lay Benedictine. When he had Christmas dinner at the monastery, he refused to look out the windows to note Allied positions lest it be construed as compromising the monks' neutrality.

Although outnumbered twenty-five divisions to eleven along the static fronts, the Allies tried three times to take the mountain. For three weeks the U.S. 34th Division fought up the towering rocks. They got to within four hundred yards of the top but no farther. Some had to be carried down the mountain.

"I thought I had never seen such tired faces," said an American who watched the men slog past. "They came from such a depth of weariness I wondered if they would ever be able quite to make the return to the lives and thoughts they had known."

The next try was by the Indian 4th Division, led by Major General F.I.S. Tuker which included two regiments of Himalayan Gurkhas, and the 2nd New Zealand. Tuker was convinced the Germans were using the monastery as an observation post and so was Lieutenant General Sir Bernard Freyberg, the New Zealand commander. They prevailed on Clark and Alexander, who did not want to destroy the building both for the bad publicity and because rubble would make an even better defensive position. The monastery, whose monks had prevailed through the long night of the Dark Ages, had almost certainly not been used by the Germans—the huge structure had only one entrance and Von Senger had posted guards to keep soldiers out—and its treasures had largely been removed. But on February 15, 1944, it was hit by 225 planes that bombed it into ruins with 576 tons of explosives. Then the troops started out. It was combat so close bodies couldn't be removed. They stayed where they fell for putrid days and weeks while rats became engorged on the rotting flesh. In the town at the foot of the mountain Kiwis and Germans sometimes shared the same buildings fighting floor to floor. Allied soldiers defecated into empty ration cans and threw them into German dugouts. But the German paratroopers couldn't be dislodged.

Said Alexander of his foe: "I doubt if there are any other troops in the world who could have stood up to it and then gone on fighting with the ferocity they have."

The Kiwis came back again. New Zealand bazooka men of the sort of bravery, one onlooker said, "who would spit in a rattlesnake's eye," blasted stone houses in the town with as many as ten rockets before making a hole three feet wide. The Germans held firm.

By now the 5th Army had become a motley assemblage of as many as twenty-six nationalities

ART AND WAR

The wandering Saint Benedict had founded the abbey at Monte Cassino on the site of an old Roman temple to Apollo. It was destroyed a few years later by the Lombards, again by the Saracens in 883 and again by an earthquake in 1349. Its scholar-monks had preserved the writings of Cicero, Saint Thomas Aquinas, Ovid and many other writers of antiquity.

Captain Maximilian Becker, a doctor with the Hermann Goering Division whose real loves were art and archaeology, had visited the monastery in October 1943 after the Germans had abandoned Naples. He knew troops had burned the city's archives out of malice before leaving and figured the war was heading towards the strategic strongpoint of Cassino. At his urging, the monks crated most of the monastery's treasures, and the Germans trucked them to Rome for safekeeping.

Ironically, Becker's divisional namesake, the head of the Luftwaffe, was a notorious looter of art for his private collection. Both sides, however, went to great lengths to safeguard Italy's priceless art treasures. American experts, dubbed Venus Fixers, often briefed bombing crews to avoid historic buildings before they set out on raids.

Germans had not occupied ancient Benedictine monastery until after Allied bombing, then fortified rubble.

in twenty-eight divisions: Poles, Basutos, Canadians, Indians, Cypriot French, Mauritians, South Africans, Brazilians, Nepalese, Greeks, Yugoslavs, Moroccans, Algerians, even some Italians. Among the fiercest were the Moroccans goumiers, hill soldiers to whom fighting was not a way of life but *the* way of life. They liked to work at night with long knives that they honed lovingly by day. An officer asked a goumier if he could come back from patrol with a wristwatch. He obliged, with the bloody arm still attached. The Poles, mostly POWs released by the Soviets via Iran, were orphans of war, fighting for a homeland they had lost, abandoned save for a visceral hatred of Germans. Same for the French from the African colonies. There were the dogged, carefree Kiwis. "Your people don't salute very much, do they?" An Englishman asked Freyberg. "You should try waving at them," he replied. "They always wave back."

Churchill growled that the Italian stalemate was "scandalous." On Christmas Day he had met with Eisenhower in Tunis to discuss outflanking the Gustav Line with a landing up the coast at Anzio. Eisenhower doubted the landing by only two divisions was enough. Four would be needed, he thought. He questioned that the movement would draw troops from the Cassino defense. Clark, too, was reluctant but took the word of British intelligence that two divisions would suffice. "And they were wrong again," he later commented. "I felt like a lamb being led to slaughter," said Major General John Lucas, the fifty-four-year-old American who would command the landing corps of the 3rd U.S. and 1st British Divisions. Truscott of the 3rd warned: "You are going to destroy the best damned division in the U.S. Army, for there will be no survivors."

For months Allied and Germans fought room by room for control of Cassino.

Ernie Pyle: "I am very sick of the war but if I left it, it would be like a soldier deserting."

BRAVE MEN

One of the most remembered and reprinted dispatches of the war was Ernie Pyle's unadorned account of the death of Captain Harry Waskow of the 36th Division.

Pyle had looked on as mules brought the day's dead down from the mountains one day in January 1944.

"The men in the road seemed reluctant to leave. They stood around, and gradually one by one I could sense them moving close to Captain Waskow's body. Not so much to look, I think, as to say something in finality to him. I stood close by and I could hear. . . . a soldier came and stood beside the officer and bent over, and he too spoke to his dead captain, not in a whisper but awfully tenderly, and he said: 'I sure am sorry, sir.'

"Then the first man squatted down, and he reached down and took the dead hand, and he sat there a full five minutes holding the dead hand in his own and looking intently into the dead face, and he never uttered a sound all the time he sat there.

"And finally he put the hand down, and then reached up and gently straightened the points of the captain's shirt collar, and then he sort of rearranged the tattered edges of his uniform around the wound. And then he got up and walked away down the road in the moonlight, all alone."

Clark cautioned Lucas: "Don't stick your neck out, Johnny." His orders were to secure a beachhead, then attack "in the direction of" the Alban Hills to the east and cut coastal Highway 7, one of Kesselring's main supply routes that followed the route of the ancient Appian Way where Hannibal's armies had once marched. The landing January 22 achieved surprise, and in fact the road to Rome was open and the Eternal City almost undefended. But Lucas stuck to his orders as he saw them and established the beachhead enlarged to seven-by-fifteen miles. Within forty-eight hours 50,000 troops were ashore, but Kesselring had promptly moved elements of eight divisions to the Anzio perimeter under General Eberhard von Mackensen with units of five more on the way. The official British history was to ask why Lucas did not move before German reinforcements arrived: "The men could not understand it. What was stopping the division?" Lucas, soon to be replaced in favor of Truscott, was to contend he would have been wiped out by spreading his men too thinly, and most historians agree with him. A battalion of 767 American Rangers reached the outskirts of Cisterna on Highway 7 on D + nine but were ambushed. Only six soldiers returned. A battalion of the 3rd almost cut the highway but were driven back, losing 650 of 800 men. Outnumbered, the Allies fought off Mackensen's attacks—Americans of the 45th Division now ashore holding firm even when surrounded. On February 20, Mackensen dug his troops into defensive positions. Anzio had become another stalemate.

The Germans had flooded marshy areas. Men slept half standing up in water up to their waists in sandbagged foxholes. In the morning the sand had leaked out through shrapnel holes left by bombardments. To break the endless diet of canned rations, some troops threw exploded German mines in the sea to harvest dead fish. Constant enemy artillery fire got a name: the Anzio Express.

German guns could reach any point of the beachhead which had become a grim replica of the trenches and dugouts of World War I. The Special Forces made night forays by stealth, leaving signs on knifed German sentries: "You may be next." Lieutenant General Kurt Maelzer, the murderous drunk who was the German commandant in Rome, said: "That the Allies did not take advantage of this great chance [to capture Rome] has to date been incomprehensible to us." He blamed the Allies' "always demonstrated" proclivity to be 100 percent certain before attacking. Kesselring called the landing "a halfway measure." Axis Sally, the German radio propagandist, pronounced Anzio "the largest self-supporting prisoner of war camp in the world."

Ironically, Clark ordered renewed attacks on Cassino to help draw off German troops around Anzio.

Ernie Pyle described the landscape in the valleys beneath the killer mountains: ". . . the limb of an olive tree broken off, six swollen dead horses in the corner of a field, a strawstack burned down, a chesnut tree blown clear out with its roots by a German bomb, little gray patches of powder burns on the hillside, snatches of broken and abandoned rifles and grenades in the bushes, grain fields patterned with a million crisscrossing ruts from great trucks crawling frame-deep through the mud, empty gun pits and countless foxholes, and rubbish-heap stacks of empty C-ration cans and now and then the lone grave of a German soldier. . . ."

By May spring had come. Poppies bloomed. Nightingales could be heard between shell bursts. It was time to move out.

Alexander's plan was to break through at Cassino, then up the valley of the Liri Valley—the old Roman Via Casilina—while the Americans moved up the west coast to link up with Anzio. The Anzio troops were to drive eastwards to Valmontone in the hills to cut off the German retreat. What Alexander did not foresee and Kesselring did in a brilliant withdrawal was that the Germans would retreat sideways, pivoting along the axis of the boot to keep their rear open.

Secretary of War Henry Stimson is briefed on hard facts of Italian campaign. Mark Clark (center).

Anzio breakthrough turned to trench warfare instead as wounded paid price of stalemate.

Bulldozer clears wreckage from Anzio street. Whole beachhead was in range of Nazi artillery.

On the east coast, Canadians, "mouseholing" as they called blasting through walls in house-to-house fighting, took Ortona to unhinge the Gustav Line. Lieutenant General Wladyslaw Anders' 40,000 Poles finally captured abandoned Cassino and its mountain May 18 and planted the flag of a homeland many would never see again atop the ruins. General Alphonse Juin's rainbow French Army of Foreign Legionnaires, Algerians, Senegals, Free French and the goumiers set off across the Aurunci mountains, thought impassable by the Germans but familiar turf to many of the North Africans. They made astonishing speed where not even mules could traverse. "It is a matter of honor," said Juin. The mouth of the Liri Valley became an impasse of tanks, trucks and troops, slowing the advance northwards. Meanwhile, preceded by air and naval bombardment 150,000 American and British, including the all-Japanese 442nd Regimental Combat Team, broke the iron ring around Anzio. The Germans moved back grudgingly. The 3rd Division took 950 casualties the first day. As if to vent the frustration of the four-month siege, Private John Dutko made a frenzied one-man attack, wiping out three machine guns and an 88 cannon as well as their crews before he in turn was killed. Along Highway 7 Lieutenant Colonel R.E. Kendall rallied his men: "C'mon, you bastards, you'll never get to Rome this way!", then charged with his carbine, grabbed a bazooka to silence a machine gun in a house, following it up with a grenade through a window before he was cut down. On May 25 Captain Ben Souza was leading a patrol south from Anzio and met Lieutenant Francis Buckley, an engineer who had stopped his jeep to inspect a bridge.

"Where the hell do you think you're going?" Souza challenged.

"I'm trying to make contact with the Anzio forces," Buckley answered.

"Boy, you've made it."

The breakout was accomplished, and Truscott wanted to keep driving east to surround the retreating Germans. But Clark, in a decision that has been argued ever since, ordered him to split his corps

EYE FOR AN EYE

A war few had relish for left the Italians demoralized. The Germans viewed the population with contempt, remembering their mass surrenders in North Africa. Many Americans found them dirty and devious.

But when Germany became an occupier rather than an ally, patriotism hardened. On March 23, 1944, a bomb went off in Rome at a point where German troops daily marched. Thirty-two soldiers died. Hitler wanted all able-bodied Roman males shipped to Germany as slave labor. Kesselring protested this would overburden rail transport. So he ordered ten Romans shot for every soldier that had died. The Germans actually gathered 335 victims in the Ardeatine Caves and shot them, then dynamited the site.

Kesselring was subsequently sentenced to death for this, but was later released to die in Munich in 1960.

and send the bulk of it towards Rome. Clark was not only racing the Germans to Rome but the British as well. He wanted his men to get the credit, not the 8th Army which he wrote in his diary ". . . has done little fighting. . . . It will not put in its full effort, for it never has." Clark reportedly ordered his advance troops to fire on the British, according to one account, if they were about to enter Rome first. Major General Geoffrey Keyes, commander of the U.S. II Corps, explained why Clark was in such a rush: "France is going to be invaded, and we've got to get this in the papers before then."

But Truscott's debated turn north ran into stiff resistance while Kesselring's main army fell back intact inland. Some of the enemy reacted to the pressure. In one German unit 130 soldiers mutinied. They were promptly shot by their officers who were shot in turn by the rest of their men who thereupon surrendered. Italian partisans began harrying the retreating Germans. With the issue seemingly decided, Italian civilians began turning on the occupiers who had oppressed them. Radio correspondent Eric Sevareid reported: "A child was vigorously kicking a dead German until a young woman shoved the child aside and dragged off the man's boots." In Rome, the Germans hurriedly packed and left any way they could. An American nun who had been in the city all during the war described the flight of "wild-eyed, unshaven, unkempt [men] on foot, in stolen cars, in horse-drawn vehicles, even carts belonging to the street cleaning department . . . handsome motor cars with Fascist dignitaries looking anything but dignified in their anxiety to get away. . . . They were frightened."

Early on June 4 Keyes reached Rome's outskirts. He encountered Brigadier General Robert Frederick, head of the 1st Special Forces who had just been wounded for his ninth Purple Heart of the campaign. Frederick told Keyes his men would need the rest of the day to get by German artillery.

"That will not do," said Keyes. "General Clark must be across the city limits by 4 o'clock."

"Why?" asked Frederick. "Because he has to have a photograph taken."

Frederick looked at Keyes steadily. Finally he said: "Tell the general to give me an hour."

Clark got his picture. The Allies got the first Axis capital to fall. For the 5th Army the price had been 20,389 lives, 11,292 of them American. They lay buried back down the newly bloodied ancient Roman roads, the latest in a long line of fallen conquerers who never reached the Eternal City from the south. But the living Willies and Joes had.

Benvenuti a Roma. Girl welcomes Mark Clark to Rome day after capture. In back seat are Major General Alfred Gruenther (l.), chief of staff, and II Corps commander Major General Geoffrey Keyes.

No hard feelings. Romans hail U.S. 5th Army troops who "liberated" them from former ally, Nazi Germany.

ITALY: YET MORE MOUNTAINS

The fall of Rome had been a climax, but the battle for Italy was not played out. The international army of Harold Alexander had been weakened by the withdrawal of all four of the French and three of the best American divisions for the invasion of France.

More on an equal footing, the Germans slowly retreated from one mountain defensive line to the next under continuing pressure from the U.S. 5th and British 8th Armies. First the Trasimene Line eighty-five miles north of Rome, then the Arno Line. The Germans withdrew through Florence blowing up all the ancient bridges there over the Arno with the exception of the Ponte Vecchio, a favorite landmark of Hitler. Along the Adriatic coast the 8th Army captured Rimini, then was bogged down in the marshes of the Romagna Plain and its thirteen rivers.

By October 1944 the Allies had pierced Kesselring's strongest prepared fortification, the Gothic Line, and Mark Clark could see the Po Valley—tank country at last—and the Alps beyond. But then the rains began. The Allies went into static positions for the winter.

Even so, the fighting continued. The 10th Mountain Division, an elite unit made up of American skiers and mountain climbers, made a formidable debut. Less successful was the 92nd Division, made up of black enlistees and mostly white officers, continuing a practice dating to the Civil War to keep black troops segregated. "The Negro soldier needed greater incentive and a feeling he was fighting for his home and that he was fighting as an equal," said Clark. The 8,400 Japanese-Americans of the 442nd Regimental Combat Team returned from fighting in France to continue their illustrious record. Lieutenant Daniel K. Inouye lost an arm knocking out three machine gun nests but continued his charge firing his tommy gun with his remaining hand. He won a Distinguished Service Cross and later a seat in the U.S. Senate.

Italian partisans, many of them communists, harassed the Germans behind the lines despite brutal reprisals. They also began attacking the remaining fascists of Mussolini, reduced now to a powerless puppet of the Nazis, his empire a paper republic he declared from his headquarters near Salo. Neither had much time left.

The Fleet

One of Ernest J. King's six daughters said of her father: "He is the most even-tempered man in the Navy. He is always in a rage."

This was unfair to the Navy's wartime leader whom Roosevelt called "the shrewdest of strategists." King was sixty and thought his career over when he was summoned by Roosevelt to become Chief of Naval Operations right after Pearl Harbor. King had excelled at Annapolis; commanded submarines, battleships and carriers; observed closely Marine experiments with landing craft; was a whiz at crosswords; knew enough about engines to take them apart and put them back together and whose only weaknesses according to an Annapolis biographer were "other men's wives, alcohol and intolerance."

It was King's fiercely held view that the Pacific was more decisive than other Allied commanders often felt. It would be essential, he was to argue almost to the point of explosion, that Hawaii be held, the shipping lanes to Australasia be kept open and the Japanese navy be kept off balance by attacks wherever and whenever possible. There was no such thing as defensive naval warfare, he believed. It invited defeat because the sea, unlike land, did not permit itself of static defense. He agreed that Europe receive primary consideration, but thought, correctly as it developed, that America could produce the men and material to mount offensives in both hemispheres. Some historians have contended that the British accepted an invasion of France in 1944 instead of a lesser operation, say in the Balkans, because they feared King would persuade Roosevelt to otherwise concentrate on the Pacific. It was King's contention that in any event Russia would be doing the bulk of the land fighting against Germany.

Army-Navy jealousies were always present at all levels during the war and Marshall and King, the respective service commanders, "probably didn't like each other much," wrote Robert William Love of the Naval Academy. But they came to appreciate the value of a united front, particularly in the face of possible British influence on the president. "King, the greater strategist, often gave way to Marshall, the greater man," wrote Love.

The Navy was very much a mixed cargo. Marc Mitscher, a slight admiral "who didn't look a day over eighty," had come up through submarines to become a brilliant carrier commander, sticking to his ship while ignoring a heart attack.

Admiral Richmond Kelly Turner, who commanded the Iwo invasion, often scraped his colleagues like barnacles. He was abrasive, outspoken and a brilliant planner. Told he was going to command the amphibious forces on Guadalcanal, he protested to Admiral King that he didn't know enough about beach warfare. "You will learn," King replied. Turner did, at Tarawa, Eniwetok, and the Marianas. "We would rather go to sea with him in command than any other admiral under whom we have served," said "Howlin' Mad" Smith. Turner liked his drinks after a hard day, but his superiors felt the same way Lincoln did about Ulysses Grant's reputed bottle problems: find out what his brand is if that's the way he fights.

Spruance, the commander at Midway, headed the fleet at Iwo, a target whose importance he had insisted upon. He had been sharply criticized for not striking at the Japanese carriers during the Battle of the Philippine Sea but insisted he fulfilled his primary duty of defending the Saipan invasion. He was a steady, painstaking leader in contrast to the more unpredictable, pugnacious Halsey, but staff preferred the former's dependability.

Spruance and Halsey alternated command of the fast carrier fleet like interchangeable quarterbacks. It was the 5th Fleet when Spruance took the Marianas, the 3rd under Halsey at Palau and the Carolines.

By either name, this was not the Navy strategists had thought a few years before would fight a war in the Pacific. The planning had been for a surface campaign with battleships being the major players. Instead it evolved into a carrier war. The result was an undercurrent of suspicion between the "brown shoe" carrier admirals and the "black shoe" battleship commanders. Spruance was suspect because he was a cruiser man. He had been Nimitz' chief of staff and was a meticulous organizer. But he was also a master tactician of the new carrier warfare. War historian Eric Larrabee wrote: "It can be said of Spruance as of no other American high commander in the war that he did not make mistakes."

By 1944 American production had produced immense naval power: eight new battleships, ninety-two carriers, thirty-five cruisers, 513 destroyers and escorts. Mitscher's Task Force 58 was at sea with nine fast carriers, four light ones and six new battleships. The carriers held 600 planes, floating air bases. They stayed at sea for months at a time—some sailors didn't put a foot on land for ten months—supplied by regularly scheduled auxiliary ships from Hawaii and the West Coast. There were seventeen carriers of the new Essex class by the war's climax. The namesake of the group was to sink twenty-five warships and eighty-six merchant vessels and shoot down 1,531 Japanese planes. The carriers were supplied with Grumman F6F Hellcats, a fighter designed to outperform the Zero after one had been captured intact in the Aleutians and

The very top of the top brass: (l. to r.) *Admiral King; Admiral William Leahy, chief of staff to the president, and George Marshall.*

intensely scrutinized and tested by the Americans. "If it could cook, I'd marry one," said an admiring Hellcat pilot.

Supervising it all back in Hawaii was the deceptively easygoing Nimitz, who brought his schnauzer Makalapa to work with him every day. Nimitz kept peace between the black and brown shoes, was always open to suggestion—and a photo with a swabee who had bet his shipmates he could get in to see the admiral—and kept on his wall reminders of his job. Will it succeed? What are the consequences of failure? Is it practicable?

Spruance, who had worked down the hall at a stand-up desk in an office with no chairs for anyone to get comfortable in, said of Nimitz: "He is one of the few people I know who never knew what it meant to be afraid of anything."

The Navy had made legend of names few Americans had ever heard of before. Even Mitscher said all he knew about Truk, the huge Japanese navy base carrier planes demolished, he had read about in the *National Geographic*.

In every sense of the phrase, the Navy had come a long way.

Saipan was different from the tiny stepping stone islands across the Pacific. It was a threshhold.

It was bigger, twenty-five miles long and shaped like a rearing rhinoceros in the Marianas Islands some 1,500 miles southeast of the Japanese port city of Hiroshima. Just south of Saipan lies the smaller, mostly flat sister island of Tinian, cliff-girt, from a distance looking like a huge carrier in the sea. In June of 1944 Saipan was garrisoned by 30,000 secondary troops and populated by about 35,000 civilians, mostly Japanese save for some native Micronesians called Chamorros. On June 15 after air and sea bombardment, units of the 2nd and 4th Marine Divisions and the 27th Division of the Army left transports for the beaches.

"Most of you will return, but some of you will meet the God who made you," said a chaplain. "Perish-the-thought-department," an officer said to a correspondent. Within twenty minutes, 8,000 Marines, a vanguard of 71,000 soldiers to come, had landed. In Tokyo the Army General Staff radioed the outgunned, outmanned and plane-less defenders: "To the very end continue to destroy the enemy . . . thus assuaging the anxiety of the emperor." The defense was suicidal. The Japanese commander, Lieutenant General Yoshitsugu Saito, ordered: "There is no longer any distinction between civilians and troops. It would be better for them to join in the attack with bamboo spears than be captured."

In intense fighting Holland Smith complained that the GIs of Major General Ralph Smith were not matching the aggressiveness of his Marines and had Smith relieved, touching off Marine-Army bitterness that was to continue in the months ahead. At sea, Vice Admiral Marc Mitscher's Task Force 58—a mammoth armada of fifteen carriers, seven battleships and eighty-nine cruisers and destroyers—had a field day when the Japanese tried to reinforce the island. In a battle to be known as "The Great Marianas Turkey Shoot" the Americans sank three enemy carriers and shot down 475 planes. Their cause lost, Japanese civilians and soldiers alike charged the Americans even with Saito's bamboo spears. The survivors, including women and children, jumped off Saipan's cliffs until the waters were so crowded with bodies small boats couldn't maneuver. Two-thirds of the civilians died and almost all of the soldiers, at a cost of 14,111 American casualties.

It was a sobering foretaste. The invaders also recaptured Guam as well as Tinian. Seabees immediately began bulldozing six runways on the latter, the island that looked like a carrier and was only a bomber's flight from Hiroshima.

Landing on Leyte went smoothly. The blood came later.

At right: *Stars and Stripes at Leyte beachhead. Next stop: Manila.*

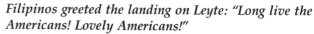

Filipinos greeted the landing on Leyte: "Long live the Americans! Lovely Americans!"

Return to the Philippines

The Japanese knew MacArthur was coming, and soon. Where, was the question.

In Washington the Pentagon favored the ultimate broad jump bypassing the Philippines to strike at Formosa. MacArthur argued stridently that the United States had a moral obligation to liberate the Philippines as soon as possible. He had never swallowed Marshall's and Eisenhower's policy that Europe came first. Meanwhile, Halsey's carrier pilots in that summer of 1944 were reporting a notable lack of resistance by the Japanese in attacks on Leyte, a 100-mile long island in the central Philippines. A Navy pilot who had been rescued from Leyte by a submarine after he was shot down reported there were fewer defenders on the island than had been thought. Weighing the risk of impertinence or even insubordination, Halsey finally decided "to stick my neck out" and recommend to Nimitz that Leyte be seized "at the earliest possible date." CINCPAC passed the recommendation on to Roosevelt and Churchill who were meeting in Quebec. Leyte it would be.

In Tokyo an embattled high command decided on an all-out gamble of desperation, a plan called Sho-1, Sho being Japanese for victory. Its naval air arm had just been decimated in the Battle of the Philippine Sea, the Great Marianas Turkey Shoot. The navy's remaining carriers under command of Vice Admiral Jisaburo Ozawa, with only 120 surviving planes, had been withdrawn to defend the Home Islands. The army protested that if the navy lost its all-out gamble, what would become of it in its last ditch fight? But oil was at stake, and so was honor. "Please give the Combined Fleet the chance to bloom as flowers of death," pleaded the Japanese operations head. The emperor gave his assent. On October 18, 1944, a fleet of seven battleships, two of them, the *Yamato* and *Musashi*, the most powerful in the world with eighteen-inch guns, put to sea from Singapore with twelve cruisers and fifteen destroyers. Notably absent, however, were any carriers.

Halsey's 3rd Fleet had already done crushing damage to the remnants of the Japanese air arm, destroying more than three hundred planes in strikes against Okinawa and Formosa. Then on October 20 the greatest armada yet of the Pacific war began landing the first of 200,000 men of Eichelberger's 6th Army. The fleet of almost 1,000 ships and landing craft pulverized the beaches of Leyte as its 20,000 defenders dropped back into what remained of the jungle. Only forty-nine GIs

Japanese faded into Leyte jungle on A (Assault) Day but later fought to last man.

died in the first day, named A Day in deference to Normandy's D Day. In Tokyo the Japanese apparently gave some credence to the entirely fictitious report of the commander on Formosa that his planes had sunk eleven American carriers, two battleships and three cruisers. With tongue in cheek, Halsey, who had not lost a ship, radioed CINCPAC: THE THIRD FLEET'S SUNKEN AND DAMAGED SHIPS HAVE BEEN SALVAGED AND ARE RETIRING AT HIGH SPEED TOWARD THE ENEMY. The Sho plan had already been badly compromised. Halsey had mostly eliminated air power in the area, and the Americans were already ashore, including the "returning" MacArthur and a provisional government. But the Japanese steamed on.

Then occurred one of the most famous foul-ups of the war: Bull Halsey's "end run." Ozawa sortied his carriers as bait to lure Halsey's Task Force 34 north to leave the American invasion fleet open to an attack around the north and south ends of Leyte by the Japanese fleet led by vice admirals Takeo Kurita and Teiji Nishimura.

"You must all remember that there are such things as miracles," Kurita addressed his men. "Banzai!" they replied, "Banzai!"

Ashore, Vice Admiral Takajiro Ohnishi had been stunned on arriving in the Philippines October 17 to take over the First Air Fleet to learn that he had fewer than 100 planes to send aloft. His solution was characteristic of Japanese tradition that put death before dishonor. He would turn his pilots into flying bombs. They would be named for Kamikaze, the Divine Wind, a typhoon that in 1281 sunk the Mongol fleet of Kublai Khan that had been on its way to invade Japan. Ohnishi asked for volunteers. Almost to a man the pilots stepped forward. Japan had a new weapon. Its first use came October 21 when a pilot flew into the bridge

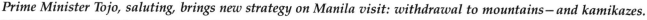

Prime Minister Tojo, saluting, brings new strategy on Manila visit: withdrawal to mountains—and kamikazes.

of the Aussie cruiser *Australia* putting it out of action.

The first knowledge that the Japanese fleet had sortied came from the American submarines *Darter* and *Dace* early on October 22 after they each sank a cruiser of a large flotilla approaching Leyte. The word came back to a divided command. MacArthur, a general, was in charge of the invasion which including a support fleet of old battleships, most Pearl Harbor survivors, and eighteen small escort carriers. The big carriers and new battleships were led by Halsey under command of Nimitz. The two vast pincers had finally met at the Philippines but interservice rivalries, personalities and spotty synchronization left too many gray areas.

"Bull" Halsey was a firm believer in the first principle of the new carrier war: get the enemy's carriers first. Even though at Leyte his orders were to protect the beachheads, his "primary task" was to attack if a "major portion" of the Japanese naval strength showed itself.

After the Navy's planes had badly mauled Kurita's fleet as it swung around through San Bernadino Strait to hit Leyte from behind, sinking the superbattleship *Musashi*, Halsey thought Kurita had been repulsed when his ships turned away. But then Kurita turned back. Meanwhile, Ozawa's six-carrier feint had been discovered by American patrol planes. Halsey saddled up his battleships and carriers and took off. "I thought Admiral Halsey was making one hell of a mistake," said Rear Admiral Gerald Bogan, head of a carrier group.

Nishimura, steaming at flank speed in the moon-lit Suriago Strait where Magellan had once sailed, ran right into the six battleships, five Pearl Harbor veterans, of Rear Admiral Jesse Oldendorf. Oldendorf performed that perfect game of naval warfare, crossing the T to bring all his guns to bear on the oncoming Japanese. A battleship blew up in two pieces. Nishimura's flagship capsized, drowning him and most of his crew. Vice Admiral Kiyohide Shima, coming up from behind, steamed into the same carnage.

Two hundred miles to the north, Kurita had wheeled his fleet and as dawn broke came down like a wolf on the fold on a group of seven destroyers and destroyer escorts and six jeep carriers, baby flattops converted from merchant vessels and armed with only 40mm antiaircraft guns and a single five-inch cannon. When the unmistakable pagoda-like masts of the Japanese battleships appeared over the horizon, Rear Admiral Clifton A. "Ziggy" Sprague radioed frantically in the clear for help and then took the only recourse a fighting admiral thought was open to him: attack. It was terriers against onrushing grizzlies, as suicidal in its

way as the kamikazes. While *Yamato* hurled 3,200-pound shells at Sprague's egg-shell fleet, the almost ludicrously outgunned destroyers charged under a smoke screen for a torpedo attack. Sprague launched all planes. The combination so astonished Kurita that he paused. A kamikaze dove into the jeep carrier *St. Lo* which exploded and sank. Head down, the destroyer *Johnston*, commanded by Ernest E. Evans, a Cherokee Indian, charged to battle against anything in sight, first a heavy cruiser, then a battleship. Repeatedly hit by the huge guns—"It was like a puppy being smacked by a truck," said one of her officers—it kept fighting until sinking. The ferocity of the attack by sea and air convinced Kurita he had run into Halsey's main fleet. Thinking he would never be able to break through to play havoc with the landing transports off Leyte, he withdrew in confusion with the fifteen ships of the thirty-two he had started out with. Without the eyes of patrol planes, he could not find Halsey, whose own planes to the north savaged Ozawa's fleet, sinking four carriers including *Zuikaku*, a Pearl Harbor attacker, whose crew saluted on the heeling flight deck as the ship went down.

Kinkaid repeatedly radioed for help from Halsey. In Honolulu where he had been monitoring the fight, Nimitz' headquarters messaged:

WHERE IS TASK FORCE THIRTY-FOUR?
THE WORLD WONDERS

The last, unfortunately worded phrase was added to confuse Japanese decoders, but Halsey, deeming it an insult, slammed his hat to the deck in rage. When history's largest naval battle ended on the 26th, the Imperial Navy had lost thirty-four warships compared to the light carrier *Princeton*, two jeep carriers and three destroyers and escort destroyers for the United States. Never again would the Japanese fleet pose a threat. Increasingly, the Japanese would fight with the one resource that remained: their lives. It was becoming a war of suicide.

The war was changing for the Americans, too. Island hopping had been fought at the divisional level, ideally suited to Navy-borne Marines. Now that large land masses were the target, armies were involved. Command was unified under generals instead of admirals. On December 26 MacArthur declared Leyte had been captured except for "mopping up." The general had become famous if not infamous for premature proclamations of victory, and Leyte was no exception. Eichelberger's soldiers still had hard fighting ahead in which 27,000 Japanese troops were killed. All told, of 70,000 enemy soldiers who eventually fought on Leyte, only 5,000 survived.

The main enemy force of 275,000 men were on Luzon commanded by Lieutenant General Tomoyuki Yamashita, The Tiger of Malaya. He had been so new to the Philippines he had to be told where Leyte was. But it was no hard guess that MacArthur would land on Luzon just where the Japanese had three years before: Lingayen Gulf. They came on January 9, 1945, 280,000 men of Lieutenant General Walter Kreuger's 6th Army and an armada of almost 1,000 ships. By nightfall 68,000 U.S. soldiers were ashore and moving inland. Yamashita's strategy was to withdraw into the mountains and fight a war of attrition. As his men fell back on Manila, he finally declared the capital an open city. MacArthur meanwhile landed troops at two points on Bataan who took the now historic peninsula in a week. A precisely timed air drop and landing recaptured Corregidor in ten days of hard fighting. The Japanese survivors blew themselves up in a tunnel.

In Manila GIs unlocked the ghastly barbarity of the Japanese conquerer when they liberated the starving POWs and civilians of Santo Tomas pris-on. In the mountains the Americans remembered, and an ugly war became uglier. Charles Lindbergh, the trans-Atlantic hero, toured the Pacific and confided to his diary: "Our men think nothing of shooting a Japanese prisoner or a soldier attempting to surrender. . . . the more I see of this war in the Pacific the less right I think we have to claim to be civilized. In fact, I am not sure that our record in this respect stands so much higher than the Japs."

The atrocities culminated in Manila where marines and sailors commanded by Rear Admiral Sanji Iwabuchi, left behind to destroy port facilities, began a massacre. Hospital patients were bound in their beds and the buildings burned. Men were mutilated and killed, women raped, infants brained. Manchester says 100,000 were killed. Yamashita was to later be hanged for war crimes.

MacArthur himself decided to revisit his old penthouse home in Manila, an enemy strongpoint. He followed Tommy-gunners up the stairs, finally crossing the threshold over a newly-killed Japanese colonel. MacArthur was, literally, home.

"Nice going, chief," said a lieutenant.

Snorkel-equipped U.S. tanks invade Luzon near beach where Japanese did three years before.

Battle for Manila left city one of worst damaged of entire war.

POWS

One of the most horrifying accounts of Japanese barbarity towards prisoners of war is related by John Toland in his history *The Rising Sun.*

As the Japanese awaited MacArthur's expected invasion of Luzon, they assembled the survivors of the Cabanatuan POW camp on that island. Of an original group of 6,500 men, some survivors of the Bataan Death March, 2,644 had died from disease and neglect in the first year. The rest survived by eating cats, dogs, rats and even garbage. Colonel James Gillespie described in his clandestine diary some new arrivals: "Faces devoid of expression. . . . Aged incredibly beyond their years. . . . Some stark naked. . . . Smeared with excreta from their bowels. . . . May I never see [this sight] again. . . ."

On December 18, 1944, some 1,300 of the prisoners were stuffed in two holds of a former cruise liner to be taken to Japan. There was little food or air, hardly any water. Men began drinking their own urine. Guards were deaf to pleas for water. Some prisoners slashed at others to drink their blood. Men began to die. Major Virgil McCollum, a Bataan veteran, recalled it as "the most horrible experience imaginable and probably unprecedented in the annals of civilization."

When American planes attacked the ship, the men were transferred to a freighter. They were issued a mess kit of rice for six men, a cup of water for six. The prisoners licked condensation from the hull of the ship. Bodies of the dead, more than ten a night, were left where they lay among feces and urine. Five hundred died in a bombing raid by U.S. planes. There was nothing to treat the wounded with. Some began freezing to death as the freighter moved north.

"About forty men died last night not buried," wrote Major Roy L. Bodine, a dentist captured on Bataan. "Hope ends soon. . . ."

On January 29, 1945, the freighter reached Kyushu. Only 450 POWs remained and 100 more would soon be dead.

Several years before, the *Nippon Times* had reported the Japanese "respected the principles contained in the international law governing the conduct of war." Americans, the paper said, were "enjoying life at the various prisoner camps."

Living skeletons survive barbarity of Japanese Santo Tomas prison camp in Manila. Lee Rogers (l.), 90 pounds, and John Todd, 102.

Ploesti in Romania was Hitler's fuel tank and U.S. bombed it regularly. The raid in 1943 was an epic of bravery.

B-24 Liberators hit Ploesti refineries at ground-level in one of war's most courageous attacks. Whole squadron was decorated.

Ploesti

Ploesti was a sprawling oil complex in southeastern Romania that, said Churchill, was "the taproot of German might." On August 1, 1943, it became a preview of hell: fire, death, chaos.

To strike at the fuel tank of the Wehrmacht, 177 B-24s flew an unprecedented 1,100 miles to bomb perhaps the most heavily defended air target on Earth. Fifty-three bombers did not return. To achieve surprise and duck beneath German radar the bombers came in from all directions just above the forests and corn fields of Transylvania. Ploesti had been the target of the first bombing raid in Europe by U.S. airmen June 12, 1942, when thirteen B-24s did slight damage to the farflung refineries. This time the well-rehearsed fliers were right on target, "like putting letters in a mail box," said one ground observer. Heroism was commonplace.

Lieutenant Addison Baker from Akron, Ohio, and Major John Jerstad from Racine, Wisconsin, continued flying their "Hell's Wench" even though it was encased in flames from nose to tail, boring in on the target to crash to their deaths just beyond it. They were awarded two of the five Medals of Honor earned that day. There were 1,620 airmen on the raid, three hundred ten of them killed. All got Distinguished Flying Crosses. Production at Ploesti was cut 40 percent temporarily, but the Germans had ample reserves to make up the loss.

The Ploesti attack—there were many more to come—was a paradigm of the air war in Europe. It was brave, dramatic, lethal and highly visible and publicized. And had mixed results.

Air power had had several passionate advocates in its infancy. Italian General Giulio Douhet in World War I had prophesized that future wars would be won by demoralizing bombing attacks on enemy civilian populations. Ulysses S. Nero, one of the Ploesti raiders' ground crewmen back in Libya had flown with then-Colonel William Mitchell when he sank a surplus battleship with bombs. Mitchell's outspoken championing of air power eventually resulted in his court-martial in 1925. When World War II began, Churchill called the proposed bombing of German cities "a well worthwhile experiment." Roosevelt, on the other hand, asked all the combatants to refrain from bombing civilians. He was not heeded. In the early days of the war, British bombers dropped only propaganda leaflets on Germany, but when German planes started the London "blitz" after the fall of France, the British retaliated immediately by bombing Berlin three times within ten days. Hitler was shocked that his capital could be vulnerable.

The first raid mounted in daylight by the Royal Air Force December 18, 1939, resulted in the loss of half of the twenty-four planes sent over Germany. The RAF soon confined its strategic bombing to nighttime with a resultant loss of accuracy. "You have not dropped 200 tons of bombs on these (target) plants," said an RAF official. "You have exported 200 tons of bombs." A photo survey indicated that only a tenth of the bombs hit within five miles of the designated objectives. Radar and electronic navigational devices improved accuracy, but when the Germans shot down thirty-seven out of 400 RAF bombers November 7, 1941, Bomber Command suspended attacks for the winter. "It is very disputable whether bombing by itself will be a decisive factor in the present war," Churchill said.

Within three months of Pearl Harbor, Brigadier General Ira Eaker had arrived in Britain to set up the 8th Air Force. The Army Air Corps, as it was then known before it became a separate service after the war, had 800 planes and 26,000 men in 1939. At the war's end it had 80,000 planes and 2.4 million men. At its peak, the huge plant at Willow Run in Detroit was turning out a B-24 every seventy minutes. The Air Force, says its official history, ". . . was young, aggressive and conscious of its growing power. It had to justify the expenditure of billions of dollars and the use of almost a third of the Army's manpower. It sought for itself as free a hand as possible . . . in accordance with its own ideas and the maximum credit for its performance." Claims of damage done and enemy planes shot down were sometimes unrelated to reality. Eisenhower, a former foot soldier, referred to the crush-hatted air generals as "the Bomber Barons." Sarcastic GIs down in the mud were often much less charitable.

The 8th Air Force staged its first raid on Rouen in France August 17, 1942. All planes returned. Eaker was soon in violent disagreement with air chief marshal Sir Arthur Harris of Bomber Command. The Americans insisted pinpoint attacks by daylight were the best use of its planes, while the British insisted on saturation bombing by night to keep losses down. Said RAF Air Vice-Marshal John Slessor of the argument: "War without allies is bad enough. With allies it is hell." The controversy was finally settled at the Casablanca conference where a policy of round-the-clock bombing was worked out. By March 1943, 8th Air Force could put 100 bombers at a time into the air. Eaker was promised 944 new bombers by that July as the quaint villages of the verdant English countryside suddenly blossomed with Yank air bases. The Elysian tranquillity belied the deadly business it produced. By the second half of 1943 almost a third

Ira Eaker led the debut of U.S. bombers in European Theater with raid on Rouen in France in 1942.

of the American airmen failed to complete the twenty-five missions that qualified them for rotation back home. And what did the loss in lives buy? Germany had access to 6 million slave laborers to repair the damage and keep the factories running.

On August 17, 1943, the Americans sent 146 B-17 Flying Fortresses to strike the Messerschmitt plant in Regensburg that made 30 percent of Germany's fighters. Another 230 B-17s bombed the ball bearing works at Schweinfurt, defended by 300 Luftwaffe planes. The Americans lost sixty bombers, the Germans twenty-five fighters. Production of vital ball bearings was cut 38 percent. A second raid October 14, 1943, by 291 B-17s interrupted production at Schweinfurt for six weeks. Again, the Americans lost sixty bombers. But the attacks did not slow German output of tanks and planes. An expert witness as to the effectiveness of strategic bombing was Albert Speer, Hitler's confidant and head of all production. He was to write after the war that the Americans "threw away success when it was already in their hands" by not continuing raids on Schweinfurt. The U.S. Economic Warfare Division said at the end of 1944 that a high degree of damage in a few essential industries was more effective than "a small degree of destruction in many industries." The idea to hit key areas of production such as ball bearings and oil "was correct," Speer was to say, "[but] the execution defective."

The Americans were aided by improvements in bombing tactics as well as Hitler's blundering. When the Germans introduced the Messerschmitt 262 jet fighter, the fastest plane by far in the sky, at the end of 1944, Hitler insisted it be used for bombing instead of the fighter role for which it was designed. Goering likewise was obtuse in the face of reality. Brigadier General Adolf Galland, the fighter commandant who had 104 kills for the war, reported an ominous development to Goering. Two American P-47s had been shot down near Aachen in German territory which suggested the Allies were developing long range fighter protection from base to target, which in fact they were. Goering was furious that Galland had worried the fuehrer with the news.

"The downed planes are there at Aachen," said Galland.

"I herewith give you an official order that they weren't there," Goering stormed. "Do you understand? They weren't there!"

"Orders are orders," said a wry Galland.

Another crucial instance of Nazi muleheadedness was the policy of flying pilots until they were killed or injured. They did not withdraw their aces to train future pilots, and the pilot pipeline dwindled. This became critical as the

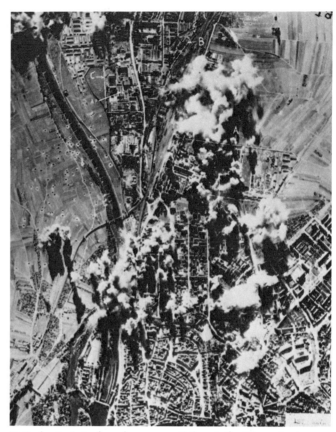

U.S. lost sixty bombers over Schweinfurt to cripple German ball bearing production but didn't press home with more attacks.

Americans began bombing with the escort of long-range P-47s and P-51s equipped with disposable belly tanks. (The North American P-51 was probably the best fighter of the war. The British ordered it based on their experience from the Battle of Britain and wanted a prototype flying in 120 days from design to completion. They got one in 117 days.) Germany lost 4,121 planes, mostly fighters, in February and March of 1944, but for the year production was 40,000 planes compared to 20,000 in 1943. There simply weren't the experienced pilots and, under constant bombing of oil facilities, the fuel to put them into the air. At the same time Hitler put plane production fifth on his list of priorities to Speer. Some aluminum, for instance, that could have gone for fighters went to make termite-proof barracks for the Third Reich's postwar tropical colonies.

Despite the horrific losses over Schweinfurt, by the end of 1943 the 8th Air Force, now under command of General Carl Spaatz, had 700 bombers available per mission. The British had pioneered the 1,000-bomber raid a year and a half earlier with an attack on Cologne that left 60,000 homeless. The Americans had refined bomber defenses with the box formation, designed by then-Colonel Curtis Le May, known in the squadrons as "Iron Ass," which stacked twenty-one bombers so as to bring all their .50-caliber machine guns to bear in self-

B-17s over Berlin fly in LeMay's box formation to concentrate flier power. On Wilhelmshaven-Schweinfurt raid, sixty bombers didn't come home.

U.S. B-17s airborne for Schweinfurt. German production actually increased despite strategic bombing but rails and oil capacity were shattered.

protection. Radar had improved as had the Norden bombsight. In a raid on the Focke-Wulf fighter factory January 11, 1944, by 663 bombers half of the bombs fell within 1,000 yards of the target. Sixty bombers were shot down despite an escort of P-47s, twin-engined P-38 Lightnings and P-51s which shot down fifteen German fighters to no American losses. One of the pilots, Major James Howard, won the Medal of Honor for single-handedly attacking thirty German planes, shooting down four even though three of his four machine guns had jammed. "I seen my duty, and I done it," he said.

In February 1944 the Americans concentrated on attacking aircraft production. At Leipzig 350 planes were destroyed on the ground. Speer dispersed production, and in May output was 2,200 planes, a new high. A Luftwaffe officer said he was "virtually drowning in planes." But his fatherland had lost 10 percent of its interceptor pilots. American fliers such as Colonel Francis Gabreski, the top American ace with twenty-eight kills, (Gabreski became a prisoner of war when he flew so low on a strafing run he bent his propeller on the ground and crashed.) were clearing the skies for the bombers.

Early in 1944 the RAF opened a sutained saturation bombing of Berlin. (They were not deceived by a nine square mile dummy Berlin Hitler constructed.) Nightly the bombers were overhead. When the campaign was called off, the British had lost 1,047 bombers, but much of Hitler's capital was in rubble. On March 30, 1944, 795 RAF bombers attacked Nuremberg, the spiritual capital of the Nazis. They were ambushed over Aachen by fighters with radar tuned to a new frequency that bypassed the aluminum strips, or chaff, that the RAF had discovered confused enemy electronics. ME-110s with cannon angled upwards atop the fuselage shot down ninety-five bombers, the heaviest toll of the war. The RAF temporarily suspended attacks.

The constant battering from the air only produced a "growing toughness," Speer claimed. "Loss of our production capacity was amply balanced by increased effort." But the need to man antiaircraft guns tied down hundreds of thousands of soldiers. Cannons that could have been firing at Russians advancing through Poland were emplaced instead around Germany's cities. Electronics that could have gone for better combat radio equipment and fire control went for defensive radar instead. (The Germans estimated it took an average of 3,343 rounds to down a bomber.)

Then the Americans began attacking where they had begun: oil, the heart blood of war. Factories could be, and were, moved into the forests and caves. Oil wells, of course, and refineries could not despite ingenious efforts by the Germans to build dummy plants. The Leuna synthetic fuel plants were hit by 935 bombers of the 8th Air Force May 8, 1944. Daily production was cut from 5,850 tons to 4,280. An attack on Ploesti cut its output by half. Raids on Ploesti from the 9th Air Force's captured Italian bases at Foggia became regular occurrences. Oil production became a sometime thing—90 percent of plane gasoline knocked out in June, production back up to 40 percent in July. German refineries were reduced to a patchwork of instant repairs. "Direct hits were no longer required to do extensive damage," Speer records. "Merely the shock of bombs exploding in the vicinity caused leaks everywhere. Repairs were almost impossible." Speer warned Hitler in that summer of D Day, of Russian's 400-mile advance to Warsaw and capture of Ploesti August 30, of the invasion of Saipan in the Pacific, that the country had reserves of oil for only nineteen more months. "If they [the bombers] persist, we will soon no longer have any fuel production worth mentioning," Speer cautioned.

Spaatz told his staff in early 1944 he needed only twenty or thirty clear days to bomb Germany into surrender. Harris agreed. They both protested vehemently when the bombing emphasis was changed from strategic bombing to attacks on rail and highway transportation in France and Germany in support of the invasion. The two bomber barons, for once in unison, thought it was an opportunity missed, and Speer was inclined to concur. The Americans had made a mistake of suspending attacks on the aircraft industry, he believed. Airplane frames could be assembled in a forest, engines could not. Yet the Allies turned on

Pilots called the Maryland-made B-26 "The Baltimore Whore" because it had no visible means of support.

the transport network with telling effect. By D Day all twenty-six bridges over the Seine between Paris and the sea had been bombed into the water. Some 1,500 locomotives had been destroyed. The B-26 Marauder, made in Maryland by Martin and a decidedly cranky if not dangerous plane to fly, came into its own as a tactical light bomber. (The sleek but small-winged plane was nicknamed "The Baltimore Whore" because "it had no visible means of support.") The German 2nd SS Panzer Division took seventeen days to reach Normandy from southern France over demolished roads and rails. On D Day alone the Allies flew 14,700 sorties to only 300 for the Germans. The embittered German soldiers grumbled a sardonic revision of airplane identification. If the aircraft was silver, it was American; dark, it was British; invisible, it was German.

With the Allies ashore in France, 1,000-bomber raids became everyday. Oil production was down to 5 percent, synthetic output at Leuna 9 percent. In October Speer visited the Italian front. Oxen were pulling trucks. There was no gas to train tank crews. The chemical industry was forced to use rock salt in ammunition, reducing its effectiveness. When the Germans attacked in the Ardennes December 16, 1944, there was only five days of fuel on hand. The offensive literally ran out of gas. That November Major Walter Nowotny, the German flier who was credited with 258 victims mostly easier pickings on the Eastern front, crashed to his death flying one of the few jets Hitler allowed to be used as fighters. There were only young, raw teen-agers to replace him. On New Year's Day Goering sortied his remaining 900 fighters in a bitter, Gotterdamerung finale. Hundreds of Allied fighters were destroyed, but Germany lost 253 irreplaceable pilots.

On April 16, 1945, the strategic bombers were grounded for the last time. There were virtually no more targets. The Allies had lost 160,000 airmen over Europe and 33,700 planes. In the rubble of German's cities lay 305,000 civilian dead. The U.S. Bombing Survey paid something of a tribute:

"Under ruthless Nazi control [Germans] showed surprising resistance to the terror and hardships of repeated air attack. . . . They continued to work efficiently as long as the physical means of production remained. The power of a police state over its people cannot be underestimated."

The Britons of London had showed a similar indominatability in their ordeal during The Blitz. Whatever the morality and effectiveness of bombing civilians had been, and both would be argued by some, one thing had been made clear by World War II. An enemy's civilians were no more and no less than its soldiers: targets.

The fastest guns in the West: U.S. fighter escorts that made long-range bombing practicable.

DRESDEN

The air war had passed Dresden by. It was not of any particular strategic significance. It was a city known more for its medieval buildings and historic art than military prominence.

On the eve of the meeting with Stalin and Roosevelt at Yalta in late 1944, however, Churchill wanted to show a measure of material support to his Soviet ally. He ordered an air strike on Dresden. Such a raid, he reasoned, would disorganize troop movements and spread confusion in the largest German city to have escaped the bombers.

On February 13, 1945, some 772 RAF planes firebombed the city. Ten hours later, 331 Flying Fortresses hit it again. German fighters based nearby didn't have enough fuel to fly without higher authorization, and that came late. In the resulting firestorm an estimated 35,000 civilians were incinerated. One of the survivors was an American POW, Kurt Vonnegut. He was to describe the attack in a novel, *Slaughterhouse Five.*

After the raid, Churchill said: "The destruction of Dresden remains a serious query against the conduct of Allied bombing."

Buildup

Safely through the killing ground of the North Atlantic, the troopship eased towards a dock in Britain. A noted jazz musician, now reissued as a GI, made his way to the bow. Jimmy MacPartland lifted his cornet and to the delight of dockside Britons played "The Blue Bells of Scotland." The Yanks were coming.

Beginning early in 1942 they were to come by the millions bearing their weapons and a brash, irreverent youthfulness to a nation that had stood alone for so long. In time the American war machine became so huge the British said the only thing that kept their island afloat was the barrage balloons tethered to it. Cultural friction was inevitable. The trouble with the Yanks, went the music hall joke, was that "they're overpaid, oversexed and over here."

"Meanest" sailor in Navy, Fleet Commander Ernest J. King.

Designer of victory, George C. Marshall. Said Stimson: "You, sir, are the finest soldier I have ever known."

There had been a deeper division among the English-speaking Allies that was anything but humorous. Almost from the beginning of their entrance into the war the Americans had pushed for an invasion of Europe at the earliest possible date. When the British balked at a 1942 landing, Marshall and King, who favored the Pacific Theater anyway, threatened to withdraw U.S. emphasis on Europe to concentrate against the Japanese. As a compromise an invasion code-named Roundup was scheduled for April 1943 by forty-eight divisions.

Churchill, always allured by the strategic and political importance of the Mediterranean to Britain, suggested an Allied invasion of the Greek island of Rhodes. Eventually the landing in Africa was to postpone the invasion of Europe until 1944.

Even so, said Stimson, "Though they [the British] have rendered lip service to the operation, their hearts are not in it." None "of these methods of pinprick warfare [such as an attack on Rhodes] can be counted on by us to fool Stalin into the belief that we have kept [our] pledge [for a second front]."

The British had reasonable cause for their reluctance. By the time the invasion of France actually occurred, they had lost 2 million men. They were simply running out of manpower. They had the highest regard for the fighting power of the German soldier who had driven their army into the sea at Dunkirk and fought a superior army to a standstill in Italy. Many of the British commanders knew first hand the bloody slaughter of Flanders in World War I. The invasion of France, said Brooke, "may be the most ghastly disaster of the whole war."

Even the bellicose Churchill told Marshall: "We are carrying out our contract, but I pray to God it does not cost us dear." Just prior to the invasion of North Africa, the suspicious U.S. Chiefs of Staff wrote privately: "The conclusion that the forces being built up in the United Kingdom will never be used for a military offensive against Western Europe but are intended as a gigantic deception plan and an occupying force is inescapable."

Even so on March 12, 1943, British Lieutenant General Sir Frederick Morgan reported for work as Chief of Staff to the Supreme Allied Commander (COSSAC) to begin planning the invasion of France. "It won't work," Brooke told him, "but you must bloody well make it."

As convoy after convoy turned southern England into an American military base, the British inevitably if grudgingly assumed the role of a slightly junior partner. On his way home from the Tehran conference, Roosevelt met with Eisenhower December 7, 1943, in Tunis. "Well, Ike, you are going to command Overlord," as the invasion was now named. It was the climax of a rocket ascent from obscurity.

Roosevelt's first choice was Marshall, but he was considered invaluable where he was, running the war in Washington. "Eisenhower is the best politician among the military men," the president told one of his sons. "He is a natural leader who can convince other men to follow him, and this is what we need."

Brooke wasn't too sure. "[Eisenhower] is just a coordinator, a good mixer, a champion of inter-Allied cooperation, and in those respects few can hold a candle to him. But is that enough?"

Genial, certainly, Morgan thought his grin alone was worth an army corps. But Omar Bradley, his West Point classmate, thought Ike "had matured into a charming man with a first class mind." True

FDR liked Ike. On way back from Cairo, president gave Eisenhower invasion command because of landing experience and team play.

he read pulp Westerns "because I don't have to think." But, wrote an anonymous observer: "Few who watched him carefully indulged the fantasy that he was a genial, open, barefoot boy from Abilene who just happened to be in the right place when lightning struck."

He showed his underlying steel as well as his dedication to the alliance when he sacked an American general and sent him home. "I don't care if you called him a limey, and I don't care if you called him a son-of-a-bitch if that's what he is. But you called him a limey son-of-a-bitch, and that's why I'm firing you."

Montgomery was selected to head the ground forces for the invasion. He was vain, self-justifying and arrogant, but dedicated to winning. Said one of his long-suffering staff: "We never lost confidence in him, but we would very often say 'Oh, Christ, what's the little bugger doing now?'" "God Almonty," others called him. Brooke confided to King George VI that he thought Montgomery was "a very good soldier, but I think he is after my job."

"I thought he was after mine," the king replied.

Montgomery looked at Morgan's plans and protested immediately that the initial landing force had to have five divisions, not three, and land on a broader front. "If you don't have enough men, get them," he said.

Bradley was given command of the Americans. A correspondent said the homespun Bradley "might have passed as an elderly rifleman." He was, said A.J. Liebling, war correspondent for *The New Yorker*, "the least dressed up commander of an American Army since Zachary Taylor, and he wore a straw hat." Compared to Patton, Bradley "seemed a man of milk." But the slapping incident had left Patton temporarily in disgrace without a command.

But what Marshall had written of Bradley in a 1930 fitness report still held true: "Quiet, unassuming, capable, sound common sense. Absolute dependability. Give him a job and forget it."

Normandy with its extensive beaches had been picked for the invasion from the start. The English Channel coast along Calais, the closest point to England, had cliffs and too few exits to the interior. The Allies would have to seize a port immediately to supply the troops. And the British embarkation ports opposite Calais were too small. The Baie de la Seine off Normandy had twenty-one-foot tides and three-knot currents. But it was more sheltered and adjacent to the harbors of Brittany. D Day had to coincide with a late rising moon for visibility for the paratroops and a rising tide just after maximum ebb so the traps of Hitler's Atlantic Wall could be cleared from the beaches. Moon and tide were synchronous only three days a month. May was initially targeted but changed to permit a buildup of more landing craft. D Day was finally set for June 5.

Morgan's planners kept very much in mind the bloody lessons of the disastrous raid by 6,000 Canadians and British commandos on Dieppe August 19, 1942. Half of the men were lost. The British learned that a seaborne invasion would have to begin on beaches, not against fortified towns. It must be preceded by an overwhelming naval barrage and bombing. Special armored vehicles would have to be designed.

D Day commanders: Bradley and Montgomery.

"For every man who died at Dieppe, ten were saved on D Day," said Lord Louis Mountbatten, head of the British special forces.

Montgomery's brother-in-law, Major General Sir Percy C.S. Hobart, devised some special tanks his men dubbed "funnies." One was a tank with a chain flail in front to explode mines. Another was a flamethrower. Another shot charges the size of an ash can against pillboxes. Some American Sherman tanks were outfitted with propellers to swim ashore enveloped in a buoyant canvas casing.

"If we can't capture a port, we must take one with us," said Rear Admiral John Hughes-Halle. Some 40,000 British shipbuilders set to work making huge concrete caissons the size of five-story buildings that would be towed across the Channel and sunk to make docks and breakwaters. Seventy-four old merchant ships were to be sunk as well to make the two artificial harbors code-named Mulberries. Each was to be the size of the port of Dover which had taken seven years to build. The shipbuilders had as many months.

Overlord called for two U.S. landings at Omaha and Utah beaches in the crook of the Contentin peninsula below the port of Cherbourg. The British were to land on Gold and Sword beaches to the east and the Canadians on Juno. The British 6th Airborne Division and the U.S. 82nd and 101st. Parachute Divisions were to jump behind their respective beachheads prior to the landing by ground soldiers. Air Chief Marshall Sir Trafford Leigh-Marshal, Eisenhower's deputy for air, protested using paratroops, but yielded when Bradley said he would scrub the Utah landing without them. Eisenhower's Supreme Headquarters Allied Expeditionary Force, SHAEF, estimated that two weeks after the landing the Allies would have twenty-eight divisions in France opposed by an equal number of Germans.

Throughout the winter and spring frogmen landed secretly on the beaches, testing the sand's compactness for tanks. Photo planes recorded gun emplacements and beach obstacles along the whole coast from Spain to the Netherlands. Vacationers were asked to turn in any post cards they might have from coastal France.

Meanwhile, southern England had been taken over by a friendly army of occupation. Crammed in among the thatched cottages and the downs and the quaint farm villages and cathedrals and the sheep and the ancient castles and curiosity shops were 1.5 million American soldiers, 1.75 million from Britain and her Commonwealth, plus 40,000 French, Polish, Norwegian and Belgian troops. Each armored division needed forty shiploads to supply it, an infantry division thirty. Farmland became tank parks. Country lanes were lined with artillery shells. The military took over schools, cottages, manors and moved into 279,000 tents and 398,666 prefabs. By April 1944 half a million tons of supplies were being landed monthly. The U.S. alone stockpiled 700,000 separate items: 8,000 planes, 1,000 locomotives, 100,000 packs of gum. A force of 54,000 men was required just to take care of the invading army—2,000 security agents, 4,500 cooks serving chow to lines that could stretch a quarter of a mile. The Army even stockpiled French phrase books for the invaders including one line instructing how to tell a jeune fille "My wife doesn't understand me" which caused a flap back home. Every other day planes landed with 730 miles of paper from the States. Paratroopers took up residence in hamlets such as Straight Stolley, Crooked Stolley, Ogbourne St. George and Mildenhall which they learned to pronounce "Minal." Twenty-five square miles of Devon were evacuated to make room for American maneuvers. Troops rehearsed again and again attacking terrain and fortifications copied from the real thing in France with only the names left out. Orders for the First Army alone made a book thicker than *Gone With the Wind.*

Instead of capturing ports, bring them along. One of two Mulberry artificial harbors off Normandy.

GIs also learned to throw darts in pubs. British kids learned to blow bubble gum. The Yanks were to come home with 70,000 war brides, although some cultural exchanges were also ludicrous, humorous, abrasive and sometimes mystifying.

British Mulberry. Long ramps lead from beach to sunken caissons behind breakwater of sunken ships protecting artificial harbor.

That an invasion was pending was no secret, as the few reconnaissance planes of Hitler's dwindling Luftwaffe that weren't shot down could attest. The secret was when. And where. To hide their hand the British waged a clever war of camouflage and deception on a massive scale.

MI-5, British counterintelligence, had located all Hitler's agents in the country and "turned" them to send back an array of half truths, mistruths and no truths to Admiral Wilhelm Canaris's Abwehr, the Nazi intelligence agency. As D Day neared, the British took the unprecedented step of forbidding foreign diplomats from leaving the country. Mail overseas was stopped.

Would it be Norway, the exposed flank of neutral Sweden which Hitler counted on for his iron ore? To make the fuehrer think so the British created a fictitious army based in Scotland. Wedding announcements of this mythical army's men were placed in local newspapers along with scores of its soccer teams. Notices of regimental dances were posted. Dummy planes and tanks were placed around the countryside. British agents in Stockholm ostentatiously bought Norwegian road maps and made pointed inquiries about railroads. The result: Hitler kept seventeen valuable divisions on guard in Norway.

Would it be Calais? The British created another fictitious army southeast of London, this one commanded by Patton. Discreet leaks indicated this army of fifty-seven divisions, forty-two of which were phony, would attack across the Channel. A movie studio built dummy landing craft that were anchored in the Thames. They even had laundry flying in the rigging, and their exhausts puffed real smoke. Other plants and leaks hinted at attacks in the Balkans. A Montgomery look-alike was sent to Gibraltar to reinforce the idea. Hitler moved three panzer divisions there.

As a result of all these ruses, called Operation Fortitude, Hitler's commanders figured there were ninety-two to ninety-seven divisions in Britain poised to strike. There were actually thirty-five.

Keeping the real secret secret was a constant preoccupation for security. Once a dozen copies of invasion plans blew out of an open window at the War Office. Employees dashed to the street and quickly retrieved eleven. For two frantic hours they searched for the twelfth until it was turned in by a Horse Guardsman who'd been handed it by a passerby. A railway worker turned in a briefcase filled with plans he had found on a train. A postal clerk in Chicago opened a package of plans a clerk in London had sent to his sister back home by mistake. The quartermaster of the 9th Air Force, a major general, was broken to lieutenant colonel

ULTRA SECRET

Perhaps the best kept—and most valuable— secret of the war was some odd machinery in a large Victorian estate forty miles northwest of London. And it was no more odd than the men who ran it.

Bletchley Park was the home of Ultra, the electric wizard that could read German codes. Its very existence was not declassified until thirty years after the war. The German codes were based on a typewriter-sized cipher machine called Enigma developed by a Dutchman in 1919. Through brilliant work, Polish mathematicians and cryptanalysts had deciphered the keys to the machine. Just before Poland fell, they gave the fruits of their ingenuity to the French and British.

At Bletchley the British assembled an exotic band of mathematicians, puzzle solvers, blackboard scribblers and assorted radio and electrical geniuses to build a machine that could read Enigma messages from daily radio intercepts. "I told you to leave no stone upturned in your recruiting," Churchill reportedly told his spymaster. "I did not expect you to take me so literally."

Foremost among them was Alan Turing, a wizard of what became computer logic and an eccentric of the highest order. He kept a long distance phone line open to his mother so they could share comments on a BBC broadcast of Larry the Lamb, a children's play. Also a pioneer jogger, he sometimes ran from Bletchley all the way to London with an alarm clock tied to his waist.

Ultra, named for an old naval code used at Trafalgar, was an invaluable source of intelligence throughout the war as were the U.S. codebreakers in the Pacific.

Only a few years before, Henry Stimson had spurned creation of a "black chamber" codebreaking organization saying: "Gentlemen do not read each other's mail." By World War II they did so, daily. Victory depended on it.

War Secretary Henry L. Stimson, a gentleman of the old school, ruefully learned rules of war had changed.

and sent home because he said at a cocktail party at Claridge's in London that France would be invaded by June 15.

In May, one Leonard Sidney Dawe, a physics teacher who composed crossword puzzles for the *Daily Telegraph,* was surprised by a visit of agents from MI-5. They were most interested to know why his puzzles over five consecutive days contained clues that were answered by Utah, Omaha, Overlord, Neptune (the code name for the naval operation for D Day) and Mulberry. They said these were all codes for upcoming but unspecified Allied operations. Just a very odd coincidence, said Dawe, which indeed it was.

So successful was Fortitude that of 250 agents reporting to deputy fuehrer Heinrich Himmler, all were wrong about the invasion but one.

Facing the Allies were fifty-eight divisions in northwestern Europe under the command of Field Marshal Gerd von Rundstedt. He was a crusty sixty-nine-year-old Prussian of the old, old school, a thorough professional who had little use for Hitler whom he called "the little Bohemian corporal." Ten of those divisions were armored including the Panzer Lehr, one of the best units in the Wehrmacht, and the Hitler Youth Division, mostly fanatic teen-agers ready and willing to die for their fuehrer. But a lot of the troops, particularly in Normandy, were second line: older soldiers, recovering wounded from the Russian front, even some captured Poles and Russians who figured fighting for Germany was preferable to life in a POW camp.

Rundstedt's strategy was to counterattack the Allies once they landed with a massive strike by his mobile reserve. Common sense, he believed, would dictate the Allies coming ashore in the Pas de Calais. Disagreeing with him on both counts was his deputy, Field Marshal Rommel who commanded the German Atlantic defense including Army Group B along the Norman coast. He was convinced (so was Hitler), that the invasion was coming his way. His strategy was to attack the beachhead at once: "The high water line must be the fighting line."

Churchill on pre-invasion inspection of U.S. troops whose helmet stencils signify: "Anywhere, Anytime, Anyhow, Bar Nothing." Shoulder patches censored.

Rommel was no admirer of Hitler, either. He called the vaunted Atlantic Wall Hitler's "cloud cuckoo land" until he was named to defend it in 1943. Rommel determined to turn the 800-mile coastline into a continuous fort. He put 250,000 men, much of it slave labor, to work around the clock to erect 15,000 strong points. Blockhouses were built with fifteen-foot thick concrete. Deadly 88s were emplaced in bunkers with their walls to the sea so they could fire down the beaches. Cannon, machine guns, mortars were hidden in existing buildings and blockhouses disguised as vacation homes and casinos. Rommel wanted to plant 200 million mines and came fairly close. Beaches were porcupined below the high tide line with steel crosses to rip the bottoms off landing craft. Inland he planted poles—"Rommel's asparagus"—to break up landing gliders. The defenses were constantly monitored by photo planes and the French underground. But Rommel had built a fort, and in May, playing his hunches, Hitler reinforced Normandy. This brought German strength there to six infantry divisions, two panzer and two more panzers in reserve.

Rommel's prior experience in France and Africa had taught him the ability of air power to create a chaos behind the lines. That was why he thought Runstedt wrong in contemplating a battle of maneuver. Allied planes wouldn't permit it.

In any event, he had done his best. He could only wait. His headquarters were midway between Paris and Normandy in the chateau of the dukes of La Rochefoucauld. Rommel could well have reflected what one duke, Francois La Rochefoucauld, France's great composer of maxims, had written 300 years before: "C'est une grande habileté que de savoir cacher son habileté." The height of cleverness is to be able to conceal it. The phantom "4th Army" would have loved the irony.

Maxims aside, Rommel decided to take a little R and R by visiting his wife Lucie in Germany on her fiftieth birthday. He had bought her some gray suede shoes in Paris. He left headquarters at La Roche Guyon on Sunday, June 4. Her birthday was Tuesday, June 6.

For the lesser generals in Normandy and Brittany Tuesday was to be a work day. They were to gather in Rennes for a staff war game. The exercise: a hypothetical parachute landing in Normandy.

Weathermen are a much maligned species and Group Captain James M. Stagg showed it. "There goes six-feet-two of Stagg and six-feet-one of gloom," they used to say around the RAF base. On the first weekend of June 1944 Stagg had about the toughest call any weatherman ever had to make.

He was Eisenhower's meteorologist for the invasion of France.

Eisenhower had moved down to Portsmouth, a major embarkation point, and was working out of a trailer parked alongside Southwick House. Stagg spent his nail-biting time studying reports from six weather stations out in the Atlantic, a luxury his German counterparts lacked. Eisenhower had set D Day for June 5 so he would have June 6 available if there was a postponement. The tides wouldn't be right again until June 19. But there would be no moon. The weathermen had said the odds were ten to one for getting the right conditions, and Stagg's forecast for the 5th was for high winds and overcast skies on the French coast.

In England's Channel ports the LSTs—"Large Stationary Targets," the sailors called them—began landing.

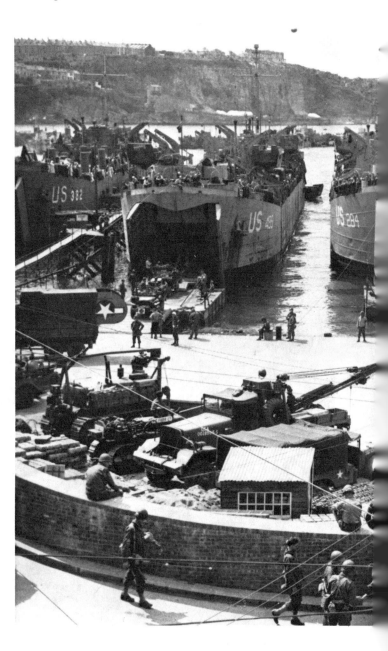

Loading for the invasion of southern France had begun months before D Day.

Some advance ships were already at sea. Pubs in the arsenal that England had become were suddenly absent of relaxing GIs and Tommies. Endless convoys snaked through the countryside towards the Channel ports.

On June 4 Stagg, speaking improbably against the reality of rain lashed horizontally by the wind against Ike's trailer, saw a silver lining. He had picked up a clearing cold front that should reach the area by June 6. Eisenhower debated the prospects with his staff; Montgomery and six other Britons and one American, his brilliant chief of staff, Major General Walter Bedell Smith. But the ultimate decision was Eisenhower's alone. How long could the men stay cooped up in their crowded transports? How long could secrecy be maintained? Could an invasion even be stopped in mid-thrust?

The small group reconvened at 4:30 a.m. June 5 in the trailer. The weather was still violent. But Stagg was firm in his forecast of improvement June 6.

Finally Eisenhower spoke: "Okay, we'll go."

There were tears in his eyes as Eisenhower watched U.S. 101st Airborne take off for Normandy.

The Allied commander talked to some Tommies loading in Portsmouth. He visited some paratroopers of the 101st Airborne, their faces blackened with burnt cork.

"Where are you from, soldier?"

"Pennsylvania, sir."

"Did you get those shoulders working in a mine?"

"Yessir."

"Good luck to you."

He played some checkers with his naval aide Captain Harry Butcher, getting a draw from what seemed certain defeat. He took a walk with Merrill Mueller of NBC. Mueller said he looked "as though each of the four stars on either shoulder weighed a ton."

Every night the BBC included in the news coded messages for the Maquis, the French underground. By prearrangement when the announcer said "The dice are on the table," it was a signal to begin the Red Plan, destruction of phone lines. "It is hot in Suez" was to start the Green Plan, sabotaging the railroads. "The Trojan War will not be held. . . . Sabine has just had mumps." Codes that may have meant nothing or something. From a captured Resistance fighter, the Abwehr learned the tipoff for the invasion. It was two lines from "The Song of Autumn" by the French poet Paul Verlaine. The first line—"The long sobs of the violins of autumn"—was the alert. When the second line came over the BBC, it meant the invasion would begin within forty-eight hours starting at midnight following the broadcast. The headquarters of the 15th Army guarding the Calais coast had picked up

the first line June 1. On June 5 they heard the second: ". . . Wounding my heart with a monotonous languor."

Immediately Rundstedt's headquarters was alerted as was Hitler's. For some undetermined reason, no one notified the 7th Army in Normandy.

Despite the warning, Rundstedt's office in the Paris suburbs told the OKW, the Armed Forces High Command, in Germany: ". . . imminence of invasion is not recognizable." The German navy thought the weather too foul to send any patrol boats into the Channel. Rundstedt didn't think anyone was so stupid as to tip off an invasion.

In Normandy Major General Wilhelm Falley, commander of the crack 91st Air Landing Division which had just moved into the area, unknown to the Allies, had already left for the exercise at Rennes. He had only hours to live.

Those who saw the armada of 5,303 ships and landing craft headed for Normandy would never forget it. For more than two hours bombers and transport C-47s flew over London in an uninterrupted stream. In the vacant pubs, in the homes near the now deserted camps, in the suddenly empty ports, Englishmen nodded to each other: "This is it."

Mueller watched Eisenhower as the paratroops took to the sky. There were tears in his eyes. Percy Wallace, a lighthouse keeper on St. Gibans Head, had watched the fleet pass in awe. He returned home and asked his wife to kneel with him.

"A lot of men are going to die tonight," he said. "We should pray for them."

10
D DAY

On June 6, 1944, waves and waves of men swept
Normandy's shore.

If war is luck improved by design, June 6, 1944, in Normandy was a textbook.

Luck was sometimes good, sometimes bad. SHAEF's intricate designs sometimes went out the window in minutes. They were replaced by improvisation. But the overall objective was to land an army in France. This was achieved. Hitler's Atlantic Wall was pierced in a day. It cost approximately 2,500 of the lives the Wallaces had prayed for, a quarter of SHAEF's grimmer estimate.

The plan was for the American 82nd and 101st Airborne Divisions to drop at night behind Utah Beach where the U.S. 4th Division was to land at H Hour, 6:30 a.m. The veteran 1st Division was to land on Omaha Beach fifteen miles to the east with the 29th Division. Next to them down the coast were Gold Beach (British 50th Division), Juno (Canadian 3rd) and Sword (British 3rd) with the British 6th Airborne Division dropping inland towards the city of Caen, a first day objective.

Things came unhinged almost immediately. Nervous pilots dodging flak dropped troopers of the 6th all over the countryside. Lieutenant Colonel Terence Otway could round up only 150 of the 700 men of his battalion. His target was the 200-man battery at Merville, its lethal guns to be out of action by 5:30 a.m. before the naval barrage was to begin. In vicious hand-to-hand fighting his men made it by fifteen minutes. Lieutenant Mike Dowling reported to Otway: "Battery taken as ordered, sir. Guns destroyed." Then he dropped dead. British glider forces skidded to a stop within feet of their objective, key bridges over the Orne Canal. They seized them at once.

To the west, 822 C-47s carried 13,000 U.S. paratroopers. To keep the Germans from copying their D Day markings, the wings of the planes had been painted with black and white stripes at the last minute—which set off a hurried hunt for 20,000 paint brushes. While the soldiers, weighted with more than 100 pounds of equipment, smoked, joked or hid their thoughts and fears in nervous silence, the pilots tried to maintain formation and avoid collision. Just before the green jump signals turned on, the planes flew into clouds. Many thirty-man "sticks" dropped blind. The paratroopers were scattered over one hundred square miles. Some didn't rejoin their units for weeks, some never. Seven had refused to jump.

Only two of the six parachute regiments landed on their drop points with any cohesion. Major General Maxwell Taylor, commander of the 101st, rounded up only 2,500 troops. Major General Matthew Ridgway, leader of the 82nd, could find 4,000. Eleven of Corporal Louis Merlano's stick fell into the sea off Utah Beach and quickly drowned. Merlano, in the dunes, heard German voices and began eating his codes.

Many other Americans fell into fields flooded by the Germans and drowned, some in only a few feet of water. One trooper remembered his comrades hitting the meadows "like large, ripe pumpkins being thrown down to burst." Men of the 101st tried to find each other by snapping toy crickets. The more experienced 82nd thought they attracted sniper fire and used a password: "Flash," response "Thunder." About all many of the soldiers knew was that if there were cows in the fields where they

D Day gliders crash-landed among the hedgerows of Normandy.

landed, they weren't mined. Major Lawrence Legere of the 101st was challenged by some Germans. He began explaining to the voices in the dark in French that he was returning from a date with his girl, all the while trying to pull the pin on a grenade. He finally managed, threw it and found three dead Germans.

Private John Steele of the 82nd had a ringside seat, as dramatized in the movie *The Longest Day* based on Cornelius Ryan's riveting account of D Day. He was hanging by his parachute from the steeple of the church of St. Mere-Eglise. A less fortunate buddy crashed through the roof of a burning house.

In these early hours the Germans were coming alert but with uncommon confusion. "The Americans knew what was happening, but few of them knew where they were," David Howarth wrote in his account of the battle. "The Germans knew where they were, but none of them knew what was happening."

Some American units, rarely with the light artillery and radioes they had jumped with, got oriented and took their objectives. Others began waging guerrilla warfare. What had seemed an unlucky drop actually confused the Germans the more. They had no concentrated targets to shoot at.

At 2:11 a.m. General Erich Marcks, commander of the German 82nd Corps around St. Lo who had been rehearsing his part in the war games at Rennes, was phoned that the real thing seemed to have happened: parachutists along the Orne. Within four minutes he phoned Major General Max Pemsel, chief of staff of the 7th Army, who awakened his commander, Colonel General Friederick Dollman: "General, I believe this is the invasion."

General Hans Spiedel, Rommel's chief of staff, was alerted at the chateau at La Roche-Guyon where he had just had drinks with officers who were conspiring to kill Hitler. "For the time being this is not to be considered a large operation," Spiedel decided. He and many other German commanders were to think, even for as long as the following month, that Normandy was a feint. The real invasion would land on the Pas de Calais. Fortitude was working.

One of those awakened was Major Werner Pluskat. He headed at once for his battery right in the middle of Omaha Beach. His binoculars ceaselessly scanned the horizon. Nothing. As dawn broke, he suddenly saw masts. Then more masts. And even more masts. He thought: "This is the end for Germany." Then he phoned in his sighting. Where were the ships heading? "Right for me!"

General Falley was on the road to Rennes, assuring his staff: "Nothing's going to happen in this lousy weather." Group Captain Stagg was a better forecaster. Skies were clearing, and the wind was ten to eighteen knots from the northwest as the greatest armada in history took up position about ten miles off the beaches. In a way it was a sail-past of the war. *Nevada*, raised from the mud of Pearl Harbor, was one of the seven battleships. *Augusta*, which had carried Roosevelt to his first meeting with Churchill, was among the twenty-three cruisers. So was Britain's *Ajax* which had hounded the German pocket battleship *Graf Spee* to her doom. There were ninety-three destroyers, 4,024 landing craft, 2,583 amphibious DUKW trucks. The Allies had intentionally not attacked some German radars on the Pas de Calais, so the Germans would pick up hundreds of decoys towed by small craft out in the Channel.

Aboard the real fleet, H Hour for the British

Coast Guardsmen steer for D Day beach under smoke screen.

beaches was 5:30 a.m., the Americans to open fire twenty minutes later. From then on, D Day became a blurred kaleidoscope of violence, smoke, fear, heroism, cowardice, chaos.

Major C.K. King recites to his men of the British 3rd Division lines from Shakespeare's *Henry V:* "And gentlemen in England now abed/Shall think themselves accurs'd they were not here . . ." Away all boats!

On another transport: "Our Father who art in Heaven. . . ." Away all boats!

And on another, a loading master: "Pick it up and put it on! You've only got a one-way ticket, and this is the end of the line! Twenty-nine, let's go!" Away all boats!

Sergeant Roy Stevens of the 29th hunts out his twin brother just before they clamber down cargo nets into the boxy landing craft. The brother offers his hand. "No, we'll shake hands at the crossroads in France just as we planned," Stevens says. "We said goodbye. I never saw him again." Away all boats!

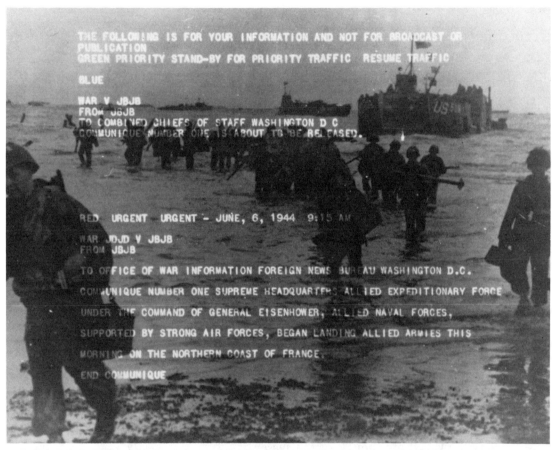

To the Far Shore: D Day announcement superimposed on landing photo.

Omaha Beach became a shooting gallery with crouching GIs the targets.

One GI is already down as Life's Robert Capa and camera hit the beach.

Life's *Robert Capa admitted to "trembling hands" as he took classic D Day photo, one of handful to survive darkroom haste.*

The guns begin firing, destroyers moving in for closer shots. The landing boats move among them like water spiders bearing 3,000 assault troops of the first wave. Many throw up in vomit bags or their helmets from sea-sickness. To them even machine guns on the beach are a welcome alternative.

The crew of a boat carrying some Rangers jumps ship into a dinghy. The Rangers have to land themselves. Other LCT crews ram their vessels up on the beach and begin firing with everything they have.

A boat begins swamping in four-foot swells. Soldiers jettison gear to lighten the vessel. Overboard goes $1,200 Private Chuck Vella won in a crap game. And Sergeant Charles Frederick's false teeth.

Men drowning with their heavy loads plead for rescue from passing boats. A coxwain swerves to pick some up. "You are not a rescue ship!" an officer commands. "Get on shore!"

Overhead, 329 heavy bombers zero in on Omaha Beach. Between bad visibility and fear of hitting their own men, bombardiers drop most of their loads ineffectually inland.

Commander Robert O. Beer to his crew of U.S. destroyer *Carmick:* "This is probably going to be the biggest party you boys will ever go to—so let's all get out on the floor and dance!"

American destroyer *Corry,* touching bottom inshore, turns seaward, hits a mine and breaks in two off Utah. A sailor grabs the flag from the aft section and raises it on the main mast now just sticking out of the water.

Captain Edmund Duckworth of the 1st steps onto Omaha and is instantly killed. He had married an English girl only five days before.

A company of Rangers loses half of its seventy men before it can reach the seawall on Omaha. By nightfall only twelve remain.

Thirty-two duplex-drive tanks, DDs, head for Omaha encased in their canvas floats. Twenty-seven founder and sink to the bottom, taking most of their crews with them.

Life magazine photographer Robert Capa shelters behind one of Rommel's beach barriers firing his camera. Only ten frames will survive darkroom haste back in London, but they will be the most memorable of the landing.

"I'll tell you what I see," a passing GI shouts to Capa. "I see my ma on the front porch waving my insurance policy!"

At the water's edge of Omaha, a soldier sits throwing pebbles into the surf "and sobbing as if his heart would break."

A medic tends a wounded soldier whose thigh is split from knee to hip. He closes the wound with safety pins.

On Utah, the current has landed the troops 2,000 yards out of position. Luckily this is the least defended part of the beach. Major General Theodore Roosevelt, second in command of the 4th, at fifty-seven the oldest man to land—his son, Quentin, a captain, is also landing—and the son of one president and cousin of another, strides the beach with a cane and a pistol loaded with seven bullets, surveying the terrain as calmly as if buying instead of invading it.

"Start the war from here!" he decides.

On Gold, Sergeant Major Stanley Hollis, who has already killed ninety Germans in the war, gets two more taking a pillbox singlehanded. He will get another ten before the day is over.

In some sectors of the fifty-nine-mile invasion front the "funnies" of General Hobart, which the Americans don't use save for the DDs because they believed them unproven—to their regret—cut through parts of the Atlantic Wall within half an hour. Things are so quiet in one sector medics are helping unload supplies.

On Juno, a battened-down Canadian tank runs over its own wounded on the beach until an officer blows off a tread with a hand grenade.

A sailor off a landing craft sees some Canadians herding six German prisoners behind a dune. Hoping for a souvenir helmet, he goes there himself. All six Germans are dead, their throats cut.

ROLL CALL

General Teddy Roosevelt, Jr., was to win the Congressional Medal of Honor for his D Day performance on Utah Beach. On July 12, Eisenhower named him to command the 90th Division. He died the same day of a heart attack.

Maxwell Taylor was to become Chief of Staff of the U.S. Army, Matthew Ridgway commander of U.N. forces in Korea. Sergeant Major Stanley Hollis survived the war to become a sandblaster. Sergeant Harrison Summers' one-man invasion earned him a battlefield commission.

Major Werner Pluskat, who saw the invasion coming his way, also survived to become an engineer.

In Caen, the Germans execute ninety-two suspected Maquis they had been holding.

Four Germans complete with packed suitcases surrender, happy to be heading to England as POWs. Other Germans surrender and are put to work clearing the mines they only recently had laid.

A Canadian hears voices shouting inside a pillbox. "I told the sergeant maybe they wanted to surrender, but the door was jammed. But the sergeant told the guy with the flamethrower to turn on the heat. You should have heard those Germans in that pillbox screaming. God, it was awful."

Photo reconnaissance has indicated six German guns at Pointe du Hoc, emplaced atop a sheer one

On D Day the bombers missed the beach; most tanks sank but the men kept coming.

hundred-foot cliff overlooking Omaha. "Three old women with brooms could keep the Rangers from climbing that cliff," says a Navy officer. But the Rangers have been training for months with extension ladders borrowed from the London Fire Brigade. With frightful losses, 220 Rangers assault the height. Once atop, they find what a Maquisard had frantically been trying to signal to London. The guns weren't emplaced yet.

Omaha Beach was the worst.

Its 300-yard deep beach at low tide was a shooting gallery. Beyond the beach was a stretch of stone shingle, then meadows rising to one hundred fifty-foot bluffs. The bluffs were cut by four valleys along their five miles, the only outlets for armor. Rommel had placed eighty-five machine gun posts and 109 artillery, rocket and mortar positions along the heights, most of them directed to the valleys. A landing had to be at Omaha because elsewhere there were only cliffs and offshore reefs.

It was no place for the bombing to have gone wrong, for the tanks to have sunk. A Company of the 116th Regiment was to suffer 96 percent casualties of its 197 men on that beach. "Within twenty minutes A Company had become a forlorn little rescue party bent upon survival," said the unit's official history. Twenty of the dead were from the same small town, Bedford, Virginia.

Three-thousand men landed in the first wave. Captain Carroll Smith of the 29th saw his friend Captain Sherman Burroughs rolling in the surf, shot through the head. At least he won't be having any more migraines, Smith thought.

Naval gunfire was not as accurate because Rear Admiral Allan G. Kirk had moved his ships twelve miles offshore instead of the recommended eight to avoid shore artillery. And the beaches by then were obscured by the smoke and dust of battle.

Engineers were to have blown sixteen channels through the underwater obstacles. But 111 of their 272 men had become casualties. Only three of sixteen bulldozers had made it. The tide was creeping up the yellow sand a yard a minute. A tank ran over a detonating wire just as it was set to blow. Only five channels had been cleared, and the

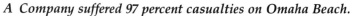

A Company suffered 97 percent casualties on Omaha Beach.

engineers had lost too many buoys to mark them properly. Tanks couldn't get traction on the loose shingle. Bradley, on *Augusta*, began contemplating withdrawing the troops. The Germans began sending troops to reinforce the British sectors, thinking the landing repulsed.

But the Americans kept coming.

Landing craft milled about "like a stampeded herd of cattle." Destroyers, some scraping the bottom, steamed in to fire point blank.

The novelist Ernest Hemingway had come ashore with the assault. "The first, second, third, fourth and fifth waves lay where they had fallen, looking like so many heavily laden bundles on the flat, pebbly stretch between the sea and the first cover."

The living took whatever shelter they could behind the shingle. Brigadier General Norman Cota strode back and forth in full view of the German gunners like a football coach, trying to prod his men from their torpor. The green troops of his 29th had not yet learned the battle wisdom that the closer you are to the guns, the safer.

"Two kinds of people are staying on this beach," cried Colonel George Taylor, "the dead and those who are going to die. Now let's get the hell out of here!"

Colonel Charles Canham urged his men forward with irrefutable Yankee pragmatism: "They're murdering us here. Let's move inland and get murdered."

One by one the men of the 29th crossed the shingle into the swampy ground beyond and towards the deadly bluffs.

By 4:15 a.m. Rundstedt had become convinced that a major operation was under way. He ordered two panzer divisions based outside Paris to Normandy, including the top-flight Panzer Lehr. Officially, however, these troops were under the German High Command, the OKW. They could only be released with direct approval of Hitler. And Hitler, a nighthawk whose nerves now had to be soothed with barbiturates before he could sleep, was still in bed in Berchtesgaden, a few miles from OKW. And furthermore, Colonel General Alfred Jodl, OKW Chief of Operations, was not about to wake him up. Instead, he countermanded Rundstedt's order. "We must wait further clarification of the situation," he said. Rundstedt's aides recall him "fuming with rage, red in the face, and his anger made his speech unintelligible." As a field marshal he could have phoned Hitler direct. But all day he did not call the man he called "that Bohemian corporal."

Speer remembered: "In recent days Hitler had kept on saying that the enemy would probably begin with a feigned attack in order to draw our troops away from the ultimate invasion site. So no one wanted to awaken Hitler and be ranted at for having judged the situation wrongly."

Offshore, Omar Bradley debates whether to pull his men off Omaha Beach.

D Day colonel: "They're murdering us here. Let's move inland and get murdered."

When the fuehrer finally awakened and was given the day's news after his breakfast, the two divisions were released. By then it was 3:40 p.m. And too late. Panzer Lehr, under constant debilitating air attack, didn't reach Normandy until June 9.

Spiedel finally managed to reach Rommel at his home at Herrlingen in Bavaria at 10:15 a.m. "How stupid of me. How stupid of me," he repeated. Later, as he and his aide Captain Hellmuth Lang sped in a car to La Roche-Guyon he interrupted his concentration to say: "I was right all along, all along."

Seven weeks earlier he had told Lang: ". . . the first twenty-four hours of the invasion will be decisive . . . the fate of Germany depends on the outcome . . . for the Allies, as well as Germany, it will be the longest day." And for his longest day Erwin Rommel had got a very late start.

Max Hastings, a British journalist and military historian, quantifies the German reaction as "lassitude that verged on incompetence."

Not everywhere.

General Falley had heard the bombardment as he was en route to Rennes and ordered his car to turn back. He was near his headquarters at Picauville behind Utah Beach when his car was hit by machine gun fire and crashed. "Don't kill! Don't kill!" the general cried as he crawled to his gun. Some troopers of the 82nd shot him dead. Lieutenant Malcolm Brannen, Ryan wrote, "wasn't sure, but it looked to him as though he'd shot a general."

Elsewhere the paratrooper had taken Ste. Mere-Eglise. They raised a Stars and Stripes they had flown over newly-liberated Naples on the flagpole outside town hall.

Closer to Utah Beach, German medic Franz Mueller tended a wounded American paratrooper. Suddenly Mueller was hit by a swarm of descending cigarettes. He looked up to see an American sniper (the paratroopers had all been issued a carton of smokes as battle rations) who had rewarded him for his deed. The sniper then shot a German who was rifling a dead trooper's pockets.

Nearby, Sergeant Harrison Summers of the U.S. 502nd Airborne Regiment had embarked on a one-man war against his assigned objective, an artillery group stationed in a series of stone farm buildings. Summers's men held back, so he began fighting house to house, kicking down a door and spraying the inhabitants with his tommygun. Private John Camien approached him.

"Why are you doing it?"

"I can't tell you. They (the others) don't seem to want to fight, and I can't make them. So I've got to finish it." Camien joined him, and they did just that, shooting a final fifteen Germans as they were at breakfast.

Troops keep coming as invasion Army fights inland.

The 4th Division on Utah had had an easier time than the men on Omaha. Most of their tanks got ashore. By afternoon a scout from the beachhead ran into Sergeant Thomas Bruff, a paratrooper of the 101st, on one of the four roadways going inland over the flooded meadows.

"Where's the war?" the scout asked.

"Keep on going, buddy, you'll find it," Bruff replied.

On the British sector north of Caen, General Marcks was organizing the one panzer attack of the day. "If you don't succeed in throwing the British into the sea, we've lost the war," he told his tank leader, Colonel Hermann von Oppeln-Bronikowski. The panzers, Mark IV tanks, aimed for a vulnerable gap between Juno and Gold beaches. British gunners blasted them to a standstill. By nightfall Marcks had lost seventy of his 124 tanks. Bronikowski watched a drunken soldier and two Wehrmacht women stagger up the road. "The war is lost," he said to himself.

By the end of D Day the Allies had 55,000 men ashore. Omaha had been enlarged to a beachhead six miles wide and two deep. Supplies were pouring ashore with almost no fear of air attack. Allied planes had flown 13,000 missions to command the beaches. The Luftwaffe could barely manage one hundred.

Montgomery, with the irksome bravado that so nettled Americans and more than a few of his countrymen, had said his men would take Caen on the first day. They had not and would not for another thirty-three days of hard fighting.

But the Allies had landed in France and stayed. "After that day there was no hope of a counterattack being decisive," said Captain Lang, Rommel's aide. "Why don't you go to bed," he told his chief. "It's been a long day." In that prediction, at least, Rommel had been dead right.

THERE'LL ALWAYS BE AN ENGLAND

Of all the days of the year—of all the days of any time—June 6, 1944, was the annual meeting of the Channel Tunnel Company, folks who wanted to connect England and France by digging under that historic barrier.

The meeting adjourned, as news of one way to cross the Channel was speeding around the world, after deciding the future of a tunnel was impossible to predict.

IKE'S NOTE

It was a measure of the man, many were to say, and his commitment to responsibility of command.

After giving the go-ahead for the invasion, Eisenhower hand-wrote a short note and stuffed it in his pocket just in case. . . . It said:

"Our landings in the Cherbourg-Havre area have failed to gain a satisfactory foothold and I have withdrawn the troops. My decision to attack at this time and place was based upon the best information available. The troops, the air and the navy did all that bravery and devotion to duty could do. If any blame attaches to the attempt it is mine alone."

He later gave the note to Captain Butcher, his aide, who came to brief him in his trailer early D Day morning and found the general in bed, smoking a cigarette and reading a Western.

The Normandy beachhead secured, the supplies streamed ashore.

British Tommies planned to capture Caen on D Day. It took a month.

Breakout

In French it is called bocage.

Literally, this translates as "grove." Actually, in Normandy it was the hedgerow, banks ten and fifteen feet high built up over centuries dividing farm plots and intertwined by a thicket of vines and scrub trees. Nature had provided the Germans a better defense after D Day than the man-made concrete of Hitler's Wall on the coast.

At the beaches, thousands of tons of equipment were piling up daily. Fifty-five thousand troops had landed on D Day with many more to follow. The artificial Mulberry at Utah was completed in ten days, remarkably ahead of schedule. LSTs could unload in sixty-four minutes and head back to England for more instead of waiting hours for the tide to lift them from the shore. Then on June 19 a four-day gale wrecked the American Mulberry and heavily damaged the British. Landing went back to the beaches, something the Americans did superbly.

In Normandy, the hedgerows made better defenses for the Germans than the concrete and steel of the Atlantic Wall.

A week after landing, D Day beaches became instant seaport.

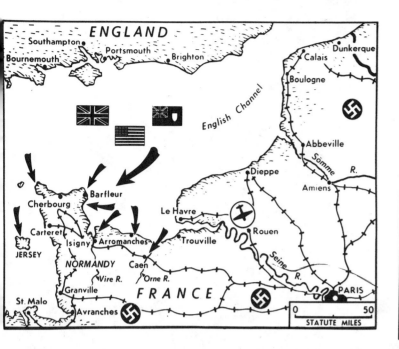

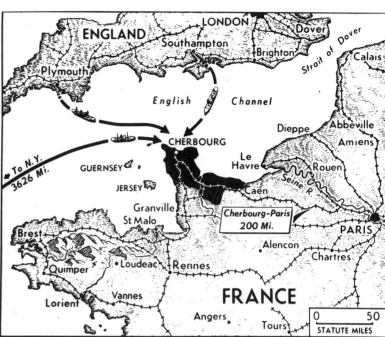

Above left: *Arrows and plane symbol indicate where confused Germans thought Allies had landed on D Day.* Above right: *With the capture of Cherbourg, supplies could reach France directly from United States.*

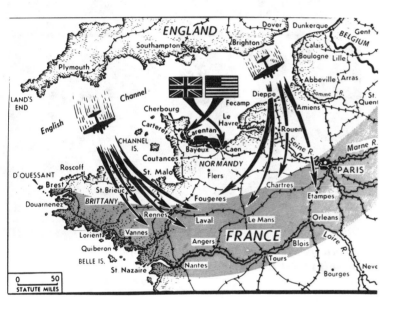

Above: *After four days Normandy beachheads had been connected as Allied bombers crippled rail networks in shaded area.* At right: *With the Normandy landing, Hitler's Reich faced attack on three fronts.*

A week after D Day, Allied buildup was nonstop.

*Allied tracers fire at one of few Luftwaffe attackers
as ships wait to unload off Normandy.*

Inland, U.S. soldiers under Major General J. Lawton Collins, "Lightning Joe," sealed off the Cotentin peninsula. Rommel had withdrawn some of his troops beforehand in defiance of Hitler's order to defend Cherbourg "to the last man." But Rommel, still fearful of a Calais landing, did not call in the reserves from the 15th Army there. The Americans fought into Cherbourg street by street. One unit burst into a German bunker just as officers were sitting down to eat a ham. "Stop!" ordered the GI commander. "I'll take that." He took the ham, and his comrades took the port June 27. But so thorough had been German destruction, Cherbourg wouldn't be operational for months.

To the east the British still had not captured Caen, further increasing dissatisfaction with Montgomery at SHAEF. But on July 1 the British held off a counterattack. "What shall we do?" Field Marshal Wilhelm Keitel, OKW chief of staff, asked Rundstedt. "Make peace, you fools," the old Prussian replied and resigned the next day after "the Bohemian corporal" intimated he was too old for the job.

Some Americans grumbled that Monty's African veterans had lost their fighting edge, feeling they had already done well—and enough—for their country. Montgomery was to rationalize then and later into ongoing criticism. One of his American aides remarked at the time: "The (British) commanders feel the blood of the British Empire, and

Hitler ordered Cherbourg garrison to fight to last man. They had other ideas.

Paratroopers check Ste. Mere-Eglise for snipers after D Day.

hence its future, are too precious to dash in battle.'' In truth Mother England had no more men left to give, and the Canadians were the last she would get from the Commonwealth.

But by July 7 the British and Canadians had a 4:1 edge over the Germans in men and 2:1 in tanks. The corresponding ratios were 3:2 and 8:1 for the Americans. And they were facing inferior, motley troops. In one regiment of Soviet ''volunteers,'' thirty-two different dialects were spoken. But the Germans proved to be masters of defense and small unit counterattack in the bocage. The hedgerows neutralized the American advantage in armor. Many of the conscript GIs were green to battle.

''The Allied soldier never seemed to be trained as we were, always to try to do more than had been asked of us,'' said Corporal Adolf Hohenstein of second line 276th German Division. ''We could not understand why they didn't break through.''

''By and large they were better soldiers than we were,'' said Brigadier Bill Williams, an aide to Montgomery. They also in many cases had superior equipment. The German Panther and Tiger tanks were more heavily armed and armored than the American Sherman. They could set the flammable U.S. tank ablaze at 4,000 yards while the Sherman had to close to within 300 to knock out a Tiger. The German Spandau machine gun was a superb weapon as was the American M-1 Garand semi-automatic rifle which, however, had a tendency to jam.

Normandy's bocage made a natural fortress for defending Germans as GIs attacked the hedgerows.

The Germans were fired by the knowledge they were now fighting for their Fatherland. But effective and abundant U.S. artillery was slowly taking its toll. And so was air power. In Normandy the lessons of close-support attacks by fighter-bombers had finally been learned. At the urging of Major General Elwood "Pete" Quesada of the 9th Air Force, one of the rare fliers who recognized wars were ultimately won by the foot soldier, tanks were given radios tuned to the fighter pilots' frequencies. It became phone and strafe. Fragile little Piper spotter planes flew back and forth for the gunners over the battle lines. Germans began to dread the sight of P-47 Thunderbolts and P-51 Mustangs armed with cannon and 2,000 pounds of bombs.

But one of the key solutions to the bocage came from a Tennessee GI named Hillbilly Roberts who asked his captain one day: "Why don't we get some saw teeth and put them on the front of the tank and cut through these hedges?" Thus was born the "rhino," a Sherman tank with welded-on horns made from Rommel's old beachhead obstacles. The rhinos began uprooting the bocage, regaining armored mobility again while the heavy panzers still had to stick to the roads and country lanes.

It all began to pay off by July 25. By then the Americans had 812,000 men ashore, the British and Canadians 640,000. Around St. Lo Bradley, who relied heavily on his tested fighters—1st, 4th, 9th and 2nd Armored—massed fifteen divisions and 750 tanks and 1,000 cannon against nine German divisions. Rommel had already lost 100,000 men and received only 6,000 replacements. He had lost 225 tanks and got only six new ones. Meeting with Hitler near Soissons July 17 he told the fuehrer Normandy was lost and he should consider negotiating with the Allies. Hitler fired Rommel forthwith and ordered his men yet again not to yield an inch. But still he didn't call in the 15th Army.

"One's imagination boggled at what the Germany army might have done to us without Hitler working so effectively for our side," Quesada said after the war.

On July 25 the St. Lo sector was attacked by 1,800 bombers of the 8th Air Force. In the dust and smoke which blew slowly back over the U.S. lines some bombers hit their own men, killing 111, including Lieutenant General Lesley McNair.

But the raid also killed half of Panzer Lehr's remaining 5,000 men. For the remainder, said Lieutenant General Fritz Bayerlein, commander of the division, "the shock effect was indescribable. Several of my men went mad." Nonetheless, Field Marshal Gunther Hans von Kluge, a veteran of the Russian front who had succeeded Rundstedt and had lost his initial optimism about the situation,

U.S. infantrymen creep through Normandy farmland past fallen comrades.

GI's bright idea used prongs made of Rommel's beach traps to cut through Normandy hedgerows.

ordered Bayerlein to hold to the last man. "Out in front everyone is holding out. Everyone," Bayerlein raged. "Not a single man is leaving his post. They are lying silently in their foxholes, for they are dead. You understand? Dead . . . the Panzer Lehr Division is annihilated!"

*Fighting was often house to house as GIs enlarge
Normandy beachhead.*

"We could only play foxes," said a German lieutenant. " 'Home to Germany' was the principal thought in many people's minds."

To the west, led by Patton returned to battle as commander of the newly-created 3rd Army, the Americans finally broke out. Patton's tanks pivoted through Avranches into Brittany as the Germans abandoned the field to withdraw into the Breton ports. Bradley has been criticized for not sending Patton on a dash to Paris at that point. Bradley, however, did not think the road to the French capital would have been any easier than Normandy had been.

Instead of fighting a rear guard action towards new lines nearer to Germany, something the Germans did brilliantly, Hitler ordered an attack from Mortain towards what he saw as an American weakpoint at Avranches. "He's mad," said one of his generals. "I'd like to meet Hitler," Brooke commented. "I'd like to shake his hand . . . worth forty divisions to us."

The Americans had already had a day's warning from Ultra intercepts when the attack came August 6. The Germans had some initial success in what was something of a trap. But the Americans, having broken free, fought with a new ardor. A battalion of the 30th Division, cut off by the advance, formed

*In the Falaise Pocket, the Allies netted more
German prisoners than the Soviets did at Stalingrad.*

a perimeter and in six days of heroic resistance helped stall the enemy. Patton wheeled and headed back towards Normandy. "Flanks are something for the enemy to worry about," he crowed, his tanks moving so swiftly they had to be fueled by parachute drop. In one of the continuing controversies of the war, Bradley halted Patton at Argentan, eighteen miles from completing a ring around the Germans at Falaise.

"Let me go on to Falaise," Anglophobe Patton pleaded with Bradley, "and we'll drive the British into the sea for another Dunkirk." Bradley held firm. Patton insisted his protest be made a matter of record. Montgomery, for his part, had set the boundary between the two Allied armies at Argentan and did not change it to let Patton move to Falaise. Nor did Bradley ask him to. He feared the Americans would be too weak once back into the bocage to withstand the fury of a trapped German army trying to get out. So Patton left some troops at Argentan and sped on towards the Seine to try for a wider encirclement.

Meanwhile, Montgomery's spearheads from Falaise to Argentan of Canadians and Poles had been stalled by fierce German resistance. The Canadian's official history commented: "German force far smaller than our own (the Canadians had 700 tanks to thirty-five for the Germans), taking advantage of strong ground and prepared positions, was able to slow our advance to the point where considerable German forces made their escape."

It was a lost opportunity but a slaughterhouse nonetheless. Allied fighters turned the so-called Falaise Pocket into an abbatoir and junkyard. It was littered with dead animals "like overturned hobby horses." Bodies and burned out vehicles littered the ground. Spotter planes flew higher to get away from the stench. But the Germans kept the gap open for thirteen days. Some 50,000 soldiers escaped. But the fighting in Normandy, culminating in a debacle nearly the equal of Stalingrad, had seen forty German divisions destroyed, 240,000 men killed or wounded, 1,500 tanks and 3,500 guns and 20,000 vehicles lost. Only twenty-four tanks and sixty guns got across the Seine.

For the Allies, 36,976 had died.

The Normandy survivors as well as the 15th Army from the Pas de Calais—some 300,000 men and 25,000 vehicles—fell back beyond Paris to regroup. One of them was Corporal Hohenstein. "After Normandy, we had no illusions any more. We knew we stood with our backs to the wall."

Paratroopers drop from sky in disputed invasion of southern France.

Navy Secretary James Forrestal (**second from right**) *and commanders of southern France invasion.*

One of the most heated battles between the Allies was settled August 15 when U.S. 6th Army Group invaded southern France. Churchill and his generals had adamantly insisted such a landing should be at the head of the Adriatic Sea in the Trieste area and thence follow an ancient invader's path through the Ljubljana Gap into Hungary and the Balkans. The objective was primarily political: to keep the Soviets from getting there first and establishing post-war dominance.

Roosevelt just as adamantly maintained the American people would have no sympathy for a Balkan excursion. They wanted Germany defeated and the war in Europe over by the most direct path as they saw it: through France. Post-war politics had little attraction to the American voter—who would decide whether to elect Roosevelt to an unprecedented fourth term that fall. "For purely political reasons over here, I should never survive even a slight setback in Overlord if it were known that fairly large forces had been diverted to the Balkans," the president told Churchill.

Undeterred, Churchill argued with Eisenhower that a leapfrog up the Italian peninsula would not diminish Alexander's Italian armies as a French invasion would. Then as a compromise he pro-

HITLER'S V FOR VICTORY

With defeat an increasing reality, Hitler desperately sought a "secret weapon" to save his collapsing Reich.

One was the V-1, a 350-mph, jet-propelled rocket launched from ramps in northern France. The first was fired June 13, 1944, at London. Hitler gambled that the flying bomb, with the moment of terror when its buzzing motor cut off and it began its dive towards earth, would demoralize the British. Using ground radar, RAF pilots found they could intercept the rockets and either shoot them down or fly alongside wing tip to wing tip and flip them off course. Before the ramps were overrun by Allied troops, 9,251 V-1s were launched against Britain; 4,621 were shot down and about 2,300 hit London destroying over a million buildings and killing 5,479, far fewer than were lost in Allied bombing raids on Germany.

One V-1 went off course June 17 and exploded on top of a command bunker near Soissons, France, where Hitler was paying his only visit to the western front. He was unhurt and never returned.

Hitler's V-2 was a true rocket, ancestor of today's missiles, and developed by German scientists who later helped produce America's first rockets. The first of these 13.6-ton, liquid-fueled missiles was fired on Paris September 6. Two days later the first of 1,359 were launched on London which were to kill about 2,500 people. Another 1,500 were fired at Antwerp, Brussels, and Liege in Belgium before the end of the war.

ATROCITIES

The close, bitter battles of the hedgerows in Normandy and sabotage of the Maquis did nothing for the rules of war.

Both sides were guilty of shooting prisoners. An American officer asked a private why he was bothering to take a surrendered German to the rear. Instead, he shot him on the spot. A British major gave some water to a wounded German— who drew a pistol and killed him. The Allies usually were greeted with wine, women and song by the jubilant Normans. But the wreckage of war caused some Frenchmen to think liberation a mixed blessing. In turn a British MP machine-gunned two Frenchmen he found going through the pockets of a dead soldier.

On June 10 at Oradour-sur-Glane, Germans of the SS Das Reich Division took revenge for the suspected kidnapping of an officer by the Maquis. They executed about half of the 600 people of the village near Limoges, then barricaded the rest including women and children in the church and torched it, gunning down any who tried to escape the flames.

Some members of the division were eventually buried in a cemetery in Bitburg, Germany, where President Ronald Reagan was to make a controversial homage many years later.

posed the troops be used to invade Brest in Brittany. Eisenhower was distressed at what he called his most difficult time with the prime minister, but he would not yield. At one point Churchill threatened to resign but finally accepted the fact that the Americans were now dominant in the Alliance. He did, however, have the French landing renamed Dragoon instead of Anvil since he felt he had been dragooned into it.

The armada of 1,800 ships including nine carriers was far out of proportion to the resistance as the U.S. 7th Army under Lieutenant General Jacob L. Devers and the French 1st Army commanded by General Jean de Lattre de Tassigny landed near Toulon and Nice. They quickly seized the port of Marseilles, the primary objective, and sped north almost unopposed to link up with Patton. Marseille was to become of great value. Through it for the rest of the year flowed one-third of all the supplies for the SHAEF armies. It also was the means of getting French soldiers into battle without clogging further the other invasion ports.

More than 800 ships took part in landing in southern France.

MEANWHILE IN RUSSIA

With pointed emphasis, the Soviet armies began their summer offensive June 22, 1944, exactly three years after Hitler invaded the Soviet Union.

A total of 118 divisions opened a 250-mile gap in the German center, advancing almost 400 miles to the gates of Warsaw in little more than a month. Germany lost 350,000 men at a time when replacements were only 60,000 a month. In the south the Russians swept through forty-seven German and Romanian divisions in August, capturing the vital oil fields of Ploesti before the Germans could destroy them. Romania, Bulgaria and Finland sued for peace with the Allies.

In August, the Warsaw Poles rose in revolt against the Nazis. The Russians stood by just outside the city despite pleas from Poles and the Western Allies. Stalin dismissed the rebels as "criminal elements" which the Allies read as a brutally cynical tactic to get rid of some Germans and non-communist Poles at the same time. About 250,000 Poles died.

If it revealed for all to see Stalin's brutal motives in Eastern Europe, the summer advance disclosed something else as well. On July 27 Russian troops reached Lublin. The Soviets took some Western correspondents on a guided tour of the extermination camp of Majdanek a mile outside the Polish town.

For the first time outside eyes saw the crematoria the Germans had kept burning day and night inside the barbed wire. There were ashen mounds with remnants of bones. An estimated 1,500,000 people had been put to death at Majdanek by a supposedly civilized state. Correspondent Raymond Davies of the New York tabloid *PM* wondered how one could get the enormity of it into a newspaper story. His home office had notified him: "Cable only if death rolls unusually large or deaths themselves unusually gruesome."

Davies was shown a warehouse that the guide said contained 820,000 pairs of shoes. That seemed about right. As the Germans abandoned yet more barbed wire camps in the face of advancing armies, Davies would not be the last to wonder what a human being could say.

GIs ignore Notre Dame cathedral to greet liberated Parisiennes.

JULY 20, 1944

There were, and always had been, those who opposed Hitler. They were centered mostly among the German aristocracy, the clergy and higher elements of the Wehrmacht.

To some he was a madman. To others he was bringing destruction to a nation they sincerely loved. And to some his fanatic obduracy stood in the way of approaching the Allies to end the war. Conspirators had made several attempts on Hitler's life, but his famous luck always seemed to protect him. A bomb planted in his plane failed to explode. An air raid cancelled a meeting where an assassin awaited.

But on July 20, 1944, Colonel Claus von Stauffenberg, an aristocrat who had lost an arm, an eye and all but three fingers of his remaining hand in a mine explosion in Africa, was to attend a meeting with Hitler and his generals at the Wolf's Lair in East Prussia. Stauffenberg had broken a vial of acid to trigger a two-pound

Eisenhower had planned on bypassing Paris, more a political than a military objective. But he did not reckon with De Gaulle, the once obscure officer whose dreams of regained glory for France included himself. When De Gaulle insisted on detaching Major General Jacques Leclerc's 2nd French Armored Division to the city, Eisenhower relented and sent the 4th Division along with it. Hitler had ordered the city burned but for once cooler Nazi heads prevailed to save a cultural treasure. Although partisans were fighting with his troops in the streets, Lieutenant General Dietrich von Choltitz opted for historical discretion over obedience to save Paris by surrendering the city. As he did so August 25 at his headquarters, 176 Germans surrendered to two American lieutenants outside the Hotel de Crillon bar nearby. The Americans told the Germans to check their weapons at the coatroom and, Paris being Paris, went inside. Ernest Hemingway, whose career had blossomed in Paris, checked in at the Ritz and ordered seventy-three dry martinis for two truckloads of French resistance men with him. Captain Raymond Sarniguet of the Fire Brigade, who had lowered the French tricolor from the Eiffel Tower when Hitler's troops captured the city in 1940, climbed the structure's 1,750 steps to put it back. And four days later, Norman Cota of Omaha Beach, now a major general in command of the 28th Division, led his men in battle equipment down the Champs Elysees and kept right on out of town.

Paris was deleriously free again.

plastic explosive in his briefcase. He placed the briefcase close to Hitler and left the room to fly to Berlin to help direct a coup by anti-Hitlerite generals. Just before the bomb exploded in a sheet of yellow flame, however, an aide of Hitler's moved the briefcase behind a stout oak table support. The fuehrer's new trousers were shredded—he proudly showed them around afterwards—and his face covered with soot, but he survived. Four died.

Uncertainty whether Hitler had been killed and failure to seize the Berlin communications center doomed the plotters who were overcome that night. Four, including Stauffenberg, were immediately shot. With typical German thoroughness the conspirators had left lists with names of co-plotters and sympathizers. Hitler thus learned that the plot, which he had blamed on a few "criminal elements" at first, was actually widespread. Kluge had known of the plot as had Rommel who had declined a role because he believed the Allies' insistence on unconditional surrender made Hitler's death immaterial. Kluge was dismissed by Hitler as the Normandy front was collapsing and ordered back to Berlin. Hitler suspected, possibly correctly, Kluge had tried to surrender. Kluge made a sentimental tour of his old World War I battlefields, then killed himself August 18 by swallowing cyanide. Rommel, who had been severely injured in a strafing run on his car in July, was given a more honorable alternative due to his renown: stand trial or kill yourself. He, too, took cyanide October 14 and died, sobbing.

Ringleaders of the plot were hung from meat hooks by piano wire and slowly strangled. The SS took movies of their death throes for the amusement and instruction of Hitler's entourage. By one account, 11,448 Germans suspected in the plot were eventually executed.

Support for the assassination attempt among the general populace and the military was minimal. The afternoon of the explosion Hitler kept to a scheduled meeting with Mussolini, now running a puppet government from northern Italy. Hitler told Il Duce that his narrow escape was certain proof that Nazism would survive its present difficulties.

American infantrymen marched through liberated Paris and right on out of town to go back to war.

Out of the dog house, Patton raced across France. Pauses with Eisenhower and Bradley (l.)

Arnhem

In September 1944, the Allies stumbled on the staircase to victory.

With Paris taken, their tanks drove past the blooded fields of World War I France, mocking that stalemate in top gear. Montgomery aimed for Holland, Patton for the Rhine at fifty miles a day limited only by fuel supplies as German resistance seemed to have dissolved. Montgomery reached Brussels September 3, and Antwerp, Europe's second largest port, the next day. Patton sped past Verdun, murderous metaphor of the stagnation of the earlier war. Then he ran out of gas, literally. And Eisenhower ran into a controversy in the person of Bernard Montgomery that was to fuel a heated argument for decades to come.

Montgomery insisted that Patton be stopped and he be given the bulk of the supplies and troops to curve northwards across the plains of Germany to take Berlin and finish the war by year's end. Eisenhower, true to his sense of his job, compromised. It led to tragedy at a Dutch river town called Arnhem.

The Americans were so euphoric at the scent of victory in 1944 that in September post exchanges were told to send Christmas packages home to the States. This disregarded two imponderables: were the Germans in fact defeated and could the Allies get sufficient supplies to their armies to prove it?

As for the enemy, Saul Padover, who was assigned to gauge German morale and was wise beyond his rank which was lieutenant colonel, quoted Napoleon: "An enemy is not defeated until he thinks himself defeated." As for being home by Christmas, Padover said of the war: "It was all over but the shooting."

And as for the supplies, the Allies had become victims of their own success. By the original Overlord plan, they were to have reached the Seine by D+90. They were then to pause to resupply until D+120. Instead they were at the Seine by D+79. Montgomery's 21st Army Group commanded by Lieutenant General Sir Miles C. Dempsey raced for Belgium at 250 miles a week. Patton at the same time ate up ground east of Paris and his 3rd Army was approaching Hitler's Siegfried Line of prepared defenses on the German border. But he needed 400,000 gallons of fuel a day to keep moving. And the farther the Allies got, the farther behind were their supply terminals at Cherbourg and the beaches of Normandy. To keep the armies supplied, 10,000 trucks of the Red Ball Express pounded the roads bumper to bumper day and night. Drivers were put on report if they couldn't maintain forty miles an hour. Marseilles was taking ships direct from New York. It was not enough. Patton had to stop in early September when he got only 32,000 gallons in a day. He told his men to drive on until their tanks were dry, then "get out and walk." His men disguised themselves as members of Lieutenant Courtney Hodges' 1st Army, his left flank neighbor, to scrounge some of their fuel.

"If Ike stops holding Monty's hand and gives *me* the supplies, I'll go through the Siegfried Line like shit through a goose," Patton boasted.

At the same time, Montgomery was telling Eisenhower: "Just give me what I need, and I'll reach Berlin and end the war." What the diminutive commander said he needed was control over Hodges' 1st Army on his flank and supplies for forty divisions for his Berlin thrust. This premissed Patton cooling his engines. And set the stage for Eisenhower's least fine hour.

On August 23, Eisenhower came to lunch with Montgomery. Ever status-conscious, Montgomery never visited Eisenhower, saying he was "too busy with the war" to call on his commander in chief. He compounded his cheek by asking that Eisenhower's chief of staff, "Beetle" Smith, leave the room although Montgomery's staff head, Major General Freddie de Guingand, stayed on. Montgomery, barely concealing his belief that Eisenhower knew next to nothing about war, began lecturing him about his upcoming drive. He asked for, and got, control over the airborne divisions now in reserve back in Britain, "operational coordination" with the 1st Army and the lion's share of the supplies. Eisenhower refused, however, to rein in Patton, noting American public opinion wouldn't stand for it "and public opinion wins wars." Montgomery demurred but had largely gotten his way.

The decision, Patton said, left Bradley "madder than I have ever seen him." Bradley wondered openly "what the Supreme Commander amounted to." Patton said they both should resign. Bradley wouldn't, talked instead to Eisenhower and got back the 1st Army, lending some weight to the barracks room gossip that Ike always agreed with the last man he talked to.

On September 1, at Marshall's insistence and to Montgomery's ill-concealed distress, Eisenhower became overall commander of the ground battle as well as head of SHAEF. To appease Montgomery, Churchill promoted him to field marshal which gave him five stars to Ike's four, technically but not actually outranking him. Eisenhower continued to plan for a two-prong invasion of Germany by Montgomery and Patton. He felt he could not risk all on one drive. Its flanks would be open to attack. His more conservative strategy called for occupation of territory to build bases for forward air support and bringing up equipment for the climactic bridging over the Rhine. He could not assume a swift stroke would be decisive. De Guingand indicated as much after the war. He noted it took 160 Russian divisions, the Western armies, Alexander's army in Italy and eight more months of round-the-clock bombing to force Germany's surrender.

Essential to Eisenhower's strategy was securing the port of Antwerp. Although the port was taken intact, its cranes stood idle against the sky, its locks empty, for the Germans had not been cleared from the Scheldt Estuary which led to the harbor. Eisen-

Patton's dash across France halted only when it ran out of gas.

Omar Bradley sometimes thought his West Point classmate, Eisenhower, was too diplomatic with British.

hower cabled Montgomery that opening Antwerp was of first importance. Without it, the Allied armies would falter and ultimately stall.

"Napoleon would have realized these things," Lieutenant General Brian Horrocks, head of Dempsey's spearhead XXX Corps, was to say, "but Horrocks didn't."

Not only were the supplies not coming in but the German 15th Army, which had been retreating from the Pas de Calais, managed to escape encirclement by the one road that led inland from the Scheldt which was left open by Montgomery pausing in Antwerp.

While the Canadians were wrenching the Germans out of the smaller Channel ports which Hitler had ordered them to turn into fortresses, Smith phoned Montgomery to ask what he was doing about Antwerp. The response so enraged Smith he

turned the phone over to Morgan, the D Day planner who was his deputy: "Here, you tell your countryman what to do." Morgan, figuring his career would be over in a post-war Montgomery army, and he was right, told Montgomery his supplies would be cut off if he didn't clear Antwerp. September 10 Montgomery again summoned Eisenhower to his headquarters and berated him like a none too bright student. He demanded control of the land battle be returned to him, charged Patton, not Ike, was running the war, that Ike had double-crossed him and that a dual offensive was doomed to failure. Montgomery derided plans that Eisenhower said he had approved as "balls, rubbish, balls." Eisenhower leaned forward and put his hand on the Briton's knee: "Steady, Monty. You can't talk to me like that. I'm your boss."

U.S. foot soldiers use tank for convoy entering Belgian town.

"I'm sorry, Ike," he mumbled, then proposed a new plan: a parachute attack, the biggest in history, in advance of his army to secure a bridgehead over the Rhine in Holland. Eisenhower later said dealing with Montgomery was "simple, give him everything he wants, which is crazy."

Montgomery was to tell his commander: "It may be that political and national considerations prevent us from having a sound organization: If this is the case, I would suggest we say so. Do not let us pretend we are all right whereas actually we are far from being all right."

In the light of such near insubordination Eisenhower much later told biographer Peter Lyon: "He's (Montgomery) just a little man. He's just as little inside as he is outside."

But on this occasion Eisenhower became an instant convert to the airborne assault. He made crossing the Rhine and then attacking southeast into Germany's Ruhr industrial belt primary over securing the Scheldt, now downgraded to "a matter of urgency."

Eisenhower's biographer, Stephen E. Ambrose, calls this Eisenhower's "worst error of the war. . . . At no other point did Eisenhower's tendency toward compromise and his desire to keep his subordinates happy exact a higher price." Patton agreed: "It was the most momentous error of the war."

But even Bradley, nonplussed at Montgomery's uncharacteristic audacity, agreed it could be a master stroke: "Had the pious, teetotalling Montgomery wobbled into SHAEF with a hangover, I could not have been more astonished than I was by the daring adventure he proposed."

It even caught Rundstedt by surprise. He had been recalled from his brief exile to resume, out of his duty to his oath as soldier, command of the West. He thought Montgomery "overly cautious, habit-ridden and systematic." He was not entirely wrong in spite of the bold plan known as Market-Garden.

There was only a week to prepare for the attack, an advanced carpet of 35,000 airborne troops laid down for sixty-four miles over five rivers and canals on which Horrocks' men would then advance. The U.S. 101st and 82nd Airborne, in reserve since D Day, were to cover fifteen miles to Eindhoven and ten miles to Nijmegen in southern Holland respectively and capture their bridges. The British 1st Airborne, the Red Devils under Major General Robert Urquhart, a hefty, likeable Scot, were to jump with a Polish brigade to take the key crossing, the Rhine bridge at Arnhem. Lieutenant General Frederick Browning, an English gentleman-officer from moustachioed head to highly polished toe, told Montgomery his Red Devils could hold out for four days until Horrocks arrived. "But I think, sir, we may be going a bridge too far."

The Polish commander, Major General Stanislaw Sosabowski, had a more pertinent question: "But the Germans, general, what about them?"

What about them?

Despite catastrophic defeats in Normandy and Russia; although the Luftwaffe had been defeated in the air; although the U-boats were a nuisance now, not a menace; although Germany proper was paved with rubble from the bombing, there were still men, production and morale. There were 3.4 million men under arms, 2 million of them on the Russian front. In late July Hitler ordered activation of twenty-five militia divisions and ordered creation of eighteen new divisions for the West. Submarine crews were given rifles and put into the infantry. So were recovering wounded, clerks, policemen who had been pounding a beat only a few weeks before, Luftwaffe pilots, middle-aged men, mid-teen boys. One division was made up of those with ulcers and other stomach problems who ate a diet of special bread. Out of the rubble, factories nonetheless were making Tiger and Panther tanks. Sixty of those superior weapons had arrived that very September to begin rearming two SS Panzer divisions.

They were based temporarily "in a peaceful sector where nothing was happening," one of their officers wrote home. From Arnhem.

Ultra intercepts had picked up the probable presence of the panzers. The Dutch underground

The smiles of Allied cooperation were only skin deep: (l. to r.) Generals Dempsey, Hodges, Montgomery, Simpson and H.D.B. Crerar of the Canadians.

did, too. But the British put little credence in them. Nazi double agents had deeply infiltrated the Dutch resistance. Nonetheless, Major Brian Urquhart of British paratroop intelligence was deeply worried about the reports. He had photo planes take oblique-angle photos of the woods around Arnhem and found the tanks he was looking for. He did not believe the Allies would walk into Germany "like a bride into a church."

Instead of heeding him, his superior suggested Urquhart had been working too hard and should take some time off.

As it enters the Netherlands the Rhine divides in two, the main flow becoming the Waal through Nijmegen and the Lower Rhine to the north through Arnhem. The southernmost of the three rivers Anglo-Americans had to cross was the Maas, the Dutch terminus of the Meuse. While it was flat countryside, there were many canals and wetlands making it poor ground for armor which had to stick to elevated roads for the most part.

To avoid the scattering of the night drops in Sicily and Normandy this one was by daylight. But due to a transport shortage the airborne force was to be delivered over three days. The first wave landed September 17, a Sunday. Holding course despite increasing flak, the pilots made the best drops of the war. An artillery unit of the 82nd, landing between Eindhoven and Nijmegen in the middle of the airborne carpet, safely got all ten of its 75s. General Browning, the husband of novelist Daphne du Maurier, landed just by the Dutch border and ran over into Germany. "I wanted to be the first British officer to pee in Germany." Within six hours the 82nd, now led by Brigadier General James Gavin, had secured crossings of the Maas and the Waal.

Dashing up its fifteen miles of highway the 101st grabbed nine of eleven assigned crossings. But the main bridge at Son had been blown by the Germans. Engineers immediately began repairs. In Eindhoven, joyful Hollanders ran into the streets to greet their liberators. The Lowlanders had been more harshly treated than the French by their German occupiers, and their hatred of them was even stronger. Everyone from tot to grandparent waved a ribbon or raiment of orange, the national color. They danced merrily in circles, hugged the soldiers and wrote their names on the tanks.

To the north the Red Devils came down in color-coded parachutes like tree blossoms in spring. Some of their gliders had been shot down in flames. Others crashed. But the first of 10,005 of Urquhart's paratroopers were down. One paratrooper paused at an inn for tea. He said he would be back for champagne with dinner. Another had to be interrupted from an amatory interlude with a

Dutch girl in a hayloft. Colonel John Frost had jumped with regulation gear but had arranged for his golf clubs and dinner jacket flown over on resupply flights. He and his men collected their gear and moved towards Arnhem.

Disastrously, as it turned out, the drop zone was six miles from town, chosen to avoid heavy antiaircraft concentrations at the bridge. A disaster because they did not know, despite Major Urquhart's warnings, that two panzer divisions really were in Arnhem. At first the paratroopers took pains to avoid trampling the neat gardens of the ecstatic civilians who actually slowed the advance. But by evening, Frost had captured buildings at the north

end of the bridge. Across from him Captain Eric Mackay of the engineers had taken up a position with his men in a schoolhouse. The Germans, reacting with great speed, fought off their efforts to get to the southern side of the bridge. Frost and Mackay and their 600 or so soldiers were to hold out until Thursday against increasingly over-whelming numbers in one of the most courageous actions of the war.

Urquhart, crippled by ineffective radio commu-nications, was unable to coordinate their relief. Cut off himself, he hid in an attic for crucial hours while Germans maneuvered against his men just below his window.

The second wave was due to drop Monday, the 18th, but the Germans had retrieved a briefcase with the full plans of the operation from a crashed glider. The Luftwaffe's remaining fighters lay in wait. Fortunately fog kept the Allied transports on the ground in England. When they arrived, most of the enemy fighters were on the ground refueling. An American crew chief aboard a C-47 told a Red Devil as he fastened his jump line: "You'll soon be down there, and I'll be heading home for bacon

Parachutes of the field: British paratroopers dot the flatland of Holland like tulips as Montgomery reaches one bridge too far at Arnhem.

and eggs." Moments later the American was dead, killed by a .50-caliber bullet.

The 82nd got 80 percent of its men and supplies, the 101st about half. But most of the British drop was out of the zone, although one gun and its crew arrived by a commercial ferry west of Arnhem that Allied planners didn't even know about. (The Dutch joked later the ferryman decided not to charge for the crossing.)

With the expedient of using the Dutch telephone system to call up for construction advice, engineers fixed the Son bridge and told Horrocks to come ahead. But his linkup with the 101st was already eighteen hours behind a tight schedule. His tanks stopped for the night after some 88s hit his column south of Eindhoven. The American paratroopers continuously fought off German attacks against the flanks of the thin highway. Private Joe Mann, his wounded arms bandaged to his side, jumped on a German potato masher grenade in fighting at a bridge near Eindhoven. Posthumously, he won the Medal of Honor. Captain LeGrand Johnson of the 101st was shot in the head. His sergeant, Charles Dohun, carried him to an aid station where a doctor hecticly tending the wounded told him he would treat Johnson "soon as we can get to him." "It's not soon enough," said Dohun, cocking his .45 and threatening to shoot the doctor if he did not take care of the gravely wounded officer at once. The physician complied. Dohun was taken before his superiors. An officer said he was going to have to place him under arrest—for one minute. Johnson survived.

The Son bridge was declared open at 6:45 a.m. Tuesday. The XXX Corps tanks got there by 8:30 that morning, now thirty-six hours behind schedule. They reached Nijmegen at noon. The Germans held the north end of that bridge.

Meanwhile Frost and Mackay were fighting under a point-blank barrage of tanks, cannon and mortars, the wounded stacked in basements as buildings collapsed around them. Urquhart had escaped from the attic, had drawn his men into a perimeter west of Arnhem and was trying without avail to fight into town.

Aware time was running out, Gavin decided to attempt a crossing of the 400-yard-wide Waal. The current was running eight knots. All he could reconnoiter were some canvas craft with flimsy plywood bottoms. The men would have to paddle with their helmets and rifle butts. Major Julian Cook led 254 men in the assault under a fusillade of Spandau fire and the killing crack of 88s. He lost 134 men, but combined with a charge by tanks of the Guards Armored Division the Anglo-Americans captured the bridge by 7:15 p.m. Only eleven miles to Arnhem.

Dempsey met Gavin and said: "I am proud to meet the commander of the greatest division in the world today." Not British understatement that day.

But in Arnhem, Frost had run out of water and was rationing bullets. After more than sixty hours across the high-level bridge approach from Frost, Mackay had told his few remaining men to fend for themselves. He was captured, told an astonished German officer, "It is all over for Germany, and I am quite prepared to take your surrender," escaped, was recaptured and escaped again, finally making it back to Allied lines.

Across the way, Major Digby Tatham-Warter strolled among exploding shrapnel and tumbling masonry carrying an umbrella. Not for protection, he said later, but for identification. "I was always forgetting the password."

Back at Njimegen Colonel Reuben Tucker of the 82nd couldn't understand why the British tanks did

Gliders are already down and paratroopers are coming in Arnhem drive, the smoothest air drop of the war—at the beginning.

not move out at once for Arnhem. "That's what Georgie Patton would have done . . . As usual, they stopped for tea."

"I can't tell you the anger and bitterness of my men," said Gavin.

"There appeared to me to be a fundamental lack of urgency in the rear areas," wrote correspondent Alan Moorhead. "We will have to wait for the tanks to clear it up."

In truth Horrocks' tanks were sitting ducks silhouetted on the raised highway. When they did get under way, the column was halted immediately as the lead tanks were hit by German guns. The armor had to wait for infantry to clear its way.

Meanwhile, Frost had finally surrendered to a respectful enemy who paid tribute to "an indescribable fanatacism. . . . Some of the British offered resistance to their last breath."

The Poles dropped in a third wave but few managed to reach Urquhart's pocket. They were meant to have landed on the third day. Bad weather, which had also grounded the Allied fighter-bombers, held them up until the sixth. On September 26 by dark of night Urquhart ordered his men to retreat across the river under cover of Allied scout patrols. He came out with only 2,163 surviving Red Devils. They had gone one bridge too far.

Arnhem cost the Allies in other ways. Because it monopolized their supplies, the Canadians were delayed in clearing German guns blocking the Scheldt from Walcheren Island at its mouth. Antwerp did not receive its first freighter until November 28.

GIs probe cautiously into Metz, France, while Hitler prepares counterattack to the north.

In his memoirs Montgomery wrote that "in spite of my mistakes, or the adverse weather or the presence of the 2nd SS Panzer Corps in the Arnhem area," Market-Garden would have succeeded if he had been given the planes and infantry "necessary for the job."

The statement does not consider, however, that Market-Garden had extended the battle line between Montgomery and Patton. An alert enemy might, if he had the resources, consider this a weak point and strike, strike so as to create a bulge in the Allied defenses, a bulge reaching all the way to Antwerp.

Battle of the Bulge

Eisenhower and Montgomery had a friendly bet: five pounds the war in Europe would be over by Christmas. Monty, who'd taken the long side, wrote Ike a chivying letter requesting payment. Eisenhower wrote back he "still had nine days left." Ten, actually. The letter was dated December 15, 1944. The next day Adolf Hitler took a far greater gamble.

Despite the setback at Arnhem, the Allies were now fighting on German soil. On September 11, Staff Sergeant Warner Holzinger of the U.S. 5th Armored Division had led a five-man patrol to the banks of the swift, brown waters of the Our River. He was back in the homeland of his ancestors. He was also the first enemy soldier to invade Germany since Napoleon. Thirty days later, Aachen, once the seat of Charlemagne when it bore its French name of Aix-La-Chapelle, became the first sizeable city in Germany to fall to the Allies. To the south French troops became the first to reach the Rhine two days before, October 19. On December 3 the American 95th Division crossed the Saar River in Germany. Other GIs fought yard by bloody yard against firm resistance through the Hurtgen Forest southeast of Aachen.

Montgomery's intelligence chief, Brigadier E.T. Williams, reported "The enemy is in a bad way . . ." Bradley's G-2 concurred. ". . . attrition is steadily sapping the strength of German forces . . ." Not euphoric but certainly confident. In the hard hills of Italy the Allies relentlessly pushed a grudging German army ever northwards. The old British 8th Army had taken Bologna. Russians had surrounded Budapest. And

MacArthur was back in the Philippines. Certainly confident.

That was a major reason not much heed was paid to Ultra intercepts of heavy train movements behind the enemy lines in Belgium and Luxembourg. They weren't audible to the Allied soldiers in the area. Even if they had been, the noise would have been drowned out by German planes that kept flying low over the area at night. Drowned out by loudspeakers that kept blaring recordings of trains and tanks and their metallic gnashings. Otherwise the Ardennes was so quiet one could almost hear the softly falling snow. So quiet it was nicknamed The Ghost Front.

This suited the Allies just fine. It was both a training camp and a rest camp, nursery and nursing home. Three of the six U.S. divisions posted along the eighty-mile sector were green as shamrocks, divisions that had never fired a shot in battle nor, more germane, had never had a shot fired at them. The 106th, the Golden Lions, was typical, made up of young draftees. Many of the GIs had been moved from specialized training programs such as ASTP on state-side college campuses into the infantry. Ground soldiers were needed now, not rear echelon technicians. Those billets were filled. The other divisions were licking their wounds from earlier battles, their losses being filled by replacements. The Ghost Front was so lightly patrolled that German soldiers crept through the lines at night to visit relatives. One such told his family he wouldn't be coming back for a while. Something was about to happen.

Whether or not Colonel General Alfred Jodl put the idea in Hitler's mind, it surfaced at a meeting September 16 when the chief of operations mentioned the word "Ardennes." Hitler, noticeably paler now, bent, with an almost uncontrollable twitching of his arm and hands, suddenly came alive. "I have made a momentous decision!" he cried. "I am taking the offensive!" Through the Ardennes.

Three times in seventy-five years—1870, 1914 and 1940—this had been the gateway through which German armies stormed into France. It was a terrain of forested hills, steep twisting valleys, rushing streams, tiny quaint villages and few good roads or even straight ones. It had taken the blitzkrieg of Rommel and Heinz Guderian three days to fight through the Ardennes until it burst out into the Lowlands in 1940.

"The coalition between the ultra-capitalists and the ultra-Marxists is breaking up," Hitler excitedly told his generals. "If we can now deliver a few more blows, this artificial front may suddenly collapse with a clap of thunder!"

His plan was to attack through the Ardennes to

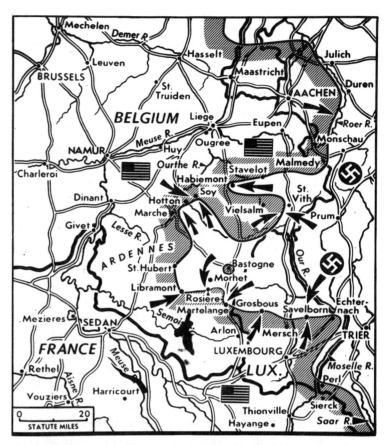

At the Bulge and in Bastogne, GIs fought their finest hour.

capture Antwerp, wiping out Montgomery's armies and forcing the Allies to negotiate. Then he would turn all Germany's energies against Russia. Perhaps, even, the Western powers would realize communism was the real enemy and join him.

His generals, who had borne the weight of Hitler's ruinous errors—declaring war on the United States, invading the Soviet Union—were skeptical.

"This damn thing doesn't have a leg to stand on," said Field Marshal Walther Model. Privately. "Antwerp?" exclaimed Rundstedt. Privately. "If we reach the Meuse, we should get down on our knees and thank God." He and Model, who was to command the attack, proposed a less ambitions "small solution" of breaking through and then curving north to encircle the Americans around Aachen. Hitler would have none of it. "This battle is to decide whether we shall live or die!" The Prussian professionalism of his generals yielded to their inbred duty to fatherland and commander in chief even if, as some thought, he was a maniac who was bringing Germany crashing down around them.

Hitler almost willed the coming battle as his nation rallied behind him. Notwithstanding the bombings, German production set new records for the year except, critically, of oil. Factories had been moved underground or to the east where Russia had no heavy bombers. With ample slave labor available, men from sixteen to sixty were drafted. Men up to sixty-five were put into the last-ditch home guard. All theaters were closed. The staff of the Berlin Opera was put to work in an electrical plant. Hairdressers were ordered into the army. And toll takers. Somehow the Germans patched together a formidable army—greater than the blitz force of 1940—of twenty-four divisions, seven of them armored, 900 guns, 970 tanks. Even the stricken Luftwaffe assembled 1,000 planes including sixty brand new jets.

It was all done with unparalleled secrecy and deception. No phones or teletypes were to be used. Generals were to type their own orders. Rumors of every conflicting sort were planted in bars. The code name of the operation—originally Watch on the Rhine—was changed every two weeks, finally becoming Autumn Mist. Field Marshal Keitel ostentatiously told commanders in the West in October that no counteroffensive was possible. Hitler held a final meeting December 12 at his new headquarters near Giessen north of Frankfurt. His condition had obviously deteriorated since the July 20 bombing. His hands shook beneath the table. The room was ringed by SS men with machine pistols. Major General Hans Waldenburg feared even to reach into his pocket for a handkerchief lest

MALMEDY

Seventy-four SS soldiers were tried for the massacre of American POWs at Malmedy, and forty-three were sentenced to death, though none was actually executed.

Surrendering soldiers faced varying fortunes on both sides. A Luftwaffe pilot who was shot down behind the lines of the Bulge on Christmas Day shared turkey dinner with American troops before being imprisoned. On D Day there was no room or mechanism to handle German captives, and none was to be taken. One GI of the 29th Division told a surrendering German to start running, shot him and then signaled a tank to run over him.

he be shot. The attack would go December 16, regardless, Hitler said.

Rundstedt dutifully issued a ringing order of the day, telling his soldiers: "We gamble everything." One of them wrote his sister:" . . . Some believe in living, but life is not everything! It is enough to know that we attack and will throw the enemy from out homeland. It is a holy task."

The Ghost Front exploded precisely on schedule at 5:30 a.m. December 16, with a violent artillery barrage including 14-inch shells from railroad guns far to the rear. Unsuspecting, slumbering Americans were blasted awake from down coverlets in

Winter in the Bulge. Bar in front of jeep is to cut wire Germans strung at neck height across roads.

On "Ghost Front" in Belgium you needed sign to tell where Germans were.

YOU ARE ENTERING
GERMANY,
AN ENEMY COUNTRY.
KEEP ON THE ALERT

comandeered inns, from haylofts, from foxholes. Out of the snow-covered trees and the mist—"it was like being in a milk bottle," one GI recalled—came hurrying figures wrapped in white. Spotlights blinded the defenders. Shooting began.

In what became known as the Battle of the Bulge, Eisenhower more than made up for his fumble over Antwerp. Almost immediately he realized, as Bradley and Patton did not, that this was a major offensive. Twenty-four divisions had struck at Troy Middleton's corps of three. From his headquarters at Versailles Eisenhower told Bradley to send two divisions to Middleton from Patton's 3rd Army which was about to strike into Germany's coal bin, the Saar. George isn't going to like it, Bradley warned. "You tell him Ike is running this damned war!" said the boss.

The only reserves he had other than troops in England, too far to be a factor, were the 82nd and 101st Airborne, recovering from Arnhem in camps around Rheims. They were ordered to move.

Any battle is bedlam. The Bulge with its snow and fog and twisty roads and suddenly key cowpaths and tiny stone villages and suddenly menacing forests and the cold and the strong points and the dreaded Panzer Tigers and troops fleeing and others trying to advance and find the enemy and colonels not knowing what had fallen and what had not or where anybody was . . . the Bulge was bedlam and then some, a swirling story of vignettes . . .

. . . Sergeant John Bannister mans a machine gun in the second floor of a house. A German runs by and shouts in English: "Take a ten-minute break. We'll be back!" "Go to hell! We'll still be here!" . . . Cooks, truck drivers, anybody, are given M-1s and ordered into line. "I've been in the Army three years, and all I've done is cook," one protests. "I'll get blown to hell." . . . Other cooks and a driver near Wirzfeld knock out six panzers, then charge, killing the infantry behind them. . . . Engineers running a sawmill near Stavelot drop their tools and blow two bridges. . . . A colonel calls in artillery to his coordinates. "It'll come right in on your head," say the gunners. "I might as well lose my head. I'm about to lose my ass." . . . A column of the 7th Armored is trying to bull its way to cut off St. Vith against the panic of retreating vehicles. Its orders: "If anyone gets in the way, run over the son of a bitch!" A sergeant jumps aboard one of the tanks: "I'm in this army to fight, not run." . . . A small detachment of English-speaking Germans, trained in American slang and wearing captured American uniforms and driving captured jeeps, infiltrates behind the battle. They are commanded by Otto Skorzeny, the man who rescued Mussolini. They cut phone lines, turn road signs the wrong way, wave an American column down the wrong road. Rumors and fear of infiltrators reach all the way to

GIs uncover grim evidence of massacre of American POWs at Malmedy.

Paris. MPs stop everybody: "How many home runs did Babe Ruth hit?" "What's the capital of Maryland?" (A correspondent from Maryland says "Baltimore" and is waved on before he can correct himself.) Brigadier Bruce Clark of the 7th Armored is briefly locked up by the MPs because he insists the Chicago Cubs are in the American League. . . . Eisenhower's security is tightened until in exasperation he tells his driver Kay Summersby: "Hell's fire, I'm going for a walk. If anyone wants to shoot me, he can go right ahead." . . . Near Malmedy 140 men of Battery B 285th Field Artillery Observation have the bad luck to run into Germans. Not trained to fight, the spotters surrender. "Kill them all," says a German. Machine guns spray the Americans as they stand in a field with their hands up. Lieutenant Virgil Lary feigns death next to a soldier shot in the head. Germans with pistols shoot the wounded. One comes near. "I lay tensely still. Could he see me breathing? Could I take a kick in the groin without wincing?" The German leaves. Lary runs for the woods. He survives as do forty-one others. Word of it drifts like fog through the Ardennes. The GIs don't forget . . .

Tanks leave tracks in snow-covered field in the Malmedy area.

Patton wheeled his Army 90 degrees in only two days to attack the neck of the Bulge.

Troops of the 7th Armored Division, wearing white camouflage suits, hug the snow-covered road to St. Vith in Belgium.

All but cut off, Americans refused to yield St. Vith on the right shoulder of the German break-through. The Germans had to divide around it like a tide around an islet. But in two days their columns penetrated up to thirty miles. Increasingly the crossroads market town of Bastogne became an obvious necessity for both armies. The 101st, the Screaming Eagles, were ordered to rush there as quickly as possible. The first paratroopers got there at dusk on December 18, just beating out the panzers of General Heinrich von Luttwitz. . . .

. . . *The paratroopers are joined by some men and tanks of the 10th Armored Division. One of their* colonels is William Roberts, who fought at Chateau Thierry in World War I. He orders Major William Desobry, too young for that war, to block a road into Bastogne from the north and gives him avuncular advice: "You'll probably be nervous. Then you'll probably want to pull out. When you begin thinking that, remember I told you NOT to pull out." Desobry holds, then gradually withdraws, reaches Bastogne where he is badly wounded by a shell burst. . . . The last road into Bastogne is cut. Lieutenant Colonel Henry Kinnard of the 101st assesses the situation: "So they've got us cut off. The poor bastards." . . .

Eisenhower admitted error in not considering that Hitler could mount an offensive, but he quickly saw that "if things go well, we should not only stop the thrust but profit from it." Two days after the attack began, he ordered Patton to get ready for an offensive to cut off the Bulge, trapping the Germans. On December 19 Eisenhower met at the old battlefield at Verdun with Bradley, Patton and Jacob Devers, whose corps was now in Alsace. How soon could Patton wheel his army 90 degrees and strike north into the southern flank of the Bulge?

"Two days," Patton replied.

"Don't be fatuous, George," said Eisenhower. "Take an extra day to make it stronger."

Patton said: "Hell, let's have the guts to let the sons of bitches get all the way to Paris. Then we'll really cut 'em off and chew 'em up." Then he left to change direction. The next day Eisenhower was faced with a cruel decision, the old one of whom to assign Courtney Hodges' 1st Army. The Americans north of the Bulge were cut off from Bradley and could be more directly handled by Montgomery. Between the 1st and Montgomery was the American 9th Army led by Lieutenant General William Simpson. (Bradley had put Simpson there so if he had to lose an army to Montgomery it would be his and not the more veteran 1st.) Eisenhower phoned Bradley he was temporarily assigning both U.S. armies to Montgomery.

"By God, Ike, I cannot be responsible to the American people if you do this. I resign." (Patton said he would, too). "Brad, I—not you—am responsible to the American people. Your resignation therefore means absolutely nothing." Bradley, who had the day before reluctantly bowed to the wisdom of the transfer, cooled somewhat. "Well, Brad, those are my orders."

Eisenhower phoned Montgomery over a bad connection. It caused Eisenhower to shout which the Englishman interpreted as Ike's "being very excited," implying battle nerves. Within two hours Montgomery was at Hodges' headquarters looking "like Christ come to cleanse the temple." Meanwhile . . .

. . . Lieutenant Jesse Morrow knocks out a tank with a rifle grenade carefully aimed at its ammo pack, then Tommy-guns Germans following behind it. He takes a bazooka to go after another, but it fires its 88 first, the shell brushing Morrow's neck. He comes to in an aid station where a crewman of the tank, captured when somebody else got it, asks from the next stretcher for a cigarette. Morrow tries to throttle him until he himself passes out. . . . Three days after they were cut off in the initial attack, 8,000 Americans surrender, the largest number to do so other than Bataan in the war. One of the GIs spots the surrendering colonel and gives him a Bronx cheer. . . . At St. Vith, holding out after five days, a German shouts through the door of Captain Dudley Britton's command post: "Cumzieout!" "Cumzieout, hell. What've you got out there I want? Cumzie in, Mac!" . . . Nearby Bruce Clark, having learned about the Cubs and the White Sox, orders his men to evacuate. An unshaven, bloody, cold sergeant hunts him out: "Me and my men don't like the idea of leaving the front, so now I just want to get it straight we were ordered out by you." . . . December 23 the weather clears and Allied planes fly 15,000 sorties. Some B-26s bomb American troops by mistake. The GIs shoot at the planes, as they had done in similar circumstances in Normandy and Sicily. They bitterly call it "the American Luftwaffe." . . . The day before Germans under a white flag approach the perimeter at Bastogne and tell the defenders to surrender in the name of "well-known American humanity" to avoid more casualties. "Aw, nuts," says Brigadier General Anthony McAuliffe, commander of the besieged 101st. Later he thinks he ought to at least answer the Germans. "What the hell should I tell them?" "The last remark of yours was hard to beat," says Henry Kinnard. "What'd I say?" Reminded, McAuliffe writes his response for then and history: "To the German Commander/Nuts/The American Commander." Colonel Joseph Harper translates it to the puzzled Germans: "In plain English it's the same as go to hell. And I'll tell you something else. If you continue to attack, we'll kill every goddam German that tries to break into this city. On your way, bud." Then, in a brainstorm, ". . . and good luck to you." . . . The next day Bastogne's garrison, outnumbered three to one by General Hasso von Manteuffel's Germans, are down to ten rounds per gun. Hitler tells his generals Bastogne must be taken. Instead the Americans get an air drop of supplies on the 23rd. The next day someone crayons "Merry Christmas" on the map of German positions in McAuliffe's headquarters. The day after Christmas Colonel Creighton Abrams idles the engines of twenty tanks and a column of halftracks loaded with infantry. Shortly after 3 p.m. he gives the order: "Let 'er roll!" One of the soldiers, James Hendrix, charges the crews of two 88s singlehanded. They surrender. Abrams rolls into Bastogne. The siege is over. . . .

On Christmas morning the 2nd Panzer Division reached a ridge overlooking the Meuse. But they had no more gas. Hitler had given his panzers enough fuel for one hundred miles, but strategic bombing had kinked the pump. Even if there were fuel, troops of Horrocks' XXX Corps had been moved into position on the other side of the river. By December 28 Major General Ernest Harmon's 2nd Armored Division had stopped the point of the Bulge. His men had knocked out eighty-eight tanks and taken seventy-five guns. It was, he reported, ''a great slaughter.''

Hitler, furious that his generals ''had not followed out orders,'' lowered his sights and now embraced Rundstedt's original ''small solution'' to turn north and trap the 1st Army around Aachen. But isolated resistance such as the stand at St. Vith, a brilliant escape of 20,000 men by Brigadier General Robert Hasbrouck from near entrapment at Vielsalm and reinforcement of the north flank of the Bulge by the 82nd Airborne had contained the offensive in its various scenarios, great and small.

Hitler told his men to rest on their guns while he unveiled another attack, Nordwind, into Alsace. Briefly successful, Eisenhower weighed a tactical withdrawal from the recently captured capital, Strasbourg. De Gaulle was enraged over the political effects of a retreat and threatened to withdraw French troops from the war. Eisenhower agreed to hold the city and then turned his attention to an even heavier cross he had to bear than the cross of Lorraine—De Gaulle's symbol—as Churchill once put it. This was, yet again, Bernard Law Montgomery.

Eisenhower had urged Montgomery to attack at the flank of the Bulge as soon as possible to cut off the Germans. The field marshal said he must first await an expected German thrust, then he would push the Bulge back from its spearhead. Eisenhower subsequently thought he had a commitment from Montgomery to strike the flank by January 1. When De Guingand came to Versailles and said his commander would not be ready until January 3, Eisenhower felt he had been lied to. He would fire Montgomery if he did not attack January 1. De Guingand, as popular at SHAEF as Montgomery was not, soothed Eisenhower, but Montgomery would not be stopped. He sent Eisenhower a letter picking an old scab: there should be one offensive into Germany and he should be in command of it. To make his point clear, he drafted such an order for Ike to sign.

German Tiger tanks had only five days of fuel in the Bulge. It wasn't enough.

Merry Christmas. When skies cleared, planes dropped supplies to besieged Bastogne.

Instead, Eisenhower returned the 1st Army to Bradley and told Montgomery the debate was over. De Guingand reported back to his boss that his ouster was imminent. "Who would replace me?" Monty huffed. Alexander, said his aide. Montgomery, who had not thought of the commander of the Italian front, paced his trailer in consternation. "What shall I do, Freddie? What shall I do?" De Guingand gave him a "Dear Ike" letter he had already drafted. Montgomery signed it. But neither that war nor the one in the Bulge was done. . . .

. . . On New Year's Day the Luftwaffe flies its remaining planes in a mass swan song. They destroy 156 planes on the ground including Montgomery's personal C-47. But the Germans lose 300 irreplaceable pilots. . . . As the Germans resume their attack, a GI with a bazooka is digging a foxhole in the snow. He says to a halftrack crew: "Just pull your vehicle behind me. I'm the 82nd Airborne. And this is as far as the bastards are going" . . . Lieutenant James Creighton is leading Fox Company of the 26th Division on their first day of battle. He leads his men forward to find none have followed him. He rousts them out with a sergeant to the rear threatening to shoot any stragglers. The next day the company repulses three German charges. They find one of their wounded has been booby trapped. So they string up the body of a dead German in a tree. After several more days of hard fighting, the twenty-seven men left of 176 originals are relieved. Now they are veterans. . . . Private First Class Kurt Gabel of the 17th Airborne is with Patton fighting towards the village of Houffalize to close the Bulge. Two medics are shot as they crawl out onto a road to retrieve a wounded GI. Gabel, born in Germany but raised in California, herds some German POWs ahead of him at gunpoint to use as a shield to get the bodies. That's not in the Geneva Convention, says his lieutenant. "Neither is shooting medics," says Gabel. . . . In the village of Bande, where the Gestapo had rounded up suspected resistance men at the start of the offensive, three Tommies digging through the rubble of a house, find thirty-four frozen bodies in the basement. All had been shot in the neck. . . . In Wiltz in northern Luxembourg, scene of some of the hardest early fighting, some women hide three wounded Americans for weeks. . . . Some civilian Luxembourgers snipe at Americans from windows with hunting rifles. Luxembourgers speak German, and a few think it. . . . Germans are surrendering in larger batches now. Private John Fague sees sixty POWs marched over a hill. The Americans had been told to take no prisoners. Remember Malmedy. Later he sees sixty dark shapes in the snow. Somebody says there's been a foulup. Orders were to take prisoners. . . . The Germans continue to press furious attacks at Bastogne, but by January 5 the momentum slackens. . . . On January 9 Hitler gives permission to Model to begin withdrawing from the Ardennes. But it will be several more hard weeks before the bulging line through the forests will be straight again. It will cost 80,000 American casualties.

In days to come a large tower will be built outside Bastogne surrounded by thousands of white crosses. This will mark the American dead. They will also mark the coming of age of the GI of World War II. . . .

The other war, with Montgomery, had one final chapter to go. On January 7 he held a press conference at Zondhoven in Holland. He entered the room jauntily, so much so that the man who had once in horror told Eisenhower to put out his cigarette in his presence, bade the newsmen to light up. What followed was a long account of the battle with the emphasis on the pronoun "I" and the implication strongly made that the British had saved the Americans' hash.

"As soon as I saw what was happening, I took certain steps myself to ensure. . . . And I carried out certain movements to meet the threatened danger . . . I was thinking ahead . . . I employed the whole available power of the British Group of Armies" bringing it "into play very gradually. Finally, it was put into battle with a bang. . . ."

Little of this bore a resemblance to the facts. By far the lion's share of the fighting had been done by the Americans. Eisenhower was the first to react. "With a bang" was not an accurate description of Montgomery's typically studied counterattack. It was Patton who had moved with a bang. "I think possibly one of the most interesting and tricky battles I have ever handled," Montgomery said. Topping that outburst of modesty, Montgomery added: "The Americans were great fighting men when given proper leadership."

Bradley was enraged. "After what has happened I cannot serve under Montgomery," he fumed. If he ever had to, "send me home," he told Eisenhower. Me, too, Patton echoed. "Monty is a tired little fart," he said. "War requires the taking of risks, and he won't take them."

It remained for Churchill to calm the waters. The Battle of the Bulge had been fought predominantly by Americans, he told Parliament, and their victory would stand high in that nation's history.

In Belgium, Hitler's last offensive died in the snow.

GI Joe

The American who dropped his rifle and ran at Kasserine Pass and the draftee who kept firing in his shallow foxhole in the Ardennes until overwhelmed both belonged to the same Army. It, and they, had come a long way in two years of war.

An early observer, Harold Alexander, commented on the American fighting men: "They simply do not know their job as soldiers. . . . Perhaps the weakest link of all is the junior leader who just does not lead, with the result their men don't really fight."

But war is a remorseless teacher. Certainly the paratroopers of Bastogne or the Marines of Iwo or the Big Red One of D Day were more than equal to the ordeal of waging war. It took uncommon command of fear to fly through the hell of Ploesti never taking an eye off the target. Terror is to lie in a fragile steel cocoon beneath the sea yet fire a torpedo knowing all too well the retribution that may come from the thudding depth charges. Yet the Americans did all these things.

In Europe they were matched against a soldier to whom his enemy paid almost universal respect. In the Pacific the enemy was a soldier to whom surrender was a cultural taboo.

An American colonel, Trevor Dupuy, made a postwar study of the German soldier: "On a man-for-man basis, the German ground soldier consistently inflicted casualties at about a 50 percent higher rate than they incurred from opposing British and American forces under all circumstances."

The Germans often had a low opinion of their American enemies. The real margin of victory, they would contend, was air superiority and the lavish

Peacetime soldiers train at Fort Dix in New Jersey early in 1941.

EDDIE SLOVIK

From Normandy to the end, about 1,200 German soldiers were tried for desertion and shot. In all of World War II, in fact since 1864, only one American soldier was executed for desertion. His name was Eddie Slovik.

Private Slovik, almost twenty-five, was shot by twelve GIs of their common 28th Division, who were handpicked for marksmanship. The incident took place January 31, 1945, in a snow-covered, walled garden of a country house near St. Marie, France, not far from the front. Eisenhower had signed the order for the execution. Major General Norman Cota, the man who had been a hero at Omaha Beach and then marched the 28th through Paris, was the officer in charge to see that sentence was carried out.

The 28th had borne the first German onslaught in the Bulge. Even the divisional band, musicians who had played with the likes of Artie Shaw, were given guns and joined the fight. While other units dropped their guns and fled, Slovik's 109th Regiment killed 2,000 Germans in an afternoon. But Slovik had not been there. Two months before, he had told his commander he would not fight and walked away. Caught, he was court-martialed and convicted.

Death sentences were handed out to forty-nine Americans during World War II. All but Slovik's were subsequently lessened. William Bradford Huie described the case in his stinging book *The Execution of Private Slovik*. A contributing factor, Huie indicates, in Slovik's case was the Army's replacement system. Slovik, a draftee from a Michigan factory town, was simply assigned to a unit like a sandbag dumped on a levee, left on his own to sink or swim.

Veteran GIs used to grumble to the rear depots: "Don't send us any replacements. We don't have time to bury them."

use of artillery. In effect, massed technology, not raw courage. Figures give some support for this. Fifty-four percent of the German Army were fighting soldiers compared to 38 percent of the Americans. Forty-five percent of the Germans were actually in fighting divisions contrasting with twenty-one percent for the United States. A German rifle company was armed with 56,000 rounds, its American counterpart only 21,000. The GI required thirty pounds of supplies a day. The Tommy took twenty pounds. At the end of the war the German got by with only four. The American did not fight lean and mean and probably never had since Valley Forge. And if he fell back on bombs and shells, he might say in his defense that all is indeed fair in

GIs fought for their buddies as much as anything.

love and war. Even so, the Bulge was won by riflemen and cannoneers on the ground. Foul weather grounded the planes.

The official U.S. history of the war noted that only 5 percent of Americans who had the choice opted for the infantry or the armored, producing "a dangerously low level of men . . . who seemed likely to perform effectively in combat." S.L.A. Marshall, the combat historian who had also been a general, made a study, later disputed, which indicated a surprisingly few infantrymen actually fired their rifles in action. Six percent of the Army took 53 percent of the casualties.

The Germans, said Colonel Wyldbore-Smith of the 11th British Armored Division, "are great opportunists. They are prepared to act—always." They came armed as well with a long military tradition and a secular religion, Nazism. The Japanese had their semi-divine emperor. Both saw the war as a crusade in defense of their homelands.

The GI was not only far from home. Who the hell had ever heard of Tulagi or Anzio or Houffalize or Pelelilu back home in Grovers Corners and what did these places have to do with his life? He had to find a map, if he could, even to know where he was.

The GI was often a stranger in his own unit. One foot soldier counted fifty-three different lieutenants at the head of his platoon from D Day to V-E Day. The British regimental system, on the other hand, wedded the same men to their units throughout their military careers. They fought with their buddies and because of their buddies. Conversely, the Americans consciously avoided where possible placing too many men from the same area together. There could be political repercussions back home.

The GI, born in a democracy, was alien to the caste system of the military. Moreover, some men never saw their colonels except at ceremonies. Said one GI of "Blood and Guts" Patton: "Yeah, our blood and his guts."

JOE AND WILLIE

Bill Mauldin said this in his book *Up Front:*

"I know of another guy—a former racketeer's bodyguard—who once found two Germans sleeping together to keep warm, remembered an old Ghoum trick and slit the throat of one, leaving the other alive so he would wake up and see his bunkmate the next morning. Most of the doggies thought it was a good stunt. . . . Joe and Willie, however, come from the other infantry— the great numbers of men who stay and sweat in the foxholes that give their more courageous brethren claustrophobia. They go on patrol when patrols are called for, and they don't shirk hazards, because they don't want to let their buddies down. The Army couldn't get along without them, either. Although it needs men to do the daring deeds, it also needs men who have the quiet courage to stick in their foxholes and fight and kill even though they hate killing and are scared to death while doing it."

Patton himself said: "It is an unfortunate and to me tragic fact that in our attempts to prevent war we have taught our people to belittle the heroic qualities of the soldier." Preponderantly, the best and brightest opted for the exotic services or the "cleanest"—the planes or the ships. The American Army was top heavy with brass compared to the German: 7 percent of the Americans being officers as to 2.86 percent in the Wehrmacht where the emphasis was on veteran non coms.

No one better captured the American's ironic, cynical vision of battle than Bill Mauldin. His Willie and Joe characters would have been convulsed if they had been there when Mark Clark, on one of his self-promoting "photo ops," had his picture taken sharing lunch with a GI. The picture taken, he handed the soldier his opened K-ration: "Here, son, eat this."

Colonel J.C. Fry noted in his GIs after four days of combat in Italy: "The complete absence of all outward expressions of mirth or anticipation left them with the overall appearance of men who had nothing to look forward to. They could only endure. Their pride anchored them to their job. Galley slaves, in ages past, must have presented a similar appearance."

And yet they fought.

Eric Sevareid wrote of his experiences as a correspondent in Italy. "A thousand times one asked oneself why they were like this. [The GIs] understood the war's meaning no more than any others—which is to say hardly at all. Their country, their families were not in any mortal danger, and

yet they plodded on. . . . They did not hate the Germans. . . . They did not hate the concept of fascism because they did not understand it. But they struggled on, climbing the hills, wading the rivers until they dropped and . . . [died] in ignorant glory."

Looking around at his artillery unit in Normandy, Lieutenant Lloyd Ratliff mused: "Nobody felt much animosity towards the Germans except a couple of German-speaking Jews in our unit. Most of our men were bewildered by the whole thing. They didn't understand what it was all about although they felt that it was a just cause because of Pearl Harbor."

Pearl Harbor certainly inspired hatred in many Americans. And to some the war was a crusade against an undifferentiated evil, Nazism. Ramsay Potts, one of the pilots of Ploesti who became a general before he was thirty (Jimmy Stewart, the actor, was his exec in the 8th Air Force), had seen Hitlerism first-hand while touring Germany one summer while in college. He saw justice in the bombs he dropped.

But for others, why did they fight?

"Some of the fellows wanted to surrender, but we'd heard the Germans were shooting prisoners," said Charles MacGillvary fighting in France on New Year's Day, 1945. "So there really wasn't much choice but to try and get out of there." His Medal of Honor citation was more explicit. MacGillvary volunteered to go out on a lone patrol. He knocked out six machine gun positions, losing an arm in the process. Not far from there, Ralph Neppel's leg had been blown off. Nonetheless, he crawled back to his machine gun and fought off a German tank, forcing it to withdraw along with its accompanying infantry. Neppel, too, won the Medal of Honor.

Why did Sergeant A. B. Sally of the American 88th Division fight? "I don't know unless it's because I feel I must because I'm expected to. If I should fail to do what is asked of me, I would betray the trust of the men fighting with me. If I betrayed this trust, in my own eyes I believe I would become despciable. There is an urge inside me that compels me to go with my buddies, to endure seemingly useless privation, all to what may be a useless end."

For all their multifarious reasons, the GIs fought, learned war and won. Probably none had a more basic reason than an anonymous GI who was at the Battle of the Bulge, one of the American soldier's proudest moments.

"I didn't have anything personal against the Krauts. But I learned something today. Now I want to kill every goddam Kraut in the world. You know why? To save my own ass."

Big Government

During World War II the federal government spent more money, hired more people and wielded more power than ever before. Its civilian payroll increased from 1 million employees in 1940 to almost four times that many in 1945; its annual spending soared from $6 billion to fifteen times that amount; and its officials exerted more control over citizens' lives than at any time before or since. Nearly every item Americans ate, wore, used or lived in was rationed, controlled or otherwise regulated. Sometimes they grumbled, but by the time the war was over people were accustomed to looking to Washington for solutions to their problems.

The government had been growing all along, of course. The cost of running the federal government had increased 350 percent between 1915 and 1930, and the New Deal years saw another expansion. But the New Deal only increased federal employment by about 400,000; the war increased it by 2.8 million.

The government would spend twice as much in the five years after 1940 as it had in the preceding 150 years, but it began the war with a puny tax structure and a fear of budget deficits. The need to come up with an extra $200 million a day produced a fiscal revolution, in the form of the expanded income tax and payroll tax withholding.

In those days the handful of Americans who had to pay income taxes did so a year late (on 1940 income in 1941, for instance) and in quarterly installments. The Revenue Act of 1942, however, required employers to subtract taxes for that year directly from employees' paychecks. The expression "take-home pay" thus entered the language. The new system didn't make taxes more popular, but it made them less conspicuous. Future tax increases became that much easier, especially as inflation eased workers into higher tax brackets.

Since Congress authorized taxes sufficient to cover less than half the war's cost, the government had to borrow the rest. The national debt soared from $47 billion—a figure that had conservatives apoplectic in 1941—to $280 billion. In 1944 alone, the gap between expenses and revenues was twice as large as the accumulated debt had been four years earlier.

Without the specific approval of any legislature, Franklin Roosevelt issued some of the most sweeping orders in American history. His administration banned pleasure driving and sliced bread, told butchers how to cut meat and couturiers how to cut clothes, limited ice cream to eight flavors and shoes to six colors. It seized Montgomery Ward from its executives and 200,000 pounds of scrap from a reluctant junkman. It took over, at various times, the coal mines, the railroads and dozens of factories. It set skirt lengths, and legally defined Santa Claus. Next, people joked, Roosevelt would require farmers to remove their horses' shoes every night to conserve iron.

Roosevelt's invasion of the fashion world was necessitated by a shortage of fabric for uniforms. Some sort of regulatory milestone was reached with War Production Board Order L-85, which set skirt lengths about three inches below the knee and banned full skirts, knife pleats and patch pockets. The WPB also ordered a 10 percent reduction in the amount of fabric used in women's bathing suits, giving a boost to the two-piece suit.

Government intervention also produced the most famous photo to emerge from the home front: two burly GIs carrying Montgomery Ward chairman Sewell L. Avery out of his office.

When Montgomery Ward head Sewell Avery said "to hell with the government" in 1944, the Army unseated him.

With 600 stores and 78,000 employees, the giant mail-order house sold a fifth of all the manufactured goods purchased by American farmers. But when its executives refused to obey a pro-union order by the War Labor Board in 1944, Roosevelt ordered the company taken over.

Sewell L. Avery was the perfect foil. "If anyone ventures to disagree with me, I throw them out the window," was his self-stated management philosophy. He was bitterly anti-Roosevelt and anti-union. Ward employees spelled his name by deleting the periods after his first two initials: Slavery. When Attorney General Francis Biddle flew to Chicago to negotiate with him, Avery refused to compromise and vowed not to leave his office. "I want none of your damned advice," he told Biddle. "To hell with the government." When Biddle told the soldiers to carry him out, Avery—a small, crusty-looking old man—spat out the worst insult that occurred to him: "You New Dealer!"

The incident amused some people but worried others. Acting under legislation designed to be used against strikes, Roosevelt had seized Montgomery Ward merely by defining it as "useful" to the war effort, even though the company dealt solely in civilian goods. The lesson was clear: the government could do virtually anything it wanted to further what it defined as the war effort.

Such government interference shocked a system that had survived even the Depression and the New Deal in a fair imitation of laissez-faire capitalism. Before 1941 people still argued about whether the government should be involved in the economy; by 1945 the point seemed moot.

The government's size was growing along with its power. During the Depression, Al Smith had said of FDR, "The Great White Father in Washington throws the alphabet out the window three letters at a time." A nation still reeling from the bureaucratic onslaught of the New Deal was served another course of alphabet soup during the war. According to one count, forty-four new agencies were created. The ultimate tongue-twister was the PWPGSJSISACWPB—the Pipe, Wire Product and Galvanized Steel Jobbers Subcommittee of the Iron and Steel Advisory Committee of the War Production Board—a plumbers' group.

Once, when asked a question by a reporter about an agency, the SPCBM, Roosevelt turned to an aide and asked, "The SPCBM—what on God's earth is that?"

Many of the rules and proclamations issued by the new agencies were bewildering, as well. Maury Maverick, a New Dealer from Texas, coined a term for the new speak: gobbledygook. This OPA regulation was issued in December, 1942: "Bona fide Santa Clauses shall be construed to be such persons as wearing a red robe, white whiskers, and other well-recognized acoutrements befitting their station of life, and provided that they have a kindly and jovial disposition and use their office of juvenile trust to spread the Christmas spirit, they shall be exempt from the wage-freezing order of October 3."

Having decided to regulate entire industries, Roosevelt soon found that few Washington bureaucrats knew how those industries operated. So he turned with some reluctance to the source. The result was the "$1-a-year man," an executive on loan to the government who continued to be paid by his company. (He also received a living allowance of $10 a day and travel expenses.)

Above: *Navy offices overflow Washington's Mall.*

Exploding Washington bureaucracy takes over hotel ballroom.

The first dollar men arrived in Washington in September 1939, and by 1943 they constituted the vast majority of War Production Board's executives. Although they were not supposed to be involved in matters directly affecting their companies, they worked in the WPB branch regulating their industry, and were usually sympathetic to its needs—

questions by mail, wire or phone, the bureacracy continued to swell. The textile division, for example, grew from two people in March 1941 to more than 500 employees a year later.

In Washington, the government was hiring as many as 5,000 new people a month, many of them secretaries and clerks. Civil service exam requirements were dropped, and just about anyone with a high school degree and some familiarity with a typewriter was hired. Veterans Administration staffers, chronically short of typists, dictated letters on crude dictaphones whose cylinders were then shipped to New York City. There, typists transcribed them and shipped the typed letters back to Washington to be signed and mailed.

Although the progress of war mobilization wasn't always swift, one wouldn't have guessed it from the hectic pace in the capital. In the early months of the war, WPB staffers frequently worked twelve hours a day and seven days a week. Donald Nelson himself put in a ninety-hour week, and more than one new arrival was put to work before she could find a place for her bags.

But some agencies were so disorganized that other newcomers found jobs with no work. According to one estimate, within six months of Pearl Harbor as many as half of the young women who had been hired in Washington as stenographers and typists quit—there was nothing for them to do. And sometimes there was no way to do it: by mid-1942, the government was short 600,000 typewriters.

Typewriters were weapons in the production war, and paper was ammunition. The government created more records in four years than in its entire previous history. OPA alone was producing more paperwork than the whole government did before the war. The national archivist warned that at the rate things were going, government records would soon fill an acre to the height of the Washington Monument. In 1941 the federal government owned $650,000 worth of printing and reproducing equipment; a year later it had $50 million worth.

The government, naturally, hired bureaucrats to deal with the problem. Legend had it that one of them finally won permission to destroy a stack of old records—as long as he made copies first.

Space was needed for all that paper, and for the men and women who pushed it around. In Washington, the government spilled into 358 buildings, including former skating rinks and basketball arenas, theaters and auditoriums, stables and tents. The Office of Price Administration rented space for a time in an apartment house; secretaries sat at typewriters that rested on boards over the bathroom sinks.

Flimsy temporary buildings—"tempos," they

sometimes too sympathetic. In March 1942, an official resigned from the textile division, complaining that the dollar men were blocking war production and diverting materials to civilian production.

Since each new government order, even one that was not gobbledygook, might generate 10,000

were called—sprung up everywhere. They lined each side of the Reflecting Pool on the Mall, connected by a pedestrian bridge over the water. Built in as little as thirty-eight days, the ugly tempos marred one of the nation's most magnificent public places. They were ricketey by design, the logic being that if they weren't torn down after the war, they'd fall down.

Space was so tight that desks in some capital offices were being used in three eight-hour shifts. Then there was the Textile Roundtable, where fourteen new dollar-a-year men played musical chairs at a twelve-seat table. Frank L. Walton, head of the WPB's textile division, recalled: "The man who got there first and put his briefcase on the table in front of a chair and sat down had a seat for the day. If he moved, he did not dare move his briefcase. That briefcase represented his right to the seat. The two men who had no chairs just sat around or stood around. Surprising as it may seem, this went on for three weeks or more before we could get desks and crowd them in, two or more men to a desk."

The war changed Washington more than any major city in America. In six years a slow, quiet Southern community was turned into the capital of the Western world.

When the war began, National Airport was being built to replace Hoover Field. A symbol of the old Washington, Hoover was little more than a landing strip. An Arlington County highway ran directly across the runway; the county refused to close the road, so the airport manager installed a red light to stop vehicles when planes were taking off or landing. But the county asserted sovereignty and removed the light, so pilots reverted to flying in and out during breaks in the traffic.

By the eve of war Washington already was booming. Its population was growing by 50,000 a year, rising from 621,000 in 1930 to slightly more than a million by the end of 1941. The war simply upped the ante. Seventy-thousand people became Washington residents in 1942. Thousands of them lived more-or-less permanently in hotels, rooming houses and houseboats, because housing was hard to find. Top bureaucrats Jesse Jones and Leon Henderson never got around to moving out of the Shoreham Hotel. A headline in the *Washington Post* read, "Newcomers Discover Private Baths Went Out with Hitler."

It seemed there was never enough of anything. When one young man took his laundry to a cleaners, he was turned away; the cleaner was taking no new customers, and suggested the fellow mail his laundry home. Hotels imposed a three-day limit on visits, but visitors bribed the staff and stayed for weeks and months. The overflow, meanwhile, spilled as far north as Philadelphia.

Space finally got so tight that Roosevelt started moving agencies out of Washington: the Securities and Exchange Commission was dispatched to Philadelphia, the Patent Office to Richmond, the Bureau of Indian Affairs to Chicago. In all, eleven agencies and more than 21,000 employees moved out for the duration.

The War Department itself planned the ultimate space, but the Pentagon was too small the day it opened. Still, some congressmen wondered what would happen when the military shrank back to its pre-war size. "What will we do with the extra space?" asked Congressman Everett Dirksen of Illinois. No problem, said Roosevelt. We'll use it to store records.

People talked the same way about the civil bureaucracy; no one seemed to realize that big government had come to stay. Despite postwar reductions, in 1949 there still were 2 million federal civil employees, twice as many as in 1940. Non-defense spending, which had risen during the war from $7 billion to $17 billion, would climb to $25 billion by 1947. But so did tax revenues, which soared from $5 million in 1940 to $49 billion in 1945—fairly painlessly, thanks to withholding.

End of the New Deal

Early in his third term, Franklin Roosevelt called Thomas Corcoran, a young aide who had come to Washington out of the Harvard Law School to become "Tommy the Cork," one of the most prominent New Dealers.

"Tommy," Corcoran says the president told him, "cut out this New Deal stuff. It's tough to win a war."

Several years later Roosevelt would spell out this attitude publicly in a sort of parable. The patient, the United States, had had a grave internal disorder which was treated by the New Deal. But in December 1941, the patient had been in a bad accident. "Old Dr. New Deal," the president said, "knew a great deal about internal medicine, but nothing about surgery. So he got his partner, who was an orthopedic surgeon, Dr. Win-the-War, to take care of this fellow." The story summed up FDR's political philosophy for the last three years of his life: everything came second to the war, including the reform movement on which his presidency was founded.

The primacy of winning the war might seem obvious, but the United States was so powerful and wealthy that it could have won the war in many different ways and at many different speeds. Some liberals, in fact, saw the new home front as an opportunity for reform. Much of their hope was born of frustration. "Dr. New Deal" never found a cure for the Depression, and now seemed gravely ill himself. Liberals told themselves that World War I had persuaded people to accept increased government regulation of the economy. This war, they hoped, would enhance Roosevelt's power and allow him to regain the initiative of his first term.

They were counting on the wrong man. Roosevelt probably was reconciled to the inevitablity of the war, but he was stunned by, and perhaps guilty about, the losses at Pearl Harbor. Henceforth, the president insisted on victory as quickly and as painlessly as possible. That meant nothing must interfere with production, morale and his own ability to govern. If reform somehow aided the war effort, he supported reform; if not, he ignored it.

Roosevelt created the Fair Employment Practices Committee to prod defense plants to hire the black workers they needed, and to forestall an embarrassing march on Washington. But the reaction to the move illustrated Roosevelt's wartime political dilemma. The committee had too little power to satisfy blacks and liberals, but enough to outrage Southern Democrats, his nominal allies and supporters of his war program.

A bipartisan conservative coalition in Congress had been gaining strength since 1936, and Republican victories in the 1942 congressional elections signaled to Roosevelt that the age of reform—or at least the age of offending conservatives—was over. The nadir was reached in early 1944, when Roosevelt vetoed a revenue bill he regarded as excessively generous to the rich; Congress overrode it, marking the first time such legislation was passed over a presidential veto. Although FDR undoubtedly benefited politically from his status as commander-in-chief (a title he preferred to president), the Republicans were helped by public dissatisfaction with shortages, rationing, wage and price controls and bureaucracy in general.

Roosevelt's preoccupation with the war meant trouble for the New Deal. When Treasury Secretary Morgenthau found his progressive tax program rebuffed by Congressional leaders and FDR's own advisers, he lamented, "I can get all my New Dealers in the bathtub now."

Much of the New Deal—Social Security, unemployment compensation, old age benefits, the TVA, securities regulation and the Labor Relations Act—had become permanent. But during the war Congress picked off other, less popular or relevant New Deal programs one by one: the Civilian Conservation Corps, in which unemployed young men had

helped conserve woodland and water resources; the Works Progress Administration, a work relief program for the jobless; the National Youth Administration, which had provided needy young people with job training; the Farm Security Administration, which protected agricultural laborers.

Other liberal causes also suffered. The Rural Electrification Administration gave up its copper wire for military use; antitrust prosecutors virtually stopped work in the new atmosphere of government-business cooperation; and Congress passed tough antistrike legislation over FDR's opposition.

Congressional animosity was the only reason for the demise of these New Deal programs. By putting people back to work, the military build-up deprived New Deal programs of their constituency. There were still plenty of people who needed help, but they tended to be those with less political clout, including blacks, women and very young or very old workers.

Republicans emerged from these victories hoping Roosevelt could be beaten in 1944. The president himself looked old and sounded tired. "All that is within me cries out to go back to my home on the Hudson River," he wrote the chairman of the Democratic National Committee. "But as a good soldier . . . I will accept and serve." His opponent would be New York Governor Thomas E. Dewey, twenty years his junior.

Vice President Henry Wallace sought renomination, but party leaders opposed him. While Roosevelt appeared to equivocate, the party finally chose Senator Harry Truman, who had distinguished himself as head of a congressional committee that exposed waste and confusion in the war effort.

New York gangbuster Thomas E. Dewey, 1944 GOP foe of failing FDR.

Whatever the Republicans' hopes, the election was never in doubt after Roosevelt's Fala speech.

The occasion was a September 23 address to the Teamsters broadcast to a national radio audience. Roosevelt had been so sick earlier in the day that his daughter wondered if he'd be able to go on. But when he took the dais that night he looked like the old warrior. He began with an vehement attack on his opponents which delighted the union audience. The president was rolling when he turned to the topic for which his speech would be remembered.

"These Republican leaders have not been content with attacks on me, or my wife, or on my sons," he said. "No, not content with that, they now include by little dog Fala. Well, of course, I don't resent attacks, and my family doesn't resent attacks, but—Fala does resent them."

As his audience roared, Fala's master proceeded to rebut the "Republican fiction" that he had left the Scottish terrier in the Aleutians and sent a destroyer to fetch him at taxpayer expense.

"Fala's Scotch, and . . . his Scotch soul was furious," Roosevelt reported. "He has not been the same dog since. I am accustomed to hearing malicious falsehoods . . . such as that old, worm-eaten chestnut that I have represented myself as indispensable. But I think I have the right to resent . . . libelous statements about my dog."

Dewey, not known for his sense of humor, was furious. "The race," someone wrote, "is between Roosevelt's dog and Dewey's goat." A reading of Dewey's subsequent campaign speeches refutes any notion that Red-baiting was a post-war invention. Two days after the Fala speech, Dewey called FDR "indispensable to Earl Browder," the head of the American Communist Party. A communist, he said in Boston, was anyone "who supports the fourth term so our form of government may more easily be changed."

In November Roosevelt recorded the most slender of his four presidential victories, but a decisive one. He won 432 of 531 electoral votes, thirty-six states, and 55 percent of the popular vote. In Mississippi, home of some of his most bitter congressional enemies, he received 94 percent of the vote. But the race really was won in the big cities. FDR got 60 percent of the vote in municipalities of more than 100,000, and won every major city except Cincinnati. One analyst called it "a victory of the city over the country."

The election also was a victory for labor. The Congress of Industrial Organization's Political Action Committee ran registration drives that helped bring out the decisive big city vote. In St. Louis, as many as 36,000 voters were registered on a single day. Labor's total campaign contribution of $2 million comprised almost a third of all Democratic spending.

Labor's economic power became apparent in 1943, when John L. Lewis led the United Mine Workers out on several brief strikes. Each time the government nationalized the mines and ordered the men back to work. Lewis complied, but made it clear that each return was provisional. Roosevelt had to face it: coal could not be mined without the cooperation of the 400,000 miners. "There are not enough jails in the country to hold these men," said Interior Secretary Ickes. "Even if there were . . . a jailed miner produces no more coal than a striking miner."

In all, union membership increased 45 percent during the war, twice as much as the labor force. By 1945 almost 15 million workers were union members, compared to 10.5 million in 1939.

The home front saw almost nothing that could be described as social reform, but the war did produce one tremendously expensive piece of social welfare legislation: the Servicemen's Readjustment Act of 1944, popularly known as the G.I. Bill.

The bill helped returning servicemen get an education, a job, a house, and medical care. Between 1945 and 1952 the government would spend $13.5 billion for education and training alone, thereby allowing a generation of young men to go to college or develop a technical skill. The bill also guaranteed comprehensive care for the disabled, and financed construction of veterans hospitals. It was an enormously popular piece of legislation, and it fostered two decades of unprecedented affluence.

America changed drastically between 1941 and 1945, but it was by accident, not reform. "The trained hounds of Congress sniffed each and every wartime innovation carefully for the forbidden New Deal scent," Richard Lingeman has written, "and when their keen noses flashed a warning, they raised a baying in committees and on the floor and in the press." Yet when the war ended, the America of 1941—the one the soldiers left behind and to which they dreamed of returning—was gone. If the new nation was not the one the reformers envisioned, it was richer, fairer and more open than anyone had dared hope.

The Last Winter

After two years of wartime austerity, summer 1944 brought a tantalizing taste of peace at home. The Allies were racing across France after D Day, and closing the net around Japan. Industry had been operating full blast for a year. Shortages began to ease and the Office of Price Administration lifted rationing on canned food and some meat. The War

Production Board prepared a plan for the resumption of office-machine production, and eased its prohibiton against using steel for non-essential purposes.

But there was to be one last, long winter of war. Shortages returned almost as soon as controls were eased, and rationing of pork loin, ham and canned fish resumed in August 1944. In December the Allied advance in Europe halted, and rationing was fully reimposed. The coldest winter in fifty years had begun.

Although the war still was being won, the national mood did not reflect it. Irritants ranged from home front czar James Byrnes' decision to close race tracks to a serious fuel shortage that had Easterners shivering in their homes. Blizzards disrupted fuel shipments, worsening the shortage. Schools closed for lack of fuel, and businesses closed an extra day or two. In New York City, the Army and Navy had to donate coal for emergency civilian use. In March Byrnes ordered a nationwide "dim-out," which soon became known as the "Byrne-out." Neon signs were banned, stores had to close at dusk, and everyone was under a midnight curfew. When Mayor Fiorello LaGuardia refused to enforce the curfew in New York, military police were sent in.

Of the 500,000 unsold cars whose sale the government had frozen after Pearl Harbor, only 30,000 were left—a three-day supply in peacetime—and old models were beginning to wear out. New York cabs had gone without spare parts for two years.

Shortages worsened. In Manhattan, lines formed for the few packs of cigarettes that went on sale each evening at 6. Even if you were lucky enough to get cigarettes, matches always seemed in short supply. At Christmas, shelves were barer and prices, black market or otherwise, higher than at any time since the war began. By New Year's, "Our standard of living was really on the verge of falling apart," according to writer Paul Gallico. "The only thing that was plentiful was printed paper laughingly called money."

Shortages begat shortages. Many lumberjacks in the Northwest who had demanded larger meat rations eventually were lured away by defense plants, leading to a shortage of paper. Paper drives followed, but Boy Scouts who collected 1,000 pounds of paper in the General Eisenhower Waste Paper Campaign of 1945 received only certificates. Since there was also a metal shortage, their General Eisenhower Medals were delayed.

The black market boomed as never before. So much poultry was being siphoned off in Delaware that the Army couldn't get any for its training camps. Armed soldiers were stationed along highways with orders to stop any trucks carrying chickens, and to commandeer their cargo if it appeared destined for the black market. By winter's end, virtually no beef was being sold legally in big cities. Cattle rustling had reappeared in the West, as had shootouts when ranchers met up with rustlers. Price controls seemed to be holding, but OPA administrator Chester Bowles admitted that the agency's assumption that 95 percent of businessmen would voluntarily comply "has proven too optimistic."

Even the home front's volunteer zeal lagged. Scrap drives fell short. The redemption rate on $25 bonds—the little man's bond—was twice as high as two years earlier. Overgrown and untended Victory gardens seemed to symbolize the nation's war weariness; more and more people bought their produce at the thousands of supermarkets that had appeared since 1939. Even members of the Ground Observer Corps strayed from their posts; they had waited long enough for enemy planes that never came.

The generals had been complaining about shortages of items such as bomber tires, heavy shells and tents, but workers already were leaving war plants for jobs with better post-war prospects. In February, Henry Stimson told Congress the home front was "on the verge of going sour." He suggested national service, which would have given the government control of defense workers, as "a step to cure that situation of anarchy and restore law and order."

The home front was never really on the verge of going sour, but there was selfishness, dishonesty and politics-as-usual almost from the beginning. The farm block in Congress, for example, held up development of synthetic rubber for months by insisting that the key ingredient, butadiene, be made with alcohol made from wheat and corn, rather than petroleum, which was less expensive.

Although the number of strikes was relatively low, the strikes that were called upset servicemen and their commanders. General Marshall called a railroad walkout in December 1943 "the damndest crime ever committed against America." The government seized the railroads briefly to solve the labor dispute.

Although plants like Willow Run got the publicity, there were others like the Brewster Aeronautical Corporation. The company's planes fared so poorly in early encounters with Japanese Zeros that the Navy took over and reorganized production. But no one seemed able to solve the basic problem: relations between labor and management were so poor, and morale so low, that absenteeism, strikes, slowdowns and plain loafing became a way of life.

Although the conflict has since come to be known as "the good war," many thought at the time that idealism and purpose were lacking. A poll

Wounded veterans watch FDR's fourth inauguration.

in March 1942 found most had "no clear idea of what the war is all about." Americans may have known why they were fighting—Pearl Harbor was as good a reason as any—but they seemed unsure of what they were fighting for. Treasury Secretary Morgenthau complained that in talking to soldiers and other young people he found "there is nothing inspirational being raised for them." Unquestionably unified, Americans were somewhat directionless.

Many liberals and New Dealers wanted to depict the war as a battle between democracy and totalitarianism, and a fight for what Roosevelt called the "four freedoms:" freedom of expression and religion, and freedom from want and fear. But the failure of Woodrow Wilson's idealistic crusade to make the world safe for democracy was fresh and obvious to many, including Roosevelt. When he viewed the movie *Wilson,* in 1944, his blood pressure soared to an ominous 240 over 130. The president knew that too specific a vision of a post-war world could be politically divisive—a liberal's heaven was a conversative's hell—so he said relatively little about what shape it would take and concentrated on winning.

Historian John Morton Blum has contended that because the government failed to enunciate war goals, Americans on the home front "in most places and at most times were fighting the war on

imagination alone." Stateside, he has written, the war "was neither a threat nor a crusade," only a painful necessity for men and women whom Frederick Lewis Allen has characterized as "disillusioned and deadpan defenders."

By 1945 much of the anger over Pearl Harbor had faded, and the war just seemed to drag on. In this darkness before dawn, air wardens were called back to duty because the threat of German missile attacks had become not only "possible but probable," in the view of the commander of the Atlantic Fleet. American battle casualties, meanwhile, approached 1 million. Americans were hungrier than ever for victory, by whatever means.

The Death of FDR

There was no inaugural parade in 1945. "Who's here to parade?" the president asked. Roosevelt took the oath of office for the fourth time in a simple ceremony on the south portico of the White House witnessed by several hundred people—probably the smallest inaugural crowd ever.

FDR looked old and tired. His health was the subject of as much speculation as when the war would end. During the campaign, the president's doctor, Admiral Ross McIntire, described his patient as a little underweight, but said there was "nothing wrong with him organically at all. He's perfectly OK."

Republicans whispered that if elected Roosevelt would not make it to the end of his term. To silence them, he led a motorcade on a four-hour, fifty-mile route through New York City that fall. It was raining and the president was riding in an open car, but he refused to cancel or shorten the trip. He wouldn't even order the top up. Twice he paused for rubdowns and a quick change of clothes, but most of the time he stood, smiled and waved in the cold rain. Six days later he repeated the same feat in Philadelphia. Newspapers marveled at his vitality.

In fact, Roosevelt suffered from cardiovascular problems dating back to 1937, and in 1943 he had been troubled by flu, an unexplained fever, and headaches. He tired easily and frequently, sometimes falling asleep in the midst of a conversation. Once he dropped off while signing his name.

Admiral McIntire to the contrary, Roosevelt was a sick man. But no one knew how sick until March 27, 1944, when the first lady forced him into Bethesda Naval Hospital for a thorough examination. A heart specialist who examined him, Lieutenant Commander Howard G. Bruenn, was shocked; Roosevelt was worn out, feverish, and suffering from bronchitis. His heart was enlarged, the arterial vessels swollen, and his blood pressure far too high. The diagnosis: hypertension, hypertensive heart disease and cardiac failure. Bruenn and the other specialists prescribed medication and told their commander in chief to cut back on alcohol and cigarettes (he smoked twenty to thirty Camels a day) and rest. FDR went off to South Carolina to do so.

Bruenn and his colleagues didn't tell Roosevelt of their diagnosis, but gave the test results to McIntire. It is unclear if he ever told FDR about his condition, or if FDR understood and accepted the diagnosis. If he did, he did not act like it. In the next twelve months Roosevelt traveled 50,000 miles, ran for re-election, and directed a world war. Everything fell to him, from naming a Supreme Allied Commander in Europe to deciding whether to cancel the Army-Navy game. "One man simply could not do it all," Henry Stimson said later. "Franklin Roosevelt killed himself trying."

The president had several painful attacks of angina pectoris during a tour of the West Coast in July 1944. By the end of the year he looked wasted. At a Cabinet meeting before his inauguration in 1945, Roosevelt's eyes were sunken and darkly circled, his lips blue; his hands shook; he had lost so much weight his suit was a size too big. "Only the jaunty cigarette holder and his lighthearted brushing aside of difficulties recalled the FDR of former days," wrote Secretary of State Dean Acheson.

This was the Roosevelt critics would later deride as "the sick man of Yalta," who they said gave Eastern Europe to Stalin in February 1945. But Roosevelt's health was a sometime thing; he had good days and bad days, and mostly the former at Yalta. Attending the conference, however, undoubtedly shortened his life. William Manchester has written that Yalta probably will be remembered not because Roosevelt sacrificed Poland or Romania, but because he sacrificed himself.

* * * *

In April 1945, the president was at his cottage in Warm Springs, Georgia, sitting for a portrait, going through his mail and signing papers. He had just lit a cigarette when suddenly he raised his left hand to his temple. "I have a terrific headache," he murmured, then slumped in his chair. Two-and-a-half hours later he was dead, the victim of a massive cerebral hemorrhage, as much a casualty of the war as any soldier who died in battle.

Again, as on Pearl Harbor day, there was a conference call for the three wire services. Again, Steve Early delivered the bad news. At 5:49 p.m. the AP sent this flash: "WASHINGTON—PRESIDENT ROOSEVELT DIED SUDDENLY THIS AFTERNOON AT WARM SPRINGS, GA."

It was the children's hour on radio, so they were the first to know. John Charles Daly of CBS, who had informed Chester Nimitz and millions of others about Pearl Harbor, now did the same when the network broke into "Wilderness Road." Many people refused to believe the news; Roosevelt was a given, like the morning sun in the east. He was, simply, The President.

Tributes poured in from unexpected sources. His voice trembling, Senator Robert A. Taft said, "He dies a hero of the war, for he literally worked himself to death in the service of the American people." Radio Tokyo quoted Admiral Kantaro Suzuki as praising Roosevelt's "great leadership" and saying, "I can easily understand the great loss his passing means to the American people and my profound sympathy goes to them." The network then played several minutes of music "in honor of the passing of the great man."

Eleanor Roosevelt telegrammed her sons that their father had done his job to the end and would have wanted them to do the same. So, off Okinawa, Lieutenant John Roosevelt, standing watch on the carrier Hornet, received a call from Lieutenant Commander Franklin D. Roosevelt, Jr., aboard the destroyer Moore. "Are you making it home, old man?" asked FDR, Jr. "No," said his brother. "Are you?"

"Nope," he responded. "Let's clean it up out here first."

On another ship in the Pacific, a signalman received the flashed message. "Who the hell is president now?" he wondered. Roosevelt was the only president the younger men on board had ever known. That Sunday the ship's weekly service got its biggest turnout, even bigger than after an air attack or a typhoon.

Back in Warm Springs, a sailor played "Going Home" on the accordian, and the presidential train with Roosevelt's body headed slowly toward Washington. North of Atlanta, a group of black sharecropper women knelt in the middle of a cotton field, holding out clasped hands. The train rolled through the day and into the warm Southern night, "a lonesome train on a lonesome track," like the one that had borne Abraham Lincoln's body home eighty years earlier at the end of another war. The last car contained Roosevelt's body, resting in a casket with an American flag draped over it. The car's lights were left on, and its blinds open, so the thousands who stood by the tracks could get a glimpse.

The train arrived in Washington the next morning, and the funeral procession moved from Union Station toward the White House. Twenty-four bombers, probably made at Willow Run, droned overhead; I.F. Stone thought of the vast number of planes Roosevelt had vowed to build in 1942, and choked up. The casket sat on a black caisson, drawn by six white horses. A seventh horse, the fallen warrior's, walked alongside, its eyes hooded, stirrups reversed, a sword and boots turned upside down hanging from the stirrups. The procession had so many soldiers and so much equipment that when the casket suddenly appeared people were surprised. It was a massive, 800-pound box, but it looked so small; somehow, they expected it to be bigger, like the man was.

When the funeral began that afternoon at 4, the nation came close to shutting down. Buses pulled over, and planes nearing their destinations circled overhead. In New York, subway trains stopped in the tunnels. There was silence over the airwaves, silence over the telephone lines. The wire service teletypes slowly tapped out the letters S-I-L-E-N-C-E.

In the East Room of the White House, 200 people gathered for a simple service. In his eulogy, Bishop Angus Dun quoted FDR's most famous words: "The only thing we have to fear is fear itself." Roosevelt's empty wheelchair stood apart from the improvised altar, a reminder of the fear he himself had confronted when he was paralyzed at thirty-nine. "If you have spent two years in bed trying to wriggle your big toe," he once said, "everything else seems easy."

On the day before he died, the president had returned to that theme in a speech he was writing for Jefferson Day. The war was almost over, and now Americans must go on "to conquer the doubts and the fears . . . which made this horror possible," he wrote. "The only limit to our realization of tomorrow will be our doubts of today. Let us move forward with strong and active faith."

Caisson carries the body of Roosevelt to the White House.

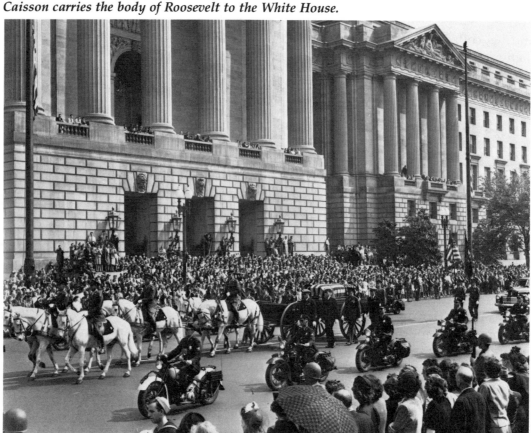

11 FINAL ASSAULT

There was no subtlety in the battle for Iwo Jima. There wasn't room for it.

The tiny island, two-thirds the size of Manhattan, became an epitome fought out on a surpassingly violent and bloody stage. Pitted in their rawest elements were the two philosophies of the warring Americans and Japanese. For the Japanese there were their ancient samurai warrior doctrine and the national belief in the power of will. The Americans brought to this island of volcanic ash— one correspondent likened it to "hell with the fire gone out"—all of the brute force of their superior industrial might, something the Japanese expected but believed their superior island people could outwill. The Americans also brought something the Japanese, perhaps, did not expect of their "soft" enemy: the unflinching, head-on valor of the Marines, Marines fighting, and dying, up to the top of their own self-image. The Americans, in the end, prevailed.

There was no surprise, either, in the battle. The Japanese knew the Americans needed the island and prepared accordingly. Iwo Jima was 760 miles south of Tokyo, a valuable haven for malfunctioning or shotup B-29s bombing Japan from Saipan and Tinian and Guam. Bombers based on Iwo could also make up in bomb weight what they saved in fuel. In time 2,251 B-29s were to make emergency landings on Iwo Jima. There was only one place to land soldiers on Iwo, the black ash beaches on the southeast side of the otherwise cliff-girt, lamb chop-shaped island. The Japanese commander, Lieutenant General Tadamichi Kuribayashi, placed his 21,000 men, hundreds of cannon and thousands of machine guns accordingly. There were pillboxes with walls five feet thick hidden everywhere in the sand and Iwo's 1,500 caves. Kuribayashi was a stern taskmaster who denied his men sake or women from the "comfort troops." He prepared for months for the inevitable landing. It came February 19, 1945.

B-24s had been bombing the island for six weeks. At dawn February 15, six battleships and five cruisers began shelling while planes from twelve jeep carriers struck from the air. Kuribayashi had told his men to hold their fire and ordered: "Every man will resist until the end, making his position his tomb. Every man will do his best to kill ten enemy soldiers." The commander had no illusions, writing his children: ". . . from now on you must reconcile yourselves to living without a father."

"Howlin' Mad" Smith, commander of the 60,000 Marines of the 3rd, 4th and 5th Marine Divisions, had no illusions, either. By now an expert on beach assault, he thought the invasion would succeed but would not be worth the price even though another battleship and three more cruisers had joined the cannonade while destroyers fired point blank off the beaches. "I can't help thinking nobody can live through this," correspondent Robert Sherrod noted. "But I know better."

The Japanese were armed with their trust in propaganda pamphlets which said the Americans ". . . have no desire for the glory of their ancestors or posterity, nor for the glory of the family name. . . . They go into battle with no spiritual incentive and rely on material superiority."

The amtracks came ashore in line trailing their

Waves of landing craft speed towards killing ground of Iwo Jima.

wakes like bridal trains towards a dread altar. They labored through the ankle-deep ash. Still no resistance. As the Marines climbed over the fifteen-foot ledge facing them onto the plateau in the shadow of Mount Suribachi, a dormant volcano, the defenders opened up from every conceivable direction. Arms and legs were blown every which way as shells and mortar rounds lobbed into the beachhead.

"C'mon, you guys, let's get these guns off the beach," cried Sergeant John Basilone, the Medal of Honor hero of Guadalcanal. A mortar shell explod-ed at his feet, killing him and four of his men. When the right wing was relieved that night, only 150 men were left of the 1,000 who had landed there. Six hundred Marines died that first day, but the rest had reached the edge of the first of the island's two completed landing strips. Kuribayashi radioed Tokyo, of which prefecture Iwo was a distant part, that the island would fall if he could not get naval support. All he got were a few kamikaze planes that crippled the carrier *Saratoga* and sank the jeep carrier *Bismarck Sea*.

Iwo Jima's strategic location made invasion
inevitable, and the Japanese knew it.

Japanese held fire until Marines topped first rise, and
then...

AP's Joe Rosenthal had doubts about famous photo—Stars and Stripes atop Mount Suribachi—because it didn't show faces.

PHOTO OP

World War II's most famous photograph was taken the second time around.

When the Marines topped Suribachi, they raised a small American flag—and shot two Japanese who charged at them from a cave. The flag was barely visible from the beachhead. Lieutenant Colonel Chandler Johnson, who had ordered his men to raise the flag when they reached the summit of the volcano, said: "Some son-of-a-bitch is going to want that flag, but he's not going to get it." He sent someone to get a much bigger flag from an LST. Joe Rosenthal, an AP photographer and veteran of Pelelieu and Guam, scrambled up the rocks just in time to fire off a photo as the new flag was raised. He took more photos of posing Marines waving their rifles which he thought would be more worthy for the photo network because they showed faces.

Secretary of the Navy James Forrestal who had just succeeded Frank Knox at his death was coming ashore with General Smith. "The raising of this flag on Suribachi means a Marine Corps for the next 500 years," Forrestal said. Rosenthal sent his film back to Guam where the darkroom showed he had done his bit for the Corps, too.

Kuribayashi had built two major defense lines across the island north of the beachhead. By the third day, Marines had fought to the top of Suribachi where the famous photograph of the flag-raising was snapped by Joe Rosenthal of the Associated Press. Up island it was a constant assault pillbox to pillbox by 60,000 Marines through scrub, rocks and sand. One bunker was blown up with 1,200 pounds of dynamite on its roof. Seabees were already clearing the first airstrip. On March 4 a B-29 almost out of gas made an emergency landing as Marines battled with bayonets and flamethrowers nearby. After a week Kuribayashi radioed he had lost 50 percent of his combat men and most of his machine guns, but he refused to let his remaining soldiers mount a suicide attack. Nonetheless, on March 8 a group of 1,000 Japanese made a banzai charge. The Marines killed 784 of them. After eighteen days, the Marines finally reached the north shore. But many defenders remained in bunkers and caves. "We have not eaten or drunk for five days," Kuribayashi radioed. "But our fighting spirit is still running high. We are going to fight bravely to the last."

There were twenty-six Marines and Navy medics who were to win Medals of Honor on Iwo Jima, seven who had thrown themselves on top of grenades. "Uncommon valor," Nimitz was to write, "was a common virtue."

On March 26, 350 Japanese soldiers and sailors made a last-ditch sword charge but died in a hard day of hand combat. The next day Kuribayashi came to the mouth of his cave, bowed north toward the Imperial Palace and then stabbed himself in the stomach. An aide slashed his bowed neck with his sword, then buried his commander. Kuribayashi's chief of staff and the island's navy commander visited the grave, then shot themselves. Only 216 Japanese had surrendered. A few thousand continued to hide in the caves. Incredibly, the last two surrendered six years after the war ended. Will power had not been enough.

The Americans lost 6,821 lives to take Iwo, the heaviest toll in Corps history. One of them was Thornton "Gus" Lyttle, hardly nineteen. A year before he had been a student at a prestigious New England prep school. He was a mature, smart, humorous lad who did not have to raise his voice to be listened to. He had an uncommonly fine artistic talent, one that had already begun to flower. But he wasn't going to college with it. He wanted to get into the war. Not for his ancestors or warrior tradition but because there was a war on, and his country was in it. For tradition or will power or whatever, dead is dead. But Gus Lyttle's painter's hands were one of thousands that helped raise the flag that stood out in the wind atop Mount Suribachi on an island called Iwo Jima.

"Like hell with the fire out." The bloody volcanic dust of Iwo Jima.

Five days after landing, supplies pour onto Iwo Jima where Marines battle cave by cave.

Okinawa

One more island to go.

While Germany twitched its last like a beheaded farm fowl and fanatic Nazis embarked on a final spasm of atrocities, the Japanese awaited their fate from the gray ships and silver bombers that pulverized their homeland. Some 13 million people poked dazedly through the ashes of what had been their homes. The food ration had fallen to 1,500 calories a day, two-thirds their accustomed diet. War production was strangled by the American submarines. Lack of bauxite for aluminum reduced plane production by a third. Steel output was down two-thirds for want of ore. Munitions were one-half for lack of coal. Tojo, the embodiment of the new martial empire that was to have fed Japan's war, had been forced out of office in the summer of 1944. He tried to shoot himself but missed his heart by inches and lived to be hanged as a war criminal. In April 1945 his successors made an approach to negotiate peace through Allen Dulles, the OSS man in Switzerland. But the Allies had said unconditional surrender and meant it. Admiral King was of the opinion that blockade and bombing would eventually force the Japanese to give up. But the island-hopping strategy he had championed had a momentum of its own. On Okinawa, its last stop before Japan, there was no surrender.

L Day on Okinawa—L for Love to the soldiers; it was Easter Sunday—was April 1, 1945. It was the biggest invasion force yet, a joint Army-Marine army of 183,000 under the overall command of Spruance. The ground troops, the 10th Army, were under General Simon Bolivar Buckner, Jr., junior because his father of the same name had been a Confederate general in the Civil War. During the Aleutian campaign Buckner slept with only a sheet to show his mettle. His Japanese counterpart was

SUBMARINES

The Navy called them the Silent Service, but in the last phase of the war in the Pacific they were increasingly heard from: the submarines.

In the war's early stages the American underseas fleet was handicapped by magnetic torpedoes that, while technologically advanced, were unreliable. Japan also had the resources to keep almost abreast of its shipping losses. By 1944, however, American subs had an improved torpedo and had adopted the German U-boat technique of hunting in wolf packs. In 1944 U.S. subs sank more than 600 Japanese ships totaling 2.7 million tons, a half-million tons more than in the war's first three years. All told the Japanese lost 1,500 vessels to submarines including eight carriers, a battleship and eleven cruisers. At the war's end the sub skippers were running out of targets on the high seas and were shooting at ferry boats in the Home Islands.

The 150 or so American subs in the Pacific operating out of Hawaii and Fremantle, Australia, were slowly choking Japan to death. To keep the oil coming from Southeast Asia, the Japanese had to curb production of bulk carriers which meant less iron ore which meant fewer ships, hence fewer tankers. The vicious circle was further compounded by the U.S. subs. Japan had to curtail its air cover for convoys at the same time America's advanced bases increased U.S. opportunities for patrol planes to spot Japanese ship movements.

The Americans paid a price. The casualty rate of 22 percent among submarine crews was the highest of any service.

Two wars in two generations. General Buchner's father had been a general in the Civil War.

Lieutenant General Mitsuru Ushijima whose 32nd Army had about 100,000 men plus sailors.

Okinawa, in the Ryukyu chain about 400 miles south of Kyushu, was Japanese territory although its 450,000 natives were poor farmers of mixed descent. Their home was about sixty miles long, two miles wide at its waist and prone to heavy rains.

The combined American force was to be the largest yet joining Marines with the Army. There had been bad blood between the services on Saipan after "Howlin' Mad" Smith had asked Spruance to relieve the commander of the Army's 27th Division for lack of aggression. Stateside

THE FLOWERS AND THE BEES

By 1945, megadeaths in bombing attacks on civilian populations had become an accepted part of war. It began during World War I with a few zeppelin raids by the Germans on London. During the Spanish Civil War, German bombers had obliterated the Basque holy city of Guernica. Coventry in Britain, Rotterdam and London had all been heavily damaged by Nazi bombers in the early days of World War II. On July 27–28, 1943, some 739 RAF bombers struck the German port city of Hamburg with 2,417 tons of incendiaries creating a new phenomenon, the firestorm, which killed as many as 45,000 people. On February 13–14, 1945, U.S. and British planes firebombed Dresden setting off a firestorm that killed as many as 100,000.

Secretary of War Stimson, a man of culture and a true Edwardian gentleman, said: "War is death."

Curtis LeMay had seen as much first hand. He had led B-17s in Europe, wrestled with the cranky new B-29s in China and in January 1945 took command of the 20th Air Force in the Marianas to step up the bombing of Japan. Japan was a different target from Germany. Its industry was scattered in small buildings among the homes of the nation's crowded, wooden-built residential quarters. Catastrophic fires were no stranger to Tokyo, particularly after earthquakes. The Japanese even had a name for them, The Flowers of Edo, the old name for the capital.

Faced with a diffuse target, LeMay began experimenting with incendiary bombing from his growing and improving force of B-29s—"Bees," the Japanese called them. A raid on Kobe from high altitude on February 4 produced promising results. LeMay decided on his own to gamble on a low-level strike on Tokyo March 9–10, 1945. By flying low the planes could save fuel by not bucking the jet stream and could carry more bombs. Over objections by his incredulous crews,

Curtis LeMay thought he had the answer to Japan's defeat: fire-bombing.

he stripped the guns of 334 B-29s so they could carry even more M-47 canisters filled with bombs of jellied gasoline: napalm. LeMay was taking another gamble: that the Japanese lacked night fighters. It was a windy night to begin with as the marker planes dropped their loads to create a flaming X across Tokyo. From as low as an unprecedented 4,900 feet subsequent bombers bucked through an updraft of hurricane intensity to feed the unstoppable holocaust. Winds sucked into the inferno threw a barrage of pebbles. Canals began boiling in the 1,000-degree heat. By dawn 83,793 Japanese by official count were dead and 1,200,000 homeless. Sixteen square miles of the city were in ashes.

The next night 313 bombers napalmed Nagoya, Japan's third largest city, then Osaka and Kobe. Forty-five square miles of urban Japan were burned out within a week.

There were those who thought Curtis LeMay had found the way to end the war.

---

newspapers got wind of the dispute and played it up, enlarging the irritation. But all was harmony as the first 60,000 troops ashore landed almost without opposition and quickly took an airfield. Marines were astonished when a Zero landed and an equally astonished Japanese pilot stepped out. He made the mistake of reaching for his pistol. "There's always some poor bastard who doesn't get the word," said a Marine.

From the beachhead the Marines moved north

and two Army divisions, the 7th under Major General Archibald Arnold and Major General James Bradley's 96th, headed south. By April 4 the Army units reported "stiffening" resistance and by the 8th "greatly increased resistance." They had reached Ushijima's in depth defense line, an intricate, deadly network of caves and pillboxes that even used the Okinawans' above-ground tombs as machine gun nests. Progress became a matter of bloody yards.

Offshore, Spruance's ships came under steady attack by kamikazes. Eager but hastily-trained pilots flying stripped-down, second-line planes dove by the hundreds at the American ships. Some had attended their own funerals, downed ceremonial sake and sometimes more, then took off. On April 6 the biggest kamikaze of all, the *Yamato*, the world's mightiest battleship, slipped its cable and headed out for Okinawa from Japan. It only had enough fuel to get there, not to return. There wasn't any more. The Japanese had planned to coordinate the attack with 5,000 kamikazes, but American bombers had destroyed many on the ground, and there was only fuel for 700 that remained. Tipped by a submarine, U.S. planes found the *Yamato* the next day and attacked in droves with bombs and torpedoes. "Banzai!" cried its doomed crew as the huge ship slowly rolled over and sank.

Rear Admiral Keizo Komura had his escorting cruiser sunk as well. He was fished out of the water by one of two surviving destroyers which continued on towards Okinawa. Then Tokyo ordered them to turn to home. Komura, who had sent out the first planes in the Pearl Harbor attack, did not protest. "I've had enough," he said.

Crew of **Hornet** *watch kamikaze just miss* **Bennington** *off Okinawa.*

Kamikaze dives for U.S. warship. Suicide pilots sank thirty-four major American vessels during war, lost 1,228 fliers. Americans called constant kamikaze attacks on Okinawa fleet "the Iron Typhoon."

Meanwhile, on Okinawa, the battle over broken terrain was beginning to resemble the mountain fighting in Italy. "I doubt if the Army's slow, methodical method of fighting really saves lives in the long run," said Spruance as the land battle passed its first month. "It merely spreads the casualties over a longer period." Offshore the kamikazes continued to take a heavy toll of sunk and crippled warships. "I see no way to get them out except blast them out yard by yard," said Major General John Hodge whose XXIV Corps ashore had to do just that. Tanks, artillery and naval gunfire from as many as six battleships could not break the Japanese defenses in front of the citadel of Shuri. Cornered, the Japanese responded with a suicidal attack like wounded lions. It failed as Ushijima thought it would. He wanted to conserve manpower for a battle of attrition, but that was not how samurai had fought.

On May 8 all American guns fired a salvo of three rounds. The war in Europe had ended. The one on Okinawa had not. Downpours bogged the battlefield to mud. On May 25 five bombers tried to land on an American strip for a death attack. Four were shot down, but a fifth landed on its belly, and its crew destroyed seven American planes and blew up a fuel depot before they were killed. At sea Vice Admiral C.R. Brown watched in awe at the repeated kamikaze attacks. "There was a hypnotic fascination to a sight so alien to our Western philosophy."

Ensign Yasunori Aoki told Toland after the war how he watched a fly on what he thought would be his last day on earth. "How lucky you are to be alive," said the twenty-two-year-old kamikaze. He wrote post cards to his family, sent them fingernail parings and a lock of hair, posed for a newsreel cameraman, drank sake, then took off for Okinawa. His plane hit the water before the destroyer it was aiming at. American sailors grappled Aoki out of the sea. He tried to bite off his tongue so he could choke to death from the blood, but it didn't work. He tried to strangle himself with a piece of string.

Marines strolled ashore on Okinawa. Then they hit the defense line.

Sometimes flamethrowers were only way on Okinawa.

One of Japanese strongholds on Okinawa was a cemetery.

First tanks on Okinawa found going deceptively easy.

That failed, too. He decided his destiny was to live.

On June 15 Buckner was watching an assault when a Japanese shell exploded nearby hurling fragments of coral. One hit him in the throat, killing him. Buckner was replaced by Major General Roy Geiger, a veteran of Guadalcanal. Like Admiral Komura, he was in on a beginning and in on an end.

Six days later a Marine patrol reached the southern tip of the island. General Ushijima, taking a fan to cool himself on a hot night, walked to a ledge outside his cave, ripped his stomach with the ceremonial knife, then an aide gave the coup de grace with his sword. Okinawa had fallen. It cost the lives of 7,000 soldiers and Marines and 5,000 sailors. Some 110,000 Japanese troops died and 75,000 civilians caught in the crossfire. The "Iron Typhoon" of Okinawa saw thirty-six U.S. ships sunk by kamikazes. Was there reason to doubt that the invasion of Kyushu on Japan proper wouldn't be worse?

MacArthur, whom Larrabee calls the "thespian general" for his melodramatics, was now commander of the Pacific Theater. The last island had been hopped. MacArthur claimed to be the originator of the strategy although he was a belated convert to it, and it really evolved out of necessity

Minutes after this photo, General Buckner (r.) was killed by shell.

Tanks became stretcher bearers in Okinawa battle.

and clever staff thinking. There was, after all, the old baseball wisdom of Baltimore Oriole Wee Willie Keeler as precedent: "Hit 'em where they ain't."

But the Americans had run out of islands where Japanese weren't. On the day Roosevelt died, the Japanese cabinet began recruiting a volunteer army of all men between fifteen and fifty-five and women from seventeen to forty-five to defend their homeland. "The strategy under which we have allowed the enemy to invade the Okinawa islands has much in common with the strategy of fighting with our backs to the wall."

ERNIE PYLE

On April 18, the GIs lost their best friend.

Ernie Pyle, now covering the Pacific, left the Marines on Okinawa to cover an action by the Army boys he had come to know so well in Europe. He had been at their side for so long, had fought as hard with Congress as they had the Germans to get them extra combat pay and creation of the Combat Infantryman's Badge. The GIs had landed on Ie Shima, a small island off Okinawa, to seize its airfield.

Pyle was riding in a jeep up to the front lines when it came under machine gun fire. Pyle hit the dirt in a ditch. Before he left for the invasion, fellow correspondents kidded him: "Keep your head down, Ernie." He didn't. A bullet hit him in the temple, killing him instantly.

The GIs put up a marker: "At this spot the 77th Infantry Division lost a buddy, Ernie Pyle, 18 April 1945."

Taps for a buddy. Ernie Pyle and 12,250 troops died in Okinawa fighting, highest toll of Pacific war.

V-E Day

Long before, in the springtime of the Third Reich, Adolf Hitler promised his people: "Give me five years, and you will not recognize Germany again."

It took longer, but for once the fuehrer was true to his word. In 1945, Germany collapsed in ruins.

As the year began the Soviet and Allied armies were poised at either extremity of the Reich like jaws of a vise. But Hitler was not without reason to hope. His army still had 260 divisions, twice the number in 1940. Despite the bombing, factories had delivered 283 new jet fighters in February. Doenitz's navy had 450 U-boats, 126 of them the new snorkel types, two of which had already put to sea. Seventy-six divisions faced the Allies west of the Rhine, twenty-four in Italy and 133 on the Eastern Front. But Hitler insisted on keeping thirty divisions in the Baltic to protect his submarine facilities beyond the reach of Anglo-American bombers. He refused his generals' advice to incorporate these units into his main armies and shorten his lines. He would not, and they would die on the vine. His creed, and it would help destroy him, was not to yield a foot. Heinz Guderian, his old tank commander who would serve at the end as chief of staff, said Hitler "had a special picture of the world and every fact had to fit that fanciful picture . . . but in fact it was a picture of another world."

Eisenhower's strategy remained as it had been: seek the Germans and destroy them. With Patton as his executioner in the Rhineland west of the river, he did just that. The Bulge having been erased and its losses quickly made up, twelve American divisions coursed through the Saar-Palatinate and in ten days, with the help of Ultra to dodge counterattacks, took 90,000 prisoners. By the time the American armies reached the Rhine in early March, they had captured 317,000 Germans including twenty-five generals and an admiral. The enemy was surrendering at a rate of 5,000 a day. They came almost joyfully, bringing wine and girl friends with them. One GI marching sixty-eight POWs to the road ended up with 1,200 by the time he got there. Field Marshal Model, the Bulge commandant, walked into the woods and shot himself.

An admiring aide of Patton's said: "Students of military history will study (this campaign) for years to come."

Brooke and Montgomery still insisted on an all-out effort to Berlin with the British-Canadian 12th Army Group plus the American 1st and 9th Armies. Eisenhower just as adamantly refused. He had only seventy-one divisions and no reserves. His plan had been to reach the Rhine so as to free twenty divisions from defensive positions to be

thrown in at any points of opportunity. He and Montgomery were no longer speaking. In any case, said Eisenhower's British deputy, Brigadier John Whiteley: "Monty was the last person Ike would have chosen for a drive on Berlin—Monty would have needed at least six months to prepare." Patton was the attacker, and his tanks were to the south.

Brooke had told Eisenhower the success in the Rhineland had proven the American right, but Ike's refusal to stack his left wing for a race to Berlin was to be argued for many years after the war. In the past Eisenhower had told Montgomery: "Clearly Berlin is the prize." But in March the Western Allies were still 200 miles from the German capital. The overwhelming Soviet offensive by 160 divisions and 22,000 guns had driven to within thirty-five miles of Berlin since it began in early January. Bradley told Eisenhower he thought a march to Berlin would cost 100,000 casualties (it was to cost the Soviet 300,000). Eisenhower felt the capital had

One GI never made it across the Rhine.

Road of retreat was lined with Nazi dead.

become just another geographical location. To get there Montgomery would have to fight across lowlands cut by many rivers. Instead Eisenhower would send the U.S. armies due east to link up with the Russians. Montgomery was to liberate The Netherlands, seize a North Sea German port for future operations against the German army in Norway and cut across the base of Denmark to prevent Russian forces from getting there first. Eisenhower saw no profit in spending blood for land he would later have to give back to the Soviets.

Montgomery took the offensive February 8 and reached the Rhine thirteen days later. Then the Allies got lucky. Very lucky.

The attack across the Rhine was to have been a waterborne operation rivaling Overlord. But on March 7 some troops of the U.S. 9th Armored Division fought their way into the river town of Remagen. Major Ben Cothran, divisional operations officer, reached town and stared: "My God!"

Patton crossed the Rhine by moonlight where Napoleon once had.

The Ludendorff railroad bridge between Bonn and Coblenz was still standing. He ran to get Brigadier General William Hoge. It was 3:15 p.m. German POWs said the bridge was to be blown up at 4 o'clock. He ordered Lieutenant Karl Timmermann to get his platoon over the span. Now! There was the thump of an explosion from the crossing. When the smoke cleared, the bridge still stood. Sergeant Alex Drabik and his platoon began running. They made it to the other side and dove into some bomb craters. "Then we just sat and waited for others to come." They came. Within ten minutes, Timmermann had 100 men across. Courtney Hodges called Bradley with the news.

"Hot dog!" exclaimed Bradley. Major General Harold "Pinky" Bull, Eisenhower's operations man, was with Bradley. Plans didn't call for a crossing at Remagen, he protested. The other side wasn't tank country. "There goes your ball game, Pink!" Bradley exulted and phoned Eisenhower. "To hell with the planners. Go on, Brad, I'll give you everything we got." Within twenty-four hours 8,000 troops crossed the bridge, in five days several divisions.

The Germans frantically tried to do what a 500-pound TNT charge on the span, its fuse cut by a lucky shell, had failed to do. The Luftwaffe attacked with twenty-one jets. Sixteen were shot down. V-2 rockets missed. Army Engineers quickly laid pontoon bridges. In time they would build forty-six floating, eleven fixed and five railroad bridges over the Rhine. While Montgomery was massing to charge to the other bank, Patton to the south took advantage of a moonlit night March 22 to cross the river without benefit of preparatory bombing or artillery. His men loaned surrendering Germans their rubber assault boats to row back across to be interned. When the river was bridged, at about the same place Napoleon had once crossed, Patton walked across and in midpassage paused to "fait pipi dans le Rhin" as an aide delicately put it in French.

Germans began surrendering in droves but a few still fought back. GIs under fire in German village.

Cologne's cathedral largely escaped but the rest of the city paid the cost of Hitler's Thousand Year Reich.

Patton urged Eisenhower to get on his horse to Berlin "quick." He replied it wasn't worth the problems. "I think history will answer that history for you," said Patton. It has, not always favorably. On March 28 Eisenhower contacted Major General John R. Deane, head of the U.S. Military Mission in Moscow, telling him to notify Stalin that the Allies were not going to Berlin. Instead they were going to make an encircling movement of the Ruhr, Germany's industrial center along with Silesia in the East. Churchill exploded. Eisenhower was making political decisions he had no right to do. It was fine for the Americans not to consider political ramifications. They would be gone from Europe after the war. But the British would not, and wanted all the territory they could get for bargaining strength with the Soviets. While the last intra-Allied fight, it was one of the most heated. Churchill, a true admirer of the SHAEF commander, simmered down but reminded him: "We should shake hands with the Russians as far east as possible."

On April 1 the Ruhr pincers closed netting 400,000 prisoners. Simpson's 2nd Armored Division raced off fifty miles in a day towards the Elbe. He had 50,000 men across it by April 12, fifty miles from Berlin. He was told to stop in place. He was now in the Russian zone as agreed to the prior November by the Allied European Advisory Commission and confirmed at Yalta.

General Alexander Patch questions surrendered foe, Field Marshal von Rundstedt, the man who dismissed Hitler as "a Bohemian corporal."

YALTA

Joan Bright of the British War Cabinet said of the Yalta Conference: "There were three cameras held by three powers with three different viewfinders." There are many more viewpoints today as to who won and why.

A thousand Soviet soldiers labored to gentrify the old Crimean resort, once the Black Sea playground of the czars. Walls were hung with the best from Moscow art galleries and museums. Log fires warmed the rooms when the Big Three met for the last time February 4, 1945. Stalin was a genial, pipe-smoking host.

Roosevelt, just turned sixty-three, was visibly failing and to the British looked "transparent." Lord Moran, Churchill's physician, presciently told Edward Stettinius, the new American Secretary of State: "I give him only a few months to live." Anthony Eden, British foreign minister, thought the American president "vague and loose and ineffective."

Conspiratorialists and Monday morning quarterbacks were to make much of the fact that one of Roosevelt's aides was Alger Hiss. But Stalin needed little help from any fellow travelers, even if Hiss, whose role was not major, was one. At Yalta he held trumps.

The Americans wanted Stalin's participation in the Pacific war. He agreed to do so conditionally in exchange for the southern half of Sakhalin Island, then in Japanese possession, the Japanese Kurile Islands, Russian co-management of the trans-Manchurian railroad and rights to the Chinese ports of Dairen and Port Arthur. Roosevelt and Churchill ceded this without even consulting their Chinese ally, Chiang Kai-shek. The Western Allies also yielded Latvia, Lithuania and Estonia to the Soviets, they being already occupied by Soviet troops. Stalin also agreed to participate in formation of the United Nations, first insisting that all of the Soviet republics must have a vote. The Americans said by that reasoning all forty-eight states should have a vote. Stalin whittled his demand down to additional votes for Byelorussia and the Ukraine. All parties agreed to a veto in the Security Council.

The Soviet-occupied lands of Eastern Europe were the sticking point. Stalin made vague promises about holding prompt elections in Hungary, Bulgaria and Romania where local communists were already in control. He insisted his puppet Polish government already spoke for the nation.

At Yalta, zones of occupation of Germany were outlined and shaded portion of prewar Germany was given to Poland.

Yalta conferees: Churchill, Roosevelt and Stalin.

"The Poles are an independent people, and they would not want to have their elections supervised by outsiders."

Churchill protested, but he was playing from a weak hand. Britain had been bled white by the war and had no reason to doubt that her American ally would pack up and go home when the war was over. Neither Churchill nor Roosevelt looked with favor on Stalin's insistence on $10 billion in reparations from Germany but surrendered the point. Roosevelt had gotten what he wanted: Russia in the U.N. and the Pacific fighting.

One of the cruelest decisions at Yalta was agreement by the Western Allies that all refugees were to be returned to their prewar homelands. Thus some 2 million people were returned to Russian hands, many to be shot outright as defectors, others to languish for years in the Soviet gulags.

Churchill said of the selection of Yalta to Harry Hopkins: "If we had spent ten years on research, we couldn't have found a worse place in the world." It soon became evident not just the surroundings had been forbidding. The Soviets had agreed to let the United States use airfields in Hungary to bomb Germany. When Americans arrived after the conference to begin preparations, they were turned away. Russia had also pledged use of bases in the East by some of LeMay's bombers. Americans became so throttled by red tape in trying to get there they gave up trying. No one was to speak optimistically of "the spirit of Yalta."

Allied photo analysts thought this 1944 aerial picture of Auschwitz only showed the sprawling I.G. Farben chemical plant. They soon learned otherwise.

Ike's face tells it all. Inmate tells of atrocities of Ohrdruf concentration camp. Patton vomited.

After tour of Ohrdruf death camp, Eisenhower wanted every soldier in his army to see what the Germans had done.

The truth about Nazi Germany unfolded in sickening bits and pieces. Sometimes it was the smell of death drifting over the countryside in contrast to the fragrance of the blossoming spring. Or the skeletal living dead staring dully from behind barbed wire. Or the bodies, thousands of them, discarded like starved and foul rag dolls in trenches and barracks where they were stacked from floor to ceiling as they died.

On April 15, Colonel Donald Taylor of the British 63rd Anti-Tank Regiment reached the German camp at Bergen-Belsen. From a distance it smelled like "a monkey house." Closer, it got worse. A Tommy was approached by a walking cadaver he took to be a woman. She was holding a dead baby and pleaded for milk. The soldier spooned some into the infant's mouth to humor her. Then the mother, too, fell dead. The 4th Armored reached the death camp at Ohrdruf near Gotha. Outraged, the liberators forced the mayor and his wife to walk through the camp. They went home and hanged themselves.

The German reaction became a universal litany: "We didn't know anything about it." . . . "We were only obeying orders." Somehow six million Jews had disappeared from the streets and villages of Germany and Europe, the smoke of their death pyres mingling in the very air camp neighbors breathed, and no one knew anything about it. If true, and few believed it among the occupying troops, the Germans soon knew it all as they were put to work burying the dead.

In mid-April, Eisenhower visited Ohrdruf. He took Patton with him. Patton was so revulsed he stepped outside and vomited. He had come, Eisenhower said, "in order to be in a position to give first-hand evidence of these things if ever in the future there develops a tendency to charge these allegations to 'propaganda'." He saw the still-smoking crematoria; butcher blocks where jaws were smashed to remove gold fillings; heaped bodies; newly killed shot in the base of the skull. He stood where menstruating women were given pads soaked in gasoline that were then set on fire.

"I want every American unit not actually on the front lines to see this place," he said. "We are told that the American soldier does not know what he is fighting for. Now at least he will see what he is fighting against."

A rabbi wrote: "If the heavens were paper and all the water in the world ink, and all the trees were turned into pens, you could not even then record the sufferings and the horrors."

NEWS OF THE HOLOCAUST

The Nazi genocide campaign against the Jews virtually dribbled into American consciousness over a period of years. British newspapers reported in 1942 that the Germans had killed a million Jews, and in 1944 the liberal New York daily *PM* printed a Soviet journalist's account of the Red Army's discoveries on the Eastern Front. But similar, if far less heinous, atrocities had been incorrectly attributed to the Germans during World War I, and now reports of a holocaust were commonly dismissed as propaganda. A poll taken in December 1944 showed that most Americans knew Hitler had killed some Jews, but could not believe that even the Nazis had methodically murdered millions.

Some journalists tried to overcome home front skepticism. After interviewing witnesses in the winter of 1942–43, Edward R. Murrow told his listeners, "What is happening is this: millions of human beings, most of them Jews, are being gathered up with ruthless efficiency and murdered. . . . The Jews are being systematically exterminated."

But confirmation would come only as correspondents visited death camps seized by Allied armies. Marguerite Higgins of the *New York Herald Tribune* described how newly liberated inmates at Dachau beat an SS guard to death. When Allied officers decided to quarantine the prisoners until they could be screened for typhus, she wrote of a suicidal protest in which the inmates "flung themselves against the electrically-charged fences, electrocuting themselves before our eyes."

In April 1945, Murrow visited Buchenwald, and on the following Sunday broadcast what he had seen: rows of bodies stacked like cordwood; children whose ribs protruded through their shirts; piles of clothing, gold teeth, human hair and children's shoes. He also recounted a conversation with a French journalist who had been imprisoned there. He told Murrow: "To write about this, you must have been here at least two years. But after that, you don't want to write anymore."

"I pray you to believe what I have said about Buchenwald," said Murrow, literally shaking with rage. "I reported what I saw and heard, but only part of it. For most of it I have no words."

Help for European Jewry was slow in coming. Roosevelt insisted on Germany's unconditional surrender—a policy that did not allow negotiations to secure the Jews' release or special military operations to save them—and the State Department refused to make it easier for Jewish refugees to enter the United States. The American Jewish community, meanwhile, was divided over how hard to press for a rescue and how it should be carried out. In spring of 1943, some Jewish groups began to call for negotiations through neutral parties, but, as Freda Kirchwey wrote in the *Nation*: "We had it in our power to rescue this doomed people and we did not lift a hand to do it."

Although public indifference to the Jews' plight can be attributed at least partly to a lack of clear information, officials had no such excuse. In the summer of 1943, Henry Morgenthau—the only Jew in Roosevelt's Cabinet—began his own investigation. He found that credible reports of Hitler's "final solution" had reached the State Department in 1942 from a representative of the World Jewish Congress who had fled to Geneva from Germany, and that an American diplomat had confirmed the reports. But Assistant Secretary of State Breckinridge Long saw to it that the department stopped relaying such information. Auschwitz, meanwhile, was executing more than 10,000 people a day.

Ordered by Eisenhower to view the horror of Buchenwald and other death camps, local officials protested "We didn't know." But Nazi leader Hans Frank said before his execution "not in a thousand years" would Germany's guilt be cleansed.

One fear that had played a role in Eisenhower's thinking was his G-2's estimate that the German armies were withdrawing into a "national redoubt" in the Bavarian Alps. The intelligence summary predicted that 100 divisions were withdrawing towards the bastion with supplies that could keep twenty SS divisions fighting for a year including "the most effective secret weapons ever invented." As the Americans plunged deeper into Germany this turned out to be a fiction. Leipzig fell April 19, Munich on the 30th. American tanks sped down Hitler's autobahns, the only resistance beings hordes of refugees and former soldiers streaming the other way.

On April 25 Lieutenant Albert Kotzebue of the U.S. 69th Division on patrol near the Elbe beyond the five-mile limit set by his commanders, met a lone Soviet horseman near the village of Strehla. This was hardly a backdrop for history which was better served later that day when Second Lieutenant Williams D. Robertson of the 69th met up with Lieutenant Colonel Alexander Gardiev of the Soviet 175 rifle Regiment 5th Guards Army at Torgau along the same river. East had met West, soon with photographers and vodka to prove it.

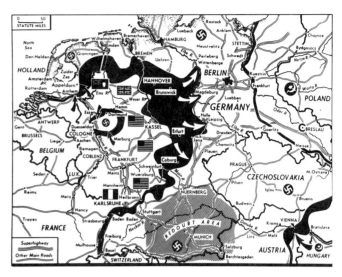

Black area shows Allied gains in first week of April 1945. Last stand in Bavarian "Redoubt Area" turned out to be myth.

As the twisted cross of Nazism crashed about him in an infernal twilight of fire, shells and bombs, Hitler alternately raged and withdrew in silence at his fuehrerbunker in Berlin. "No, never!" he shouted over what communications remained to him to the commanders of armies that had become

GI Joe meets Ivan near Torgau on Elbe River.

myths or soon would be. "We may be destroyed, but if we are, we shall drag a world with us, a world in flames!" He ordered Speer to burn everything and dismissed him in March when he wouldn't.

Old men armed with nothing but hunting rifles against Russian tanks were fighting in the militia alongside Hitler Youth, children armed with nothing but conditioned hate. No one was to retreat.

Alfred Jodl, now Hitler's chief of staff, set off another tirade when he said: "For 80 million people to fight to the death is not practicable."

Hitler had refused to leave his bunker for his Berghof and its communications center near his alpine retreat at Berchtesgaden in Bavaria. "How can I call on the troops to undertake the decisive battle if I myself withdraw to safety?" He had ordered his mistress, Eva Braun, to stay in Bavaria, but she insisted on coming to Berlin to share her lover's fate. Knowing well what that fate undoubtedly would be, the others beneath the sixteen-foot thick walls of the bunker called her The Angel of Death.

Through bungled communications, Goering, in Bavaria, thought Hitler had abdicated in his favor. Hitler's aide, Martin Bormann, whom Guderian called "a sinister guttersnipe," persuaded the fuehrer Goering was committing treason. Hitler ordered his old friend arrested. He had heard, correctly, that Himmler, the SS head, was negotiating with the Allies through a Swedish intermediary. Hitler fired him. Meanwhile, he issued barrages of orders to armies that didn't exist to stand and fight. Most had done so and been annihilated by the onrushing tanks that were already fighting in the outskirts of blazing Berlin.

In his Berlin bunker Hitler wrote a final diatribe against Jewry, married his mistress, Eva Braun, then took out his old pistol and ended his murderous life. Outside the bunker, Allied armies encircle Berlin.

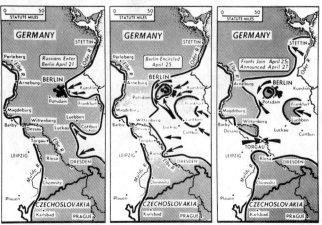

On April 22, Hitler erupted in a frenzied tantrum, the worst yet; his eyes bulging, his face purple. "Either I win this battle for the Reich's capital or I shall fall as a symbol of the Reich!" Then: "The war is lost!" It was the first time he had said as much.

In the crescendo of fire and battle in the streets above the bunker, young SS troops, to the disgust of many veterans, were summarily "court-martialing" anyone they suspected of deserting the Reich—women, clerks—and shooting them on the spot. Hitler, himself, couldn't locate Major General Hermann Fegelin of the SS, Eva Braun's brother-in-law. He was found elsewhere in the city dressed in civilian clothes. Hitler had him shot as a deserter.

In this madhouse denoument, Hitler decided to marry Eva Braun. A petty city official who had worked with Joseph Goebbels in the Propaganda Ministry was found fighting in the rubble with the militia. On April 28 he married them. Eva wore a black taffeta dress, Hitler's favorite. The official was killed making his way back to his post. The wedding party sipped champagne, the groom Tokay.

Hitler now, with Soviets fighting only blocks away, drew up his last testament. He declared that he would take his own life "to escape the shame of overthrow or capitulation." His possessions he left to the Nazi Party. He appointed Doenitz, bottled up near Hamburg, to be his successor. "If the state, too, is destroyed, there is no need for any further instructions on my part." His last words to his people—and the world—were to declare the first principle of good government. This was persecution of "the universal poisoner of all nations, international Jewry." The author of *Mein Kampf* had adhered to his own poison to the very end.

To test the efficacy of the cyanide pellets in the bunker, Hitler had one forced down the throat of his beloved German shepherd, Blondi. The dog died instantly. He ordered his aides to burn his body and Eva's. "I don't want to be put on exhibition in a Russian wax museum." He gave his favorite portrait of Frederick the Great to his personal pilot, Hans Baur. "Baur, I want them to put on my tombstone, 'He was the victim of his generals'." Then he solemnly shook hands in farewell. Eva gave her silver fox coat to a friend. They retired to their suite. Some say they heard a shot. Somebody thought it might have been a direct hit on the bunker. Aides opened the door. Eva was curled up on the couch, dead. She had taken cyanide. Hitler was slumped at a table, a bullet hole in his temple and his favorite 7.65mm Walther pistol, the gun he had carried so long ago in the beer hall in Munich, at his feet. Nearby in a silver frame was a picture of his mother as a young woman.

It was April 30.

A day later, Goebbels' wife, Magda, had a doctor inject their six daughters with morphine. Then she crushed cyanide pellets in their teeth. She and her husband walked upstairs from the bunker to what remained of a garden to save others the trouble of having to carry their bodies. An SS orderly shot them. Their bodies were burned with gasoline as the Hitlers' had been.

As their leaders died so did the nation, in blood, fire and fury. The Soviets, as many invaders from the East had been before them going back through the ages, were merciless avengers of 20 million Soviet dead. In Berlin alone 90,000 women were raped. In farmyards women were raped, killed and nailed to doors. In Prague partisans turned on the Sudeten Germans whose "oppression" had led to Munich and the occupation of Czechoslovakia and killed 30,000 of them. Soldiers and civilians alike streamed to the West to flee the Soviets and seek sanctuary and surrender with the Anglo-Americans. In Italy, Mussolini and his mistress, Clara Petacci, were caught by partisans and shot as she cried, "You can't do this." Their bodies were taken to Milan nearby. Men fired bullets into the corpses. Women urinated on them. Then they were hung up by their heels in a gas station like slaughtered beef. An English soldier decorously pinned up Clara Petacci's skirt. For the Jews there was none left to give revenge or justice. That would come, such as it would be, such as it ever could be.

For their part, the Western Allies were observant of the Yalta agreements, as they interpreted them. When Himmler tried to give up what had become the disorganized rabble of the Wehrmacht to the Allies en masse, Harry Truman stuck to the policy of unconditional surrender. "I don't think we ought to even consider a piecemeal surrender," he told Churchill. Himmler then shaved his Hitler-like mustache, donned civilian clothes and tried to lose himself in the milling mobs of refugees. He was nonetheless caught after several weeks and cheated the hangman of retribution for the countless crimes of his SS by biting a vial of cyanide.

On May 4, Patton, who had been chafing with his tank engines silent, was given permission to move forward several miles into Czechoslovakia. To assist him, the corps of Major General Ralph Hubner, who had fought with Patton in Sicily, was switched to him from the 1st Army. Hubner had no sooner said Patton would be asking him to attack within twelve hours when the phone rang. It was Patton asking if he could take Pilsen. Sure, Hubner said, and hung up. "Well, I missed that one. Instead of twelve hours it was twelve minutes."

Patton moved ahead, the road to Prague open. Eisenhower asked the Russians if it was acceptable for him to take the capital since Czechoslovakia had not been allocated to any zone of occupation. The Soviets asked him not to. Eisenhower complied.

On May 2, after more than a month of secret negotiations with Allen Dulles of the OSS in Switzerland, Kesselring surrendered the German

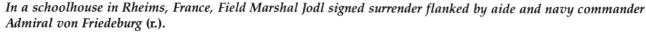

In a schoolhouse in Rheims, France, Field Marshal Jodl signed surrender flanked by aide and navy commander Admiral von Friedeburg (r.).

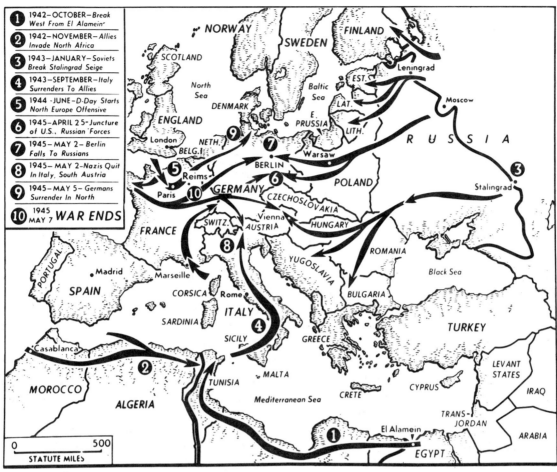

1 1942—OCTOBER—*Break West From El Alamein*
2 1942—NOVEMBER—*Allies Invade North Africa*
3 1943—JANUARY—*Soviets Break Stalingrad Seige*
4 1943—SEPTEMBER—*Italy Surrenders To Allies*
5 1944—JUNE—D-Day *Starts North Europe Offensive*
6 1945—APRIL 25—*Juncture of U.S., Russian Forces*
7 1945—MAY 2—*Berlin Falls To Russians*
8 1945—MAY 2—*Nazis Quit In Italy, South Austria*
9 1945—MAY 5—*Germans Surrender In North*
10 1945 MAY 7 WAR ENDS

The Allies' long journey to V-E Day.

armies in Italy. Shortly afterwards soldiers of the U.S. 88th Division in Italy met troops of the 103rd Division of the 7th Army at Vipiteno near the Brenner Pass.

Doenitz had begun negotiations with Montgomery through Admiral Hans-Georg von Friedeberg. On May 5 Friedeberg was escorted to SHAEF advanced headquarters in a boys' school in Rheims in France. The Allied negotiators were a grim-faced Bedell Smith and Major General Kenneth Strong, Eisenhower's intelligence chief who had been a British diplomat in Berlin before the war and spoke immaculate German. Jodl joined the parley. He reported the terms back to Doenitz who called them "sheer extortion." The Allies were blind to who the real enemy was, Soviet Russia, he felt. But there was little alternative. At 2:41 a.m. May 7 Jodl signed the surrender.

The surrender was not to be made public until the following day to allow for common release. But when a German radio station announced the war had ended, Edward Kennedy of the Associated Press considered that broke the embargo and released the news to an immediately joyous world. The Russians insisted a subsequent document be signed in the ruins of Berlin. This was done a day later which is why the Russians celebrate V-E Day one day after the Western Allies.

After Jodl affixed his signature at Reims, he made a brief statement:

"With this signature the German people and the German armed forces are, for better or worse, delivered into the victors' hands. In this war, which has lasted more than five years, both have achieved and suffered more than perhaps any other people in the world. In this hour I can only express the hope that the victor will treat them with generosity."

Then Jodl was taken before Eisenhower who had been pacing and smoking in an adjacent room. He asked the German if he was aware of what he had signed. Jodl said "Ja," saluted and left.

Bone tired, Eisenhower gathered his staff. Probably tradition required some champagne, he said. Some was procured. It was flat. Eisenhower asked for ideas for the victory announcement. Each suggestion was more purple than the next. The small-town soldier from Abilene decided to write his own:

"The mission of this Allied force was fulfilled at 0241, local time, May 7, 1945."

Omar Bradley, no less an unembellished product of the American Plains, took out his map board and wrote for the last time: "D+335."

Manhattan Project

In 1939 Niels Bohr said bomb-grade uranium 235 could be made only by turning the United States into a giant factory. Years later he told physicist Edward Teller: "You see, I told you it couldn't be done without turning the whole country into a factory."

Scientists had estimated it would take twenty-seven years to produce a kilogram—2.2 pounds—of U235 and 20,000 years to make a kilogram of plutonium. The United States made considerably more in four years. At one point 539,000 people, few of whom knew what they were making, were on payrolls of the Manhattan Project, as the bomb program was coded. The cost was $2 billion, peanuts today, a whole herd of elephants then. No one knew if it could be done. No one was sure how it could be done. It was a voyage into the unknown made desperate by another unknown: would the Germans get there first?

The Manhattan Project was run by perhaps the oddest couple to appear in American history. One half was J. Robert Oppenheimer, the brilliant, bone-thin son of wealthy New York Jews whose love in life was physics but whose loping gait also marched to interests in Sanskrit, poetry, music and women with communist backgrounds. They did not include telephones or radios or newspapers of which he had none. He didn't learn of the Crash of '29 until 1930. The other was General Leslie R. Groves, a bulldozer-blunt Army Engineer who insisted his staff keep a two-pound box of candy in his safe which did little to sweeten his disposition or "the biggest ego since Napoleon."

Kenneth Nichols, his chief aide during the project, remembers Groves as ". . . the biggest sonovabitch I've ever met in my life, but also one of the most capable individuals. . . . He was absolutely ruthless in how he approached a problem to get it done. He had absolute confidence in his decisions . . . but that was the beauty of working for him . . . I hated his guts and so did everybody else, but we had our form of understanding."

Groves was to say of the thousands of scientists and technicians Oppenheimer gathered at Los Alamos in New Mexico to bring a bomb out of the wilderness: "At great expense we have gathered on this mesa the greatest collection of crackpots ever seen." But the butt-chewing general and the gentle genius worked in perfect harmony, one of the lesser miracles of the bomb but perhaps the perfect marriage to achieve the impossible.

Groves, second in command of the Army's construction, had already approached that by building the Pentagon in eighteen months. Fourth in his class at West Point where he was known as "Greasy," he was forty-six on September 17, 1942, when told he would be kept in Washington instead of his desire to go overseas. Told if he did his job right, he could win the war, Groves, the good soldier, replied: "Oh."

The next day he sent Nichols to New York to meet a refugee Belgian, Edgar Sengier, whose mine in the Belgian Congo produced by far the richest uranium in the world. Having been told by French and British scientists that uranium might be vital to the Allies, Sengier had arranged to ship 1,200 tons of the high-grade ore to a warehouse in Staten Island where it had remained despite Sengier's efforts to interest the U.S. government. Within days after Nichols' uranium buy, Groves bought 50,000 acres along the Clinch River near Knoxville, Tennessee, as a site for a huge complex to separate U235 from U238 in ways yet to be decided. Named Oak Ridge, the site was chosen because it had water, ample electricity from the New Deal's Tennessee Valley Authority, cheap land, a mild climate for year-round construction, a nearby work force and was distant from any enemy-threatened coastline. In January 1943 MED paid $5.1 million for 780 square miles of scrubland near the hamlet of Hanford in the arid southwest of Washington state to build reactors to make plutonium. There again

In his ivory tower, Openheimer didn't learn of 1929 crash until 1930, but he knew how to create a bomb.

there was ample water, hydroelectricity and a safe separation should there be a disaster at Oak Ridge. Within no time 45,000 workers were brought into Hanford. "It was a tough town," Leona Woods remembered. "After work there was nothing to do but fight."

Rumors among the locals abounded. One wag at Oak Ridge said they were building windshield wipers for submarines. Someone in Knoxville said the factories were being built by Eleanor Roosevelt to turn black people white. Stone & Webster, the construction firm, began work on the Y-12 complex at Oak Ridge before knowing for certain what it would be used for. Eventually it would become a complex of 268 permanent buildings, two the size of twenty football fields each, to separate U235 electromagnetically. When copper was short for wiring the hundreds of huge magnets, Groves sent Nichols to the Treasury Department to get silver. How much, Nichols was asked. About 15,000 tons, he replied. "Colonel," said the Treasury official, "here we don't speak of tons of silver. Our unit is the troy ounce."

Eventually MED used 13,450 tons, all of it scrupulously accounted for and returned by Groves at the end of the war.

By October 1943 Tennessee Eastman, a working arm of Eastman Kodak, had 4,500 people working separators at Oak Ridge even though the employ-

Atom bomb scientists (l. to r.) E.O. Lawrence, Enrico Fermi and Isidor Rabi at Los Alamos.

ees didn't know what they were separating. At Hanford, Du Pont had agreed to build the reactors for $1 above costs. (It was only paid, eventually, 66 cents.) Ultimately there would be 10,000 subcontractors. On June 27, 1944, contracts were let at Oak Ridge to build a uranium enrichment plant 500 feet long, eighty feet wide and seventy-five feet high. Preliminary production began September 15, and the whole plant was in operation within six months. There was a war on.

Los Alamos was the key, a scientific wonderland in the wilderness that officially didn't exist. And Oppenheimer was the key to Los Alamos. By the time Pearl Harbor was attacked, the National Defense Research Committee had budgeted $300,000 to sixteen atomic projects around the country, mostly at universities. Oppenheimer was in California working on theory. Central nationwide authority was lacking. Groves' predecessor, Colonel James C. Marshall, had deferred buying the Oak Ridge land, for instance, until the scientists had a firmer idea of how to proceed. It was into that sea of uncertainty and hesitation that Groves dove head first. It was obvious military authority was needed to expedite procurement and build. But the scientists had to be corralled, too. Groves felt Oppenheimer out on a long train ride in the fall of 1942. The thirty-eight-year-old physicist had drawbacks even though Groves thought him a genius.

"He can talk to you about anything you can bring up. Well, not exactly. He doesn't know anything about sports."

But in spite of a broad education in science, Oppenheimer had not won a Nobel Prize and would be in charge of many who had. He was a theoritician, not an experimenter like Fermi. He had had a girl who was a communist and had married a woman who had been one. Could he come down from his ivory tower to lead people? Groves decided to pick him to direct the lab that would design and build the bomb "irrespective of the information you have concerning Mr. Oppenheimer," he told some of the worried security people. "He is absolutely essential to the project."

In November 1942, Oppenheimer toured possible sites for the lab in New Mexico where he had a retreat. He had once said: "My two great loves are physics and New Mexico. It's a pity they can't be combined." That's why Groves bought 54,000 acres in the Jemez Mountains northwest of Santa Fe for a "demolition range." The only habitation was a toughen-Junior-up boys school where winter exercise was held outdoors in the snow in shorts. The only phone line belonged to the Forest Service. This no place quickly became a non-place.

All over the United States physicists recruited by Oppenheimer packed the wife, kids and bags and disappeared as over the edge of the Earth. They were told to report to Santa Fe to a Dorothy McKibbin who became den mother to the leading scientific brains of the nation from her small office in an old adobe building. Their addresses became simply P.O. Box 1663 Sante Fe. The kids went to school without any last names. No one could open a bank account or register a car or send in a tax return lest evil eyes guess what was going on. The baseball team of the MP guards at Los Alamos never could see their feats in the local paper. The bartender at the La Fonda hotel in Sante Fe really worked for the FBI. The scientists and their families crowded into hastily built Army barracks on the Los Alamos mesa. The elite, and you almost had to have a Nobel to qualify, lived on the obviously named Bathtub Row. Less than laureates made do with showers that caked the body with salts, if they ran at all.

Freedom of scientific inquiry clashed daily with military security as Groves' "plumbers" struggled with Oppenheimer's "longhairs" in a war of lifestyles. Richard Feynman, a free spirit physicist from New York, used to decipher safe combinations and leave "Guess Who?" notes inside. Teller played the piano at all hours, adding to the personal discord. The garden of discontent, frigid in winter and roasting in summer, also had serpents. Fuchs, the shy physicist on loan from Britain's atomic effort who was a much demanded babysitter, was also a Russian spy. So was David Greenglass, an Army machinist from New York who told his brother-in-law Julius Rosenberg what was going on behind the barbed wire of Los Alamos.

Santa Feans thought the place might be a camp for unwed, pregnant WACs or an internment camp for Republicans. Instead it was where Oppenheimer with his brilliance, his pipe, his porkpie hat and his God-given genius for command was trying to turn theory into a bomb.

To a considerable extent the bomb was an Allied effort. Atomic research in Britain was very advanced under the code-named Tube Alloys program. For security, many of the British brains, including the German-born Fuchs, were moved to America. But the Allies had agreed at Quebec in August 1943 that the bomb would not be used against a third power without mutual consent. A year later an Anglo-American understanding was reached at Roosevelt's home at Hyde Park, New York: ". . . a bomb, if finally available, might perhaps after mature consideration be used against the Japanese who should be warned that this bombardment will be repeated until they surrender."

"Now we're all sons of bitches." Trinity fireball begins atomic age at 5:29:45 a.m., July 16, 1945.

At Los Alamos it was becoming increasingly possible that a bomb would be finally available. And by August 1944 Groves reported several plutonium bombs could be ready between March and July of the next year and a gun bomb that August. He predicted they would have the power of "several thousand tons of TNT." By December 1944 the Hanford piles were producing plutonium. The couriers were bringing their suitcases of uranium from Oak Ridge weekly. Conant wrote in his diary it was a race whether a Little Boy or Fat Man—nicknames for two different designs of the bomb—could be dropped July-September 1945.

The site chosen for the first test of an atomic bomb was a mountain-ringed desert in southern

New Mexico so unforgiving the Spanish colonists centuries before called it Jornada del Muerto—Trail of the Dead Man. After months of wiring and testing, an implosion device atop a 100-foot tower was ready to fire July 16, 1945.

Kistiakowsky had bet a subdued Oppenheimer a month's pay against $10 the device would work. In a pool the late-arriving Rabi had picked 18,000 tons of TNT as the force of the explosion. Fermi had filled his pocket with pieces of paper to measure the blast by how far they were blown by the shock wave. Sam Allison, a physicist from the Met Lab in Chicago, intoned the countdown of a new age.

Teller earlier had asked colleague Bob Serber what he planned to do about all the rattlesnakes on this desert of Alamogordo. "I'll take a bottle of whiskey." And what if the bomb ignites the atmosphere? "I'll take another bottle of whiskey." Such an occurrence had been deemed most unlikely although there had been discounted speculation the explosion might wrench the Earth off its axis. But no one could say, for sure, how the dragon would respond to the ultimate twist of its tail. As Allison counted off the last seconds, Oppenheimer remembered a verse from the ancient Hindu scripture, the *Bhagavad Gita:* "I am become Death/The shatterer of worlds."

With a second to go, Allison was gripped with the fear that the blast might send electrocuting shocks into his microphone. He thrust it from him as he shouted "Zero!"

It was 5:29:45 a.m. local time when a dawn that may never set exploded on the world.

Cranes at Trinity test site begin raising bomb to top of tower which it eventually vaporized.

The light from a core hot as the sun was seen 250 miles away. Fifty miles to the north Georgia Green, a school girl being driven to Albuquerque by her brother-in-law, felt the surge of heat on her face. "What's that?" she asked. She was blind. Kistiakowsky gleefully reminded Oppie he owed him $10. Oppenheimer said he had no money and would have to pay him later. Fermi's paper and his ever-present slide rule told him the force was 10,000 tons. But Rabi actually won the pool. Groves said: "The war is over as soon as we drop two of these on Japan." But the most memorable remark, for Oppenheimer, came from Kenneth Bainbridge, director of Trinity:

"Now we're all sons of bitches."

As the dust settled over the melted sand of Jornada del Muerto, as the soon-to-be-familiar mushroom cloud dissipated into the upper atmosphere, as the Associated Press in Albuquerque transmitted a prepared cover story from Groves' office that an ammunition dump had exploded at Alamogordo, Robert Oppenheimer, who loved hiking in the outdoors, took a ruminative walk into the desert. He saw a turtle that had been blown helplessly on its back by the blast. He set it upright.

"It was the least I could do," he said later.

Trinity explosion left crater half mile wide and up to ten feet deep.

12 THE BOMB

Paul W. Tibbets, Jr., had divided loyalties.
There had always been a doctor in the family and he was taking pre-med at the University of Cincinnati. But he had an itch to fly. The itch won out in 1937 when he dropped out of school to become a flight cadet in Texas. His father thought he'd be killed, but his mother, named for the Indian midwife who delivered her in a covered wagon—Enola Gay—told him: "You go ahead and fly. You'll be all right." She knew her son. He became a superb bomber pilot, calm, self-assured as the pipe he quietly smoked. He had flown General Mark Clark to Gibraltar for his submarine mission before the invasion of Africa. He flew Ike to take command of the same invasion.

Aged twenty-nine in the summer of 1944, he was test flying the new B-29 Superfortresses at Alamogordo Air Base when he received orders to report immediately to headquarters in Colorado. There he was questioned intensively by a stranger who seemed to know a great deal about him. Had he ever-been arrested? Well, there was one time as a teen-ager when he was caught in the act in the back seat of a car with a girl. The inquisitor knew that. He was testing Tibbet's honesty. He took him to the commandant: "I'm satisfied, general."

Then Tibbets met with Navy Captain William "Deac" Parsons and a civilian physicist, Norman Ramsey. They told him about a new weapon, something called an atomic bomb. Parsons said he had been picked to arm the first one. Tibbets would fly the plane to drop it.

Like most things associated with the Manhattan Project, Tibbet's new command, the 509th Composite Group, was stationed in the back of beyond and surrounded by secrecy, rumor and barbed wire. Their base was Wendover Field in Utah near the Nevada line. Hardened veterans were outraged the 509th's B-29s had been stripped of all armaments except for twin .50s in the tail. You couldn't fight a war with your hands tied. And you couldn't win it taking off every day and flying hundreds and hundreds of miles to drop a huge bomb with hardly anything in it. Each time they dropped what they called "the pumpkin," the 509th pilots wheeled at a sharp 158 degrees and dove to gather speed. They had to be eight miles from the target within forty-three seconds. Even the ground crewmen were forbidden to talk to one another once they left the 509th's compound. On a train once the dining car had been closed until 509th personnel had finished eating.

The 509th flew its Superforts all over the country, even as far as the Virgin Islands, Cuba and Bermuda, dropping pumpkins visually from 30,000 feet. Back on the ground at Wendover on the other side of the barbed wire they inspired a bit of doggerel:

Into the air the secret rose.
Where they're going nobody knows.

On April 5, 1945, an operations officer at the War Department in Washington assigned a code name for something so secret he didn't know what it was for. Centerboard. Whatever, later that month the 509th began flying brand new B-29s out of Wendover. Destination: Tinian.

Several hours after the Trinity test, a 200-pound, lead-lined cylinder about the size of a can of potato chips was hefted aboard the heavy cruiser *Indianapolis* in San Francisco by two sailors. Carrying it on their shoulders slung from a crowbar, they took it to the flag officer's state room where the canister was secured to the deck by welded straps. Two officers from Los Alamos were to sleep with it, standing alternate four-hour watches. The captain was only told this secret cargo was to be first into a lifeboat in case of emergency. *Indianapolis* headed out through the Golden Gate into the Pacific, her destination the same as Tibbets': Tinian.

History's first atomic bomb was on its way.

Above: *"Fat Man," the plutonium implosion bomb dropped on Nagasaki.*

The decisive argument for dropping the bomb had been there all along: it would win the war. Americans might not have understood what inspired the fanatical defense by the Japanese of Saipan and Okinawa. But they could count. Whatever the casualties the United States had suffered in taking the outlying islands, they could only be greater in invading the Japanese home islands. The United States had already lost 250,000 men in Europe and the Pacific. The Pentagon estimated casualties from an invasion of Japan at 1 million. It calculated the Japanese still had 5,000 kamikaze planes left and 5 million soldiers. Plans were already far advanced for Operation Downfall, the invasion of Japan. The first phase was scheduled November 1, 1945, with the invasion and occupation of the lower half of the southern island of Kyushu, Operation Olympic. Four months later would come Operation Coronet, landings on the main island of Honshu.

Oppenheimer estimated 20,000 Japanese civilians might die from an atomic bomb if they were inside bomb shelters. If. Bombing civilians had become commonplace in World War II. The Germans attacked Britain with bombers and later rockets. Some 45,000 died in the Allied fire bombing of Hamburg, perhaps twice that many in a repeat raid on Dresden. When General Curtis Le May of the 20th Air Force sent 334 B-29s loaded with napalm to firebomb Tokyo the night of March 9-10, 1945, as many as 100,000 people died and 1 million were injured in the flaming hurricane that burned out sixteen square miles of the Japanese capital. If $E=mc^2$ was a fateful equation, so were American lives against Japanese. Americans did remember Pearl Harbor.

Oddly, one of the most persistent opponents to using the bomb was its first advocate, Leo Szilard. Szilard had once again approached Einstein asking him to send another letter to Roosevelt cautioning against first use of a weapon by a country that had so many vulnerable cities of its own. The letter was in Roosevelt's office in Warm Springs, Georgia, when he died April 12.

Harry Truman

Harry Truman took the White House elevator to the second floor and stepped into Eleanor Roosevelt's study. The first lady put her hand on his shoulder and said, "Harry, the president is dead." Truman, who had been summoned from the Capitol, was as stunned; he had heard FDR was recuperating nicely. Finally, he asked Mrs. Roosevelt, "Is there anything I can do for you?" She turned his

"Little Boy." As the seconds passed over Hiroshima one crewman thought it must be a dud.

"You are the one in trouble now," his wife told Truman, here taking the oath, and burden, of president.

question around. "Is there anything we can do for you? For you are the one in trouble now."

Vice President Harry S. Truman took the oath of president that evening at 7:09 p.m. When later told of the Manhattan Project, it was the first he had heard of it. At the urging of the War Secretary, the aged but wise Henry Stimson, he named an Interim Committee to counsel him on atomic matters. Stimson added an advisory panel of scientists including Compton, Fermi, Ernest Lawrence, head of the Berkeley Radiation Laboratory, and Oppenheimer. The committee met in Washington May 31, and Stimson said the United States should be sensitive to the verdict of history in use of the bomb. Compton suggested a demonstration before a group of foreign observers. Others at the table asked what would the Japanese reaction be if the bomb proved a dud. Would it persuade them to surrender even if it weren't? Would it make it more likely they would increase air defenses against solitary bombers? Would they move Allied prisoners into likely targets?

The committee unanimously approved dropping the bomb as soon as possible. On June 1, Truman said he had no alternative but to agree. The targets—all of which had escaped major attack—were selected: Kyoto, Hiroshima, Yokohama, Kokura Arsenal and Niigata. Stimson insisted Kyoto, the ancient cultural center of Japan, be eliminated. It was.

In Chicago, Szilard and other scientists of the Met Lab drew up a report under James Franck, a refugee German Nobelist that said: "If the United States were to be the first to release this new means of indiscriminate destruction upon mankind, she would sacrifice public support throughout the world, precipitate the race for armaments and prejudice the possibility of reaching an international agreement on the future control of such weapons."

George Harrison, head of the Interim Committee and president of the New York Life Insurance Company, replied June 16: ". . . we can propose no technical demonstration likely to bring an end to the war. . . ."

Then on June 27 Under Secretary of the Navy Ralph A. Bard wrote Harrison he had been having second thoughts: "I have had a feeling that before the bomb is actually used against Japan that Japan should have some preliminary warning for say two or three days in advance. . . . The position of the United States as a great humanitarian nation and the fair play attitude of our people generally is responsible in the main for this feeling. . . . It seems quite possible to me that this presents the opportunity (to surrender) which the Japanese are looking for."

At Potsdam in Germany where Truman had gone for a meeting with Churchill and Stalin, "Hap" Arnold, head of the Army Air Force, was also having second thoughts. He had been to Tinian where Le May said his B-29s were bombing the Japanese "back to the Stone Age." Arnold thought air power plus a naval blockade would make both an invasion and use of the atomic weapon unnecessary. But it was not his decision.

On July 12 Dr. Farrington Daniels, new head of the Met Lab, polled 150 scientists. Twenty-three votes were for use in the most effective way to cause prompt Japanese surrender; sixty-nine votes were for a demonstration in Japan; thirty-nine for a demonstration in the United States with Japanese observers present; sixteen voted to withhold use but make a demonstration and three voted to not use the bomb and keep the whole thing as secret as possible.

The day after Trinity, Compton forwarded several petitions from the scientists to Harrison in Washington. Szilard had written one that first asked that no bomb be dropped on Japan, then modified it to urge no bomb be used until Japan had been specifically warned.

At Potsdam, Stimson had briefed Eisenhower on the bomb and the Trinity results. The Allied commander said he hoped the bomb would not have to be used as he did not want his country to be the first to employ it. Admiral Leahy, who had stayed as Truman's chief of staff, had first doubted the bomb would go off. When Trinity did, he still opposed use on moral grounds. Stimson's Assistant Secretary of War, John J. McCloy, favored use

'Dozers were still adding runways on Tinian as B-29s began using base to bomb Japan "into the Stone Age."

only if Japan were given sufficient warning.

The votes were in. It was up to Truman to decide. On July 24 he told Stalin about the bomb. He replied noncommittedly as if he had no spies at Los Alamos. He hoped good use would be made of the weapon. Truman later told Churchill: "He never asked a question."

Back in Washington, target selector Brigadier General Thomas F. Farrell argued against including Nagasaki in the list of targets. It had already been attacked and its hills would minimize the bomb's power. Nonetheless Nagasaki was included. A top secret message was sent to Tinian: "The 509 Composite Group, 20th Air Force, will deliver its first special bomb as soon as weather will permit visual bombing after about 3 August 1945 on one of the targets: Hiroshima, Kokura, Niigata and Nagasaki. . . .''

On July 26 Truman, Chiang Kai-shek of China and Britain's brand new prime minister, Labor Party leader Clement Attlee, who had just unseated Churchill, issued the Potsdam Declaration calling on Japan to surrender unconditionally or face "prompt and utter destruction." The nature was unspecified. Two days later the Japanese, whose government was torn between hawks and doves, rejected the ultimatum.

The *Indianapolis* had already dropped anchor off Tinian.

Hiroshima

It was a strange time, that August of 1945. Half of a world war was over, its veterans beginning to

come home. At the same time, their sons and younger brothers, many who had been pre-teens when the war in Europe began in 1939, were marshalling into position for the biggest invasion of all. *Olympic* was to land six divisions on the beaches of Kyusha on D Day. Offshore would be an armada of forty-two carriers, twenty-four battleships, 212 destroyers and 183 destroyer escorts. In all 750,000 men were involved. The military estimated 100,000 would die or be wounded. At bases around the Pacific and in the United States plans had been completed—the invasion details covered 400 single-spaced pages—and training was well advanced.

Halfway around the world in the rubble of the Thousand-Year Reich that had lasted but twelve, there was a strange silence of defeat and despair. Mingled with the smoke from the ruins was that of the crematoria, the death pall of six million people murdered by state policy. The realization of this was something that would not soon blow away. But it provided a cold proof of why, in part, this war had been fought.

In the Pacific the second half of the world war was reaching a crescendo. LeMay's bombers had dropped 40,000 tons on the cities of Japan in July. (There was an unintended irony: if Japan was ever allowed to rebuild, its infrastructure—and Germany's—would be the most modern in the world.) The B-29s had dropped so many incendiaries on Japan's tinderbox cities they had temporarily run out of bombs. On August 5, nonetheless, 600 B-29s had sortied over Japan. Tinian with its multiple runways was one of the major launching platforms. In all this hubbub the 509th was an anomaly. Their almost defenseless Superforts left their guarded section, flew out to sea and returned hours later seeming to have done nothing but consume fuel.

On August 4 Parsons gathered seven of the 509th's fifteen crews and tried to show a film of the Trinity test. The projector jammed, so he gave a verbal account. It was obviously a weapon of awesome power, but the word "atomic" was never mentioned. Tibbets, who knew, decided to give his Superfort something more than its tail number, 82. He got a sign painter out of a softball game and had him paint his mother's name on the nose, *Enola Gay.* Others had crayoned comments on Little Boy in its hoist in the bomb assembly shed. One paid tribute to the crew of the *Indianapolis,* most of whom had just died in a torpedoing. An officer wrote "No white cross for Stevie" in remembrance of his young child at home. The men wondered whether the bomb contained some new type of TNT. Major Ralph Taylor, one of the pilots, said he'd bet a month's salary that it had something to do with splitting the atom, a once much-discussed topic that nothing had been written about for years.

The weather forecast for August 6 was favorable. At 0227 hours Tibbets started the engines of the *Enola Gay*. His plane was eight tons overloaded. It took almost all the runway before easing slowly into the air. It was 0245. Parsons began arming the four-ton bomb. It had not been wired fully before takeoff lest it might explode in event of a crash. Sergeant Bob Caron, the tail gunner who was wearing a Brooklyn Dodgers baseball cap, talked to Tibbets who was checking out the crew.

"Say, Bob, you figured out what we're doing yet?" the colonel asked.

"Hell, Colonel, I don't want to get shot for breaking security."

"We're on our way. You can talk now."

"Is it some kind of chemist's nightmare?"

"No, not exactly."

"How about a physicist's nightmare?"

"That's about it."

"Say, Colonel, are we splitting atoms today?"

"You're pretty close, Bob."

Flying at 9,000 feet to husband fuel, the *Enola Gay* droned northwards past milestones—and headstones—of America's long, bloody journey across the Pacific. Saipan with its bamboo spear charge. Iwo and flag-topped Suribachi where blood so recently flowed on the black sand beaches. "I had some classmates who were beheaded by some Japanese practicing their swordsmanship," Tibbets was to say. But he did not fly on in vengeance. "We were at war. You only fight a war to win it. You use anything at your disposal. There are no Marquis of Queensberry rules in war."

The *Enola Gay* was climbing to bombing altitude as it crossed the Japanese coastline at 7:50 a.m. Tibbets ordered the crew to don flak suits although no Japanese fighters rose to meet them. There wasn't fuel or ammunition to waste on a lone bomber and its two escort B-29s.

A weather B-29 flew over Hiroshima a little after 7 a.m. and reported clear skies, a warm, calm summer morning. An air raid alarm sounded when the solitary plane was sighted. The all clear blew when it left. The life of the city beginning its day resumed.

At 8:11 a.m. Tibbets started the bomb run, holding altitude at 31,600 feet. At 8:15:17 a.m. the bombardier, Major Thomas Ferebee, opened the bomb bay and Little Boy, which one crewman likened to a "trash can with fins," fell out, turned broadside and then nosed towards the earth. An ordnance lieutenant, Morris Jeppson, who had helped Parsons arm the weapon, mentally counted off the forty-five seconds before the bomb was meant to explode.

At "43" he thought: "It's a dud."

Tibbets waves farewell as he prepares to take off into history.

Colonel Tibbets got sign painter out of softball game to name fateful B-29 for his mother.

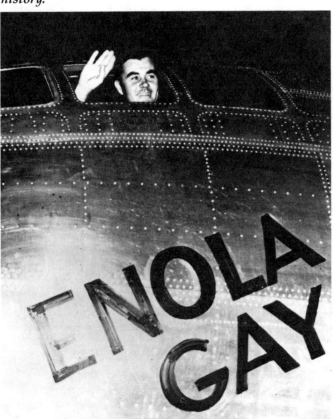

Although it was a manufacturing city and a major embarkation port of supplies and soldiers, Hiroshima was largely unscathed by the war. Navy planes had dropped two bombs in March 1945. A B-29 dropped ten bombs six weeks later when it couldn't reach its main target. About twelve people were killed. About 380,000 people once lived in Hiroshima, but the population was down to about 250,000 civilians. Thousands had been evacuated and their homes razed to create fire lanes should the Superforts finally focus on the city. Conceivably they never would.

Some 300 miles to the northeast in Tokyo there was strong sentiment in the Japanese government to end the war. On June 22 Emperor Hirohito called the Supreme War Council to tell them it was time to consider the possibility of ending the conflict. The Council was divided three to three. Shigenori Togo, the foreign minister, had directed his ambassador to Moscow, Naotake Sato, to approach the Soviets as to their becoming a mediator for a peace. The Soviets were noncommittal.

Hirohito was revered as a semi-divine person by his subjects, but his power was only moral, not actual. The Americans, deciphering Japan's diplomatic code, knew of Togo's feeler to the Soviets through intercepts. But they themselves were divided on the status of the emperor. Ex-ambassador Grew, who was now undersecretary of state, was probably the man who knew Japan best. He urged Truman to assure the status of Hirohito in any ultimatum for unconditional surrender. Stimson favored some concession on the royal role in a future Japan. Some saw the emperor as a useful tool to maintain order in Japan after a surrender. The fate of the emperor also stayed the hand of the doves of the War Council in Tokyo. On July 11, Togo cabled Sato that ". . . as long as America and England insist on unconditional surrender, our country has no alternative but to see it through to an all-out effort for the sake of survival and the honor of the homeland."

The Potsdam Declaration made no mention of the emperor. Japanese Prime Minister Baron Kantaro Suzuki in Tokyo said ". . . there is no other recourse but to ignore it (the ultimatum) entirely and resolutely fight for the successful conclusion of the war." The word he used in Japanese was *mokusatsu*—to kill with silence—which the American code breakers translated as "ignore." The Americans interpreted it also as a rejection.

Hiroshima's fate had been sealed well before Morris Jeppson began his countdown.

The clocks of Hiroshima never reached 8:17.

Little Boy exploded at 8:16:02 in a huge, boiling, purplish fireball at 1,850 feet over the awakening city. It's light rivalled anything in the heavens, its horror on the ground surpassed any concept of hell. Many people simply vanished, leaving only a shadow on the pavement. Perhaps they were the lucky ones. The survivors who bore witness:

". . . all had skin blackened by burns" ". . . you couldn't tell whether you were looking at them from in front or in back" ". . . their skin all hung down" ". . . they didn't look like they were people of this world" ". . . I discovered I had tripped over a man's head" ". . . from their whole bodies something like thin paper is dangling—it is their peeled-off skin" ". . . hanging from them like rags" ". . . people with their bowels and brains coming out" ". . . a man with his eyes sticking out two inches" ". . . a streetcar all burned and inside it all the passengers burned to a cinder" ". . . the peculiar odor of burning human flesh rose everywhere" ". . . I had the feeling that all the human beings on the face of the earth had been killed" ". . . all become corpses and their bodies carried by the (river) toward the sea . . ."

On board *Enola Gay* co-pilot Captain Robert Lewis looked back as a roiling cloud quickly rose to 40,000 feet: "My God, what have we done?"

"Holy Moses!" said tail gunner Caron.

"The war's over!" cried a voice on one of the two observer B-29s.

Not quite.

The work done, **Enola Gay** *and crew return to Tinian from Hiroshima.*

As back-up tail-gunner, Caron was given camera in case photoplane fouled up. It did, and amateur Caron came back with this historic shot of Hiroshima.

In Tokyo there was renewed consternation in the War Council. The ministers had no confirmation that the unprecedented disaster that struck Hiroshima was an atomic bomb other than President Truman's announcement in the United States. The next day Japan's leading physicist Yoshio Nishina, who had studied with Niels Bohr, flew to Hiroshima and confirmed it could have been no other weapon. Togo cabled Sato in Moscow to redouble efforts for Russian mediation. Instead Soviet Foreign Minister Molotov said Russia was declaring war on Japan. Meanwhile Fat Man, the plutonium implosion bomb, was being hurriedly assembled on Tinian. Stimson, alone, argued against its use. Despite his shock at pictures of Hiroshima taken by the observer planes, Truman was convinced his paramount responsibility was to save American lives. Fat Man would be dropped August 9 Washington time on Kokura Arsenal. The secondary target was Nagasaki where the Pearl Harbor torpedoes had been made. Kokura was obscure from clouds and smoke, so Major Charles Sweeney, flying *Bock's Car*, a B-29 borrowed from another crew, bombed the secondary. Perhaps 100,000 had died at Hiroshima, 35,000 at Nagasaki with double that to die later from radiation.

The Japanese still could not decide. The status of the emperor was the major sticking point. The Council met repeatedly. War Minister General Korechika Anami still insisted Japan's will power would yet prevail. Prevail despite the Americans' new weapon. Prevail despite the uncontested shelling that had begun by U.S. warships along the coasts of the Home Islands. Prevail although American bombers were flying with impunity at smokestack height to attack what targets remained. Prevail despite the three Soviet armies that had begun advancing into Manchuria. Late on August 12 the Council met before the emperor deep in his bomb shelter at the Imperial Palace. Two hours after midnight, Hirohito, the man who was to reign, not rule, spoke.

By ancient Japanese tradition a command from the Throne was the Voice of the Crane, a voice heard from on high even if the source could not be seen. To continue the war, the emperor said quietly, would be suicide, hara-kiri for the whole nation. ". . . the time has come when we must bear the unbearable. . . ." Then Hirohito left the room, leaving behind his sobbing council. The decision was relayed through the Swiss government. At 2:49 p.m. Tokyo time on August 14 the Japanese news agency Domei sent a flash: "It is learned an imperial message accepting the Potsdam Proclamation is forthcoming soon." The Japanese people, who were not by tradition even to look on the emperor, were stunned to hear his voice on the radio in high-pitched stilted court formality:

". . . the enemy has begun to employ a new and most cruel bomb. . . . This is the reason why we have ordered the acceptance of the provisions of the Joint Declaration of the Powers. . . ."

The Voice of the Crane had surrendered. It was August 14 in the States, V-J Day. The nation erupted in a frenzy of celebration, and the guns fell finally silent.

Enola Gay *navigator Theodore Van Kirk* (map) *explains mission after return.* Tibbets **(far left),** *General Spaatz* **(head of table),** Caron **(baseball cap at bottom).**

The Big Three (l. to r.), Prime Minister Attlee, President Truman, Premier Stalin, set the unconditional surrender terms at Potsdam—accepted by Japan after the bomb dropped.

Sweeney (squatting) explains second atomic mission to crew.

It's over Over There!

At a country estate outside Cambridge, England, the interned German scientist Otto Hahn, the man who had split the atom, did not want to believe the news. "The thought of the unspeakable misery of countless innocent women and children was something that I could scarcely bear." His interned colleagues thought Hahn might take his life but, pacified by gin, he eventually went to bed. Admiral Leahy was to say: "My own feeling was that in being the first to use it, we had adopted an ethical standard common to the barbarians of the Dark Ages. I was not taught to make war in that fashion and wars cannot be won by destroying women and children. . . ."

Stimson was to say: "My chief purpose was to end the war in victory with the least possible cost in the lives of the men in the armies which I had helped raise. . . . I believe that no man in our position . . . holding in his hands a weapon of such possibilities for accomplishing this purpose and saving those lives could have failed to use (the bomb) and afterwards looked his countrymen in the face."

Many years after World War II had ended, Norris Bradbury, the man who had directed assembly of the Trinity bomb and succeeded Oppenheimer as director at Los Alamos, considered a question. There was a small museum there with replicas of the casings of Little Boy and Fat Man. Do any of the few visitors who make their way up to the mesa ever say thank you, thank you for the atomic bomb?

"Yes," said Bradbury, "yes, some do."

Although many Americans did not fully appreciate the theory behind, or the potential of, the new weapon, they were inundated with predictions about the significance of atomic energy. Some analysts said it was the crowning achievement of science; others said it meant the end of civilization. That the future of nuclear power might be more complex and less dramatic seems to have been lost in the excitement. Americans made jokes—the Japanese had "atomic ache," they chuckled—and prayed that the bomb would end the war. But the peace for which they had waited so long now had an unexpected edge.

Peace was peace, however, and when Truman announced at 7 p.m. on August 14, 1945, that Japan had surrendered, the nation embarked on a celebration that lasted all night, all the next day (V-J Day) and well into the following night. New York made its V-E celebration look like a pep rally. This time 5,000 tons of litter—not only paper, but hats, bottles, wastepaper baskets and underwear—were dumped out windows, and an estimated 2 million people jammed into Times Square to cheer each bit of V-J news on *The New York Times'* electric sign. In Los Angeles, revelers commandeered trolley cars and played leapfrog in the middle of Hollywood Boulevard. Thousands of people in Salt Lake City snakedanced through the rain, and a crowd in St. Louis persuaded a minister to hold services at 2 a.m.

In Washington, people had waited outside the White House for two days for word of peace. Now they formed a conga line and kept chanting "We want Harry!" so finally Truman and his wife Bess walked onto the lawn and shook hands through the fence. Then, speaking into a microphone under the portico, he told them, "This is the great day." But his smile vanished as he warned of "an emergency ahead—a crisis as great as December 7, 1941."

He was not alone in his reticence. One reporter wrote from Chicago that it seemed "a peculiar peace. . . . And everyone talked of 'the end of the war,' not of 'victory.'" When the celebration was spent and the sun rose on August 16, when their heads and eyes cleared, Americans beheld a world that was almost frighteningly new.

Even Miss Liberty raised arm in salute as Times Square celebrates V-J Day.

At the same time, the nation to which 13 million servicemen would return was not the one of December 7, 1941. Business was bigger, labor was bigger and government was bigger. If it was no longer a man's world, it was less of a white one, too. Blacks had served notice they would no longer conspire in their own subjugation.

The war shattered the depression in agriculture—farm income had risen 250 percent since 1939—but the farm population declined by 17 percent in just three-and-a-half years. The 3 million who left tended to settle not inside the big cities but on their outskirts. The suburbs also seemed like a promised land to veterans returning to crowded old cities, where few houses were for sale or apartments for rent. Within two years 6 million families would be doubling up with relatives, and another half million living in quonset huts and other temporary quarters, including retired trolley cars, surplus grain bins, chicken coops and old iceboxes. In New York, two newlyweds set up housekeeping in a department store window to publicize their need for an apartment.

Thanks to the GI Bill, under which veterans were eligible for a federally-insured mortgage with little or no down payment, their dreams of a suburban house filled with appliances were realized. Single family housing starts would surge from 114,000 in 1944 to 937,000 in 1946 and 1.9 million in 1948.

But new social problems also developed during the war. In 1941 Los Angeles was a fecund

Ever the stage manager, MacArthur pauses at personal plane ramp after landing in Japan.

paradise—the nation's leading agricultural county and No. 8 in industrial production—but in 1943 the city had its first smog attack. Back in New York, there were more and more reports of an old crime with a new name: mugging.

But America's new problems were nothing next to its vast new wealth. If "Dr. New Deal" put Band-Aids on ailing American capitalism, "Dr. Win-the-War" cured it. Private enterprise regained the prestige and self-confidence it had lost in 1929. More new industrial plants were built during the war than in the fifteen preceding years, and four-fifths of it was adaptable to peacetime production. Meanwhile, almost everyone else was poor. The United States held two-thirds of the world's gold reserves and was doing more than half of its

manufacturing. The American nation had seen an Era of Good Feelings and a Gilded Age, the Gay '90s and the Roaring '20s, but it had never known anything like the wealth and power it inherited in 1945.

Surrender

The first foreign invader to step on Japanese soil in all the nation's ancient history came in peace.

Just after dawn on August 28, 1945, Colonel Charles Tench stepped from an American C-47 at Atsugi Air Base outside Yokohama. A mob of Japanese ran towards him. Tench reached for his gun. Bowing, they offered him orangeade. A Japanese general drank a glass to show it wasn't poisoned. Then Tench warily took a sip. More C-47s landed on the war-ravaged runway. Smiling Japanese cheered as technicians removed the propellers from rows of parked kamikaze planes. They cheered again as Americans raised their flag over a hangar. American planes began coming in every two minutes disgorging paratroopers. Two days later MacArthur's C-54 *Bataan* touched down in "a rubbery landing" on the last island of the general's long road. Melodramatic as ever, the khaki-clad commander posed for photographs in the door of the plane, hat tilted, corncob puffing. He stepped to the ground bringing with him not revenge but a resolve to provide his fallen foe a firm but enlightened example of democracy and renewal.

Correspondents rushed to the capital where they located Tokyo Rose. To their surprise she was a graduate in zoology from UCLA named Iva Ikuko Toguri who had been caught by the war in Japan while visiting an aunt. She had taken up broadcasting for $6.60 a month because the only option was work in a munitions factory. She was subsequently sentenced to ten years in prison.

Tokyo Rose was actually UCLA graduate who preferred propaganda work to a factory assembly line.

The formal surrender took place in Tokyo Bay aboard Halsey's flagship, the battleship *Missouri,* September 2, 1945. Overhead was the American flag that had flown over the Capitol in Washington the day Pearl Harbor was attacked. Others on board had also come full circle. In one of two places of honor was gaunt and prematurely aged General Wainwright, the surrenderer of Corregidor and just released from a Japanese prisoner of war camp. In the other was Lieutenant General Arthur E. Percival who had given up Singapore. Colonel Ichiji Sugita, who had interpreted at that surrender, stared across the crowded deck of the battleship at the Englishman. Among the broadcast correspondents was Webley Edwards who had radioed on that December 7 in Honolulu: "This is the real McCoy!"

Some of the Japanese leaders had already committed suicide. Others could not bear the shame of attending the ceremony. Admiral Sadatoshi Tomioka attended in lieu of Navy Chief of Staff Soemu Toyoda. "You lost the war," Toyoda had told him, "so you go." New Foreign Minister Mamoru Shigemitsu, who had lost a leg long before in an assassination attempt, headed the eleven-member delegation. Colonel Sidney

Mashbir, their Japanese-fluent liaison, told them to "wear a shiran kao (nonchalant face)." Shigemitsu's secretary, Toshikazu Kase, a graduate of Amherst and Harvard, noted the Rising Suns painted on a bulkhead to count the *Missouri's* victories. His throat tightened. "Never have I realized that the glance of glaring eyes could hurt so much. We waited . . . standing in the public gaze like penitent boys awaiting the dreaded schoolmaster." An Allied delegate, drunk, made rude faces at the top-hatted Japanese.

Shigemitsu limped forward, uncertain where to sign. Halsey wanted to slap him for stalling, but the diplomat was simply confused. Then MacArthur, intentionally wearing a shirt with no medals or ribbons, signed his name using five pens. Then came representatives of Britain, China, France, Canada, Australia, New Zealand, The Netherlands and the Soviet Union. Shigemitsu slowly put his top hat back on as he stared down the leering drunk.

Opposite page: *Shigemitsu signs surrender papers on* **Missouri** *as MacArthur (l.), Halsey and others look on.* **Below:** *MacArthur signs as Wainright and Percival stand by.*

The Japanese signatories stepped back from the simple mess room table with its coffee-stained green cover. MacArthur said it was his hope "and indeed the hope of all mankind that a better world shall emerge."

It was a world that had just seen 50 million of its people die in six years of war. Nearly 300,000 of them had been Americans killed in battle. And yet the conqueror had spoken in words of peace to the conquered. As he did so the clouds lifted and the sun glistened off the ancient symmetry of Mount Fuji in the distance. Kase was "thunderstruck" as MacArthur spoke. "MacArthur's words sailed on wings. This narrow quarterdeck was now transformed into an altar of peace."

Later the general spoke by radio back home to his America whose long night had finally dawned with victory:

"And so, my fellow countrymen, today I report to you that your sons and daughters have served you well and faithfully with the calm, deliberate, determined fighting spirit of the American soldier and sailor. Their spiritual strength and power has brought us through to victory. They are homeward bound. Take care of them."

Foreign Minister Shigemitsu marks the end of the war for Japan.

MacArthur hands surrender pen to Percival.

EPILOGUE

Was it fated to be that way: Pearl Harbor, Auschwitz, Hiroshima? What, after all, was World War II? And why?

History can record no better argument for the effect of one single individual on events than Adolf Hitler. But if there are men who lead the world into war, there are also followers.

Hitler may have exploited but did not invent the traumas that afflicted the Germany of 1933. He manipulated the humliation of German pride and nationalism by what he called the *diktat,* the Treaty of Versailles. Germany tried democracy with the well-intentioned but ineffective Weimar Republic. Hitler scoffed at that attempt. He played on fears, fear of a recurrence of the communist uprisings of 1919, fear of the inflation of the 1920s that left the mark worth less than the paper it was printed on. He offered a rebirth through battle. He offered scapegoats: the oppressive victors of World War I, the Russian bear in ominous new clothing. And the Jews. His people willingly followed this Pied Piper of Death to the very last.

The United States had its trauma as well: the Depression. But it chose a different path. Franklin Roosevelt came to power within days of Adolf Hitler—and died within days of him. Both had twelve years. But one led his people in consonance with their constitution and the other led his to genocide and devastation.

As the smoke of war settled over the rubble of Europe, as the crematoria of the Holocaust cooled, could any justice be found? Could the enormity of Nazism be reduced to human scale in a court of law? The judgment at Nuremberg was an attempt. Goering committed suicide before he could be hanged, but ten others of the twenty-two Nazi leaders tried went to the gallows including Keitel, Jodl and Joachim von Ribbentrop. The Allies hoped to create a precedent to outlaw wars of aggression, to turn a new leaf in history's heavy book of barbarity. Perhaps the collective force of

world opinion in the new United Nations would see to this. It did not. In the years to come there would be incessant wars and genocide in Cambodia, genocide even in tiny Rwanda and Burundi in Africa.

Japan had no Hitler. Its imperial lunge after millenia of cocooned isolation left the nation pulverized and stunned. Tojo and Homma of the Bataan Death March were executed as war criminals. The Japanese compliantly accepted MacArthur as an Occidental potentate who tried with considerable success to sow more democratic seeds in the ashes. It was only one of many twists in the aftermath of the war that Hirohito paid a courtesy call on his nemesis rather than the other way around.

For Britain, World War II cost it its Empire. Its gallant stand had spent the blood and wealth necessary to sustain it. Its early defeats had exposed Britain as vincible. A new nationalism germinated by war's disruption did not forget it. Britain descended through threadbare crises in the post-war years to a rank of the second level.

The United States, on the other hand, stood alone at the pinnacle of world power. American industry and American fighting men had achieved this. An atomic monopoly confirmed it. The war had taken 292,131 of its lives, but an American century was at hand. So trumpeted the magazines. In an act of unexampled magnanimity—along with some self-interest—the U.S. Marshall Plan gave billions to rebuild Europe. Truman received the credit. But before he died, Roosevelt had already ruled out a proposal by Treasury Secretary Henry Morgenthau to reduce post-war Germany to an agrarian state stripped of any war-making ability. The American vision was a world at war becoming

Above: *History would long debate role of Hirohito in starting war but even emperor agreed who won when he paid call on MacArthur.*

317

a world at peace and a limitless market for the new colossus. So it happened, but not for a century. The United States fought a stalemate in Korea, then encountered the setback of Vietnam. It saw its highways crowded with Japanese and German autos, symbolic of the economic rivalry of its former enemies. Who had won the war, anyway?

The GIs? They did not all come marching home. Almost half a century after V-E Day, American troops were still stationed in Europe. The enemy was a former ally, the new ally a former enemy. Hitler had been right. Where a few years earlier GIs had beaten the Germans into unconditional capitulation, Americans took up positions, positions their sons in turn would hold, in Germany alongside Germans across a wall from the new enemy, the Soviet Union. It was to be called a Cold War.

It remained cold because of a legacy of World War II, the atomic bomb. The Soviet Union broke the U.S. monopoly in 1949 with its own nuclear explosion. At that instant war took on a new definition: world annihilation. Twenty million Soviets had died in World War II. German scientists had helped both sides develop rockets. For long, dreadful years neither side dared reach for the trigger. Maybe Leo Szilard had not foreseen this mutual terror as he waited for the light to turn at that London crosswalk. But certainly Oppenheimer did at Trinity when he cited Hindu scripture contemplating the fury he had helped wrought. The race for the bomb had been won as had the war. But perhaps next time there would be no winner.

Perhaps, too, that was the legacy of World War II. The graves of Pearl Harbor and Guadalcanal and Midway and Kasserine Pass and the Rapido River and Anzio and D Day and Schweinfurt and Ploesti and the Bulge marked the limits of one kind of war. The skeletal outline of the peace dome at Hiroshima marked the boundary of another. Mankind could no longer think it could have one without the other.

Should that prove so, the graves of World War II may speak for more than the 50 million dead who lie there.

So many did so much....

Index